Martin Pring on Price Patterns

The Definitive Guide to Price Pattern Analysis and Interpretation

Martin J. Pring

McGraw-Hill
New York Chicago San Francisco
Lisbon London Madrid Mexico City Milan
New Delhi San Juan Seoul Singapore
Sydney Toronto

The McGraw-Hill Companies

5 6 7 8 9 10 QVS/QVS 19 18 17 16 15

P/N 144194-8
PART OF
ISBN 0-07-144038-0

McGraw-Hill books are available at special quantity discounts to use as premiums and sales promotions, or for use in corporate training programs. For more information, please write to the Director of Special Sales, Professional Publishing, McGraw-Hill, Two Penn Plaza, New York, NY 10121-2298. Or contact your local bookstore.

This book is printed on recycled, acid-free paper containing a minimum of 50% recycled, de-inked fiber.

Library of Congress Cataloging-in-Publication Data

Pring, Martin J.
Martin Pring on price patterns : the definitive guide to price pattern analysis and interpretation / by Martin J. Pring.
p. cm.
ISBN 0-07-144038-0 (hardcover : alk. paper)
1. Stock price forecasting. 2. Investment analysis. I. Title: on price patterns. II. Title.

HG4637.P75 2004
332.63'222—dc22 2004004831

Contents

Introduction

In 2002, McGraw-Hill published eight of my books and book/CD-ROM tutorial combinations. As an author, I can tell you that that was a lot of work, and one of my 2003 New Year's resolutions was that enough was enough and I would not write another book for many years. So much for resolutions, because 2003 has seen the birth of this book and the DVD presentation that is enclosed in the back, and 2004 will see their publication.

I first got the idea of writing this book after bumping into Rick Escher of Recognia. Recognia is an Ottawa-based software company that is dedicated to offering scanning techniques for investors and traders. Its principal vehicle for this was originally chart pattern recognition, although this has been and will be expanded to include other technical and possibly fundamental indicators. Accurate scanning software for chart pattern recognition has been one of the dreams of technicians for years, and the opportunity to work with Recognia on this project and the ability to offer it on our Web site at pring.com got me excited enough to come up with this book.

For those interested, the DVD enclosed at the back of the book offers a one-hour presentation taken from my *Live in London* video series. The contents have been selected to reinforce many of the topics covered in the book.

Several classic books on technical analysis have covered the subject of price patterns in depth. In the 1930s, R. W. Shabacker wrote several books on the stock market, of which *Technical Analysis and Stock Market Profits* is the most relevant. H. M. Gartley included a large section on this subject in *Profits and the Stock Market.* Perhaps the most notable has been Edwards and Magee, *Technical Analysis of Stock Trends,* originally published in 1951 and now, under the new editorship of Charles Basatti, expanded to include other technical and portfolio management subjects. There is therefore a raft of information available on this subject, so why offer more? The answer probably lies in the statement, "There is more than one way to skin a cat." In the old days, when charts were plotted by hand, time horizons were much longer. Today, with the advent of intraday trading, more emphasis is being placed on the short term. While a substantial number of the examples featured here rely on daily and weekly charts, quite a few intraday situations have also been included.

The more I study market action, the more I am impressed by the fact that prices are determined by the attitudes of market participants toward the emerging fundamentals. Consequently, I have tried to expand on the discussions in other books concerning the psychological rationale for many of the patterns. If it's possible to understand the logic behind these patterns, there is a greater probability that they will be more accurately—and, hopefully, more profitably—interpreted.

A whole section of the book has been devoted to what I call one- and two-bar price patterns. These formations typically indicate exhaustion and are often followed by sharp and timely reversals in trend. They are especially suited to the swing and day trader, who is forced by time constraints to act quickly. Earlier books covered some of these patterns, but one of the objectives of this book is to expand on this coverage with some ideas of my own.

In addition, I have tried to include a few patterns that are not described in the classic texts, along with a few personal variations. Also, there are some patterns that are described in other books, but that you will not find here. There are two reasons for this. First, it may be that they do not appear in the charts very often. If I have to hunt through hundreds of years of daily data and am hard-pressed to find an example of a specific pattern, that pattern is hardly of practical day-to-day use. Second, some patterns, such as orthodox broadening tops and bottoms, trigger signals so far away from the reversal point that much of the new trend's potential has already been achieved. Discussion of such formations has been kept to a minimum or eliminated altogether. So, too, have explanations of patterns where the demarcation boundaries cannot easily and conveniently be drawn. Diamonds and rounding formations come to mind.

No indicator used in technical analysis is perfect, including price patterns. In this respect, Chapter 18 summarizes some of the research that Pring Research and Recognia have undertaken through the identification of 5,000 patterns between 1982 and 2003. The results indicate that the two types of formation tested, head-and-shoulders and double tops and bottoms, generally work when the signals develop in the direction of the primary trend. This demonstrates that correct interpretation and application, when combined with other indicators, will put the odds in your favor. I say *odds* because technical analysis deals only in probabilities, never in certainties. Because of this, it is of paramount importance for all market participants to first ask the question "What is my risk?" before asking the obvious "What is my reward?" This involves mentally rehearsing where the price would need to go in order to indicate that a pattern had failed. Any good driver looks through the rearview mirror prior to overtaking the car ahead. Traders and investors should do the same by identifying risk before assessing any potential reward

Acknowledgments

There are several people whom I would like to thank for their help and encouragement in writing this book. The idea originally came to me after I bumped into my new friends at Recognia, a Canadian software company devoted to pattern recognition software. In particular, I would like to thank the president of Recognia, Rick Escher, who has provided me with several ideas and has made possible the launching of a pattern recognition subscription service at our Web site, pring.com. My thanks go also to Bob Pelltier at csidata.com for kindly providing the historical data used for the research in Chapter 18.

The DVD at the back of the book was shot as part of a *Live in London* video series. Permission to include the excerpts featured in the DVD was generously given by my friend and the sponsor of the conference, Vince Stanzione, at www.commodities-trader.com. United Kingdom–based traders looking for some quality instruction may well want to look him up.

Finally, and as usual, exceptional thanks goes to my wife, Lisa, who steadfastly applied herself to re-creating all the illustrations featured in the book from my miserable original specimens despite a house move and personal sadness caused by a close family bereavement.

To Lisa, who never fails to surprise me on the upside

PART I
Basic Building Blocks

1

Market Psychology and Prices: Why Patterns Work

The more I work with markets, the more it becomes apparent that prices are determined by one thing and one thing only, and that is people's changing attitudes toward the emerging fundamentals. In other words, prices are determined by psychology. The great technician of the 1940s, Garfield Drew, once wrote, "Stocks don't sell for what they are worth, but for what people think they are worth." If it were not for the fact that these changing attitudes move in trends and that trends tend to perpetuate, market prices would be nothing more than a random event, which would mean that technicians would be out of business.

Changing Attitudes and Changing Prices

A classic example of changing attitudes that affected prices developed in the 1970s and early 1980s. In 1973, a group of stocks known as the "Nifty Fifty" peaked after a phenomenal rise during the 1960s. These were known in the trade as "one-decision" stocks, because their earnings went up every year, as did their prices. People came to the conclusion that there was only one decision to make where these stocks were concerned: just buy! These stocks included such growth names of the time as Kodak, Xerox, McDonald's, and IBM. During 1973 and 1974, they declined substantially in price, along with the rest of the market. Over the course of the next nine years or so, the earnings for the group as a whole continued to rise, but the index did not make a new post-1973 high until nine years later.

Thus we arrive at a situation where prices bear no reality to the earnings trend. Perhaps prices were too high in 1973 relative to the earnings; perhaps they were not, and they should have continued rising throughout the 1970s as earnings rose. Who knows? Who can tell? Technicians would say, "Who cares?" Why? Because technical analysis assumes that the changing attitudes toward these emerging fundamentals are reflected in price action as displayed in charts. It's not dissimilar to a medical technician looking at a patient's chart. He doesn't have to know that the patient is groaning with pain to diagnose a problem. It's all there in the chart. The chart tells him that the patient's vital signs are deteriorating to the point where danger lies ahead and that remedial action should be taken. In a similar way, to the technician, poor price action signifies a weak price trend and the probability of trouble ahead in the form of a serious price decline. The technician does not have to know the reason why; he merely observes the condition and takes the necessary action.

Chart 1-1 shows the 1990s price action for Key Corp., a money-center bank. The bank's earnings are shown in the lower panel. Note that there are two periods when the price came down for a prolonged period, the first in the 1980s and the second in the late 1990s. In both cases the earnings rose, demonstrating once again that it is the attitude of market participants toward the emerging fundamentals rather than the fundamentals themselves that is important. This is not the same thing as saying that earnings are not important; of course they are. If we had known that earnings were

Chart 1-1 Key Corp. 1990–2002 vs. earnings. (*Source: Telescan.*)

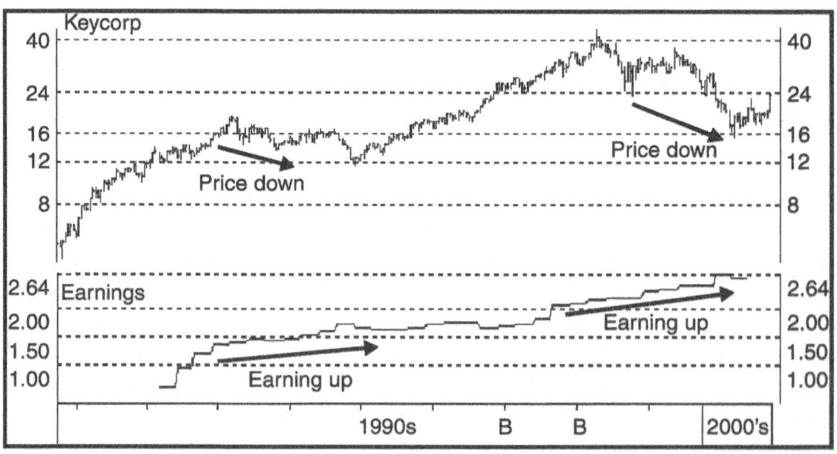

Chart 1-2 eBay 1998–2003 vs. earnings. (*Source: Telescan.*)

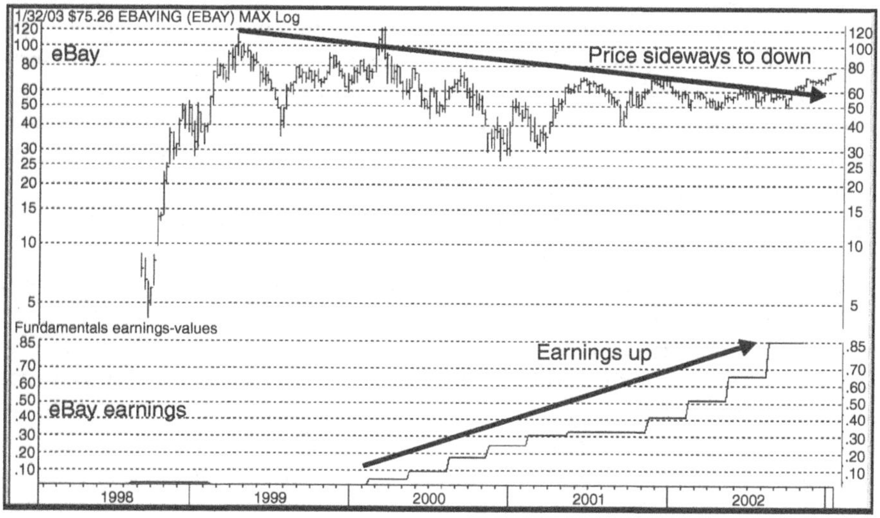

going to rise at the beginning of both these periods, it would have been reasonable for us to assume that the price would rally as well. Only a review of the technical position could have helped us to conclude otherwise.

Chart 1-2 shows another example, featuring eBay. Once again we can see that the earnings increased pretty dramatically throughout the period covered by the chart. However, the price fell slightly, showing the futility of buying and selling stocks based purely upon accurate earnings estimates.

History repeats, but never exactly, and as prices approach a turning point, people react in roughly the same way. It is this similarity of behavior that shows up in identifiable price patterns or formations, and that is the subject of this book. Later on we will classify these various formations, establish their reliability, and explain how they can be used as a basis for trading.

Technical Analysis Defined

At the outset, it is very important to understand that technical analysis is an art form. Indeed I define it as "the art of identifying a trend reversal at a relatively early stage and riding on that trend until the *weight of the evidence* shows or proves that the trend has reversed." You have probably noticed that I have emphasized the words *weight of the evidence.* This is because price patterns should be looked upon as one indicator in the weight-of-the-evidence approach. In other words, we should not look at price patterns in isolation, but consider them in conjunction with several other indicators. Over the years, technicians have developed literally thousands of indicators, so it is obviously impossible to follow them all. By "weight of the evidence" I mean four or five indicators that the user feels comfortable with. The world's great religions are all primarily concerned with finding the truth, but each has its own way of getting there. So, too, with technical analysis; what one person sees as a great indicator another may discard as useless. It's important for you as an individual to decide which indicators to adopt in your trading by testing them over a period of time. If you do not have confidence in your choices, I can assure you that you will make wrong trading decisions once the trend goes against you.

By this point you may be asking, "What does he mean by indicators?" Well, I mean oscillators such as the RSI, stochastic, KST, and so on. Other approaches include Elliott, Gann, or the Wykoff method. Still others rely on cycles, volume, or trend-following indicators, such as moving averages and trendlines. Price patterns are therefore one indicator in this weight-of-the-evidence approach. I strongly believe that they should not be used in isolation, but rather should be used in conjunction with several of these other indicators with which you feel comfortable. Price patterns should not be used blindly; they should be interpreted and applied with a full understanding of the underlying psychology that gives rise to their development. If you understand roughly how and why they work, you will be in a better position to interpret them in difficult situations.

Price Patterns and Psychology

I have used the word *trend* several times, but what is a trend? In my view, a trend is *a period in which a price moves in an irregular but persistent direction.* There will be a lot said on the subject of trends in the next chapter, but for now all we need to know is that there are various classes depending upon the time frame under consideration. For example, a 60-minute bar chart will reflect very short trends, and a monthly bar chart will reflect trends of much greater duration, lasting for years. However, the principles of interpretation are identical. The only difference is that reversals of trends on intraday charts have nowhere near the significance of those on the monthly charts. It should be assumed that the longer the time span, the more reliable the signal. It is important to understand that this last statement is a generalization, since some short-term signals can be very reliable and some long-term signals less reliable. The reason why longer-term trends have a habit of being slightly more reliable is that they are less subject to random noise and manipulation.

When a trend is underway, it means that either buyers or sellers are in control. During an uptrend, it is the buyers, and during a downtrend, the sellers.

I have often heard people respond to the question, "Why is so and so going up?" with the flippant answer, "Because there are more buyers than sellers!" Well, strictly speaking, this is not true, because every transaction must be equally balanced. If I sell 1,000 shares, there must be one or more buyers who are willing to purchase that 1,000 shares. There can never be more, and there can never be less. What moves prices is the enthusiasm of buyers *relative* to that of sellers. If buyers are more motivated, they will bid prices higher. On the other hand, if sellers are more motivated, then the savvy buyers will wait for the sellers to come down to their bids, and prices will decline.

Technicians have noted over the years that prices do not usually reverse on a dime. There is usually a transitional period between those times when buyers have the upper hand and those when sellers are pressing prices lower. During these transitional phases, prices experience trading ranges. This ranging action often takes the form of clearly identifiable price patterns or formations. If these transitional periods are classified as a horizontal trend, it follows that there are three possible trends: up, down, and sideways. Occasionally prices will resolve these horizontal price movements in favor of the previous prevailing trend. In this case, the temporary battle between buyers and sellers turns out, in retrospect, to be a period of consolidation. Such formations would then be termed *consolidation* or *continuation patterns,* since the prevailing trend would continue after their completion. By the same token, if a pattern separates an uptrend from a downtrend or a downtrend from an uptrend, the formation would be called a *reversal pattern.*

It is a generally known fact that rising prices attract bullish sentiment and vice versa. When prices begin their ascent, most people do not anticipate a large sell-off. This is because the news background remains very positive and people generally extrapolate the recent past. It is only after prices have been falling for some time that bad news becomes believable. This means that when we spot a bearish-looking pattern after a previously bullish trend, it is unlikely that we will believe its bearish omen. In fact, we could say that the less believable the pattern, the greater the odds that it is going to work.

Let's look at it another way. Say the gold market has been rallying for months and there are widespread media reports telling us that gold and gold shares have outperformed the stock market. In this kind of environment, analysts and other market participants typically expect more of the same. It's possible that there is also a scary geopolitical background; for example, oil supplies may be threatened. However, the gold price forms a reversal price pattern. At the time it would be inconceivable that this pattern could "work," but that is precisely the time when it is most likely to do so. The tip-off might come if the news becomes exceptionally bullish as a result of some destabilizing geopolitical event, but the price does not make a new high. That will give the bearish technical case substantial credibility, for if unexpected "good" news (for gold) cannot send the price higher, what will? Nothing, *because this news is already factored into the price.* Such action tells us that the underlying technical position is not as strong as it appears on the surface. It's the market's way of saying, forget the media hype, bullish sentiment, and what you *hope* will happen. Instead, focus on what the market is actually telling you and act on that. The problem is that when everyone around you is convinced that a specific trend is going to extend, it is very difficult to take a different stance. Only after taking a series of losses because you believed the crowd rather than the market action are you likely to learn the lesson that the market speaks the truth and crowds speak with forked tongues.

2 Three Introductory Concepts

Introduction

Before we proceed to a discussion of price patterns themselves, it is important for us to lay the groundwork by describing a few introductory concepts. By doing so, it is possible to obtain a firmer foundation and a better understanding of how markets work, and we will then be in a better position to interpret and apply price patterns for more profitable trading and investing. This chapter will describe the importance and implications of time frames and trends. It will conclude with a discussion of peak-and-trough analysis and the pros and cons of logarithmic versus arithmetic scaling. Incidentally, I will be using the word *security* extensively. This term is a generic one and avoids the constant use of stocks, commodities, currencies, bonds, etc. Just think of a security as any freely traded entity and you will be on the right track.

Time Frames

We have already established the link between psychology and prices. It is also a fact that human nature (psychology) is more or less constant. This means that the principles of technical analysis can be applied to any time frame, from one-minute bars to weekly and monthly charts. The interpretation is identical. The only difference is that the battle between buyers and sellers is much larger on the monthly charts than on the intraday ones. This means that any trend-reversal signals are far more significant on the longer charts. As we proceed, it will be evident that this book contains a huge variety of examples featuring many different time frames. *For the purpose of interpretation, the time frame really doesn't matter; it's the character of the pattern that does.* For example, if you are a long-term trader and you see a particular example featured on a 10-minute bar chart, the example is just as relevant as it would be to an intraday trader. The long-term trader would never initiate a trade based on a 10-minute chart, but that trader can and should take action when that same pattern appears on a weekly or monthly one, and vice versa.

Trends

A trend is a period in which a price moves in an irregular but persistent direction and is a time measurement of the direction in price levels. There are many different classifications of trends in technical analysis. It is useful to examine the more common ones, since an understanding of them will give us perspective on the significance of specific price patterns. The three most widely followed trends are primary, intermediate, and short-term trends. Whenever we talk of any specific category of trend as lasting for such and such a time period, please remember that the description is offered as a rough guide, encompassing most, but not all, trends of that particular type. Some trends will last longer, and others for less time.

Primary

The primary trend revolves around the business cycle, which extends for approximately 3.6 years from trough to trough. Rising and falling primary trends (bull and bear markets) last for 1 to 2 years. Since building takes longer than tearing down, bull markets generally last longer than bear markets.

The primary trend is illustrated in Fig. 2-1 by the thickest line. In an ideal situation, the magnitude and duration of the primary uptrend (bull market) are identical to those of the primary downtrend (bear market), but in reality, they are usually very different. Price patterns that offer reversal signals for primary trends usually take longer than three months to complete.

Intermediate

It is unusual for prices to move in straight lines, so primary up- and downtrends are almost always interrupted by countercyclical corrections along the

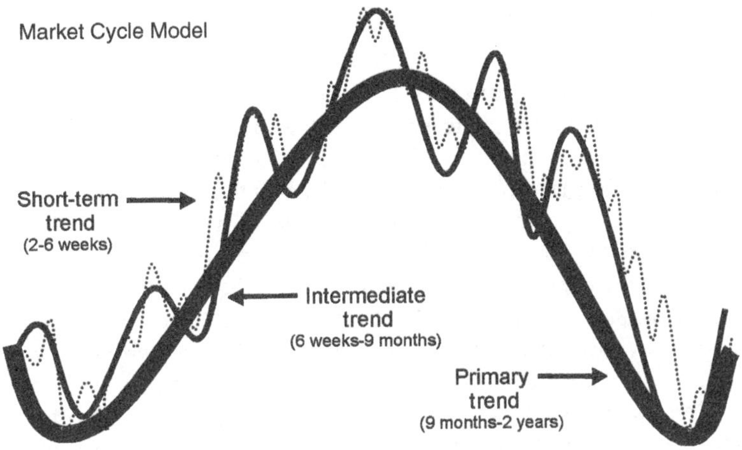

Figure 2-1 The market cycle model. (*Source: pring.com adapted from Yelton Fiscal.*)

way. These trends are called *intermediate price movements*, and they last anywhere from six weeks to as long as nine months. Occasionally they last even longer, and some writers classify some trends that take as little as three weeks to complete as intermediate price movements. The intermediate trend is represented in Fig. 2-1 by the thinner solid line. Price patterns that signal reversals in intermediate trends do not take as long to form as those reversing primary price movements. As a rough guide, I would say three to six weeks. A lot will depend on the magnitude and duration of the intermediate trend leading into the formation.

Short-Term

As a rough guide, short-term trends (the dashed line in Fig. 2-1) typically last three or four weeks, although they are sometimes shorter and often longer. They interrupt the course of the intermediate trend, just as the intermediate trend interrupts primary price movements. Short-term trends are usually influenced by random news events and are far more difficult to identify than their intermediate or primary counterparts. Price patterns in this case would take one to two weeks to develop.

The formation time varies a great deal, so the estimates provided here should be used as approximate guides. Quite often almost the whole of the trend is taken up by the formation of the pattern. We will show some examples later on when some of these formations have actually been defined.

The Interaction of Trends

It is apparent by now that the price level of any security is influenced simultaneously by several different trends. Indeed, there are many more types of trend, some longer and some shorter than the three we have just been describing. These too have an influence on price. Whenever we are considering a specific price pattern, our first objective is to understand which type of trend is being reversed. For example, if a reversal in a short-term trend has just taken place, a much smaller price movement may be expected than if the pattern was reversing a primary trend.

Short-term traders are principally concerned with smaller movements in price, but they *also need to know the direction of the intermediate and primary trends.* This is because these longer-term trends dominate near-term price action. This means that any surprises will develop in the direction of the primary trend. In a bull market, the surprises will be on the upside, and in a bear market, they will be on the downside. Just think of it this way: Rising short-term trends that develop in a bull market are likely to be much greater in magnitude than short-term downtrends, and vice versa. *Trading losses usually happen when the trader is positioned in a countercyclical position against the main trend.* The implication for price patterns is that if a false signal is to be given, it will almost always develop in a manner countercyclical to the trend above it. For example, a security may be in a primary bear market. If it then traces out a bullish intermediate price formation, chances are that this breakout will turn out to be false because it is countercyclical in nature. We cannot say that all bullish patterns that develop in bearish trends will fail. What we can say, though, is that if a failure is going to take place, it is most likely to happen following a countercyclical breakout.

Intraday Trends

What is true for longer-term trends is also true for intraday data. In this case, the short-term trend in the daily charts becomes the long-term trend in the intraday charts. Figure 2-2 represents three rough time approximations for the short-term, intermediate, and long-term trends in intraday charts. Patterns on these charts have two principal differences from those appearing on the longer-term ones. First, their effect is of much shorter duration. Second, extremely short-term price trends are much more influenced by instant reactions to news events than are longer-term ones. Decisions, therefore, have a tendency to develop as emotional, knee-jerk reactions. Also, intraday price action is more susceptible to manipulation. As a consequence, price data used in very-short-term charts are much more erratic and *generally* less reliable than those that appear in the longer-term charts.

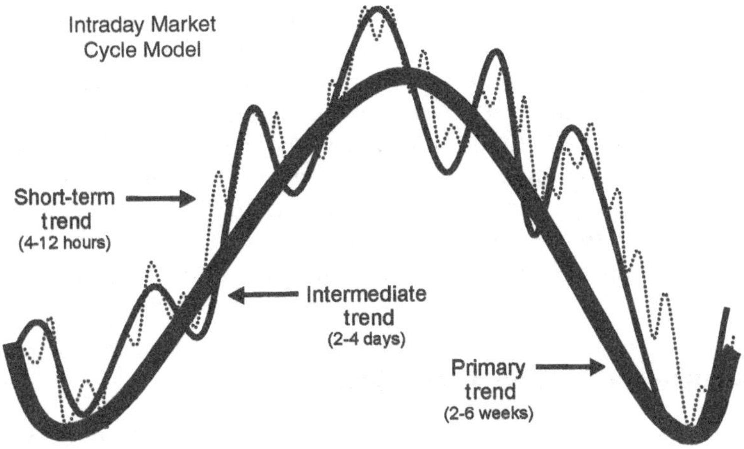

Figure 2-2 The intraday market cycle model.

The Secular Trend

The primary trend consists of several intermediate cycles, but the secular, or very-long-term, trend is constructed from a number of primary trends. This "super cycle," or long wave, extends over a substantially greater period, usually lasting well over 10 years and often as long as 25 years. A diagram of the interrelationship between a secular and a primary trend is shown in Fig. 2-3. It is certainly very helpful to understand the direction

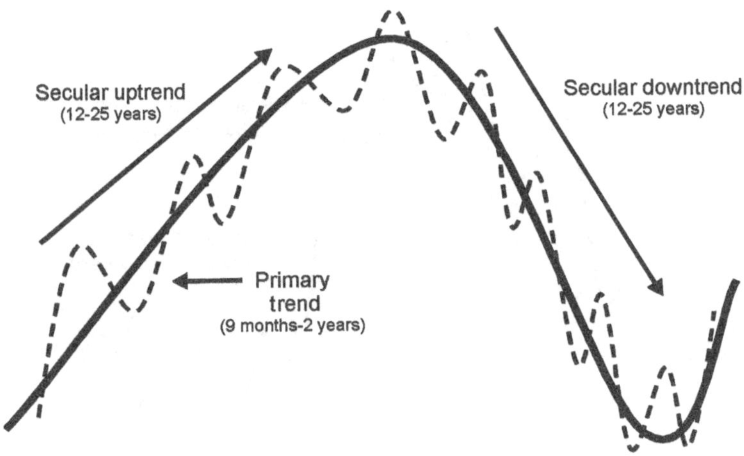

Figure 2-3 The secular versus the cyclical trend.

of the secular trend. Just as the primary trend influences the magnitude of the intermediate-term rally relative to the countercyclical reaction, so the secular trend influences the magnitude and duration of a primary-trend rally or reaction. For example, in a rising secular trend, primary bull markets will be of greater magnitude than primary bear markets. In a secular downtrend, bear markets will be more powerful, and will take longer to unfold, than bull markets. Price patterns that reverse secular trends are obviously much larger than those that separate a primary bull and bear market, often forming over many years. By the same token, they are also much rarer.

Peak-and-Trough Progression

Widespread use of computers has led to the development of very sophisticated trend-identification techniques in market analysis. Some of these work reasonably well, but most do not. In the rush to develop these more complicated approaches, the simplest and most basic techniques of technical analysis are often overlooked. One of these is the peak-and-trough approach. It is one piece of evidence in the weight-of-the-evidence approach described earlier, but it is also the building block for several price patterns.

The concept is very simple. A rising trend typically consists of a series of rallies and reactions. Each high is higher than its predecessor, as is each low. When the series of rising peaks and troughs is interrupted, a trend reversal is signaled.

In Fig. 2-4, the price has been advancing in a series of waves, with each peak and each trough being higher than its predecessor. Then, for the first time, a rally fails to move to a new high, and the subsequent reaction pushes

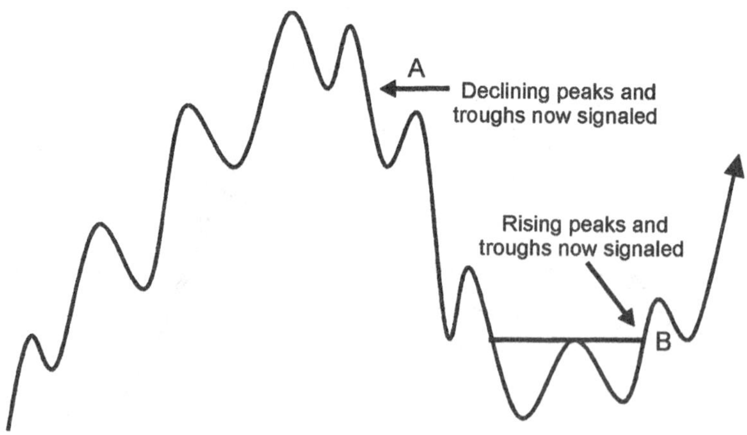

Figure 2-4 Peak-and-trough reversal signals.

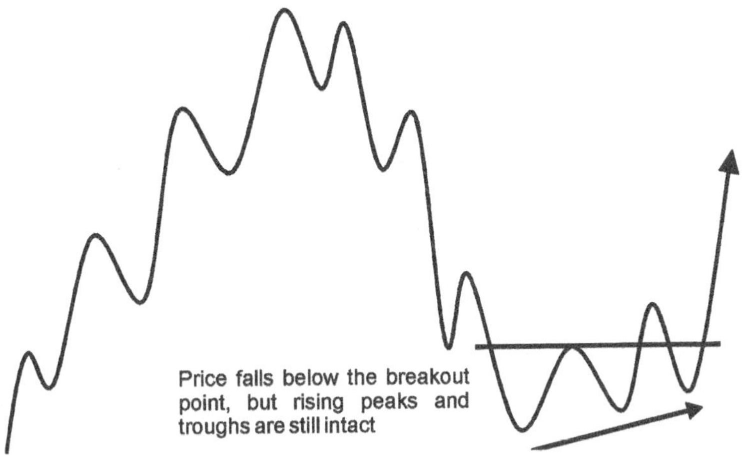

Figure 2-5 Peak-and-trough reversal and test.

it *below the previous trough.* This occurs at point *A* and gives a signal that, as far as the peak-and-trough indicator is concerned, the trend has reversed. Point *B* in Fig. 2-4 shows a similar situation, but this time the trend reversal is from a downtrend to an uptrend.

The significance of a peak-and-trough reversal is determined by the duration and magnitude of the rallies and reactions in question.

For example, if it takes two to three weeks to complete each wave in a series of rallies and reactions, the trend reversal will be an intermediate one, since intermediate price movements consist of a series of short-term (two- to three-week) fluctuations. Similarly, the interruption of a series of falling intermediate peaks and troughs by a rising one signals a reversal from a primary bear to a primary bull market.

In Fig. 2-4 the price falls back to the level of the initial recovery high, but in Fig. 2-5 it drops below it. This is still a bullish situation because the rising peaks and troughs remain intact.

A Peak-and-Trough Dilemma

Occasionally, peak-and-trough progression becomes more complicated than the examples shown in Figs. 2-4 and 2-5. In Fig. 2-6, the market has been advancing in a series of rising peaks and troughs, but following the highest peak, the price declines at point *X* to a level that is below the previous low. At this juncture, the series of rising troughs has been broken, but *not* the series of rising peaks. In other words, *at point* X, *only half a signal has been generated.* The complete signal of a reversal of both rising peaks and troughs

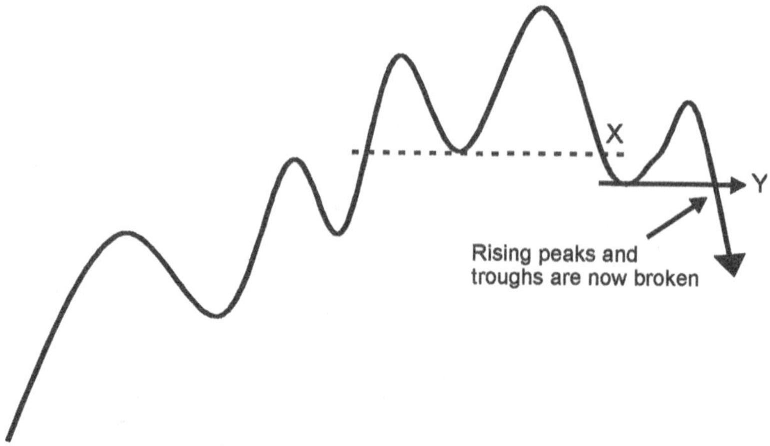

Figure 2-6 Peak-and-trough half signal at a top.

arises at point *Y*, when the price slips below the level previously reached at point *X*, having failed in its attempt to register a new high.

At point *X*, there is quite a dilemma because the trend should still be classified as positive, and yet the very fact that the series of rising troughs has been interrupted indicates underlying technical weakness. On the one hand, we are presented with half a bearish signal, while on the other, waiting for point *Y* could mean giving up a substantial amount of the profits earned during the bull market. The problem is that if we do not wait, the price could well extend its uptrend, as in Fig. 2-7.

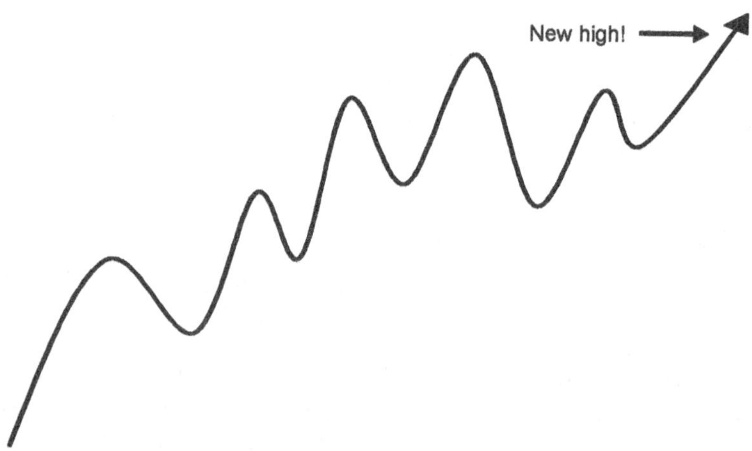

Figure 2-7 Peak-and-trough continuation.

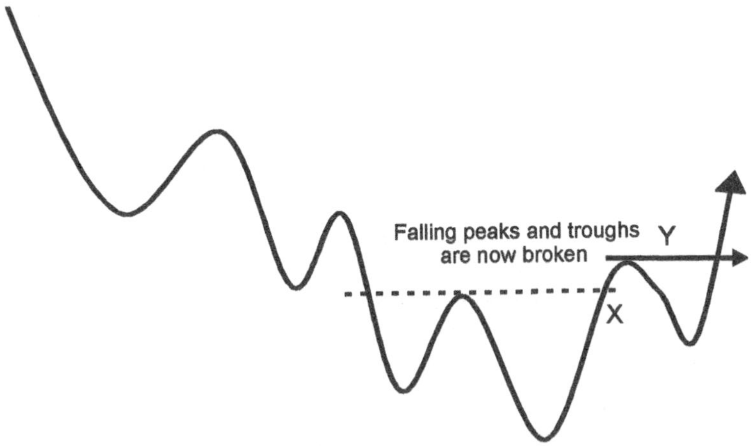

Figure 2-8 Peak-and-trough half signal at a bottom.

That's why the dilemma is probably best dealt with by referring to the weight of the evidence from other technical indicators, such as moving averages (MAs), volume, momentum, and so on. If these other techniques overwhelmingly indicate a trend reversal, it is probably safe to anticipate a change in trend, even though peak-and-trough progression has not completely *confirmed* the reversal. It is still a wise policy, though, to view this signal with some degree of skepticism until the reversal is confirmed by an interruption in *both* the series of rising peaks and the series of rising troughs.

Figure 2-8 shows this type of situation for a reversal from a bear to a bull trend. The same principles of interpretation apply at point *X* as in Fig. 2-6.

What Constitutes a Legitimate Peak and Trough?

Most of the time, the various rallies and reactions are self-evident, so it is easy to determine that these turning points are legitimate peaks and troughs. It is generally assumed that a reaction to the prevailing trend should retrace between one-third and two-thirds of the previous trend. This means that if we take the first rally from the trough low to the subsequent peak in Fig. 2-9 as 100 percent, the ensuing correction should be anywhere from one-third to two-thirds of that move. In this case it appears to be just over one-half, or a 50 percent retracement of the previous move. Occasionally, the retracement can reach 100 percent. Technical analysis is far from precise, but if a retracement move is a good deal less than the minimum one-third, then the peak or trough in question is held to be suspect.

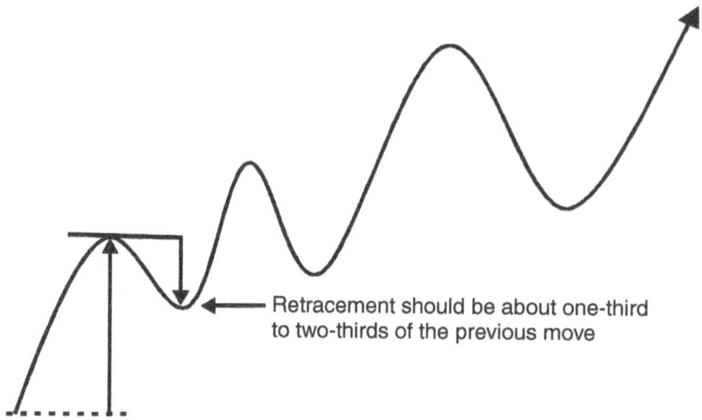

Figure 2-9 Peak-and-trough determination (magnitude).

There is one exception to this rule. Occasionally a correction takes the form of a sideways trading range rather than an advance or decline. Since the trading range is still an interruption of the dominant trend, and therefore reflects a psychological correction, we can still use the one-third to two-thirds rule, but in this instance substituting time for magnitude. This idea is shown in Fig. 2-10, where the correction should last between one-third and two-thirds of the time taken to complete the rally leading up to it. The

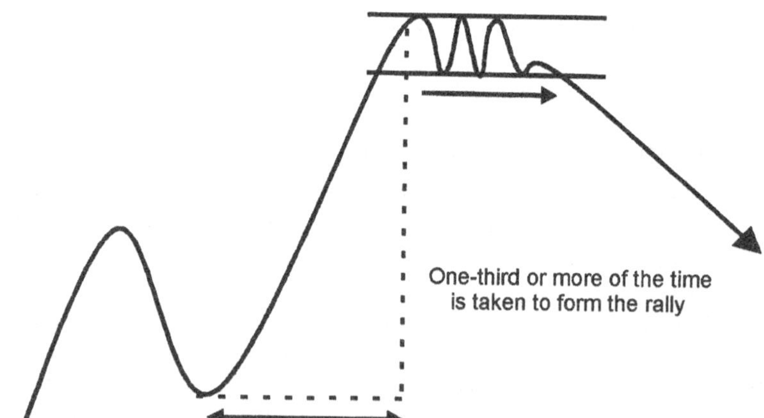

Figure 2-10 Peak-and-trough determination (time).

same principles are applied to trading ranges and rallies that develop within downtrends.

It is also important to categorize what kind of trend is being monitored. Obviously a reversal derived from a series of rallies and reactions each lasting, say, two to three weeks would be an intermediate reversal. This is because the swings would be short-term in nature. On the other hand, peak-and-trough reversals that develop in intraday charts are likely to have significance over a much shorter period. How short would depend on whether the swings were a reflection of hourly or, say, five-minute bars.

Arithmetic or Logarithmic Scaling?

There are two axes on any market chart. The *x* axis, along the bottom, registers the date (except in point-and-figure charting), and the *y* axis, the price. There are two methods of plotting the *y* axis, arithmetic and logarithmic. And which one is chosen can have very important implications.

Arithmetic charts allocate a specific *point* or *dollar* amount to a given vertical distance. Thus, in Chart 2-1, each arrow has the same vertical distance and reflects approximately 200 points. That will be true at any price level.

Chart 2-1 S&P Composite, 1900–2003, arithmetic scale.

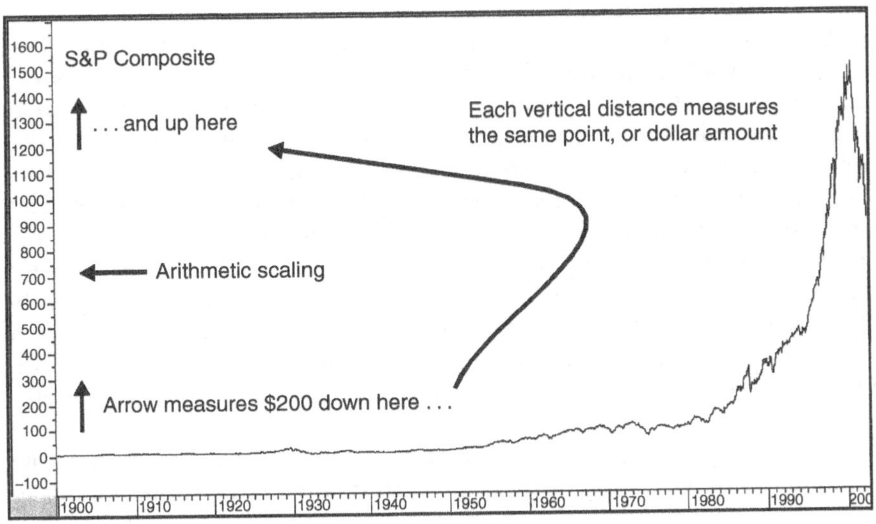

Chart 2-2 S&P Composite, 1900–2003, logarithmic scale.

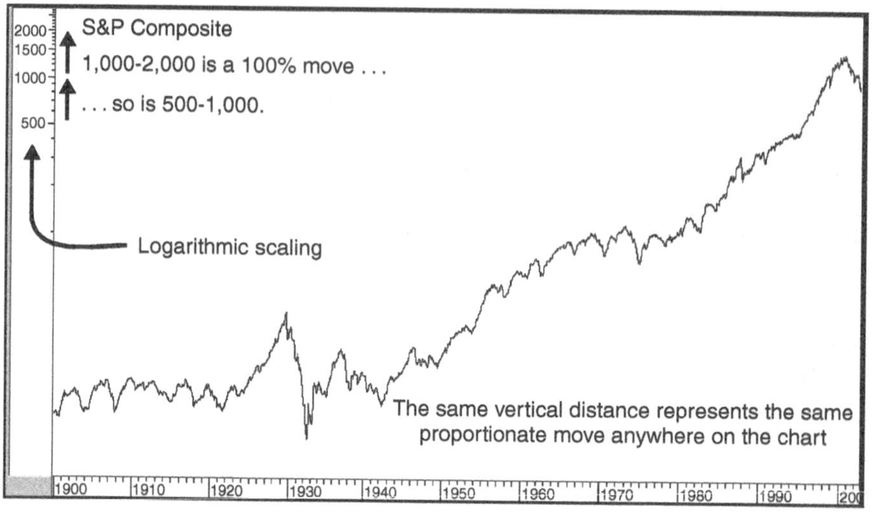

A logarithmic scale, on the other hand, allocates a given *percentage* price move to a specific vertical distance. In Chart 2-2, each arrow represents a move of approximately 100 percent, whether it is at lower prices or higher prices. There is very little noticeable difference between the scaling methods when charts are plotted over short periods of time, where price fluctuations are relatively subdued. However, with large price fluctuations, there are considerable differences.

The arithmetic scale suppresses price fluctuations at low levels and exaggerates them at high points. Thus the 85 percent 1929–1932 decline hardly shows up at all in Chart 2-1, but the 40 percent late 1990s–early 2000s retreat (no small decline) is greatly exaggerated. Chart 2-2 shows that the logarithmic scaling brings back 1929 and does not exaggerate the turn-of-the-century bear market. The media love to hype stories and news because that is what sells. You will find that charts featuring financial markets or economic numbers are almost always plotted on an arithmetic scale because this has the effect of exaggerating the most recent changes. Another hyping technique used by the media is to present the data for a short period using a very limited scale. The reader is then left with the sense of a dramatic move. This would not be the case if the data were displayed over a much longer period using a wider price scale.

As you can appreciate, I am very much in favor of using a logarithmic scale because it displays price trends in a proportionate way. Psychology tends to move proportionately as well, so it makes perfect rational sense to use logarithmic scaling. Having said that, when price fluctuations are relatively small, say over a three-month period, there is very little difference between the two scaling methods. As a purist, though, I still prefer the log scale at all times.

There is an even more important advantage of the logarithmic scale, which we shall learn when the concept of pattern price objectives is discussed later.

Summary

- The principles of technical analysis can be applied equally to any time frame.
- The longer the time frame the greater the significance of any technical signal.
- A number of different trends simultaneously influence the price level of any market; primary, intermediate, and short term are the most important.
- Peak-and-trough progression is the most basic trend-identification technique and is a central building block of price pattern analysis.
- In order to qualify as a new legitimate peak or trough a good rule of thumb is that the price should retrace between one-third and two-thirds of the previous move.
- Arithmetic scaling suppresses price fluctuations at lower price levels and exaggerates them at higher levels.

3 Support and Resistance Zones: How to Identify Them

Support and resistance are two more building blocks of the technical arsenal used in price pattern analysis. A discussion of these two concepts will therefore help us greatly in our understanding of how price patterns work. A lot of people use the term *support* when they really mean resistance and use *resistance* when they really mean support. It's no wonder that there is a lot of confusion. Basically, these are points on a chart where the probabilities favor at least a temporary halt in the prevailing trend.

Support and Resistance

In their classic book *Technical Analysis of Stock Trends*, Edwards and Magee defined *support* as "buying (actual or potential) sufficient in volume to halt a downtrend in prices for an appreciable period," and *resistance* as "selling (actual or potential) sufficient in volume to satisfy all bids and hence stop prices from going higher for a time."

A support zone represents a *concentration of demand*, and a resistance zone represents a *concentration of supply*. The word *concentration* is emphasized because supply and demand are always in balance, but it is the relative enthusiasm of buyers as compared to sellers, or vice versa, that is important because that is what determines trends. If buyers are more enthusiastic than sellers,

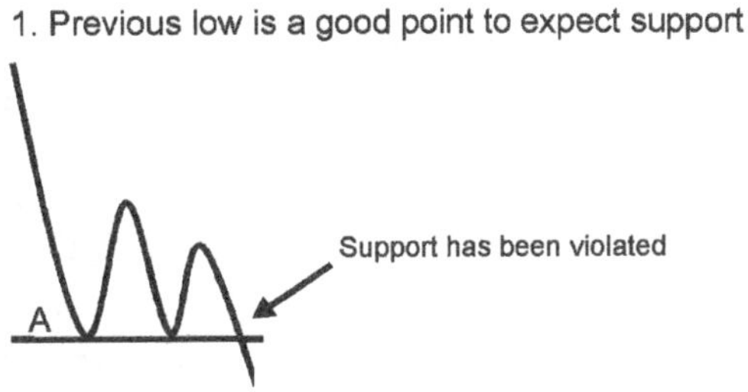

Figure 3-1 Previous low is a good place to expect support.

they will continually increase their bids until their purchasing demands have been satisfied. On the other hand, if sellers are the more anxious, then they will be willing to liquidate at lower prices and the general price level will fall.

If in doubt, think of support as a temporary floor for prices and resistance as a ceiling.

At the beginning of Fig. 3-1, the price is declining. It finds a bottom at *A* and then moves up. The next time it falls to *A*, it again rallies, so *A* may now be said to be a support area. This establishes our first principle of support/resistance analysis: *A previous high or low is a potential resistance/support level.* The third time the price slips to *A*, it goes through or, as we say, violates support. One of the first principles of identifying a potential support level, then, is to look for previous lows. In the case of potential resistance, this would be in the area of a previous high.

Figure 3-2 shows a more extended example. This time the price found temporary support at *B*. *C* also proves to be a support point, but note that

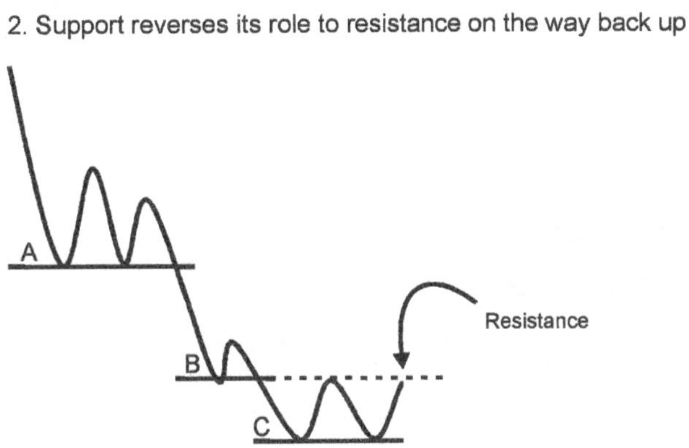

Figure 3-2 Support reverses its role to resistance on the way back up.

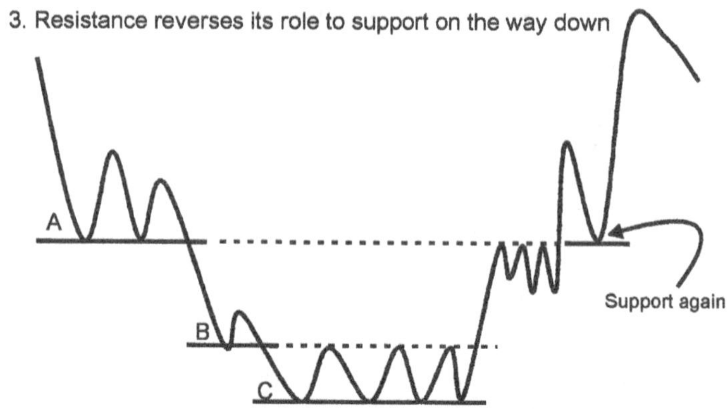

Figure 3-3 Resistance reverses its role to support on the way down.

the rallies are reversed at support level *B*. Thus the second principle is that *support reverses its role to resistance on the way up.* Just think of it this way: A floor in a building acts as a support zone, but when you fall through it, the floor now becomes resistance, called a ceiling. The reason why support and resistance reverse their roles can be appreciated with an explanation of some elementary psychology. No one likes to take a loss, and while some people overcome this feeling by cutting their losses at an early stage, others hold on until the price comes back to where the security in question was originally bought. At that point they are able to break even and sell, thereby creating a quantity of supply sufficient to temporarily halt the advance.

Finally, in Fig. 3-3 we see the price rally through resistance at *B* and *A* (the former support level). The ensuing decline then finds support at *A* again. Thus our third principle is that *resistance reverses its role to support on the way down.*

Rules for Determining Potential Support/Resistance Points

1. Previous Highs and Lows

We have already established that previous highs and lows are potential support or resistance levels. Highs are important because many market participants may have bought close to or at the actual high for a move. When prices decline, the normal human response is not to take a loss but to hold on. That way, it is felt, there will not be the pain of actually realizing a loss.

Consequently, when the price returns to the old high, those who bought at that level have great motivation to sell in order to break even, so they begin to liquidate. Also, those who bought at lower prices have a tendency to take profits at the old high, since that is the top of familiar ground. By the same token, any prices above the old high look expensive to potential buyers; consequently, there is less enthusiasm on their part, so they begin to pull away from the market.

When a price rallies and then falls back to the previous low, these bargain basement prices appeal to potential buyers. After all, they missed the opportunity the first time prices retreated to this level, and they are therefore thankful to have another chance. For the same reason, sellers are reluctant to part with their securities as prices approach the previous low, since they saw them bounce before and naturally wonder why the same process should not be repeated.

Chart 3-1 shows the sugar price for a period spanning 2002–2003. Note how previous highs and lows offer good support/resistance points for future trading. Unfortunately, there is no way of knowing whether a particular level will turn out to be support or resistance, or even whether it will be a pivotal point at all. That's why these are merely intelligent places for anticipating a temporary reversal. Resort to other indicators such as oscillators is therefore required.

Chart 3-1 Sugar, 2002–2003, daily.

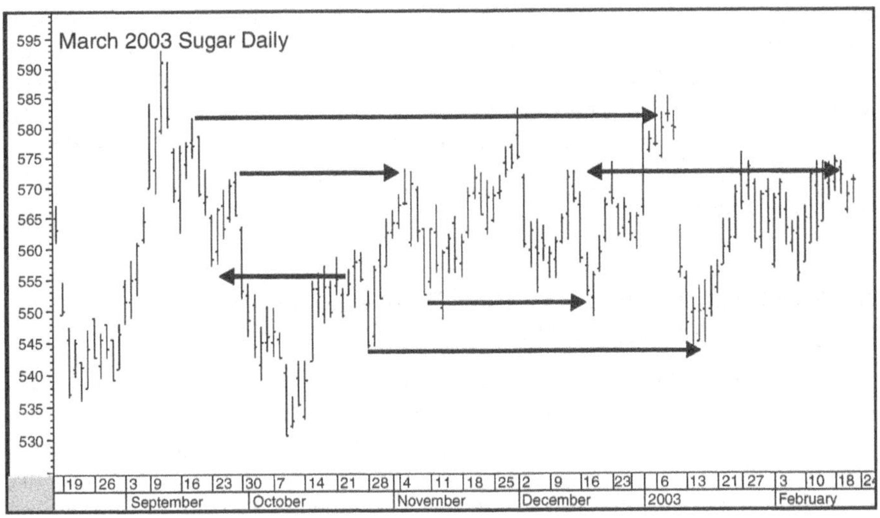

2. At Round Numbers

Support and resistance zones have a habit of forming at round numbers. This is probably because numbers such as 10, 50, or 100 represent easy psychological points upon which traders and investors often base their decisions. In the 1970s, for example, the Dow Jones Industrials had a great deal of difficulty surpassing the 1000 level. For gold in the 1980s and mid-1990s, the magic number was $400, and so forth. The guide for potential turning points, then, is to look for round numbers.

3. Trendlines and Moving Averages Represent Dynamic Levels of Support and Resistance

A good trendline should reflect the underlying trend. One of the rules for assessing the significance of a line relates to how many times it has been touched or approached. The more the merrier in this case. If a price falls back to a specific low on several occasions, this makes that particular price level a strong support zone. The same is true of trendlines and moving averages (MAs). Every time a price moves back to an up trendline or a rising MA and bounces, it is reinforced as a dynamic level of support. The same would be true in reverse for a declining trendline or moving average. It therefore makes sense to buy as the price falls to an up trendline (or rising MA) and to sell when it rises to a down trendline (or rising MA). A low-risk stop may then be placed just beyond the line or MA in case the support/resistance zone is violated.

Chart 3-2, for Hewlett-Packard, shows a very good example of how a down trendline acted as resistance. Note also that the interaction of a reliable MA, such as the 200-day MA featured in this chart, acts as reinforcement of the resistance zone. This works in the same way as if we were building a house and doubled the thickness of the roof. The identical principle holds when a moving average and a trendline are at the same level; they double the strength of the resistance (or support in the case of an up trendline and MA intersection).

4. Emotional Points on a Chart Represent Potential Support/Resistance Levels

This concept will be covered in subsequent chapters when we consider gaps, extreme points of Pinocchio bars, two-bar reversals, key reversals, and so forth. For the moment, suffice it to say that most emotional points are those at which prices following a strong and persistent trend experience a strong extension of that trend. During the course of the bar's formation, they then abruptly reverse their direction.

Chart 3-2 Hewlett-Packard, 2001–2002, daily.

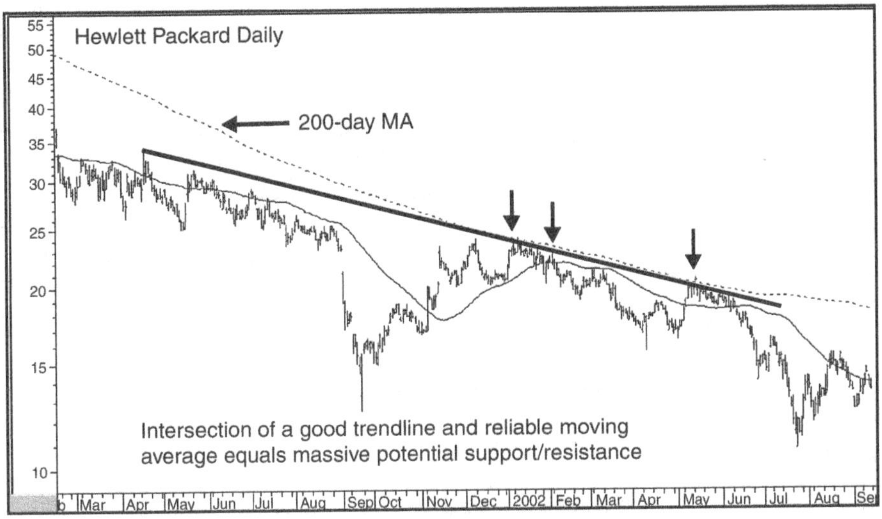

Gaps represent another example of emotional points. They are formed when buyers or sellers respond so emotionally to news that a blank space, or gap, is left on the chart. In Chart 3-3, probably because of unexpected bad news, the sugar price experiences three downside gaps. Later on, when emotions become more stable, the price rallies and tries to "close" each of

Chart 3-3 March, 2003, sugar.

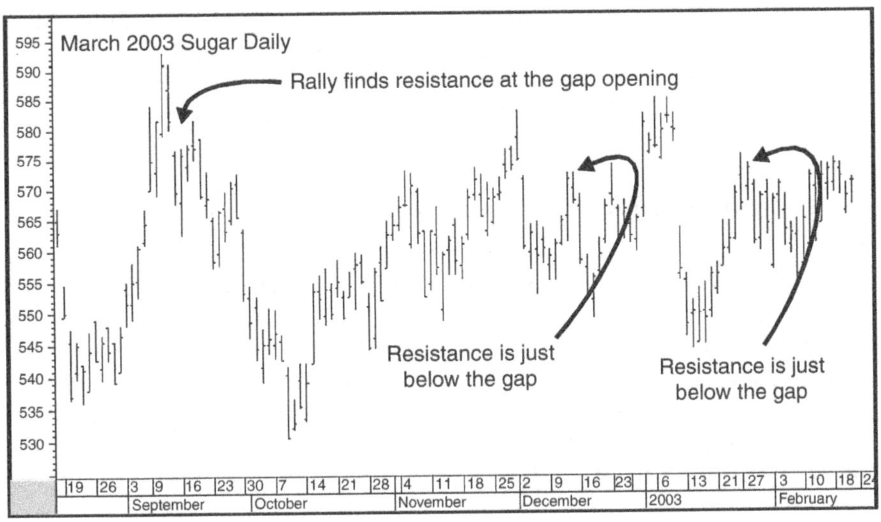

Chart 3-4 Boeing, 1998–2003, weekly.

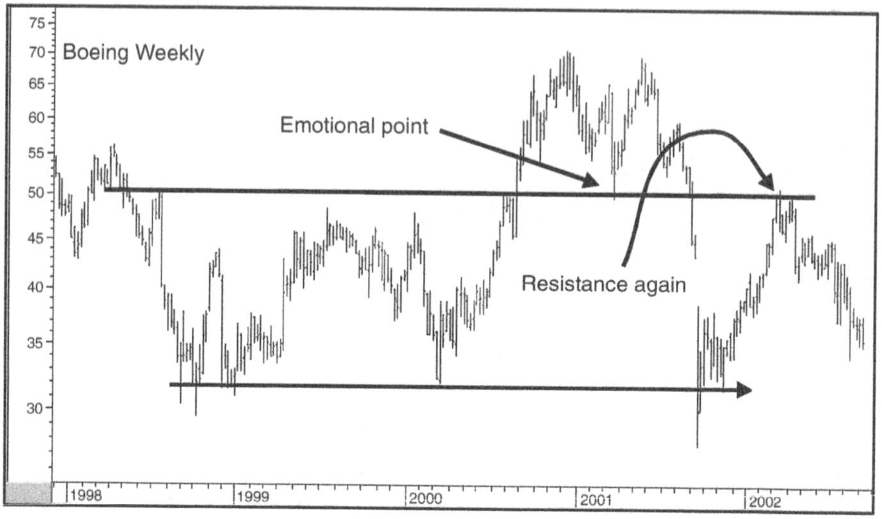

the gaps. In the case of the gap on the left, resistance is found at the gap's opening. In the other two examples, resistance forms at the lower part of the gap. Gaps are one of the most reliable technical concepts from the point of view of projecting potential support or resistance areas.

Chart 3-4, for Boeing, shows another emotional point. This time it's the bottom of a very wide bar in early 2002. Note that this low developed at a round number, $50. Normally this would have been a support level the next time the price fell to $50, but in the fall of 2002 the price went right through it. Even so, $50 did turn out to be a pivotal point the next time Boeing rallied. It goes to show that even if a support/resistance zone is violated once, it can still turn out to be a pivotal point in subsequent price action.

5. Proportionate Moves, Retracements, and So On

The law of motion states that for every action, there is a reaction. Price trends established in financial markets are really the measurement of crowd psychology in motion and are also subject to this law. These swings in sentiment often show up in proportionate price moves.

Perhaps the best-known principle of proportion is the *50 percent rule.* For instance, many bear markets, as measured by the DJIA, have cut prices by half. As examples, the 1901–1903, 1907, 1919–1921, and 1937–1938 bear markets recorded declines of 46, 49, 47, and 50 percent, respectively. The first leg of the 1929–1932 bear market ended in October 1929 at 195, just over half the September high. The halfway mark in an advance sometimes represents the point of balance, often giving a clue to the ultimate extent of the move in question or, alternatively, indicating an important juncture point for the return move. Thus, between 1970 and 1973, the market advanced from 628 to 1067. The halfway point in that rise was 848, or approximately the same level at which the first stage of the 1973–1974 bear market ended.

By the same token, rising markets often find resistance after doubling from a low; the first rally from 40 to 81 in the 1932–1937 bull market was a double.

In effect, the 50 percent mark falls in the middle of the one-third to two-thirds retracement described in Chapter 2 in the discussion of peak-and-trough progression. These one-third and two-thirds proportions can be widely observed in all securities and also serve as support or resistance zones.

Ratio-scale charts are helpful in determining such points, since moves of identical proportion can easily be projected up and down. Moreover, these swings occur with sufficient consistency to offer possible reversal points at both peaks and troughs. Remember, technical analysis deals with probabilities, which means that forecasts should not be made using this method in isolation.

In addition, when undertaking a projection based on the rules of proportion, it is always a good idea to see whether the price objective corresponds to a previous support or resistance point. If it does, the odds are much higher that this zone will represent a reversal point, or at least a temporary barrier. When a security price is reaching new all-time high ground, another possibility is to try to extend up trendlines. The point at which the line intersects with the projection using the rules of proportion may well represent the time and place of an important reversal. Experimentation will show that each security has a character of its own, with some lending themselves more readily to this approach and others not at all.

Chart 3-5, for Dollar General, shows an example using one-third, two-thirds, and 50 percent retracements. In this instance, the decline from *A* to *B* is 100 percent of the move. If we want to establish possible resistance points for subsequent rebounds, then the intelligent places to monitor are these one-third, two-thirds, and 50 percent retracements. As you can see, the rally ending at *C* represents a 50 percent retracement and that ending at *D* a 66 percent or two-thirds retracement.

Many technicians use a sequence of numbers discovered by Leonardo Fibonacci, a thirteenth-century Italian mathematician. The sequence has many properties, but a key one is that each new number is the sum of the two previous numbers in the series. Thus 5 and 8 = 13, 8 and 13 = 21, and so on. The significance of this sequence for our purposes is that it offers

Chart 3-5 Dollar General, 1999–2000, daily.

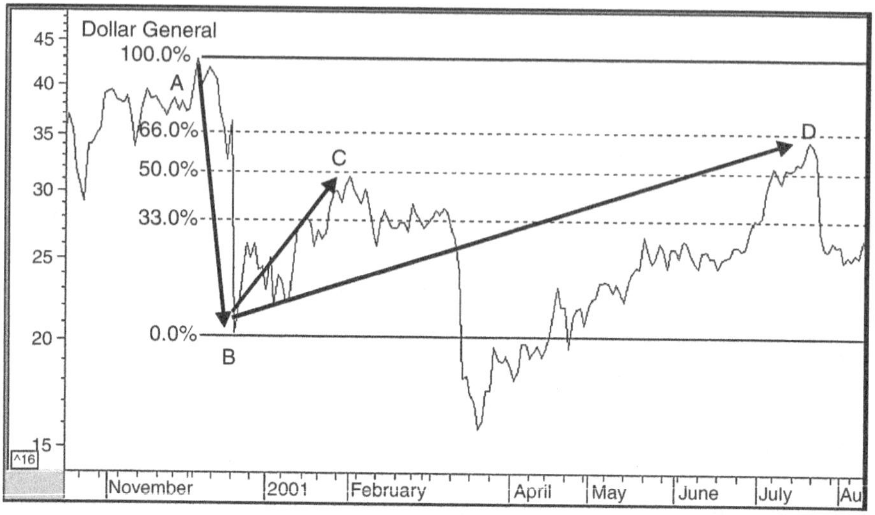

some guidelines for proportionate moves. For example, each number in the sequence is 61.8 percent of the next number, 38.2 percent of the number after that, and so forth.

In this respect, Charts 3-6 and 3-7, for Palladium, show some possibilities. In the case of Chart 3-6, the huge 1997–1998 rally represents 100 percent of

Chart 3-6 Palladium, 1997–2000, daily.

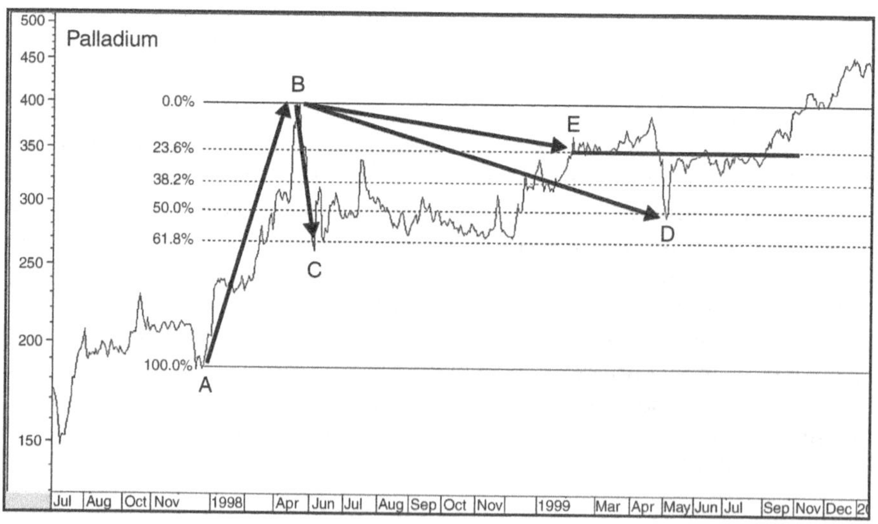

Chart 3-7 Palladium, 1996–2000, daily.

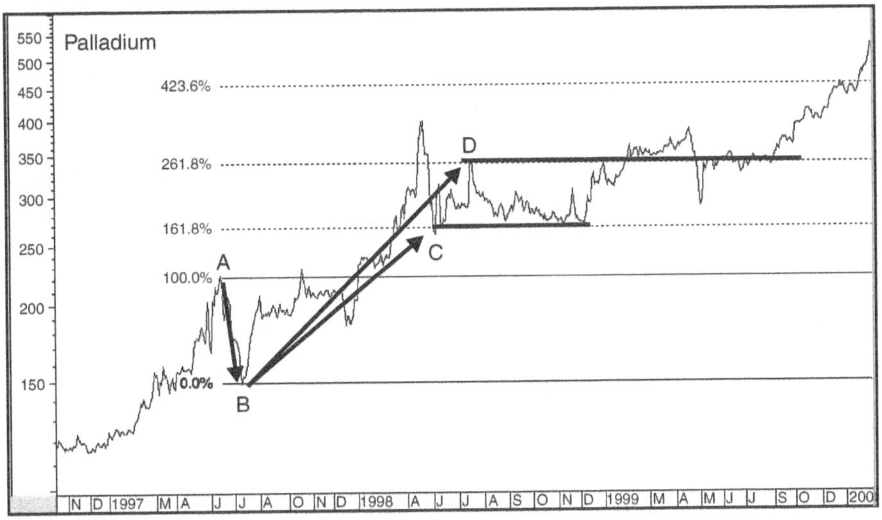

the move. *BC* and *BD*, which turned out to be support levels, were really 61.8 percent and 50 percent retracements, respectively. Note how the 61.8 percent level became support for an extended period in 1998. Also, the 23.6 percent (one Fibonacci number divided by two later ones in the series) level was pivotal in 1998 and 1999, as reflected by the thick black line beginning at *E*.

Finally, Chart 3-7 shows the same principle applied to upside projections. Once again, *AB* represents 100 percent of the decline and lines are drawn at upside Fibonacci proportions. In this case, the next higher number divided by the current number is 1.61, then 2.61, and so on. It is self-evident how the 161.8 percent and 261.8 percent proportions become key pivotal points in future price action. Once again, these levels are not guaranteed to become important pivotal points but are intelligent places on the chart to anticipate that possibility.

Rules for Determining the Probable Significance of a Potential Support or Resistance Zone

At this point you are probably asking, "How do I know how important each support and resistance level is likely to be?" Unfortunately, there is no hard and fast answer, but there are some general rules that can act as guidelines.

1. The Amount of a Security That Changed Hands in a Specific Area—the Greater the Activity, the More Significant the Zone

This is fairly self-evident, for whenever you have a large number of people buying or selling at a particular price, they have a tendency to remember their own experiences. Buyers, as we have already established, like to break even. Sellers, on the other hand, may have bought lower down and recall that prices previously stalled at the resistance level. Their motivation for profit taking becomes that much greater.

2. The Greater the Speed and Extent of the Previous Move, the More Significant a Support or Resistance Zone Is Likely to Be

The attempt to climb through the resistance level here can be compared to the efforts of a person who tries to crash through a door. If he attacks the door from, say, 10 or 12 feet away, he can propel himself with lots of momentum, and the door will probably give way. On the other hand, if he begins his attempt from 100 feet away, he will arrive at the door with less velocity and will probably fail in his attempt. In both cases the door represented the exact same resistance, but it was the resistance relative to the velocity of the person that was important. The same principle can be applied to the market, in that a long, steep climb in price is similar to the 100-foot run, and the resistance level resembles the door. Consequently, the more overextended the previous price swing, the less the resistance or support that is required to halt it.

In this respect, Chart 3-8, for the Bank Commerciale Index (an Italian stock average), falls to a low in August and then rallies. However, the subsequent decline is extremely steep, so by the time the index reaches the support level at around 880, it is completely exhausted and sellers are unable to push prices below this level.

Chart 3-9 features the gold price. Note how it makes a high in January 1986 and then falls away. The subsequent rally is quite steep, then the price runs out of steam and declines again. Finally, in late July, it works its way higher in a fairly methodical manner. This time the same level of resistance is easily overcome because buyers are not as exhausted as they were in their March attempt.

3. Examine the Amount of Time Elapsed

The third rule for establishing the potency of a support or resistance zone is to examine the amount of time that has elapsed between the formation

Chart 3-8 Bank Commerciale, daily.

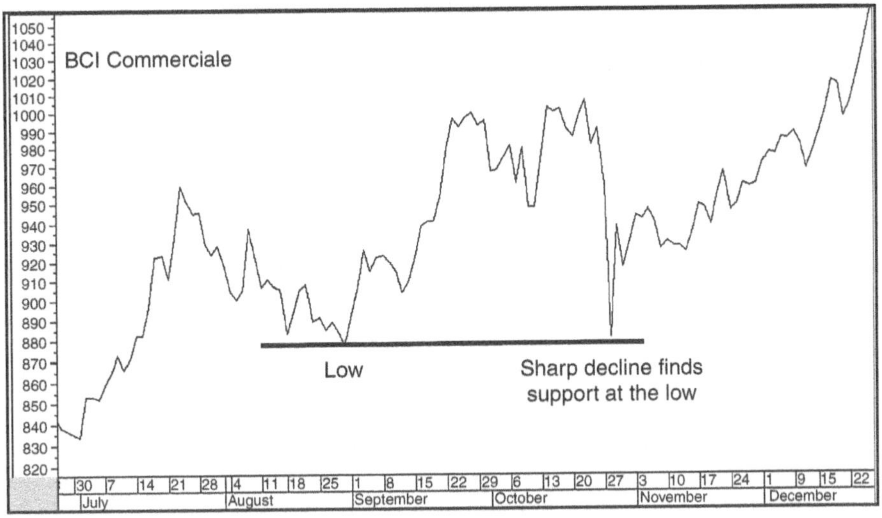

Chart 3-9 Gold, 1985–1986.

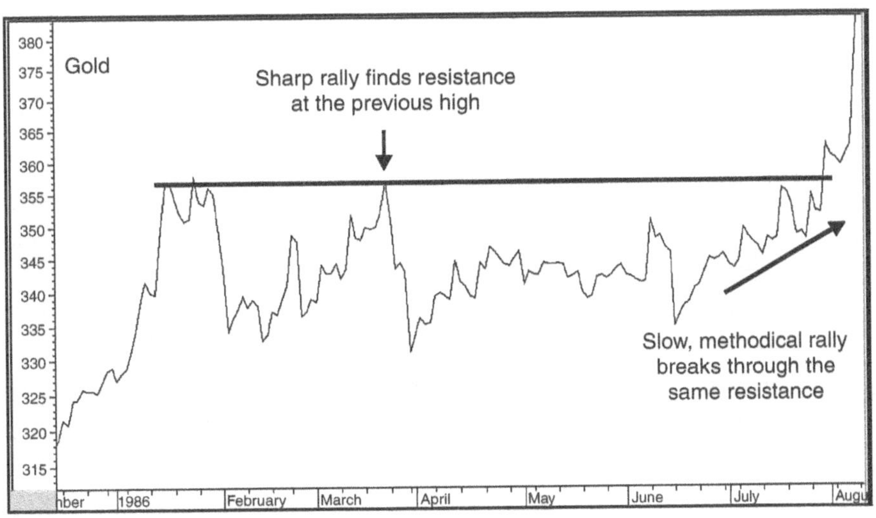

of the original congestion and the nature of general market developments during that period. A supply that is 6 months old has greater potency than one established 10 or 20 years previously. Even so, it is almost uncanny how support and resistance levels remain effective time and time again, even when separated by many years.

Summary

- Support and resistance represent a concentration of demand and supply sufficient to halt a price move at least temporarily.
- They are not signals to buy or sell but rather are intelligent places for anticipating a reversal. They should always be used in conjunction with other indicators.
- Potential support/resistance zones develop at previous highs and lows, round numbers, trendlines and MA's, emotional points on charts, and retracement points such as Fibonacci proportions.
- The significance of a support or resistance zone depends upon the amount of an asset that previously changed hands in that area, the speed and extent of the previous price move, and the period of time that has elapsed since the zone was last encountered.

4 Trendlines

Trendlines are perhaps the simplest of the tools in our technical arsenal and are arguably one of the most effective. *Since the construction of nearly all price patterns requires the use of trendlines, this concept is a fundamental building block of pattern identification and interpretation.* In this chapter we will describe the characteristics of trendlines and explain how the significance of individual lines can be determined.

A trendline is a straight line connecting a series of ascending bottoms in a rising market or the tops of a descending series of rally peaks. Those trendlines joining the lows are called *up trendlines* and those connecting the tops are referred to as *down trendlines*. Typically a down trendline is constructed by joining the final peak with the top of the first rally, as in Fig. 4-1. When the price breaks above the trendline, a trend change signal is given. The opposite is true for an up trendline (see Fig. 4-4).

How Should Trendlines Be Drawn?

In order to be a true trendline, a line must connect two or more peaks or troughs. Otherwise it will be drawn in space and will have no significance. You will often see people constructing lines that touch only one point, as in Fig. 4-2, or even no points at all, as in Fig. 4-3. Such lines have no meaning whatsoever, and are really worse than drawing nothing at all. This is because by simply appearing on the charts, such lines give the observer the impression that they actually have some significance. This is a fundamentally important point because *a true trendline is a graphic way of representing the underlying trend.* Consequently, if a line touches only one point, it cannot be a true trendline.

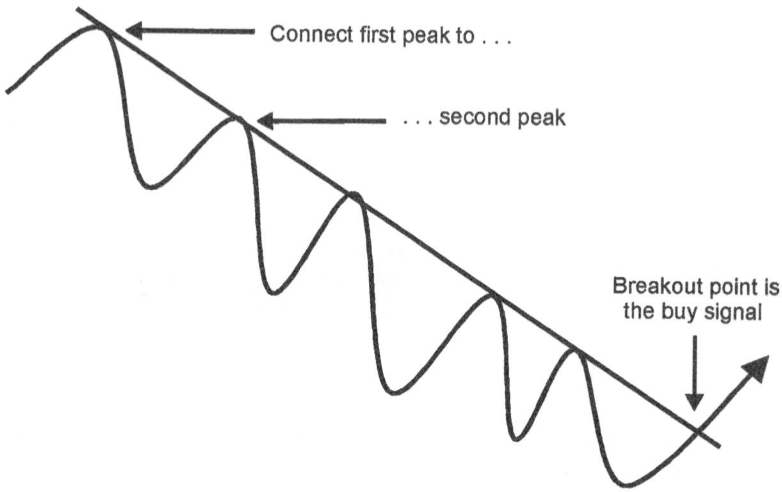

Figure 4-1 Down trendline.

Ideally, an up trendline is constructed by connecting the final low with the first bottom following the initial rally, as is done by line *AD* in Fig. 4-4. This is called the *primary trendline.* In the case of a primary trend, this would be the bear market low and the first intermediate bottom. The example shown here offers a fairly shallow angle of ascent. Unfortunately, the price rallies sharply, which means that the violation develops well after the final peak.

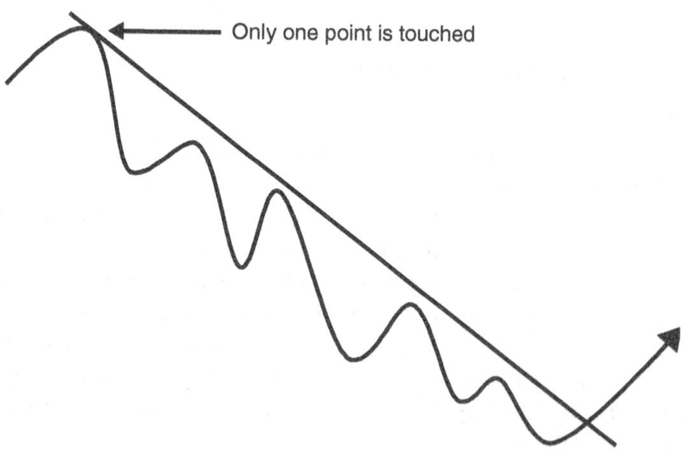

Figure 4-2 Trendline connected once.

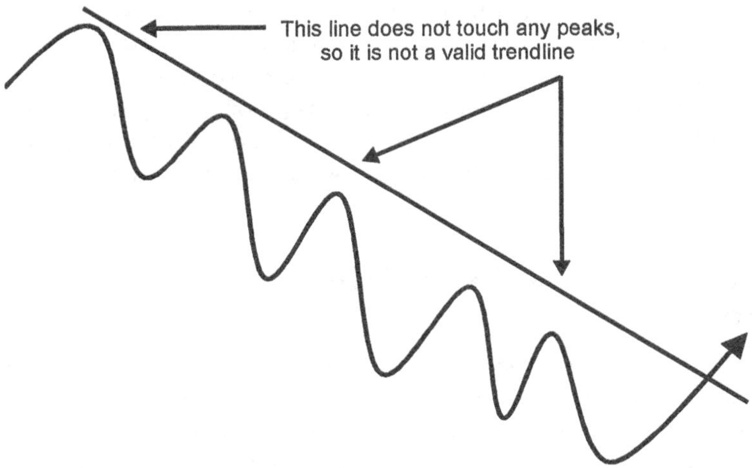

Figure 4-3 Trendline not connected.

In such situations it is better to redraw the line as the price moves up. In Fig. 4-4 this new line is line *BC*, which is obviously a better reflection of the underlying trend. This is called a *secondary trendline.* Down trendlines are constructed using the same principles, but in reverse.

Since trends can be sideways, it follows that trendlines can also be drawn horizontally. This is often the case when we construct price patterns such

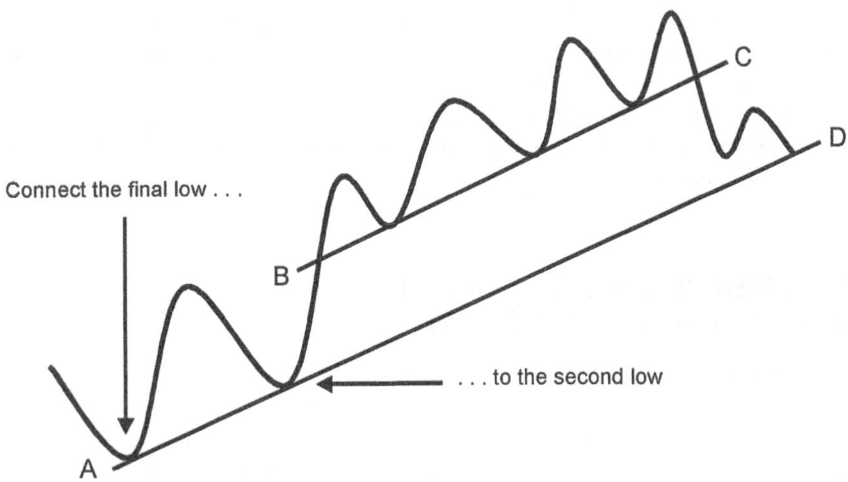

Figure 4-4 Primary and secondary up trendlines.

as the neckline of a horizontal head-and-shoulders (H&S) pattern or the upper or lower boundaries of rectangles (described in later chapters). In the case of price patterns, the penetration of these lines usually warns of a change in trend, as does the violation of rising or falling trendlines.

It's important to understand at this point that drawing trendlines is more a matter of common sense than of following a set of hard and fast rules.

Bar versus Line or Close-Only Charts

Some charts are plotted with bars and others are line charts. The question naturally arises, "Which form should be used for the purposes of trendline analysis?" In most cases, bar charts offer more timely signals, whether the signal is a peak-and-trough progression, price pattern completion, or trendline violation. In technical analysis, timeliness comes at a price, and the price in this case is more whipsaws. With traditional daily or weekly charts, the closing price is very important because it sorts out the men (i.e., those who are willing to take home a position overnight or over a weekend) from the boys (i.e., those who are not). This has become a less important factor in some markets, as they trade for 24 hours Sunday through Friday. (However, since all markets are closed over the weekend, Friday closes continue to maintain their importance.) Even so, *closing prices are, for the most part, more important chart points than highs or lows.* Also, since there is much excitement during the day as unexpected news breaks, highs and lows often represent random points on the chart. For this reason, it is often a better idea to construct trendlines using closing data. I am not going to say that this is always the case because some bar trendlines have greater significance than close-only ones, based on the rules for significance described later in this chapter. Thus, it is always crucial to apply common sense as much as strict technical rules. The question you should be constantly asking is, "Which line better reflects the underlying trend?"

Trendline Breaks Can Signal Reversals or Consolidation

The completion of a price pattern can signify either (1) a reversal in the previous trend, which is known as a *reversal pattern*, or (2) a resumption of the previous trend, which is called a *consolidation* or *continuation pattern.* Similarly, the penetration of a trendline will result in either a reversal of that trend or its continuation. Figure 4-5 illustrates this from the perspective of

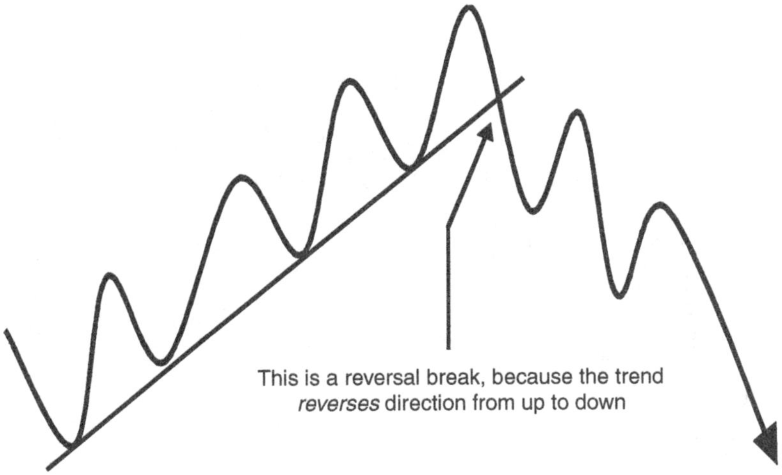

Figure 4-5 Reversal up trendline break.

a rising price trend. In this case, the trendline joining the series of troughs is eventually penetrated on the downside. The fourth peak represented the highest point in the bull trend, so the downward violation of the trendline signals that a bear move is under way.

The upward price trend and trendline penetration in Fig. 4-6 are identical to those in Fig. 4-5, but the action following this warning signal is entirely

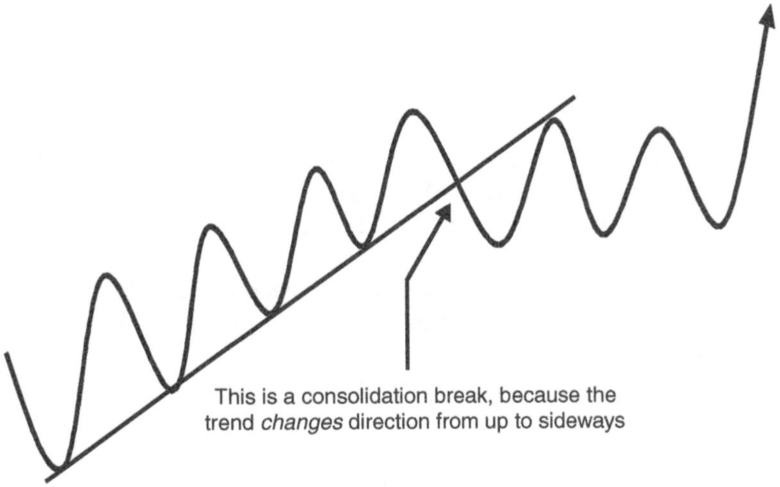

Figure 4-6 Consolidation up trendline break.

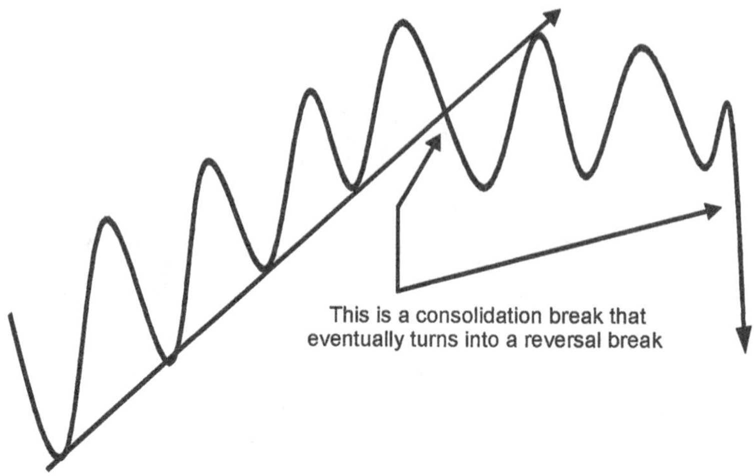

Figure 4-7 Consolidation turns into a reversal break.

different. This is because the trendline violation results in the advance continuing, but at a greatly reduced pace. The third alternative is that the price consolidates in a sideways trading range prior to reversing. This is shown in Fig. 4-7. Thus, whenever a trendline is violated, the odds strongly favor a *change* in trend. That change can be either an actual reversal or a (sideways) trading range following an up- or downtrend.

In most instances, there is, unfortunately, no way of telling at the time of the violation which possibility will prove to be the outcome. One clue may be provided by the trendline's angle of ascent or descent. Since sharp-angled trendlines are less sustainable, their penetration has a tendency to be followed by a consolidation rather than a reversal.

Valuable clues can be gleaned by evaluating the state of health of the market's overall technical structure. Also, a trendline penetration may occur at the time of, or just before, the successful completion of a reversal price pattern.

If a series of ascending peaks and troughs is accompanied by progressively lower volume, this is a sign that the advance is running out of steam (since volume is no longer going with the trend). In this situation, a trendline violation is likely to be of greater significance than if volume had continued to expand with each successive rally. It is not necessary for a downside penetration to be accompanied by high volume, but a violation that occurs as activity expands emphasizes the bearish undertone because of the obvious switch in the demand/supply balance in favor of sellers.

Extended Trendlines

Most people observe the violation of a trendline, assume that the trend has changed, and eventually forget about the line. This is a mistake, because an extended line can become just as important as the violated line itself.

If an up trendline is violated, for instance, the price often returns to the extended line. This is known as a *throwback* move. Figure 4-8 shows a trendline reversing its previous role as support when the throwback move turns it into an area of resistance. Figure 4-9 shows the same situation for a declining market.

Chart 4-1, for instance, shows an up trendline break for the U.S. government 20-year bond yield. The penetration of this relatively steep line was followed by a small decline. However, the cyclical rally peak in 1984 was turned back by the extended line, which reversed its role and proved to be strong resistance. Chart 4-2 shows the same idea, but for a down trendline for the Eurodollar yield. In this instance it was violated in 1987. Later the extended line proved to be support for the 1993 decline.

Logarithmic (Ratio) versus Arithmetic Scales

The importance of plotting charts on a logarithmic as opposed to an arithmetic scale was discussed in Chapter 2. The choice of scale is even more critical for a timely and accurate use of trendline analysis. This is because prices tend to

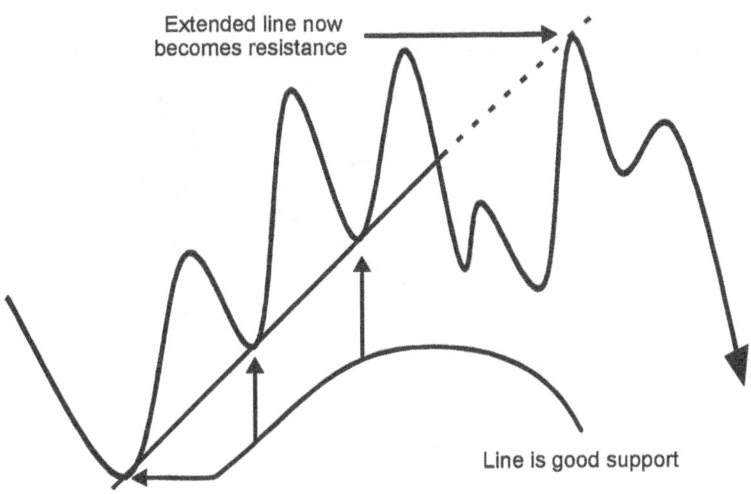

Figure 4-8 Extended up trendline becomes resistance.

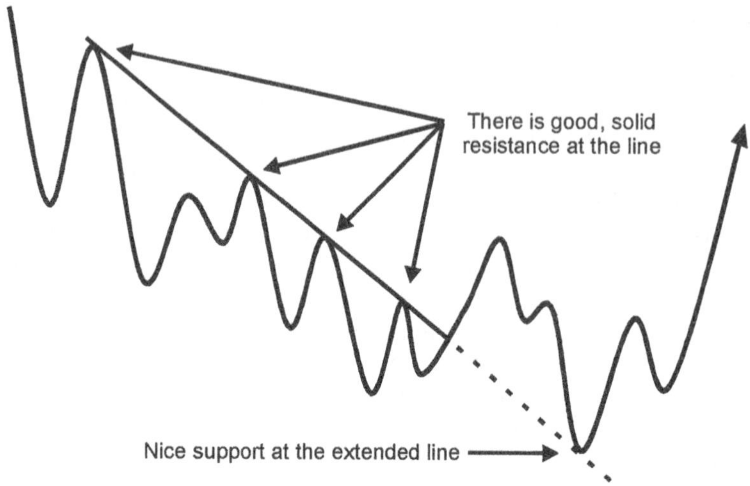

Figure 4-9 Extended down trendline becomes support.

accelerate in the direction of the prevailing trend at the end of a major movement; i.e., they rise faster at the end of a rising trend and decline more sharply at the termination of a bear market. In a bull market, prices rise slowly after an initial burst, then advance at a steeper and steeper angle as they approach

Chart 4-1 U.S. government 20-year bond yield, 1975–1986, weekly.

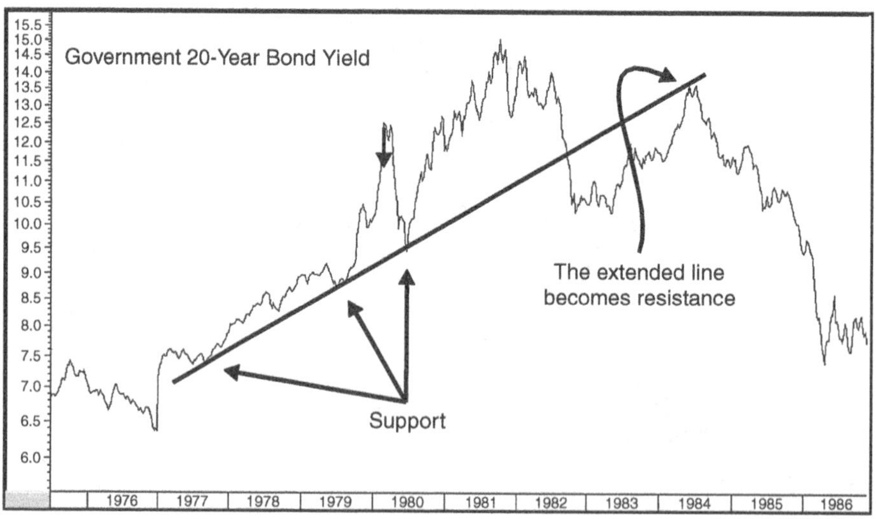

Chart 4-2 Cash Eurodollars, 1980–1994, weekly.

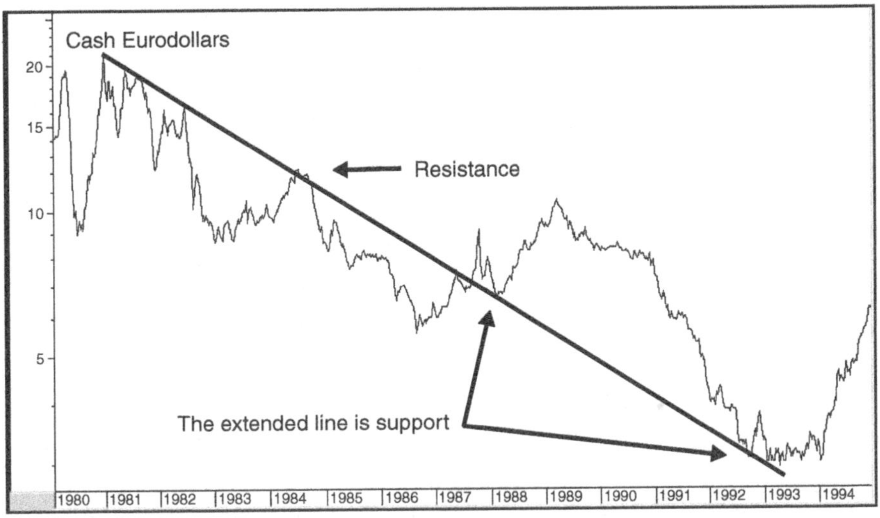

the ultimate peak, looking rather like the left-hand cross section of a mountain.

Chart 4-3 shows an up trendline break for Intel based on a logarithmic scale. Note that the downside penetration develops in mid-December. Chart 4-4 shows exactly the same period, but this time the scaling is arithmetic. The

Chart 4-3 Intel, 2001–2002, daily (logarithmic).

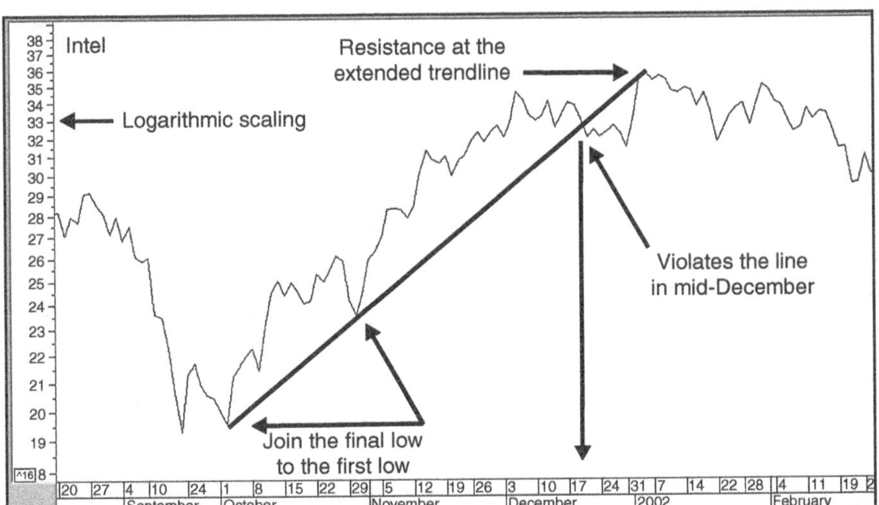

Chart 4-4 Intel, 2001–2002, daily (arithmetic).

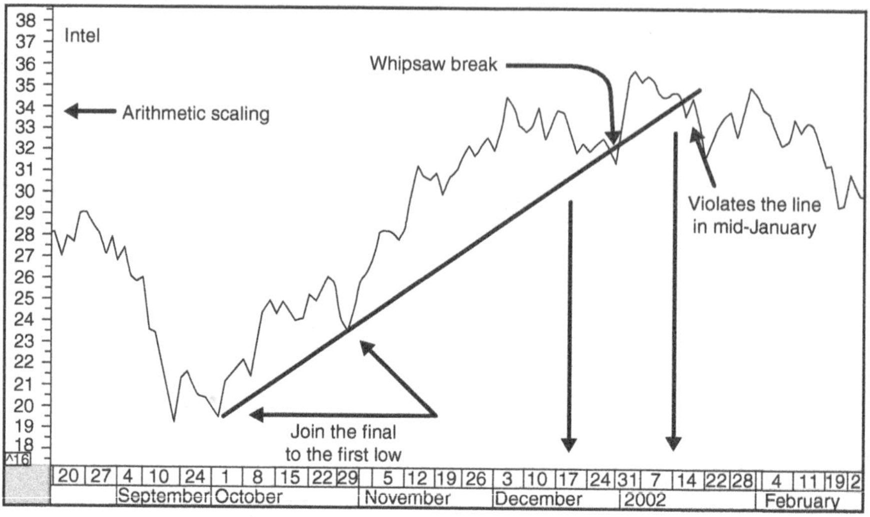

trendline break is entirely different, since it initially comes as a whipsaw in late December, followed by a valid break in mid-January. The downward-pointing arrow on the left marked the logarithmic break. Thus it is apparent that up trendlines are violated more quickly on a logarithmic than on an arithmetic scale.

Chart 4-5 IBM, 2001–2002, daily (arithmetic).

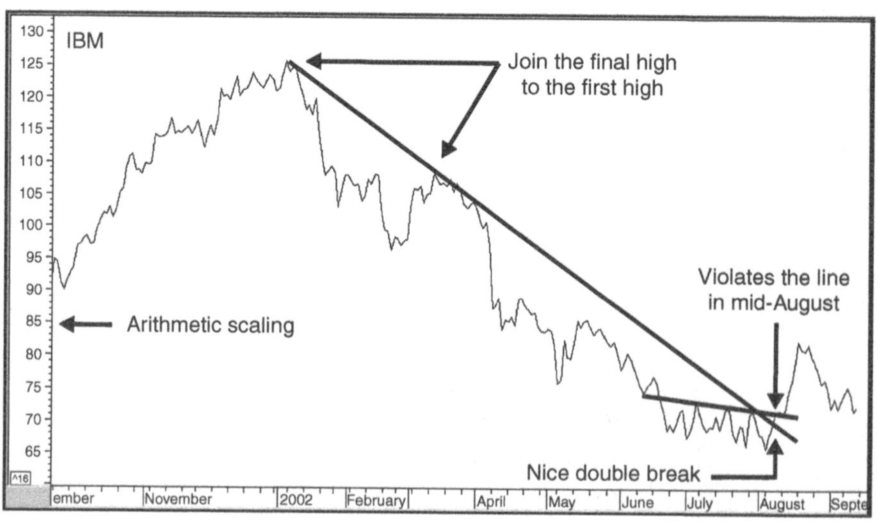

Chart 4-6 IBM, 2001–2002, daily (logarithmic).

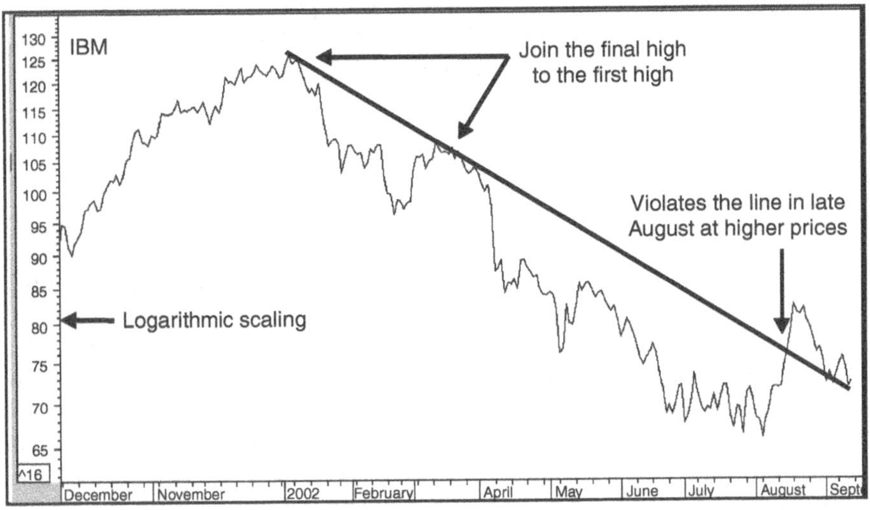

Conversely, down trendlines are violated sooner on an arithmetic scale. This can be seen from a comparison of Charts 4-5 and 4-6, for IBM.

Generally speaking, penetration of a logarithmically drawn trendline is more accurate in reflecting trend reversals than is penetration of an arithmetically drawn trendline, although in both these examples the final penetrations came at more advantageous prices for the arithmetically scaled chart.

Significance of Trendlines

It has been established that a break in trend caused by penetration of a trendline results in either an actual trend reversal or a slowing in the pace of the trend. Although it may not always be possible to determine which of these alternatives will develop, it is still important to understand the significance of a trendline penetration; the guidelines described next should help in this evaluation. Essentially, this evaluation depends on three factors: the length of the line, the number of times it has been touched, and the angle of ascent or descent. Let's consider each of them in turn.

1. Length of the Line

A trendline measures a trend, so the longer the line, the longer the trend it is monitoring and the more significant the trendline. If a series of ascending bottoms occurs over a three- to four-week span, the resulting trendline is only of minor importance. If the trend extends over a period of one to three years, however, its violation marks a significant juncture point. Just remember, big trends result in big signals, small trends in small ones.

2. Number of Times the Trendline Has Been Touched or Approached

A trendline derives its authority from the number of times it has been touched or approached; i.e., the larger the number, the greater the trendline's significance. This is because a trendline represents a dynamic area of support or resistance. Each successive test of the line contributes to the importance of this support or resistance role, and thus the authority of the line is a true reflection of the underlying trend. Just remember that a move close to the line (an approach) is almost as important as an actual touching because it reflects the line's importance as a support or resistance area.

Also, if a line gains significance from the fact that it has been touched or approached on numerous occasions, the extended line will become equally as important, but from a reverse point of view. This is because extended lines reverse their support/resistance role. For example, if a good up trendline has been violated, the price is now below it. Any rally will therefore find resistance at this line, which had, of course, previously been support.

3. Angle of Ascent or Descent

A very sharp trend, as shown by the dashed line (*AB*) in Fig. 4-10, is difficult to sustain and is liable to be broken rather easily, even by a short sideways movement. It is then necessary to draw a line with a smaller angle of ascent or descent (*AC*).

All trends are eventually violated, but the steeper ones are likely to be ruptured more quickly. The violation of a particularly steep trend is not as significant as the violation of a more gradual one. Penetration of a steep line usually results in a short corrective movement, following which the trend resumes, but at a greatly reduced and more sustainable pace. Usually, the penetration of a steep trendline represents a continuation rather than a reversal break.

Measuring Implications

Trendlines have measuring implications when they are broken. The measurement is the maximum vertical distance between the price and the

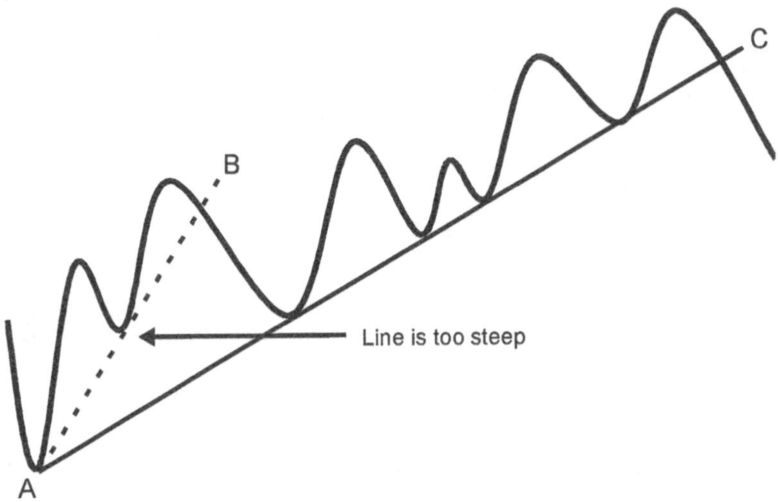

Figure 4-10 Steep angles of ascent.

trendline. An example for a rising trend is shown in Fig. 4-11. This distance is then projected in the direction of the new trend from the point of penetration.

The term *price objective* is perhaps misleading. Objectives are usually reached when a trendline violation turns out to be a reversal, but because they are more often exceeded (as we shall learn with price patterns), the

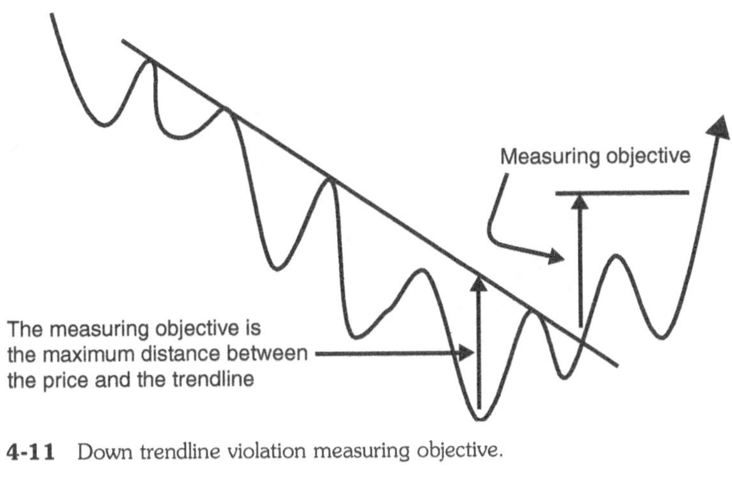

Figure 4-11 Down trendline violation measuring objective.

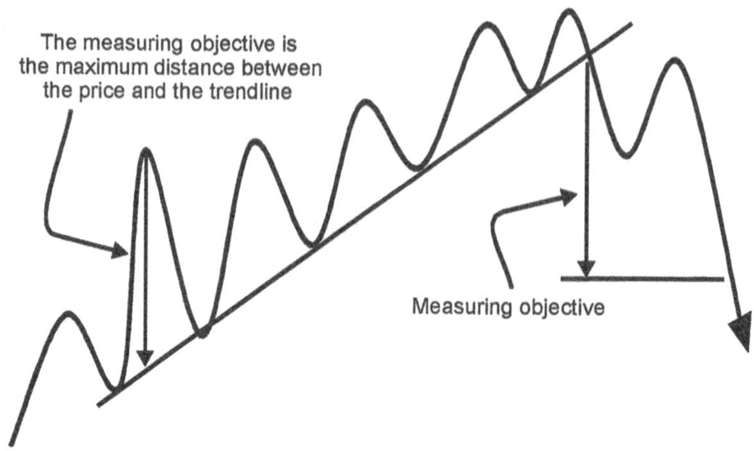

Figure 4-12 Up trendline violation measuring objective.

objective becomes more of a minimum expectation. An objective for a downside reversal is illustrated in Fig. 4-12.

Trend Channels

So far, only the possibilities of drawing trendlines joining bottoms in rising markets and tops in declining ones have been examined. It is also useful to draw lines that are parallel to those basic trendlines, as shown in Fig. 4-13. In

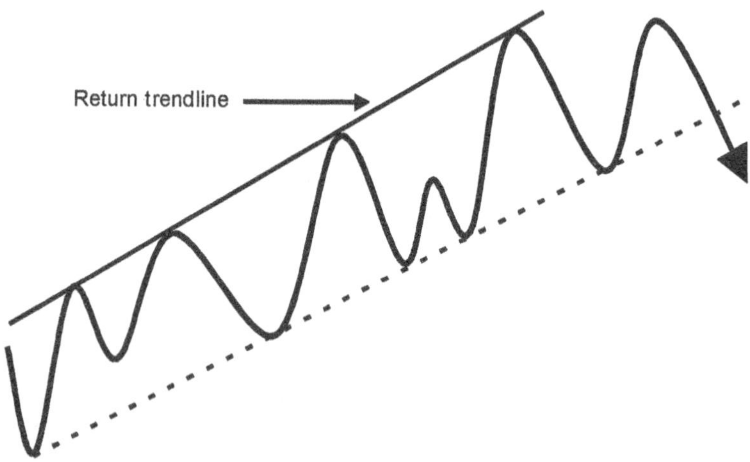

Figure 4-13 Up trend channel.

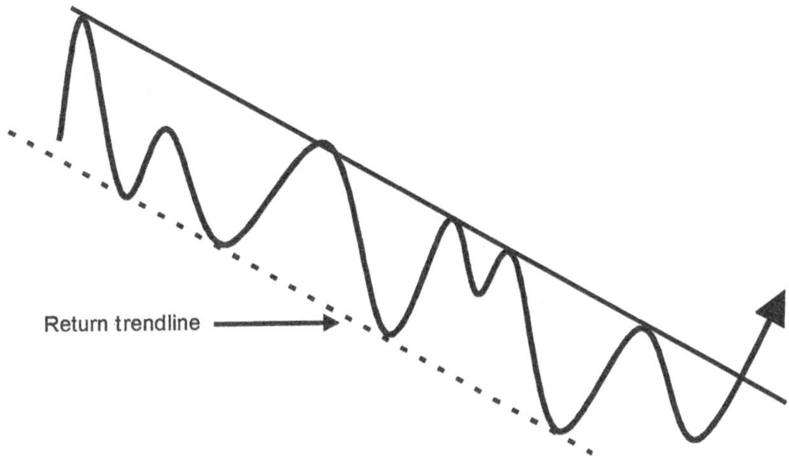

Figure 4-14 Down trend channel.

a rising market, the parallel line known as a *return trendline* joins the tops of rallies, and during declines the return line joins the series of bottoms (see Fig. 4-14). The area between these trend extremities is known as a *trend channel.*

The return line is useful from two points of view. First, it represents an area of support or resistance, depending on the direction of the trend. Second, and perhaps more important, penetration of the return trendline represents a signal that either the trend will accelerate or a reversal in the basic trend of at least a temporary proportion is about to take place.

In Fig. 4-15, the violation of the return line signifies that the price advance has begun to accelerate. In effect, the channel in Fig. 4-15 represents a rising trading range, and the trendline violation is a breakout from it.

Exhaustion

On the other hand, if the angle of the trend channel is much steeper, as in Figs. 4-16 and 4-17, the violation of the return line represents an exhaustion move. The failure of the price to hold above (below) the return line then signals an important reversal in trend. This is often the case if the break through the return line is accompanied by high volume.

Consider a situation in which a person is sawing a thick piece of wood. At first the sawing strokes are slow but deliberate, but gradually the person realizes that this task is going to take some time, becomes frustrated, and slowly increases the speed of the strokes. Finally the person bursts into a

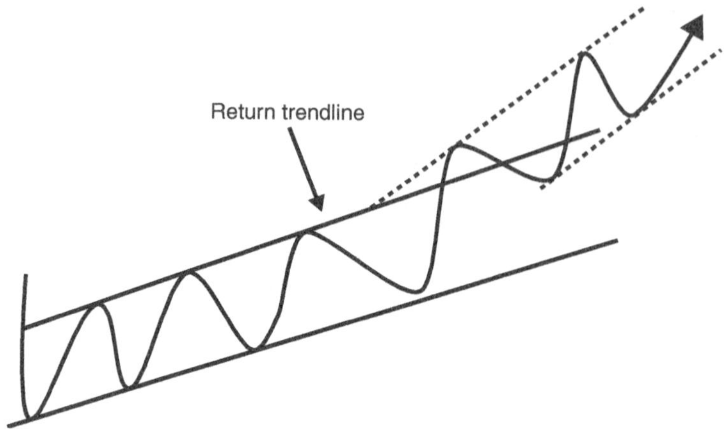

Figure 4-15 Up trend channel breakout.

frantic effort and is forced to give up the task at least temporarily because of complete exhaustion. The same principles hold true in a declining market. In this case, the expanding volume at the low represents a selling climax. As a general rule, the steeper the channel, the more likely it is that the breakout will turn out to be an exhaustion move.

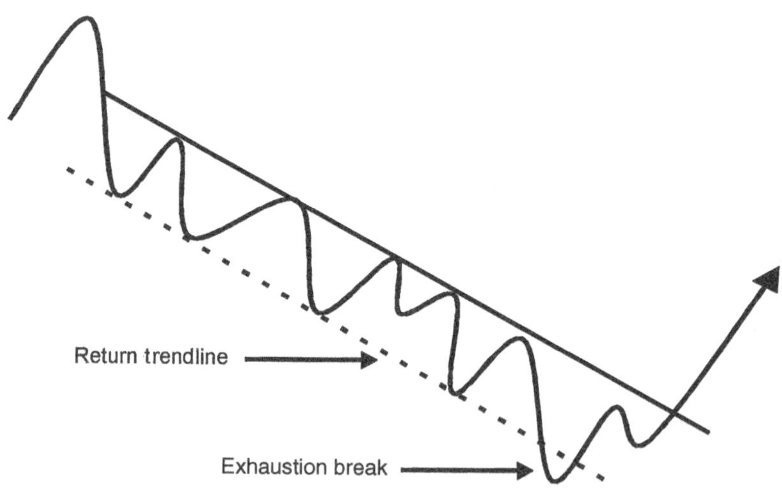

Figure 4-16 Down trend channel exhaustion break.

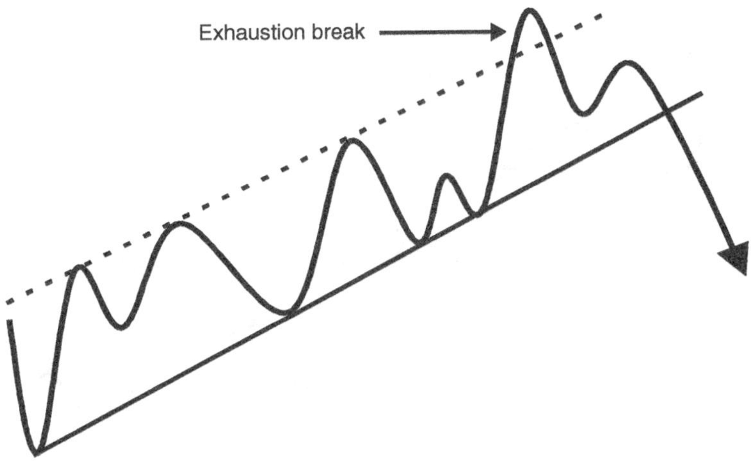

Figure 4-17 Up trend channel exhaustion break.

Exhaustion also develops when a price rallies temporarily above a regular down trendline (or below an up trendline), then breaks back below (above) it. In the case of a down trendline, the situation is akin to someone jumping up and temporarily pushing through the ceiling. He is able to pull his head through to the next floor for a few moments, but he then falls sharply back to the floor below. At this point he has used up all his spare energy in the attempt to move to the next floor and is totally exhausted. Before he can make another attempt he will need some time to gain some new energy. The same is true of the price, which makes an effort to rally above the trendline but is unable to maintain the breakout.

This temporary break often indicates that the prevailing trend has much further to run. It also raises a dilemma concerning the way in which a trendline should be constructed. In Fig. 4-18, for instance, we see a false break above trendline *AB*. Should *AB* now be abandoned, or should the peak of the exhaustion break be connected to the rally high to form a new (dashed *AC*) trendline? Again, it's a matter of common sense. On the one hand, the top of the whipsaw break is technically the correct place to draw the line, but common sense suggests that the original line is a better reflection of the underlying trend. After all, at the time of the whipsaw, it had been touched three times. If a new line is then drawn to reflect the break, that line will have been touched only twice, once at the outset and once at the whipsaw peak. In a sense, the whipsaw is adding further credibility to the initial line because the price was unable to hold above it. If we had come upon this situation after the whipsaw break and tried to construct a line, it

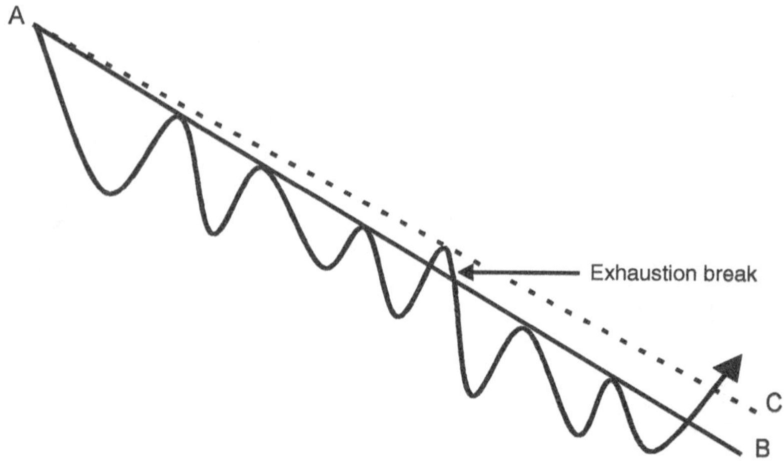

Figure 4-18 Down trendline construction.

would have been even more obvious that line *AB* was far superior to line *AC* because it has been touched or approached on far more occasions.

The same principles are true in reverse for an up trendline. When you think about it, *a whipsaw break actually adds credibility to the trendline.* This is because the price is able to violate the line, but this line is so significant as

Chart 4-7 Microsoft, 1998–1999, daily.

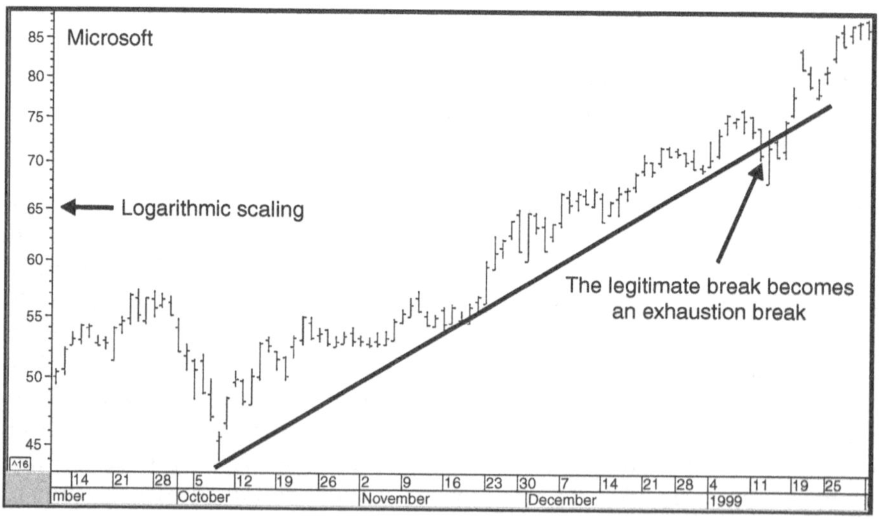

a support/resistance area that the price is unable to hold the break. If it were not such a significant barrier, the break would have held and the whipsaw would have been avoided. Consequently, when the price is able to experience a valid break, the signal is that much stronger.

Chart 4-7 shows an example of a whipsaw downside break for Microsoft in 1998.

Summary

- Trendlines are an easy tool to understand, but they should be used with a strong dose of common sense. Considerable experimentation and practice are required before the art of interpreting them can be successfully mastered.
- Trendline violations signal either a temporary interruption or a reversal in the prevailing trend. It is necessary to refer to other pieces of technical evidence to determine which is being signaled.
- The significance of trendlines is a function of their length, the number of times they have been touched or approached, and the steepness of the angle of ascent or descent.
- A good trendline reflects the underlying trend and represents an important support and resistance zone.
- Extended trendlines reverse the former support/resistance role and should not be overlooked.
- Exhaustion breaks are usually followed by sharp moves in the opposite direction to the break. Exhaustion breaks enhance the significance of a trendline.

5 Volume Principles as They Apply to Price Patterns

Almost everything that technicians use in plotting a specific security involves either the price itself or a statistical variation on it. Volume can offer a new dynamic in our interpretation of crowd psychology. Therefore, analyzing volume trends gives us a better understanding of how and why price patterns work. In effect, the study of the characteristics of volume gives greater depth to the weight-of-the-evidence approach described earlier. Volume not only measures the enthusiasm of buyers and sellers but is a variable that is totally independent of price. In this chapter we will discuss some general principles of volume interpretation. However, this is not the final word, because I will have more to say on this subject as we expand the discussion to include individual price patterns.

Benefits of Volume Studies

Volume studies offer three major benefits.

1. When price and volume patterns are compared, it is important to see whether they are in agreement. If they are, the probabilities favor an extension of the trend.
2. If price and volume disagree, this tells us that the underlying trend is not as strong as it looks on the surface. If a breakout from a price pattern develops with such a disagreement, a warning of a potentially invalid signal is being given.

3. Occasionally, price action offers mild signs of an impending trend reversal, but volume can throw up characteristics of its own that literally shout this message. In such cases, a study that was limited to price action would fail to uncover a really good and obvious warning or opportunity.

Principles of Volume Interpretation

1. The first and most important principle is that *volume typically goes with the trend.* It is normal for activity to expand in a rising market and to contract in a declining one (see Fig. 5-1). In this sense, volume is always interpreted in relation to the recent past. Comparing twenty-first-century 1 billion-plus share days on the NYSE with early-twentieth-century levels of 5 or 6 million is of little help. Such a comparison reflects institutional, not psychological, changes. Volume is higher today because of more companies being listed, the advent of derivatives, lower commissions, and so forth. On the other hand, a 3 billion share day this week compared to a recent 1.5 billion share day last month is relevant, because it shows a significant change in activity over a period in which institutional changes will be nonexistent.

   We know that when prices move in trends, this does not occur in a straight line. Instead, the price works its way up and down in a zigzag

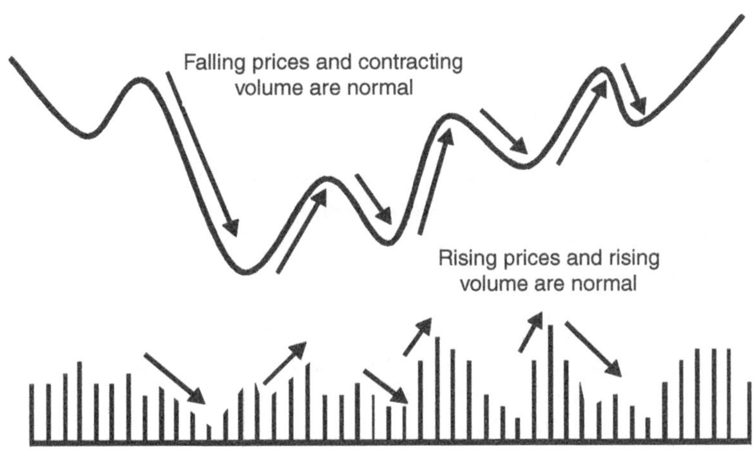

Figure 5-1 Volume goes with the trend.

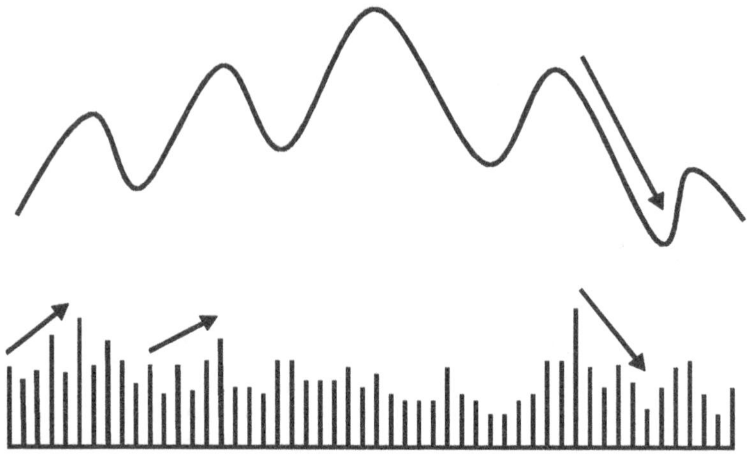

Figure 5-2 Volume moves in trends.

fashion. Volume trends are similar. On the left side of Fig. 5-2, for instance, the arrows indicate an expanding volume trend. It is apparent that the level of activity does not expand in every period. There are quiet periods and active ones, but the general thrust is up. The right-hand part of the figure features a downtrend in volume. It too is irregular. When we talk about volume rising or falling, we are usually referring to its trend. It is normal for such trends to be interrupted by aberrations in volume levels. Volume trends, like price trends, can be intraday, short, intermediate, or long, depending on the nature of the chart.

2. The amount of money flowing into a security must always equal the amount of money flowing out. This is true regardless of the level of volume.

Consequently, it is the level of enthusiasm of buyers or sellers that determines the course of prices.

If buyers are bullish, they will raise their bids until their demands are satisfied. If sellers react to bad news, they may panic, pushing prices down sharply, but at all times the amount of a security being sold is equal to that being purchased.

3. The combination of rising volume and rising price is normal. It indicates that things are in gear. Such a state of affairs has no forecasting value, except to imply that it is likely that a negative divergence between price and volume lies ahead.
4. Volume normally leads price during a bull move. A new high in price that is not confirmed by volume should be regarded as a red flag, warning

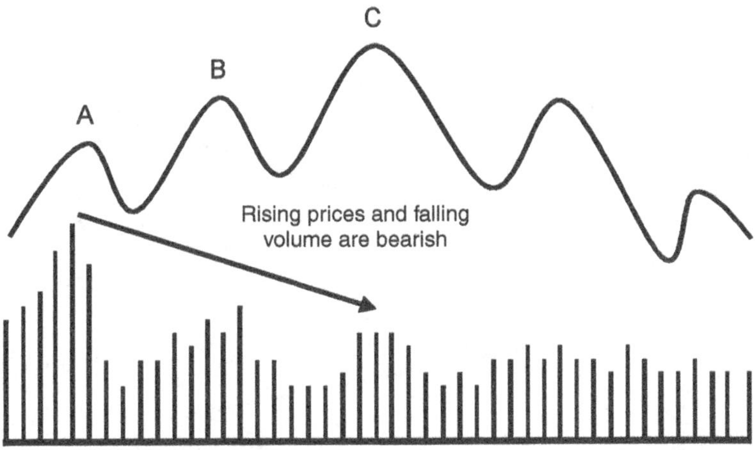

Figure 5-3 Volume leads price in uptrends.

that the prevailing trend may be about to reverse. In Fig. 5-3, the price peaks at point *C*, yet the average volume reached its maximum around point *A*. Such action is normal; the declining volume peaks warn of underlying technical weakness. Unfortunately, there are no hard and fast rules about how many divergences precede a peak. Generally speaking, though, the greater the number of negative divergences, the weaker the underlying technical picture. Also, the lower the peaks relative to each other, the less enthusiasm is being generated, and the more vulnerable the technical position becomes, once buying dries up or selling enthusiasm intensifies. A new high that is accompanied by virtually no volume is just as bearish as a new price high with virtually no upside momentum.

An example is shown in Chart 5-1, for the Mexico Fund, where you can see that the volume clusters gradually become smaller as the price rallies. Eventually this negative technical characteristic is confirmed as the price violates the March/May up trendline.

5. Rising prices accompanied by a trend of falling volume (Fig. 5-4) is an abnormal situation. It indicates a weak and suspect rally and is a bear market characteristic. When it is recognized, it can and should be used as a piece of evidence pointing to a primary bear market environment. Volume measures the relative enthusiasm of buyers and sellers. When volume shrinks as prices rise, the advance occurs because of a lack of selling rather than because of sponsorship from buyers. Sooner or later the trend will reach a point where sellers become more motivated. After

Chart 5-1 Mexico Fund, 1995–1996, daily.

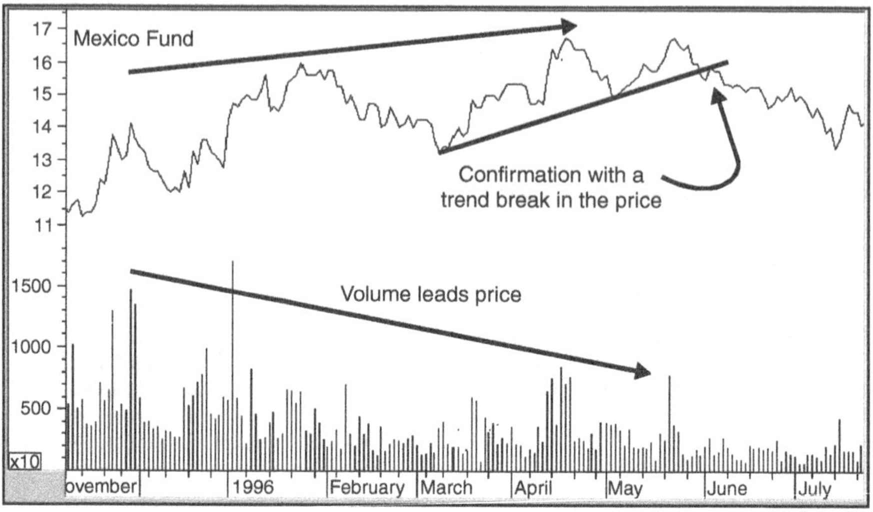

that, prices will start to pick up on the downside. One clue is provided when volume increases noticeably as the price starts to decline. This is shown in Fig. 5-5, where you can see that volume starts to pick up as the price starts a sell-off. In such situations, it is not necessary for volume to expand throughout the decline, as it does in this example. It could

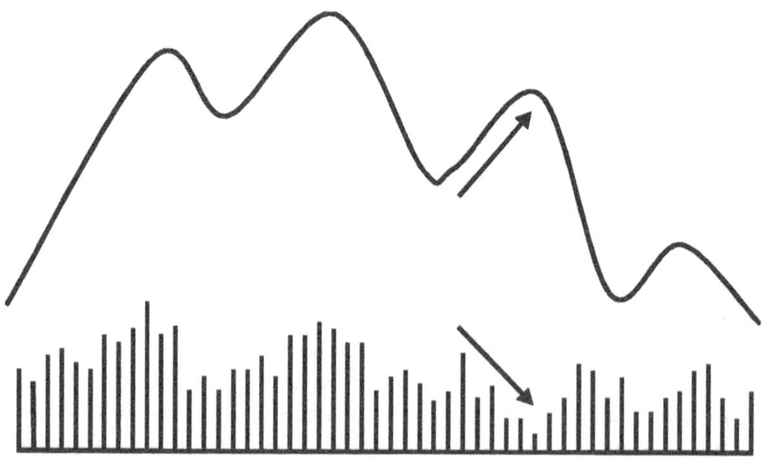

Figure 5-4 Rising price and falling volume are bearish.

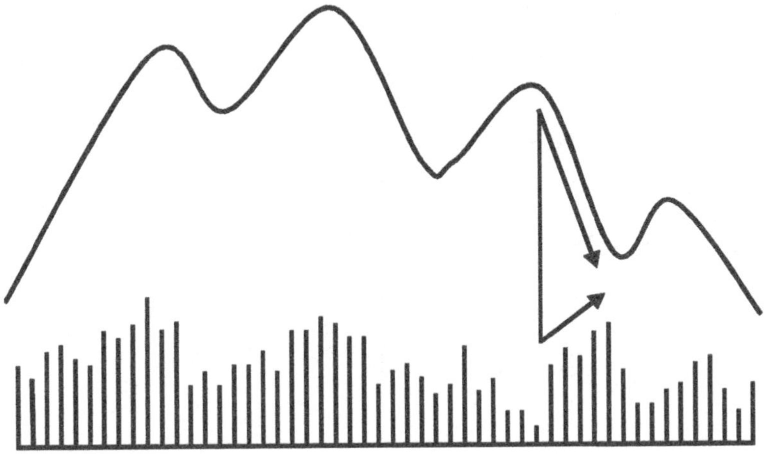

Figure 5-5 Falling price and rising volume are bearish.

be that it picks up for two or three bars just after the peak. In fact, this would be a more typical situation.

Figure 5-6 shows how the volume configurations change between a bull market and a bear market. Chart 5-2, for Coors, shows the final rally being accompanied by a trend of declining volume. When the lower trendline is violated, volume picks up noticeably. In this instance, we

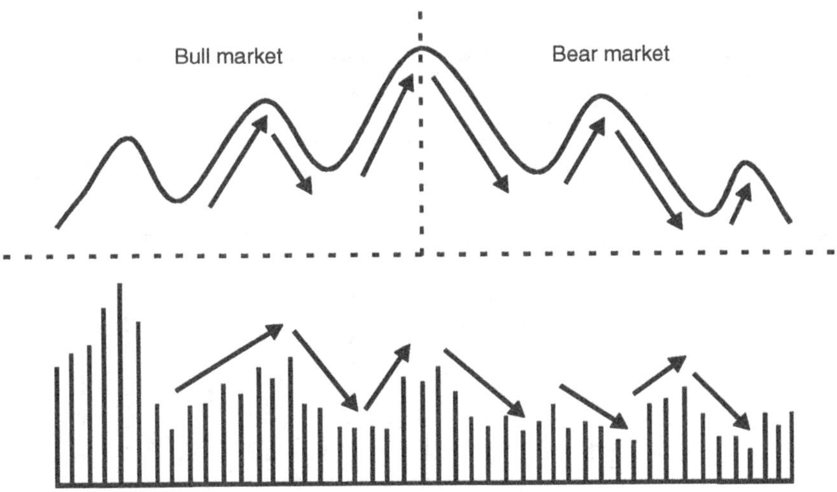

Figure 5-6 Volume characteristics change in bull and bear markets.

Chart 5-2 Coors, 2000–2001, daily.

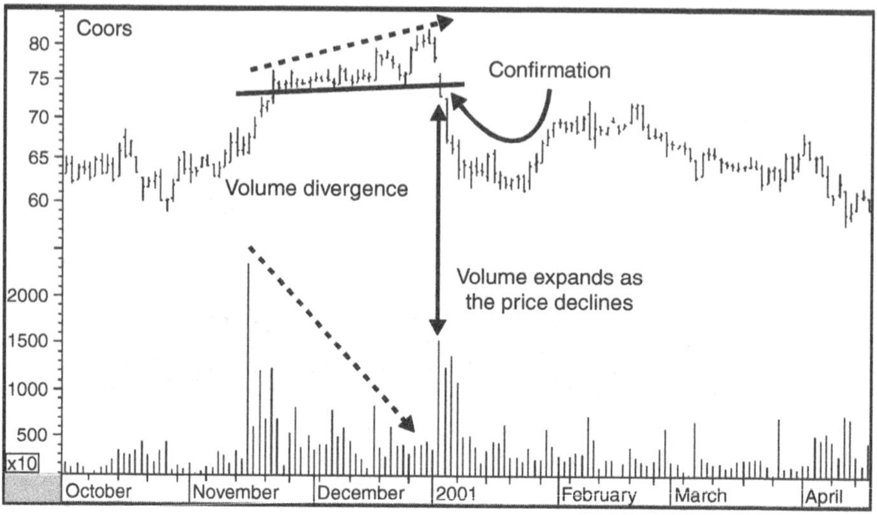

have one bearish volume configuration that is instantly followed by another. Chart 5-3, for Radio Shack, shows several bear market rallies in which the rising price trend is accompanied by declining volume.

6. Sometimes both price and volume expand slowly, gradually working into an exponential rise with a final blow-off stage. Following this development,

Chart 5-3 Radio Shack, 2000–2001, daily.

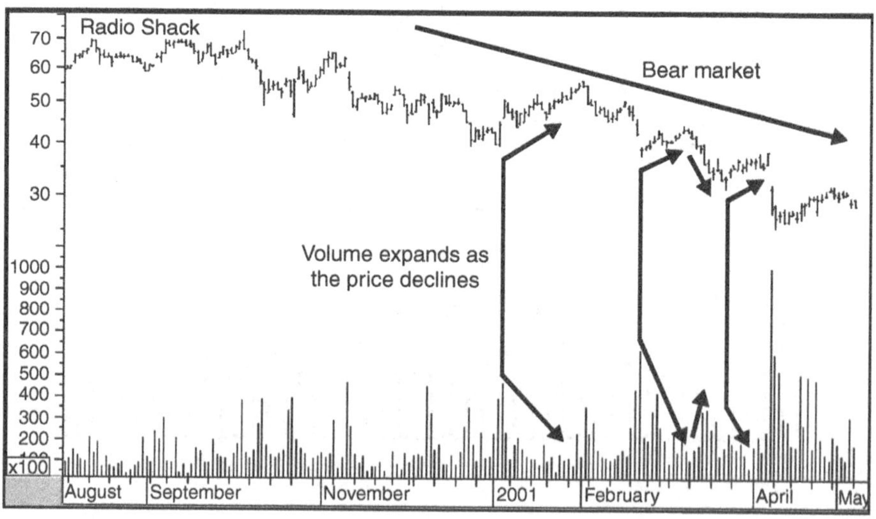

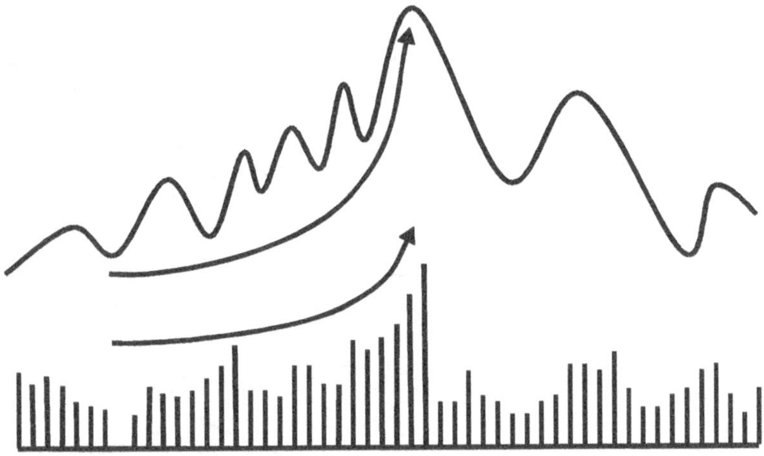

Figure 5-7 Volume and a parabolic blow-off.

both volume and price fall off equally sharply. This represents an exhaustion move and is characteristic of a trend reversal, especially when it is supported by a one- or two-bar price pattern (discussed in subsequent chapters). The significance of the reversal will depend upon the extent of the previous advance and the degree of volume expansion. Obviously an exhaustion move that takes four to six days to develop will be nowhere near as significant as one that develops over a matter of weeks. This phenomenon is termed a *parabolic blow-off* and is featured in Fig. 5-7. Unfortunately, exhaustion, or blow-off, moves such as this are not easy to define in the sense that it is possible to construct clearly definable trendlines or price patterns. For this reason, it is usually not possible to spot the terminal phase until a period or so after volume and price have reached their crescendos.

Newmont Mining, in Chart 5-4, offers a classic example of an exponential increase in both price and volume that ends in tears in the form of an abrupt reversal in late September 1987.

7. A *selling climax* is the opposite of a parabolic blow-off. It occurs when prices fall for a considerable time at an accelerating pace, accompanied by expanding volume. Prices typically rise after a selling climax. The low that is established at the time of the climax is unlikely to be violated for a considerable time. A price rise from a selling climax is by definition accompanied by declining volume. This is the only time when contracting volume and a rising price may be regarded as normal. Even so, it is important to make sure that volume expands on subsequent rallies, as indicated in Fig. 5-8. The termination of a bear trend is often, but

Chart 5-4 Newmont Mining, 1986–1987, daily.

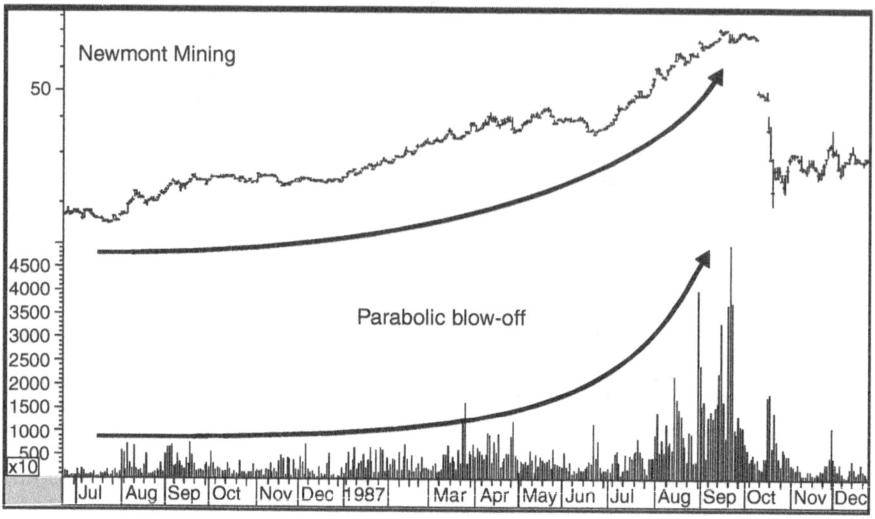

not always, accompanied by a selling climax. Having said that, it is important to note that in many instances the selling climax, after a rally, is followed by new lows.

In Chart 5-5, for Dresser Industries, we see a selling climax develop in the late summer. This is then followed by a rally, but in this instance the

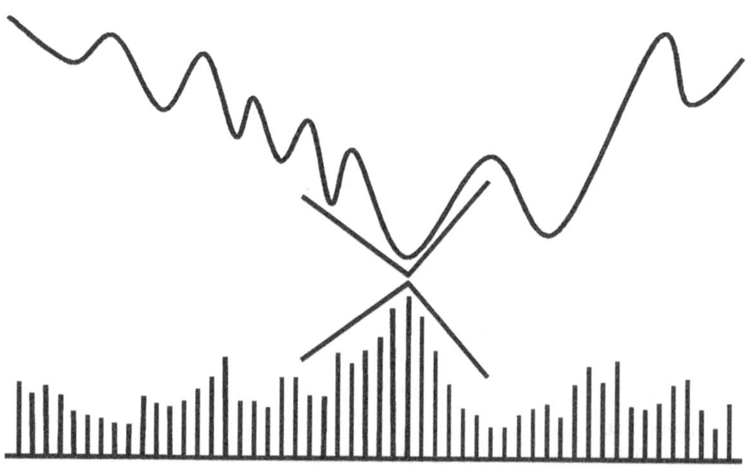

Figure 5-8 A selling climax.

Chart 5-5 Dresser Industries, 1994–1995, daily.

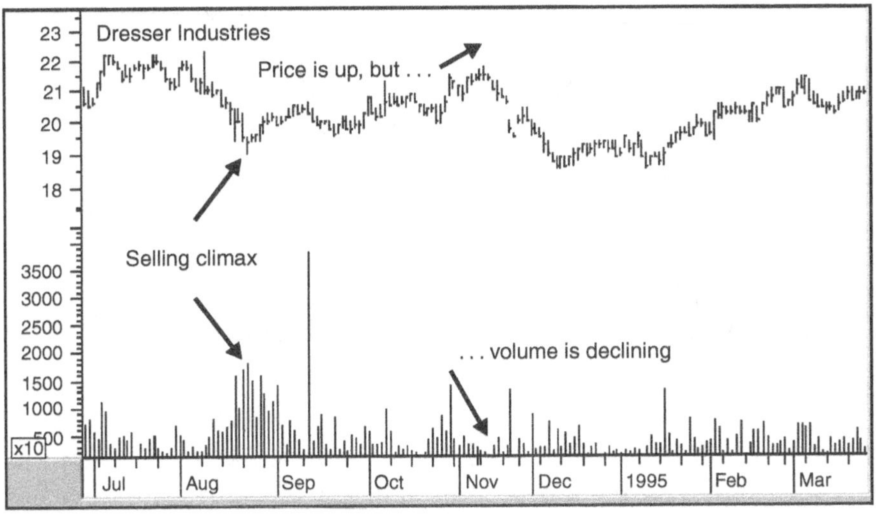

climax is not the final bottom. At the peak of the rally, rising prices are accompanied by declining volume, a typical bear market characteristic.

8. When prices advance following a long decline and then react to a level at, slightly above, or marginally below the previous trough, this is a bullish sign if the volume on the second trough is significantly lower than the volume on the first. There is an old saying on Wall Street, "Never short a dull market." This saying applies very much to this type of situation, in which a previous low is being tested with very low volume. Such a situation indicates a complete lack of selling pressure (see Fig. 5-9).
9. A downside breakout from a price pattern, trendline, or moving average (MA) that occurs on heavy volume is abnormal and is a bearish sign that confirms the reversal in trend (Fig. 5-10). When prices decline, it is usually because of a lack of bids, so volume contracts. This is normal activity and does not give us much information. However, when volume expands on the downside, it is because sellers are more motivated, so the decline, other things being equal, is likely to be more severe.
10. When the price has been rising for many months, an anemic rally (Fig. 5-11) accompanied by high volume indicates *churning* action and is a bearish factor.
11. Following a decline, heavy volume with little price change is indicative of accumulation and is normally a bullish factor (Fig. 5-12).

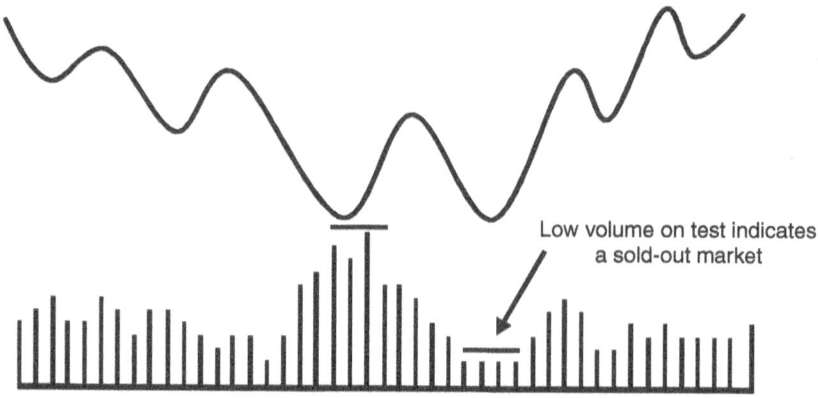

Figure 5-9 Look for low volume when testing lows.

12. Record volume coming off a major low is usually a very reliable signal that a significant bottom has been seen. This is because it indicates that an underlying change in psychology has taken place. Such reversals in sentiment are usually of a primary trend magnitude. Examples in the U.S. stock market developed in March 1978, August 1982 and 1984, and October 1998. A similar pattern also developed at the 1987 low in bonds and eurodollars. This is not an infallible indicator, though, because record volume was achieved in January 2001 for both the NYSE and Nasdaq, yet this did not turn out to be the final low for the move.

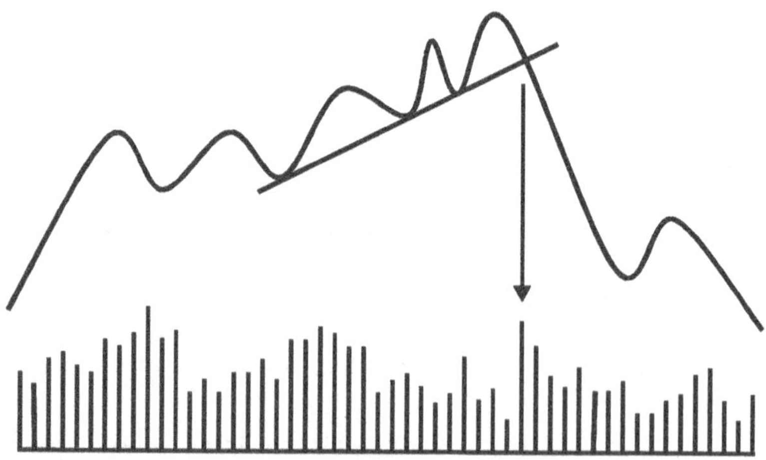

Figure 5-10 Rising volume on a downside breakout is bearish.

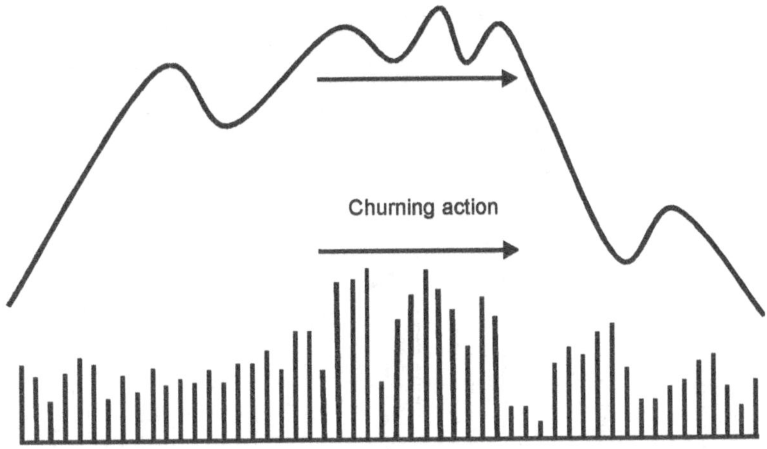

Figure 5-11 Churning is bearish.

13. When volume and price expand at a sharp pace, but short of a parabolic blow-off, and then contract slightly, this usually indicates a change in trend. Sometimes this is an actual reversal and at other times a consolidation. This phenomenon is featured in Fig. 5-13 and represents a temporary exhaustion of buying power. It is associated with several one- and two-bar price patterns discussed in later chapters.
14. When the price experiences a small rounding top and volume a rounding bottom, this is a doubly abnormal situation, since price is rising and

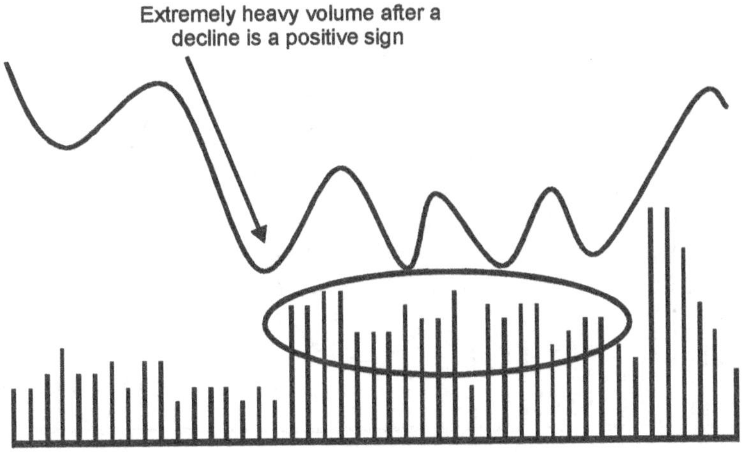

Figure 5-12 Accumulation is bullish.

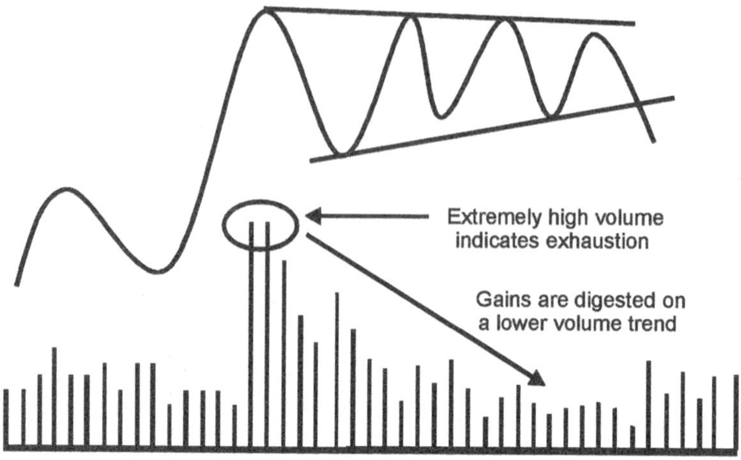

Figure 5-13 High volume after a rally indicates exhaustion.

volume falling as the peak is reached. After the peak, volume expands as the price declines, which is also abnormal and bearish. An example is shown in Fig. 5-14. An example featuring Microsoft is featured in Chart 5-6. Note how the letter *n* characterizes the price action, whereas the volume configuration is closer to a rounded letter V.

None of the indicators in the technical arsenal is guaranteed to work every time. This is certainly true of volume characteristics. However, when volume is used in combination with price characteristics in pattern

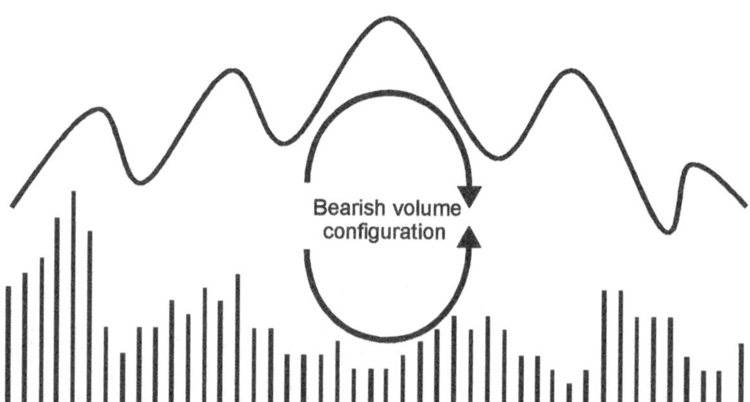

Figure 5-14 Watch volume on rallies and reactions.

Chart 5-6 Microsoft, daily.

interpretation, it greatly enhances the probability that a specific formation will work. As we discuss specific formations, the basic volume principles described here will be expanded to suit individual cases.

Summary

- Volume is a totally independent variable from price.
- It is normal for volume to go with the trend. When these characteristics are present, they have little forecasting value.
- When volume trends are moving in a direction opposite to that of price, this is abnormal and either warns of an impending trend reversal or emphasizes the significance of any breakout.
- Volume trends experience exhaustion phenomena. These are called parabolic blow-offs at tops and selling climaxes at lows.

PART II
Traditional Patterns

6 Using Rectangles, a Case Study for All Patterns

This chapter will explain the basic principles of price pattern interpretation that apply to most formations by using one formation as an example. It will then be possible to expand the discussion to include other patterns in subsequent chapters. Our chosen vehicle is the rectangle, so let's take a closer look at it.

Basic Concepts

Price trends do not usually reverse on a dime. Instead, the up- and down- or down- and uptrends are typically separated by a transitional period or trading range, where buyers and sellers are equally matched.

The two possibilities are shown in Figs. 6-1 and 6-2. Figure 6-1 represents a typical cycle consisting of three trends: up, sideways, and down. Then two more trends develop as the price experiences another horizontal trading range, followed by a renewed uptrend. Figure 6-2 shows a highly emotional market that changes without warning. This is by far the exception, since most trends are separated by some form of trading range. An oil tanker takes a long time to slow down and then go into reverse. The same is normally true of financial markets. Generally speaking, the longer the trend, the more time spent in the reversal (turnaround) process.

This transitional or horizontal phase has great significance because it is the demarcation between a rising and a falling trend (or vice versa). If prices have been advancing, the enthusiasm of the buyers has outweighed

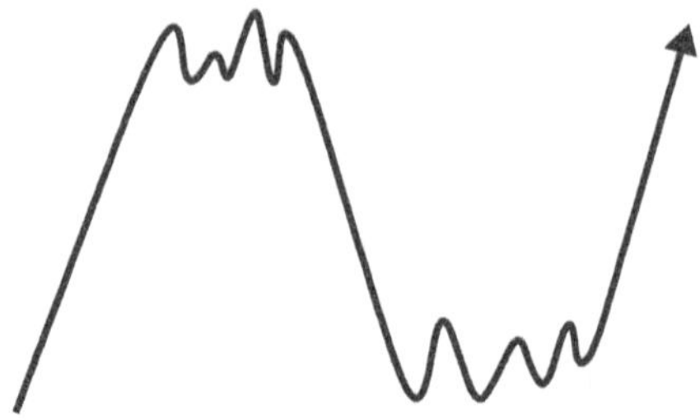

Figure 6-1 Top and bottom reversals.

the pessimism of the sellers up to this point, and buyers have optimistically bid prices higher. During the transition phase, the battle between optimism and pessimism becomes more or less even, until finally, for one reason or another, it is tipped in a new direction as the relative weight of selling pushes the trend (of prices) down. It is the breaking to post-transitional new low ground that alerts the trader to the fact that a reversal in trend has taken place. In other words, when prices fall below the trading range, a sell signal is given. At the termination of a bear trend, the reverse process occurs.

Over the years, technicians have noted that such ranging action at both tops and bottoms has taken the form of clearly definable price patterns or price formations.

The Transitional Turning Point

Figure 6-3 shows the price action at the end of a long rising trend. As soon as the price rises above line *B*, it is in the transitional area, although this is apparent only after prices have begun to fluctuate sideways.

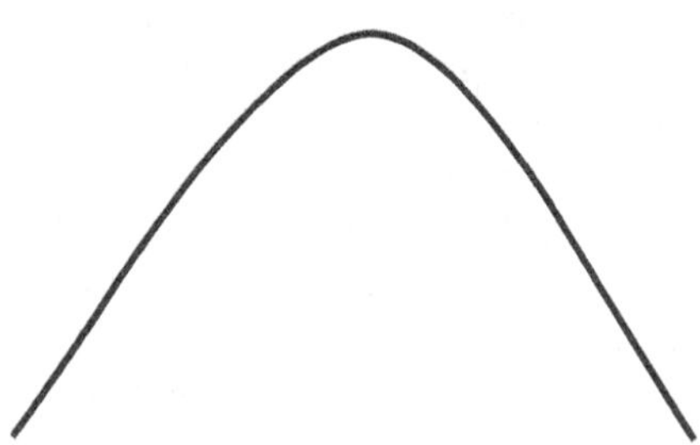

Figure 6-2 Reversal on a dime.

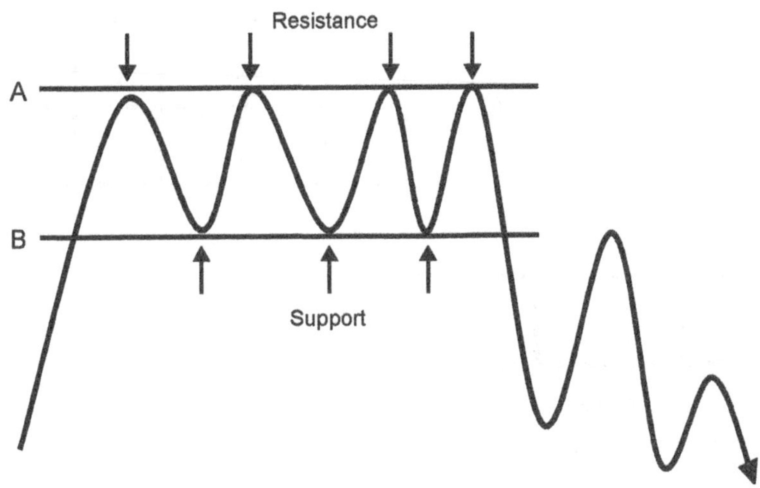

Figure 6-3 Trading range reversal.

Once the price is in this trading zone, it rises to line *A*, which is a *resistance area.* The resistance is not initially identifiable, but after the price has backed off from the initial high, it is evident that the price level at *A* represents a previous high. This makes it a potential candidate for a resistance point. When the next rally also fails at *A*, it is possible to construct a horizontal trendline. The same thing can be done at *B* when the subsequent reaction finds support at that level for a second time. The demand/supply relationship comes into balance in favor of the sellers whenever the price reaches *A*. This temporary reversal may occur because buyers refuse to pay up for a security, because the higher price attracts more sellers, or for a combination of both reasons.

Just as the price level at *A* reverses the balance in favor of the sellers, so does the support level *B* alter it once again. This time, the trend moves in an upward direction, for at *B*, prices become relatively attractive to buyers who missed the boat on the way up. Also, sellers who feel that the price will again reach *A* hold off. For a while, there is a standoff between the two parties within the confines of the area bounded by lines *A* and *B*. Finally, the price falls below *B*, and a new (downward) trend is signaled.

The contest between buyers and sellers is like a battle fought by two armies engaged in trench warfare. In Fig. 6-4, example A, armies A and B are facing off. Line *AA* represents army A's trench line of defense, and *BB* is army B's. The arrows indicate the forays between the two lines as both armies fight their way to the opposing trench, but are unable to penetrate the line of defense. In example B, army B finally pushes through army A's line of

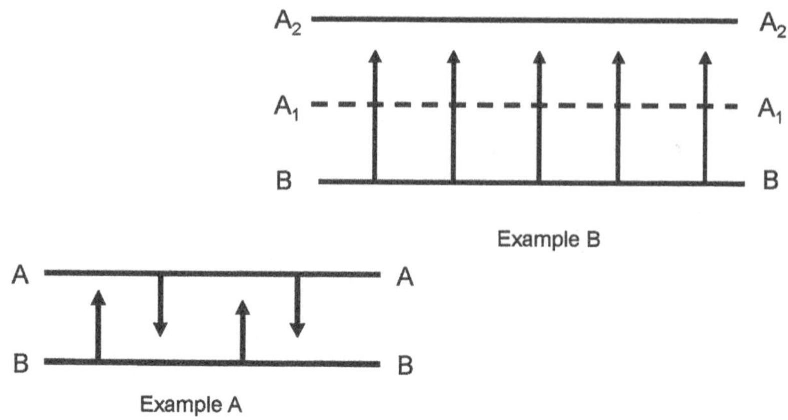

Figure 6-4 Trench warfare.

defense. Army A is then forced to retreat and make a stand at the second trench (line A_2). In the stock market, line A_1 represents resistance, and once it is overcome, this signifies a change in the balance between buyers and sellers in favor of the buyers, so that prices will advance quickly until new resistance is encountered. The second line of defense, line A_2, then represents resistance to a further advance.

On the other hand, army B might break through A_2 quite easily, but the farther it advances without time to consolidate its gains, the more likely it is to become overextended, and the greater is the probability of its suffering a serious setback from a counterattack when it reaches the next line of defense. At some point, therefore, it makes more sense for this successful force to wait and consolidate its gains.

If prices in financial markets extend too far without having time to digest their gains, they too are more likely to face a sharp and seemingly unexpected reversal. This is another application of the second rule for identifying the significance of a support or resistance level described in Chapter 3.

Introducing the Reversal Rectangle and the Psychological Conditions Contributing to Its Formation

The trading range separating rising and falling price trends discussed here is a pattern known as a *rectangle*. The rectangle in Fig. 6-5, which marks the turning point between the bull and bear phases, is termed a *reversal* pattern.

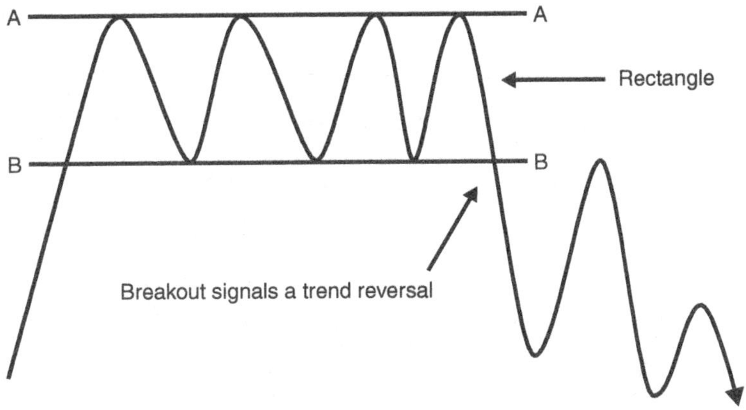

Figure 6-5 Downside breakout signal.

The actual reversal signal is given when the price breaks decisively through the lower horizontal trendline. Reversal patterns at market tops are known as *distribution* because the security is said to be "distributed" from strong, informed participants to weak, uninformed ones. The underlying psychology is that during the formation of the rectangle, the news is good, and uninformed market participants, hearing it for the first time, are encouraged to buy. Forecasts are also quite rosy at this time, so little risk is perceived from the long side. Every transaction has to have two parties, a buyer and a seller. For their part, the sellers, or distributors, have a different idea. They had been carefully buying on the way up in *anticipation* of the good news. Now that the news is materializing, it is time to sell, and who better to sell to than those uninformed participants who are hearing the good news for the first time? This kind of activity has given rise to the well-known expression "buy on the rumor, sell on the fact."

Price patterns, including rectangles, that develop at market bottoms are called *accumulation* formations (where the security passes from weak, uninformed participants to strong, informed ones; see Fig. 6-6). In this situation, the underlying psychology is reversed: The sellers, having seen the price of their security move lower, decide to sell when the bad news and forecasts of more to come start to filter through the investment community. By the same token, potential buyers had previously held off because they wanted to get the bad news out of the way. The emergence of discouraging reports is therefore one of the signals that these so-called strong buyers had been waiting for. Another might be a sign that things are going to improve down the road. This process is called accumulation because informed buyers are said to be accumulating the security in anticipation of better times ahead. These are

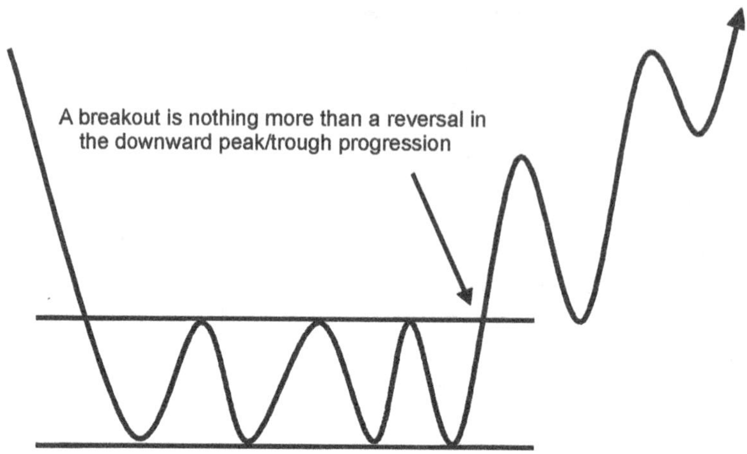

Figure 6-6 Upside breakout signal.

said to be strong buyers because they are not easily put off by discouraging news. Their focus is on the future, and only when they see signs of poorer than expected developments down the road are they likely to liquidate.

When you think of it in very simple terms, the top reversal rectangle is nothing more than a sophisticated variation of a signal that a series of rising peaks and troughs has been reversed. A bottom formation is simply the opposite.

We can also appreciate that these patterns incorporate all the basic building blocks that have already been covered: peak-and-trough analysis, support and resistance, and trendline analysis. It is also important to understand that a reversal pattern must have something to reverse. In other words, all reversal patterns must be preceded by a prior trend in the opposite direction from the reversal signal. Tops must be preceded by uptrends and bottoms by downtrends.

Consolidation Rectangles

If the rectangle following an uptrend is completed with a victory for the buyers as the price pushes through the upper line *AA* (see Fig. 6-7), a reversal does not develop because the breakout above *AA* reaffirms the underlying trend. In this case, the corrective phase associated with the formation of the rectangle temporarily interrupts the bull market and becomes a *consolidation* pattern. Such formations are also referred to as *continuation* patterns.

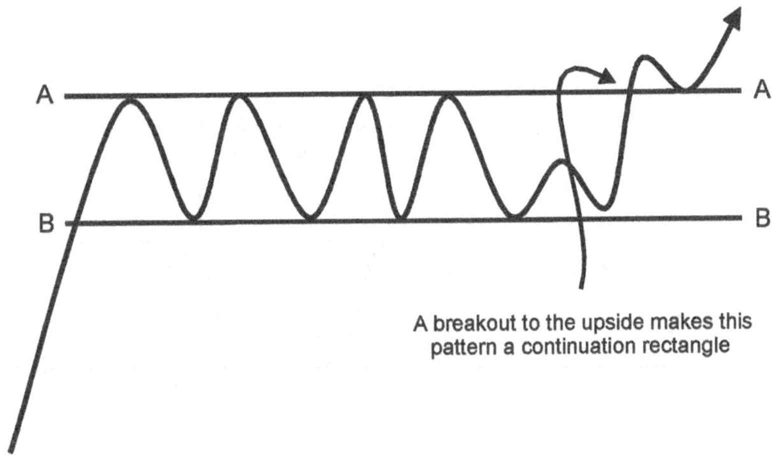

Figure 6-7 Upside continuation breakout signal.

Some price patterns show up only in a continuation mode; these are discussed in Chapter 12.

During the period in which the pattern is being formed, there is no way of knowing in advance which way the price will ultimately break. It should always be assumed, then, that *the prevailing trend is in existence until it is proved to have been reversed.* If we are faithfully applying the weight-of-the-evidence approach, it may be possible to anticipate a possible reversal if the other indicators are pointing in that direction. However, *the pattern itself can never be categorized as a reversal type until the reversal is actually signaled.*

A continuation or consolidation rectangle in a downtrend is shown in Fig. 6-8. An example is featured in Chart 6-1, for the copper price.

What Constitutes a Rectangle?

In the example in Fig. 6-5, the upper and lower boundaries of the rectangle were each touched on at least three occasions by the two horizontal trendlines. However, it was also possible to construct the rectangle using the first two points. Would that have constituted a valid pattern? The answer is yes. For the rationale for this, we need to examine the psychology underlying the formation of the pattern. Remember, the transition period is nothing less than a battle between buyers and sellers. If the battle is extended by the two boundaries being touched or approached on more than two occasions, this means that the conflict between the two parties is more

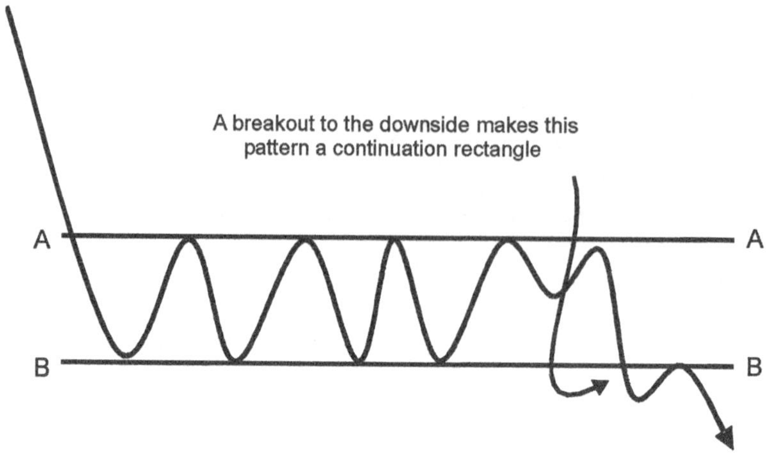

Figure 6-8 Downside continuation breakout signal.

significant. It also implies that the bearish implications of the rectangle will be stronger. We can even go so far as to say that *the more times the outer boundaries of a rectangle have been touched or approached, the greater the significance of the pattern.* It goes back to the second rule described in Chapter 4 concerning the significance of a trendline. The same holds true for the horizontal trendlines that form a rectangle. Let's return to our military analogy again.

Chart 6-1 Copper, daily.

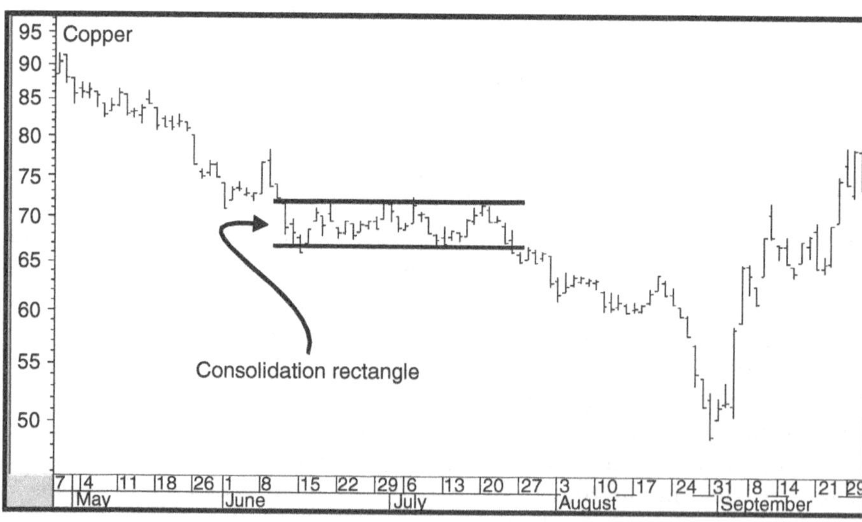

The longer the battle between the two trenches, the more exhausted the combatants will be. Thus the victory, when it comes, will be that much more decisive.

You may have noticed that I have used the word *approached* as well as *touched.* This is important, because in real life you will often find that the construction of the upper and lower boundaries of a rectangle is not as precise as that in Fig. 6-5. I regard a close approach to any trendline, including the outer boundaries of a rectangle, as being almost as valid as an actual contact. After all, if the price comes close to a boundary and then reverses, it definitely reinforces this level as a support or resistance zone.

The Significance of Any Given Price Pattern

The principles of price pattern construction and interpretation can be applied to any time frame, from one-minute bars all the way to monthly or even annual charts. However, the significance of a price formation for a specific time frame is a direct function of the formation's size and depth.

We have already established that a rectangle whose boundaries have been touched many times is more significant than one whose boundaries have been touched only twice. We can extend this idea by saying that *the longer a pattern takes to complete, the greater the number of fluctuations within it; and the deeper its trading range, the more substantial the following move is likely to be.*

Let's consider these three factors in turn.

1. Time Frames

The longer the time frame, the more significant the pattern. A pattern that shows up on a monthly chart is likely to be far more significant than one on an intraday chart, and so forth. In addition, the longer a pattern takes to develop in a particular time frame, the greater its significance within that time frame. Let's say we are looking at a daily chart and we spot two formations. The first takes ten days to complete and the second four weeks. Clearly the four-week battle between buyers and sellers is much greater and more involved than the ten-day encounter. Consequently, when the outcome is resolved, the ensuing price move is likely to be much greater. I use the word *likely* because this is a generality. Most of the time the larger pattern will be more important, but not every time. *In technical analysis, we are dealing in probabilities, never certainties.* This means that small patterns will occasionally be followed by large moves, but normally it is the larger ones that are.

Let's compare an accumulation pattern at a price low with the construction of a building. It is just as important to build a strong base from which prices can rise as it is to build a large, strong, deep foundation upon which to construct a skyscraper. In the case of security prices, the foundation is an accumulation pattern that represents an area of indecisive combat between buyers and sellers. During an accumulation phase, more sophisticated investors and professionals are positioning or accumulating the security in anticipation of improved conditions six to nine months ahead. As mentioned earlier, ownership is being transferred from weak, uninformed traders or investors to strong and knowledgeable hands. Consequently, the longer the pattern takes to complete and the greater the level of activity within it, the more significant the accumulation process and therefore the stronger the technical position.

The reverse is true at market tops, where a substantial amount of distribution inevitably results in a protracted period of price erosion.

2. The Significance of Pattern Fluctuations

The greater the number of fluctuations within a pattern, the greater the significance of that pattern. When the price action has been at a stalemate for a long time and investors and traders have become used to buying at one price and selling at the other, a move beyond either limit represents a fundamental change and has great psychological significance.

In 1972 and 1973 the commodity markets experienced a huge run-up. Chart 6-2 shows the CRB Composite. You can see that the rally was preceded by a multiyear trading range. There was no way of knowing that the breakout from the range would be followed by such a spectacular advance. Even so, the sheer size of the battle between buyers and sellers over many years would have indicated that when a resolution finally did take place, it would most likely signal an above-average price trend.

3. The Significance of Pattern Depth

The deeper a pattern, the greater its significance. The depth of a formation also determines its significance. Consider the trench war analogy once more. If the opposing trenches are very close together, say within 100 yards, this means that the victorious assault, when it comes, will be less significant than if they are separated by several miles. In that case, the battles will have been much more intense and the victory that much greater. The same is true in the financial markets. The breaching of a wide trading range generally has far greater psychological significance than the breaching of a

Chart 6-2 CRB Composite, 1957–1982, daily.

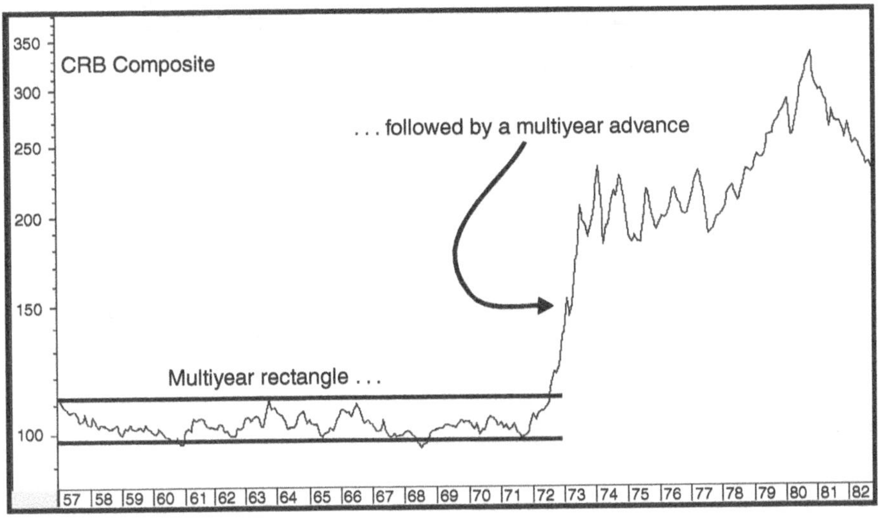

narrow one. Psychology, as expressed in market prices, tends to move in proportion. The greater the (proportionate) swing within the pattern, the greater the subsequent move is likely to be. If you get wide price swings during the formation of the pattern, you are also likely to get wide swings after it has been completed.

Having said that, it is also important to note that whenever you see a very tight and constrained trading range, this indicates that the battle between buyers and sellers is very evenly balanced. This is especially true when the level of activity shrinks to almost nothing. When that balance is tipped one way or the other, you will often find that prices move quite quickly and to a greater degree than is suggested by the measuring implication. We see an example in Fig. 6-24, where a pretty sharp decline follows the relatively narrow rectangle. Perhaps the guiding light in this is to see how many times the upper and lower boundaries have been touched or approached. The greater the number of times, the greater the significance of the line as a support or resistance zone, and therefore the more decisive the victory.

Measuring Implications

Technical analysis is best at identifying trend changes at an early stage and not so useful in forecasting how far a trend will extend. Price pattern

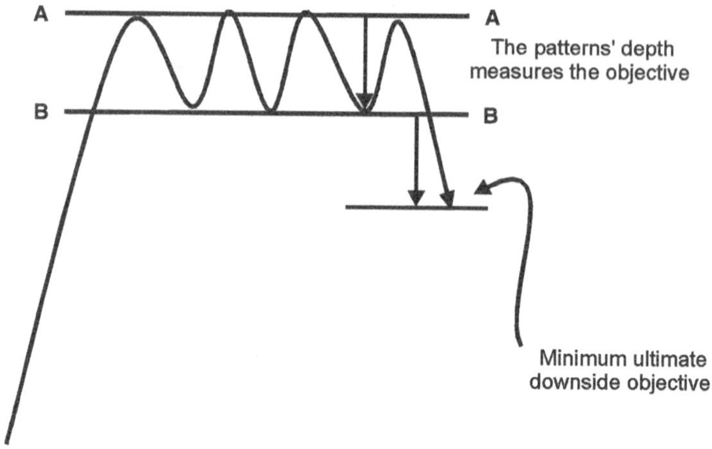

Figure 6-9 Rectangle top measuring objective.

interpretation is one exception, since the construction of these formations offers some limited forecasting possibilities.

Nearly all price patterns obtain measuring objectives from their depth. The rectangle is no exception. Figure 6-9 shows a rectangle that has formed and completed a top (distribution). The measuring implication of this formation is the vertical distance between its outer boundaries, i.e., the distance between lines *AA* and *BB* projected downward from line *BB*.

In many cases, the price trend will extend beyond the objective. In really strong moves, it will achieve multiples of it. We can take the process a step further by stating that the various multiples of the objective can become important support and resistance areas in their own right. Time and again, these price objective areas turn out to be important support or resistance points. Unfortunately, there is no way to determine where the actual juncture point will be for any rally or reaction. This emphasizes the principle that in technical analysis, there is no known way of consistently determining the duration of a price movement. It is possible only to speculate on the *probability* that a specific area will prove to be a support or resistance zone.

Consequently, while this measuring formula offers a rough guide, it is usually a *minimum* expectation. An example for a multiple-objective downside break is shown in Fig. 6-10. Here we see the price sink by three times the original objective. These multiples of the objective can be just as important in forecasting a probable pivotal point on the way back up, as we can see in the very right-hand part of the chart.

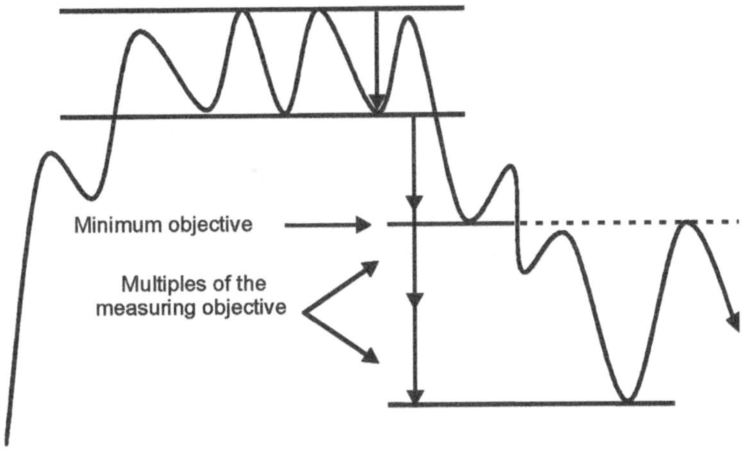

Figure 6-10 Rectangle top multiple measuring objective.

Arithmetic versus Logarithmic Scaling

The choice of arithmetic or logarithmic scaling is really important when measuring implications are being considered. This is because the method used determines the actual level of the objective. To recap, in arithmetically scaled charts, any given vertical space reflects the same dollar or point amount. Thus, we'll say that one inch represents $2, both at the lower end of the chart, in the $2 to $5 range, and at higher levels, such as the $100 to $110 range. All units of measure are plotted using the same vertical distance. Prices plotted on a ratio or logarithmic scale show identical distances for identical percentage moves. Thus, one inch could represent a 20 percent move anywhere on the chart.

Fortunately, almost all computer software gives the user the option of choosing between arithmetic and logarithmic scales.

The importance of using logarithmic scales whenever possible is shown in Fig. 6-11*a* and *b*. In *a*, the price has traced out and broken down from a rectangle. Projecting the vertical distance between 200 and 100 downward gives an objective of 0, clearly a very unlikely possibility. On the other hand, Fig. 6-11*b* gives the same projection based on a logarithmic scale. In this case, a more realistic objective of 50 is obtained.

If a rectangle appears as a bottom reversal pattern, the measuring rules remain consistent with those given for the distribution formation. The only difference is that we project the objective and multiples of the objective in an upward, not a downward, direction. The exact same principles also apply

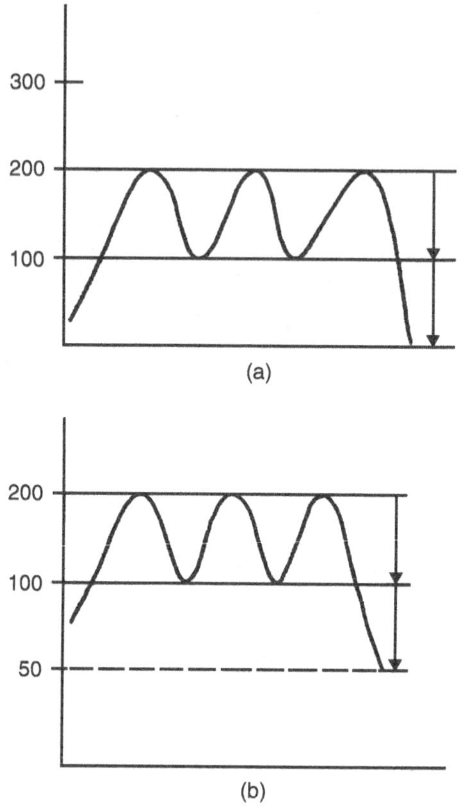

Figure 6-11 Measuring implication. (a) Arithmetic. (b) Ratio.

to continuation rectangles. Figure 6-12 shows an upside breakout from a rectangle that forms during a bullish trend. Note that in this case, the price does not reach its upside objective immediately, but does so after a small rally and reaction. This is why the objective is described by the term *ultimate.* Most people buy the breakout on the assumption that they will make more or less instant profits as the price moves straight to the objective, but that is not necessarily the case.

Retracement Moves

A great deal of the time, when the price breaks out from a pattern, the initial thrust is followed by a corrective move back to the upper or lower reaches of the formation, depending on the direction of the breakout. This

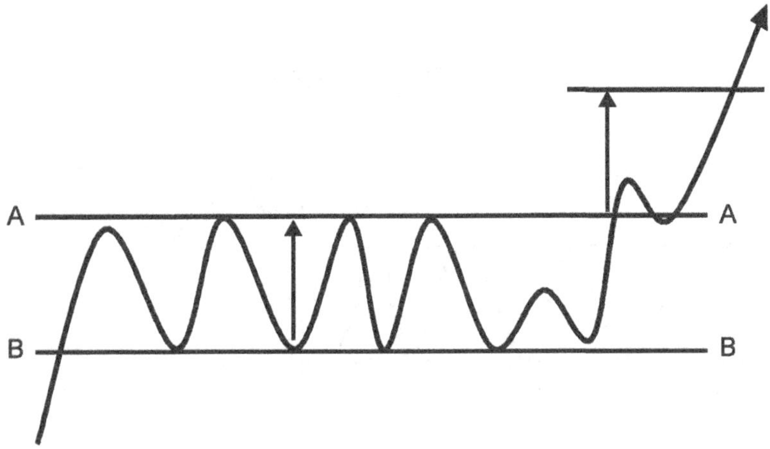

Figure 6-12 Upside continuation rectangle measuring objective.

is known as a *retracement* move, and it offers an additional entry point, often under substantially less emotional conditions. The retracement serves two functions. First, it helps to correct the excessive emotion associated with the breakout and bring people back to earth. From here, it is possible for the new trend to extend on a more sound basis. Second, it acts as a test of the breakout. A downside retracement will find support at the breakout point, and an upside one will find resistance at the lower boundary of the pattern as these two zones reverse their former roles.

Retracements, then, represent normal price behavior, and although they can be frustrating, they are nothing to get concerned about. Indeed, the breakout itself is often a volatile, illiquid affair as one side or the other heads for the entrance or exit, depending on the direction of the breakout. As a result, orders are often executed with horrendous fills. Price activity during the retracement process, on the other hand, is relatively quieter. This means that buying or selling can be undertaken in a much more controlled environment. Figure 6-13 shows that it is often a good idea to wait for a retracement in a rising trend and buy as the price signals that the retracement is over.

Cancellations

If the minimal objective proves to be the ultimate extension of the new trend, a substantial amount of accumulation or distribution, whichever is appropriate, will typically have to occur before prices can move in their previous direction. Thus, a two-year rectangle might be completed and the upward

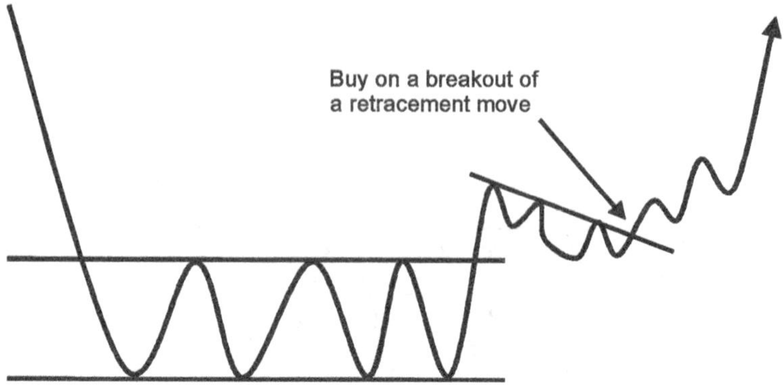

Figure 6-13 Buy on the retracement breakout.

price objective reached. Even though a further price rise does not take place, it is still usually necessary for a top (distribution) of approximately the same size as the previous accumulation (in this case, two years) to be formed before a valid downtrend can take place. An example is shown in Fig. 6-14.

Confirmation of a Valid Breakout

So far, it has been assumed that any move out of the price pattern, however small, constitutes a valid signal of a trend reversal (or resumption, if the pattern is one of consolidation). Quite often, misleading moves known as whipsaws occur, so it is helpful to establish certain criteria to minimize the possibility of misinterpretation. Conventional wisdom holds that you should wait for a 3 percent penetration of the boundaries before concluding that the breakout is valid. A rule of this nature filters out a substantial number of misleading moves, even though the resulting signals are less timely.

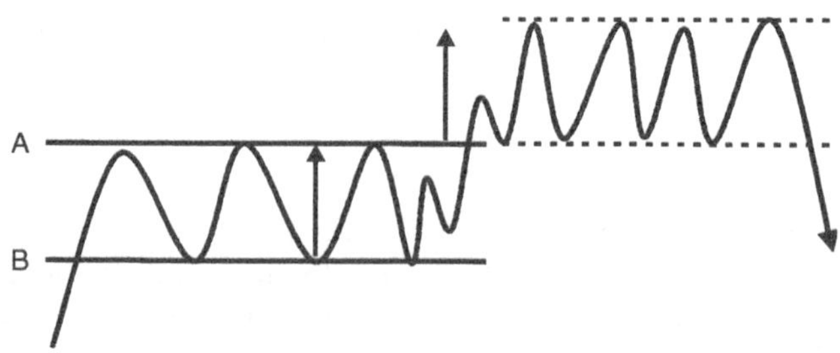

Figure 6-14 The cancellation effect.

The 3 percent rule was developed in the first part of the twentieth century, when market participants' holding periods were much longer and weekly and monthly charts were more popular. Today, with the use of intraday charts, 3 percent could represent the complete move and then some! I have no basic objection to the 3 percent rule for longer-term price movements, where the fluctuations are much greater. However, the best approach is a commonsense one based on experience and judgment in each particular case. It would be very convenient to be able to say that anything over a specific percentage amount represents a valid breakout, but unfortunately, a lot depends on the time frame being considered and the volatility of the specific security in question.

For example, electric utilities are very stable in their price action compared to mining stocks, where the volatility is far greater. Applying the same percentage breakout rule to both obviously doesn't make sense. What constitutes a decisive breakout, with the chances of a whipsaw being considerably reduced, is thus very much a matter of personal judgment based on experience, trial, and error. This judgment should take into consideration such factors as the type of trend being monitored, the volatility of the security, volume, and momentum characteristics.

Ironically, a false breakout here and there actually adds validity to a specific support or resistance zone. Say, for example, that after great effort I am able to jump from the basement through the ceiling of the ground floor, but the effort to do this leaves me with just my head above the floor and my arms and hands also resting on the floor. Technically, I suppose I am on the ground floor, but it's still taking an awful lot of effort to maintain this position. Unless I am able to drag my feet up and actually stand on the ground floor, I am likely to slip back through the ceiling and end up where I started. In this situation, my false "breakout" above resistance (the ceiling) has emphasized the importance of that resistance. It also means that I have expended a great deal of effort trying to get to the ground floor, and, as a result, I now need an extended period in which to gain enough strength to make another attempt. Figure 6-15 shows an example of a rectangle containing a whipsaw breakout.

Another factor that can help in deciding early on whether a breakout is valid is that a valid breakout should hold for several periods. For example, you may observe a decisive upside breakout from a rectangle on a daily chart, but if the price cannot hold above the breakout level for more than one day, the signal is highly suspect. Often the technical position is worse after such breakouts because those that cannot hold indicate exhaustion, and *exhaustion moves are often followed by strong price trends in the direction opposite to that indicated by the (false) breakout.* At the very least we would expect an exhaustion breakout to be followed by an extended period of trading within the body of the pattern until the technical structure can regroup.

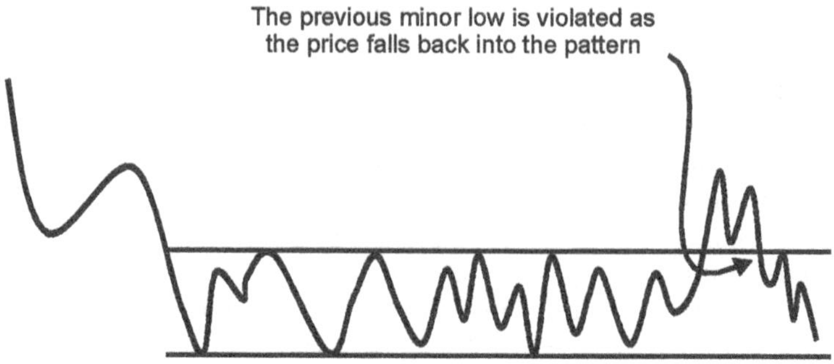

Figure 6-15 Identifying a whipsaw breakout.

Once the price moves away from the pattern, the odds favor a valid breakout. But what happens if the price breaks back into the body of the pattern again? Is the breakout still valid? If not, where is the point at which you pull the plug on the whole thing?

Anticipating When Things Might Go Wrong

One of the first things that should be done upon entering any business venture is weighing the possible risk against the potential reward. The same is true in the financial markets. Most people, upon seeing a price break out from a pattern, focus on potential profits as they calculate the probable upside objective. Experienced professionals, on the other hand, always consider the risk as an equal, if not a more important, part of the equation. If the reward/risk ratio is not greater than 3:1, the trade or investment is probably not worth initiating.

This means that whenever you are planning on opening a new position based on a price pattern breakout, it is important that you *decide ahead of time what type of price action would cause you to conclude that the breakout was a whipsaw.* In this exercise, we need to remember that when an upside breakout develops, the probabilities favor higher prices. This continues to be the case during the retracement move. However, as soon as the price moves back into the body of the pattern, the odds of higher prices begin to narrow. The question is, "When do the odds move below the 50 percent point?" Unfortunately, there are no hard and fast rules that can be said to work on all occasions. Each situation has to be judged on its own merits, and it's better to do the exercise before you enter the position than while you are holding it. Otherwise emotion will creep into what will probably turn out to be an ad hoc decision.

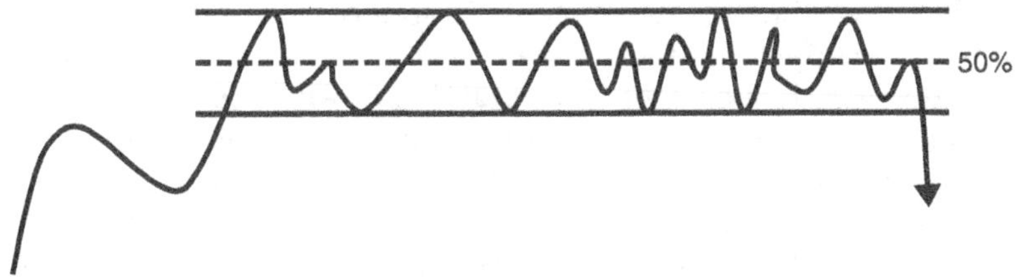

Figure 6-16 Identifying a whipsaw breakout.

The first step is to bear in mind that once the upper boundary of the pattern has been breached following an upside breakout, this is similar to saying that support has been violated. The same will be true, but in reverse, for a downside breakout. This puts us on red alert until either the price breaks back out of the pattern again or other support areas are violated. You can see that in Fig. 6-15, the breaking of the upper boundary of the formation also signals a series of declining peaks and troughs. In my view, this would be sufficient evidence to exit the position. Markets are no more and no less than an expression of people in action. *Since individuals can and do change their minds, so can markets.* You will be far better off paying attention to the market's message than to your own personal hopes and fears. When the situation is no longer flagging high probabilities of a price rise, it is better to take a small loss than to let pride and stubbornness lead to a big one.

Let's say that the price fell straight back into the pattern without the benefit of a peak-and-trough reversal. What should we do then? It very much depends on the chart. If there are no obvious support points, many traders believe that a penetration of the 50 percent mark is the place to exit. In this case, the 50 percent mark is the central point between the two horizontal lines that make up the rectangle. An example is shown in Fig. 6-16. In this case, the signal to sell would develop as the price crossed the 50 percent level.

Figure 6-17 shows another example in which the price breaks below a previous minor low. In this instance, the break develops within the pattern.

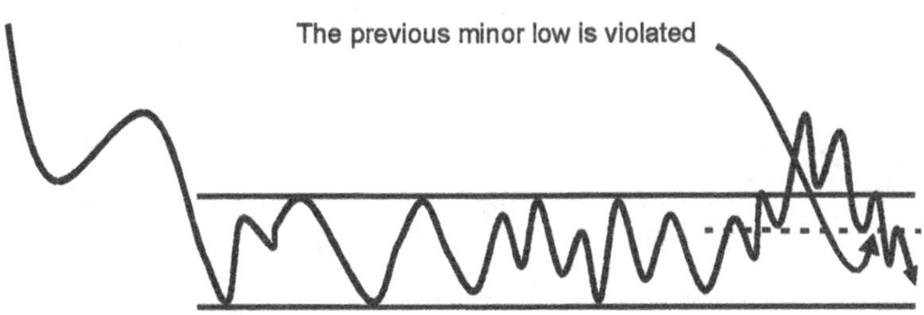

Figure 6-17 Identifying a whipsaw breakout.

Remember, the minor low is a potential support point. If the price breaks below both the upper boundary and the minor low, then two support points have been violated. Such action is certainly not what was expected during the original breakout. If you were considering a purchase, there would be no grounds for buying at this point. Why, then, if you are long, should the decision be any different? It shouldn't, of course, but it is often difficult to take a loss. Invariably hope of a rally seeps into the psyche, and a rationale for staying with the position develops. Unfortunately, markets are not as sentimental as their participants and often show no mercy. That's why it is important to take quick action as soon as the probabilities of an advance decrease.

Another possibility is shown in Fig. 6-18, where it was possible to construct a small up trendline and observe its violation. The penetration of that line then serves as a support violation and a sell signal.

In all these examples, it would be important to place a stop *below* the various support points: the 50 percent mark, the previous low, the up trendline, and so on. As previously mentioned, these stop points should be set *ahead* of time. By doing this, you will have calculated the loss that you are willing to accept and the point at which the original premise for the trade—i.e., the breakout—is no longer operative. Failure to take such action ahead of time means that when things go wrong, the actual decision to sell is more likely to be based on emotional stress caused by a reaction to a news event or something similar rather than on a logical, preset plan.

The examples we have dealt with here relate to upside breakouts, since that is the direction in which most market participants look. However, in the case of short positions initiated through downside breakouts, the principles remain the same, except that the direction is reversed. In this situation, resistance areas are substituted for support. An example is shown in Fig. 6-19 where a stop would be placed above the last rally experienced by the pattern prior to the downside breakout. A move above this point would not necessarily invalidate the formation. However, it would certainly place

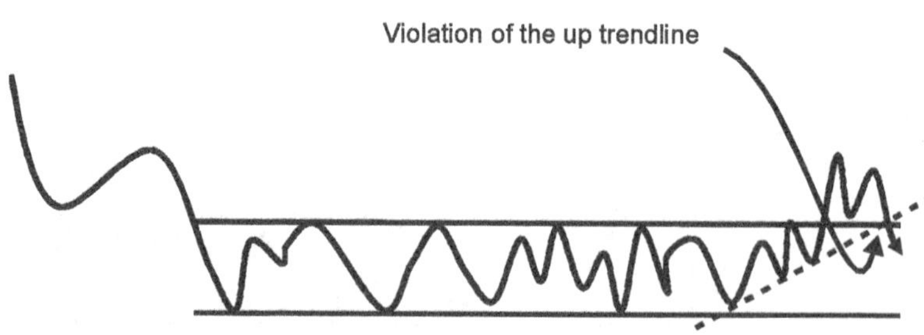

Figure 6-18 Identifying a whipsaw breakout.

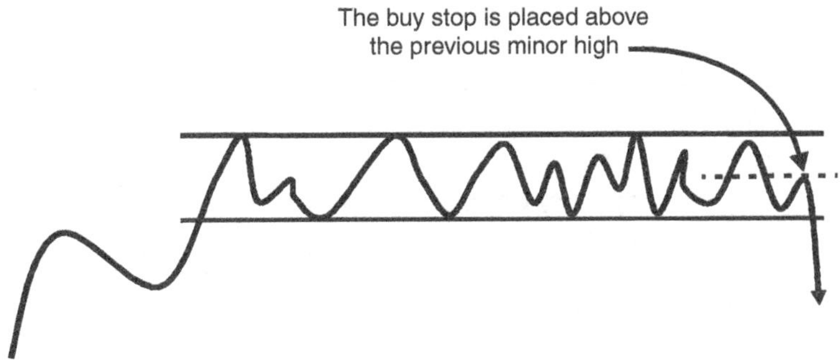

Figure 6-19 Placing a stop after a downside breakout.

the odds of its succeeding below 50/50, whereas at the time of the downside breakout they would have been well above 50/50. Consequently, if the advance above the dashed trendline invalidates the reason for going short, why continue to hold the trade?

Volume Considerations

So far we have considered only price in our analysis, but volume is an important independent variable that can help us obtain a more accurate reflection of crowd psychology. To quickly recap, volume usually goes with the trend, i.e., it expands with a rising trend of prices and contracts with a declining one. This is a normal relationship, and anything that diverges from it should be considered a warning sign that the prevailing price trend may be in the process of reversing. Volume is always measured in relation to the recent past. Thus, heavy volume is related to volume 20 to 30 bars or so ago, not to volume, say, 10 years ago, as institutional changes may have permanently increased the level of activity.

In the case of the rectangle, and with most other patterns, it is normal for the trend of volume to contract as the formation develops. Activity may continue to fluctuate along with the price, but with the benefit of hindsight, we would expect to see the various peaks and troughs of volume shrink as the pattern develops, along the lines of Fig. 6-20. As the pattern nears completion, disinterest prevails and volume often dries up.

The quality of an accumulation formation is certainly improved if volume expands on the upside break. Sometimes it is even possible to draw a trendline joining the lower-volume peaks, as shown in Fig. 6-20. It is the upward surge in trading activity that confirms the validity of the breakout because it signals the enthusiasm of buyers. A similar move on declining volume

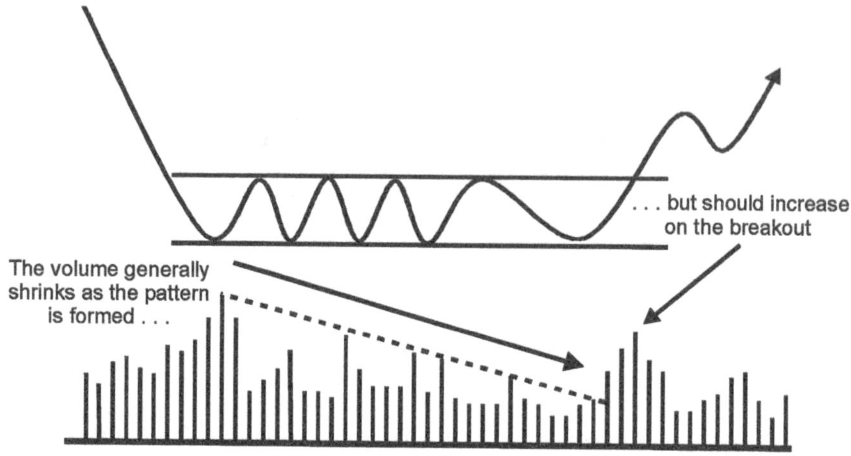

Figure 6-20 Volume trend shrinks as a rectangle is formed.

would be suspect and would indicate a failure of volume to move with the trend. An example is shown in Fig. 6-21. In this instance, volume definitely declines as the price is breaking out. Such action typically signals that prices are advancing more because of a lack of sellers than because of strong, enthusiastic buyers. As the price starts to slip, volume picks up noticeably, suggesting that the price is slipping because of selling pressure. This is a definite sign that increases the possibility that the breakout is a whipsaw.

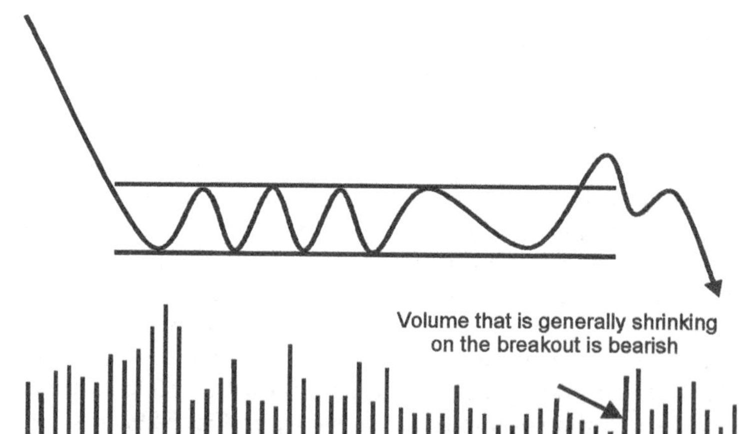

Figure 6-21 Shrinking volume on an upside breakout is bearish.

You will often see charts in which successful breakouts develop with no obvious change in volume, either on the upside or the downside. Unfortunately, this is a fact of life. Thus a good expansion is a desirable, but not necessarily a mandatory, condition for a valid breakout. It certainly increases the odds, but other indicators, such as oscillators, could also tip the balance. If volume actually declines on the breakout, as in Fig. 6-21, this is more than a missing piece of positive evidence; it is an actual negative factor.

Figure 6-22 shows a downside breakout from a rectangle. The same shrinking volume characteristics are present during the development of the pattern as were present for the bullish variety. However, volume characteristics on a downside breakout are less critical. This is because it is normal for volume to contract as prices decline. Thus, contracting volume on a breakdown is perfectly normal. What is not typical, though, is for volume to expand on a downside move. This in itself suggests that sellers are more motivated and therefore adds an additional negative flavor to the pattern.

More often than not, prices will reverse and produce a small recovery or retracement rally following the downside breakout (Fig. 6-23). This advance is invariably accompanied by declining volume, which itself reinforces the bearish indications. It is halted at the lower end of the rectangle, which now becomes an area of resistance. The same idea of declining volume should accompany a retracement move that follows an upside breakout.

Figure 6-24 shows an example in which both price volatility and volume shrink dramatically. This combination indicates an extremely fine balance between buyers and sellers that exists over an extended period. Normally a price objective is determined by the depth of the formation. In this case,

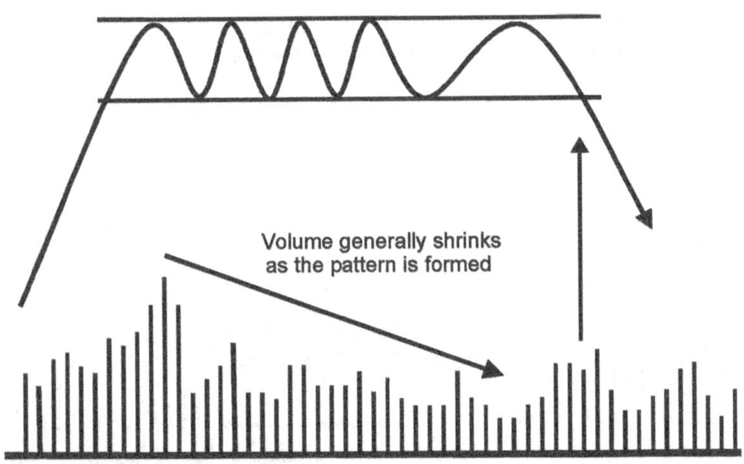

Figure 6-22 Expanding volume on a downside breakout is bearish.

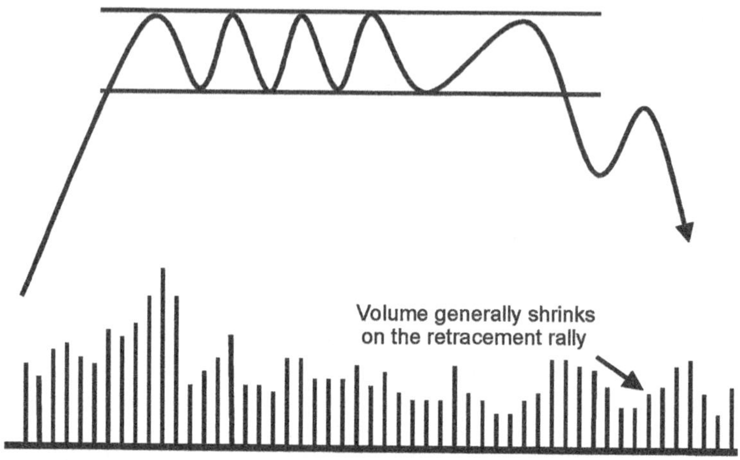

Figure 6-23 Volume should shrink on a retracement rally.

though, the finely balanced supply/demand situation is usually followed by a far greater and sharper move than would be indicated by the normal measuring techniques. Figure 6-24 shows a sharp downside breakout, but the principle of rapidly declining volume followed by a huge expansion applies equally as well to an upside breakout. In this instance, volume typically explodes as we move from a situation in which there is virtually no interest by either party to one in which buyers cannot get enough of the security at any price. Such are the ingredients for the start of a dramatic rally. An

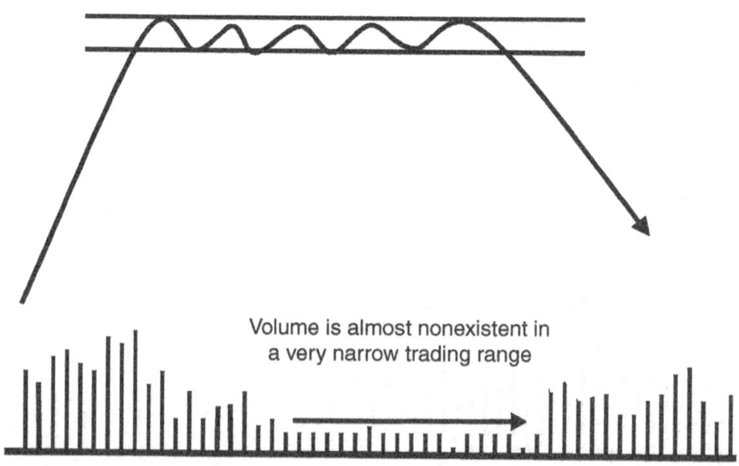

Figure 6-24 Narrow rectangle and nonexistent volume are often followed by a sharp move.

Chart 6-3 St. Jude Medical, daily.

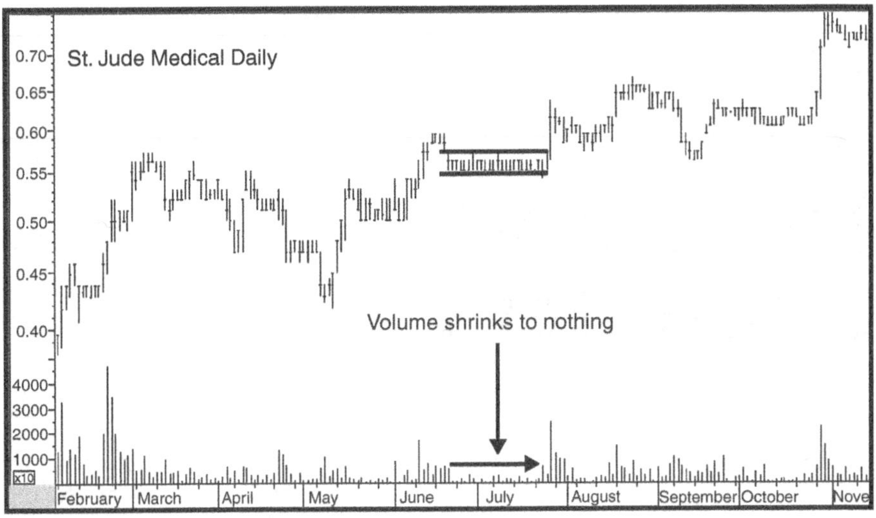

example is shown in Chart 6-3, for St. Jude Medical, where a very narrow rectangle developed with a dramatic drop in volume. When the volume expanded, a short but sharp rally followed.

Summary

- *Price characteristics:* A trading range bounded by two parallel trendlines.
- *Volume considerations:* Volume shrinks as the pattern is formed. It is better if it expands on an upside breakout; it is immaterial on a downside breakout.
- *Measuring implications:* The depth of the pattern is projected in the direction of the breakout from the breakout point.
- *Signs of false breakouts:* Shrinking volume on an upside breakout.
- *Benchmarks for upside failure:* The price falls back into the pattern and violates a previous minor low, violates an up trendline joining previous minor lows, or crosses below the 50 percent level of the pattern.
- *Benchmarks for downside failure:* The price rallies back into the pattern and breaks above a previous minor high, violates a down trendline joining previous minor highs, or crosses above the 50 percent level of the pattern.

7
Head and Shoulders

The head and shoulders is probably the most notorious of all patterns. It forms at tops and bottoms as a reversal formation and also develops during an ongoing trend as a continuation or consolidation phenomenon. Compared to other patterns, such as triangles, the head and shoulders has the reputation for being one of the most reliable.

Head and Shoulders as a Reversal Pattern

Figure 7-1 shows a typical head-and-shoulders (H&S) distribution pattern. It consists of a final rally (the head) separating two smaller, although not necessarily identical, rallies (the left and right shoulders). If the two shoulders were trends of intermediate duration, the first shoulder would be the penultimate advance in the bull market, and the second would be the first bear market rally. The head would, of course, represent the final intermediate rally in the bull market. The line joining the bottoms of the two shoulders is called the *neckline.* When the neckline is violated on the downside, the pattern is completed and a reversal signal is given. To be valid, any reversal pattern must have something to reverse. A head-and-shoulders top must therefore be preceded by a strong inbound uptrend.

Volume characteristics (see Fig. 7-2) are important in assessing the validity of these formations. Activity is normally heaviest during the development of the left shoulder and also tends to be quite heavy as prices approach the peak. If the left shoulder rally is accompanied by a higher level of activity than the head, this fits nicely into the principle, outlined in Chapter 5, that

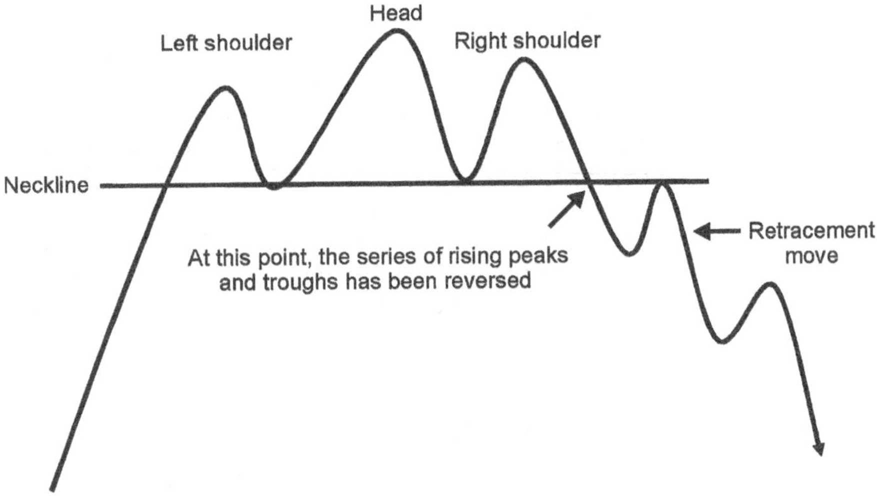

Figure 7-1 Classic head-and-shoulders top.

volume leads price. The real tip-off that an H&S pattern is developing comes with the formation of the right shoulder, which is invariably accompanied by distinctly lower volume than the head or the left shoulder. Ideally, the level of volume contracts as the right-shoulder rally unfolds. In many market place examples you will find that even though the volume characteristics differ from

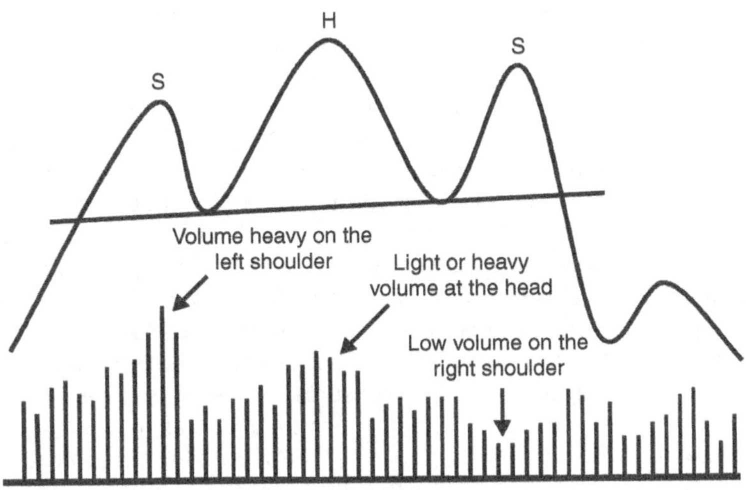

Figure 7-2 Classic head-and-shoulders top with volume.

those described here, the pattern still "works." Thus, the volume patterns are a guide. If they are present, the formation is more likely to work, but just because they are not present doesn't mean that the pattern should be ignored. Alternatively, if you can spot the price and volume action that are representative of a head-and-shoulders top, this can be used as a guide in order to anticipate the final completion of the pattern.

Figure 7-1 also illustrates the fact that the violation of the neckline represents a signal that the previous series of rising peaks and troughs has now given way to at least one declining peak and trough. The right shoulder represents the first lower peak, and the bottom of the move following the breakdown, a lower trough.

Possible Psychology Causing These Formations

The psychology underlying a head-and-shoulders formation will depend very much on the time frame under consideration. If it develops on a weekly chart following an extended rally lasting several months or more, bullish sentiment is likely to be far more embedded in crowd psychology than if a head-and-shoulders top is identified in, say, a chart of 10-minute bars. Not surprisingly, the decline signaled by a head and shoulders on a weekly chart will be far greater, since the bullish psychological pendulum epitomized by the pattern will take far longer to swing to the bearish extreme from which an upside reversal could be expected. However, there are common characteristics in the development of these patterns that apply to all time frames. The difference is that smaller patterns on intraday charts are like a quick slap on the wrist that is quickly forgotten, whereas multiyear patterns on the monthly charts are more akin to an amputation.

Let's consider how this might be applied to a daily chart. In Fig. 7-1, the left shoulder was really the end of a pretty good rally. The psychology at this point is pretty bullish, so when a setback develops and prices take out the left-shoulder high, market participants expect the trend to continue, which it does. In most cases, the rally that forms the head is quite large. Since rising prices promote bullish sentiment, the crowd is pretty happy at the top of the head. Often the level of volume is smaller on the head than on the left-shoulder rally. This is a sign that under the surface there is less buying power supporting the advance than was previously the case. Also, if you are tracking an oscillator, it may form a negative divergence between the two rallies, thereby pointing up other subsurface problems. [For a complete description of oscillators, please see *Martin Pring on Market Momentum* (McGraw-Hill, 2002) workbook/CD-ROM tutorial.] These volume and oscillator discrepancies are not signals to sell but more of a warning that prices are vulnerable in the case of a trend-reversal signal by the price itself.

When the head rally is over, prices fall back to support around the level of the previous low. At that point, buyers who missed the advance are encouraged to enter the market. If prices rose from this level before, surely this represents a bargain and they will rise again. Owners of the security, for their part, feel the same way and are less inclined to sell. Each rally up to this point has taken prices progressively higher, so there is no reason to suspect that the next advance will be any different. However, this one turns out to be quite weak. Volume shrinks as it progresses, indicating that the rise is caused more by a lack of selling than by an influx of buying. When selling does start to pick up, the price reaches the top of the right shoulder and begins to slip. Participants are still bullish at this point, expecting a small pullback before a rally to new highs. However, to the technician, a decline in volume as prices rise on the right shoulder is a bearish sign because it indicates far less enthusiasm than was indicated by the higher volume on the left shoulder and head. Finally, when the price breaks below the level of the two previous bottoms, the multitude of buyers who bought on the left shoulder and head are locked in with a loss. There is a tendency to sell, but where are the buyers? As it turns out, they expended their potential on the way up, when the news was good and bullish sentiment contagious. In some instances bad news surfaces and the price experiences a very sharp sell-off. Alternatively, we may see a series of sharp rallies and reactions taking the form of a downward zigzag. Hope alternates with despair as prices gradually work their way lower.

People can and do change their minds, and events also change. For this reason, quite a few head-and-shoulders tops are quickly cancelled out as a base is built just below the neckline. Then the bearish psychology associated with the head-and-shoulders breakdown is replaced with positive sentiment emanating from the breakout from the base. Prices are then free to rise again, but more on that later.

Measuring Implications

The measuring formula for this price formation is the maximum depth of the pattern, which in the case of the head and shoulders means the distance between the top of the head and the neckline. This objective is then projected downward from the neckline at the breakdown point (Fig. 7-3). It follows that the deeper the pattern, the greater its bearish significance once it has been completed. Sometimes a head-and-shoulders completion will be followed by a fairly extensive downtrend; at other times the negative effect of the pattern will be quickly cancelled by the completion of a base. This means that you should not assume that all breakdowns lead to large profits (from the short side). Always keep an open mind as the technical condition changes.

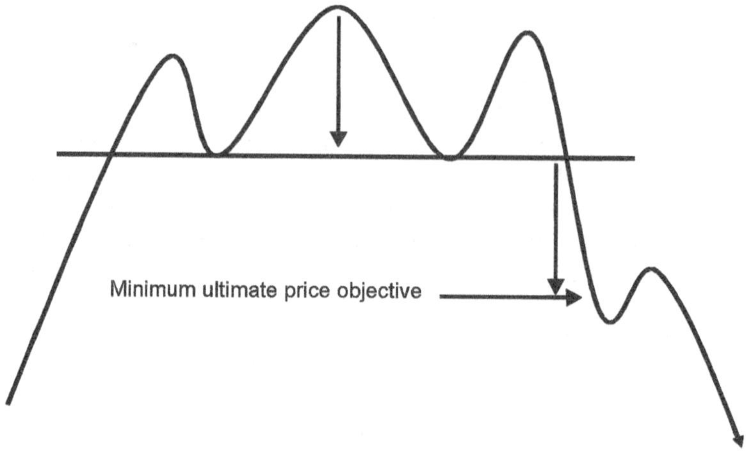

Figure 7-3 Head-and-shoulders top measuring implications.

Arithmetic versus Logarithmic Scaling

For longer-term charts, the choice between arithmetic and logarithmic scaling can be of critical importance. Where large price movements are involved, the difference in the price objectives can be considerable. Charts 7-1 and 7-2 offer an extreme example. Chart 7-1 shows the three-month commercial

Chart 7-1 Commercial paper yield, 1910–2003, monthly (arithmetic scale).

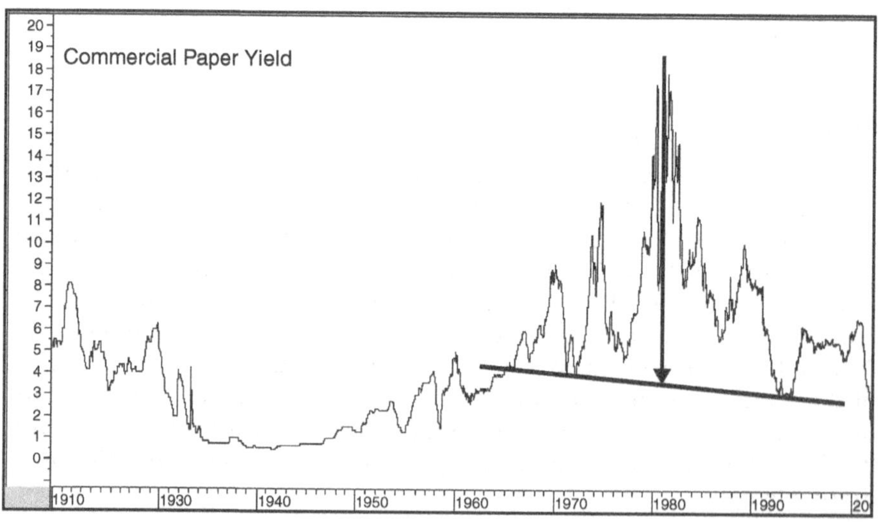

Chart 7-2 Commercial paper yield, 1910–2003, monthly (logarithmic scale).

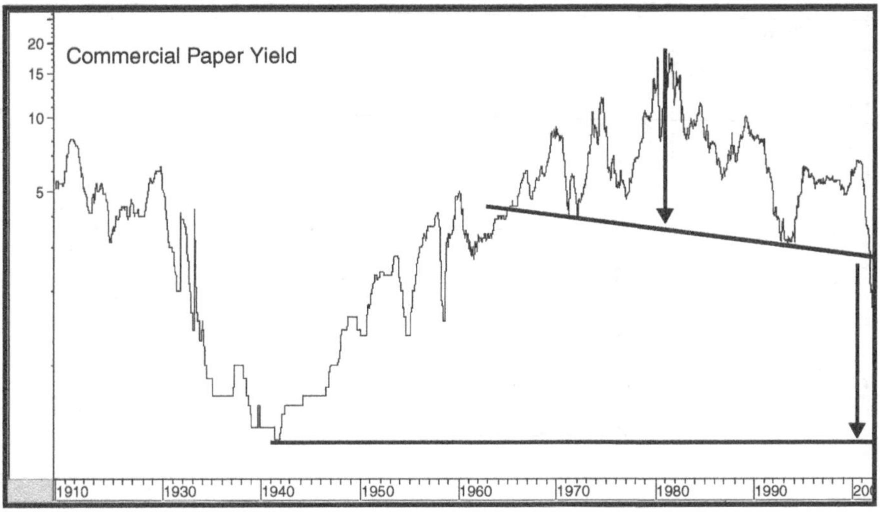

paper yield plotted on an arithmetic scale. The head-and-shoulders projection calls for the rate to decline to a negative number, clearly a very unlikely scenario. (I say unlikely because Switzerland had negative rates in the late twentieth century to discourage foreigners from investing in Swiss francs.) Chart 7-2, on the other hand, shows the same period in a logarithmic mode. Note how the downside objective was far more realistic, calling for the yield to fall to support in the area of its 1940s low.

The objective is called a "minimum ultimate" target because prices often move much further than the objective. Indeed, they often progress in multiples of it. Chart 7-3, featuring the German government bond (Bund), shows that the price declined by three times the amount of the objective. Notice that the horizontal line marking the initial objective became a resistance point later on as the price rallied again. Therefore, when you are looking for potential support areas following a downside head-and-shoulders breakout, it's a good idea to use multiples of the head/neckline measuring objective as a guide. In this case it would have worked quite well. The problem, of course, is you do not know ahead of time which, if any, multiple of the price objective will turn out to be support.

Bar Charts versus Close-Only or Line Charts

Bar charts have the advantage that they reveal all of the price action that takes place in the specific period covered. One of the problems is that prices

Chart 7-3 German Bund, 1998–2003, weekly.

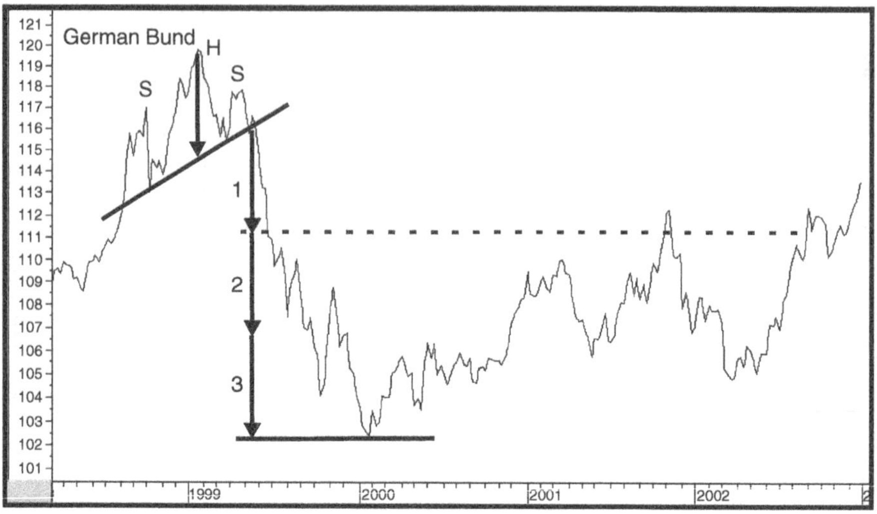

are often subject to rumor and random events that have little or nothing to do with the trend. This means that bar charts are far more susceptible to false or misleading moves.

Line charts are not immune to whipsaw signals, but they certainly filter out a lot of them. Often it is easier to spot a pattern using close-only charts, since they show the underlying trend in a more graphically pleasing manner. Charts 7-4 and 7-5, featuring XL Capital, represent the same time period in a bar and a line format. Notice that there were two whipsaws in the head-and-shoulders formation in the bar chart, but these do not appear on the close-only chart.

The neckline for the subsequent reverse head-and-shoulders was also easier to construct on the close-only chart, since it was a more horizontal and therefore significant line.

Often, traders observe the formation of a head-and-shoulders top and take action in anticipation of a breakdown. This is an incorrect tactic because *based on this evidence alone* it is not known until later whether the prevailing trend will continue, or whether a reversal signal will be given by a decisive break below the neckline. If a substantial number of other indicators are pointing in the direction of a trend change, that is another matter. Taken on its own, though, an incomplete pattern cannot signify a trend reversal. Over the years, I have seen many analysts who should know better forecast a bearish trend based on an incomplete head-and-shoulders top. Remember, *in technical analysis, the prevailing trend is assumed to be in force until the weight*

Chart 7-4 XL Capital, 1997–2002, weekly.

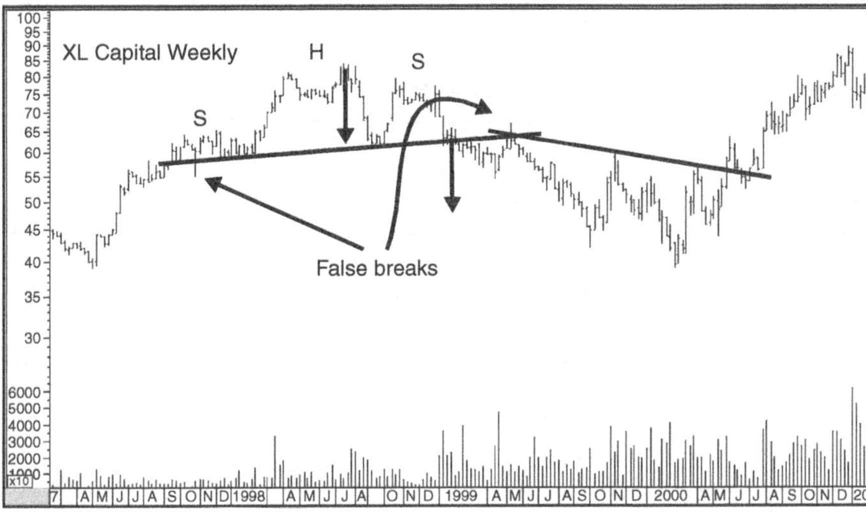

of the evidence proves otherwise. An incomplete head and shoulders is not evidence, just a possible scenario.

H&S patterns can be formed in 10 to 15 minutes or take decades to develop. Generally speaking, the longer the period, the greater the amount of distribution that has taken place, and therefore the longer the ensuing

Chart 7-5 XL Capital, 1997–2002, weekly.

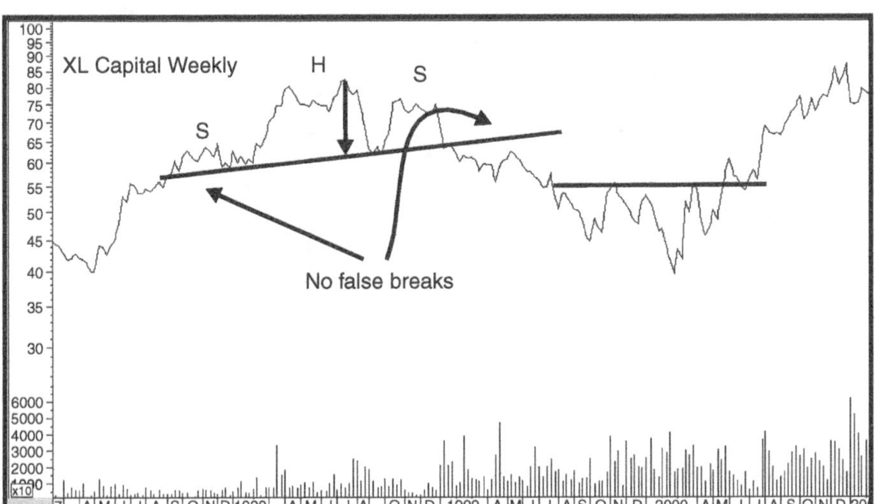

bear trend. The larger H&S formations are often very complex and comprise several smaller ones, as shown in Fig. 7-6.

Upward- and Downward-Sloping Patterns

The H&S patterns illustrated in Figs. 7-1 and 7-2 had a horizontal neckline, but there are many other varieties, all of which have the same bearish implications as the horizontal variety once they have been completed.

When the neckline of a horizontal pattern has been violated, a series of declining peaks and troughs is signaled. Not so with the upward-sloping variety shown in Fig. 7-4, because at the time of the breakout the price is still above its previous low. By the same token, the series of declining peaks and troughs has already been set in motion when the neckline of a downward head and shoulders (Fig. 7-5) has been violated. Chart 7-3, for the German Bund, shows an upward-sloping pattern, and Chart 7-6, for Union Planter's, features a downward-sloping variety. In this instance, the price eventually sold off to a four times multiple of the measured price objective. In terms of pure price objective, the downward-sloping formations for any given depth are more bearish than their horizontal or upward-sloping counterparts. This is because the breakdown from the neckline takes place at the lowest point of the pattern. By the same token, we must be careful with a neckline that has an extremely sharp angle of descent, as it is more likely to be followed by a false break. This is an extension of the rule relating to the steepness of the angle of ascent or descent of a trendline, discussed in Chapter 4. After all, a neckline is nothing more than a special trendline.

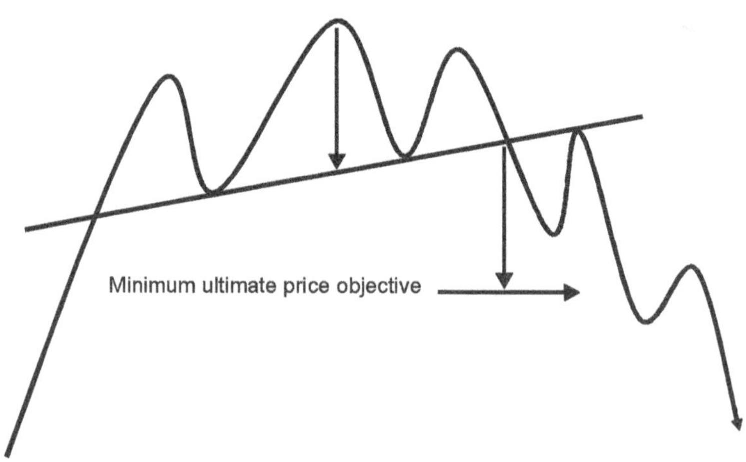

Figure 7-4 Upward-sloping head and shoulders.

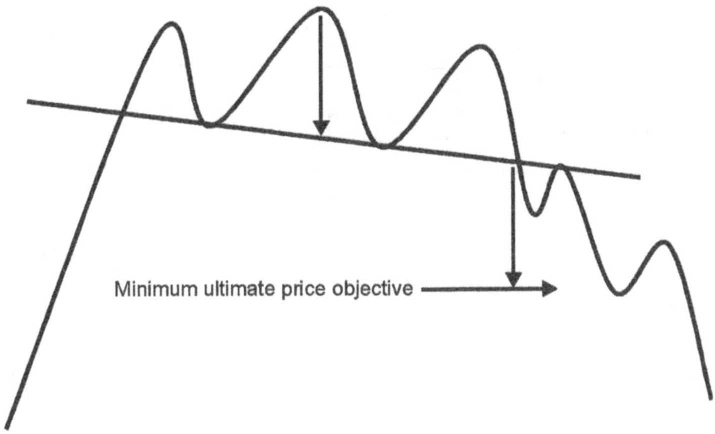

Figure 7-5 Downward-sloping head and shoulders.

Complex Patterns

Occasionally the battle between buyers and sellers is exceptionally complicated. This leads to the formation of what we call a complex head and shoulders, in which there could be more than one right or left shoulder. Alternatively, the head itself could be a head-and-shoulders top in its own

Chart 7-6 Union Planter's, 1986–2000, weekly.

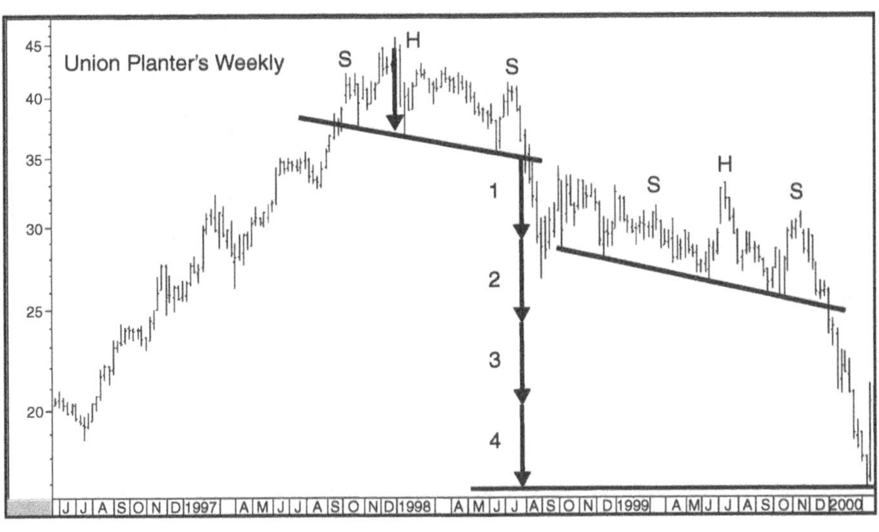

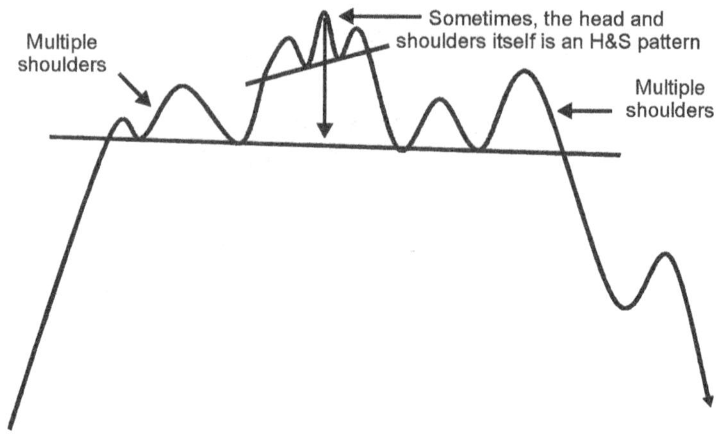

Figure 7-6 Complex head-and-shoulders top.

right. The possibilities are enormous, so Fig. 7-6 is offered as a starting point. Notice that the top shown in Chart 7-7 contains two right shoulders and therefore qualifies as a complex pattern. There is no theoretical limit to the extent of complexity in a pattern. Chart 7-7, for Watson Pharmaceutical, in fact shows a very intricate pattern consisting of four

Chart 7-7 Watson Pharmaceutical, 1999–2002, daily.

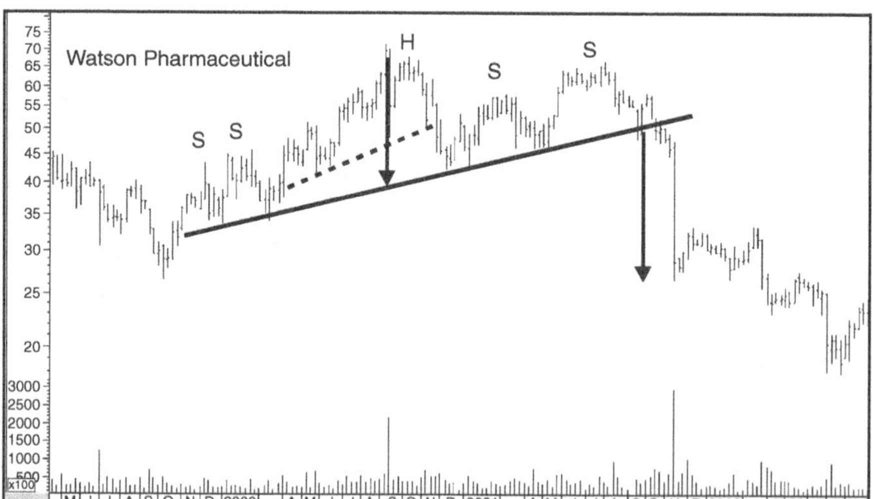

shoulders, two on the left and two on the right. You can also see that the dashed trendline is really the neckline of a small head-and-shoulders top that forms the head. As a general rule, the more complex the pattern, the more intense the battle between buyers and sellers, and the more intense the battle, the greater the implied significance of the new trend when it begins.

Characteristics of the Formation

A head-and-shoulders formation can take on many different characteristics. Since the breakdown point is the critical one, the nature of the right shoulder deserves some additional attention. After all, this is the trapdoor through which prices will drop. Figure 7-7 shows three possibilities that indicate a particularly interesting battle between buyers and sellers. The first displays what I call "a right-shoulder shakeout." This develops when it looks as if the shoulder is developing in a fairly controlled way. Then the price falsely breaks above resistance in the form of a previous trendline or high. This whipsaw action is unnerving for bull and bear alike. As a result, this unwanted volatility results in an unusually nasty decline. An example is shown in Chart 7-8, for Anheuser Busch just prior to the 1987 crash. The false dashed trendline break on the right shoulder is quickly followed by a decline. Then the trading action goes very quiet; the price barely moves and volume shrinks to almost nothing, indicating a fine balance between buyers and sellers. However, it is the calm before

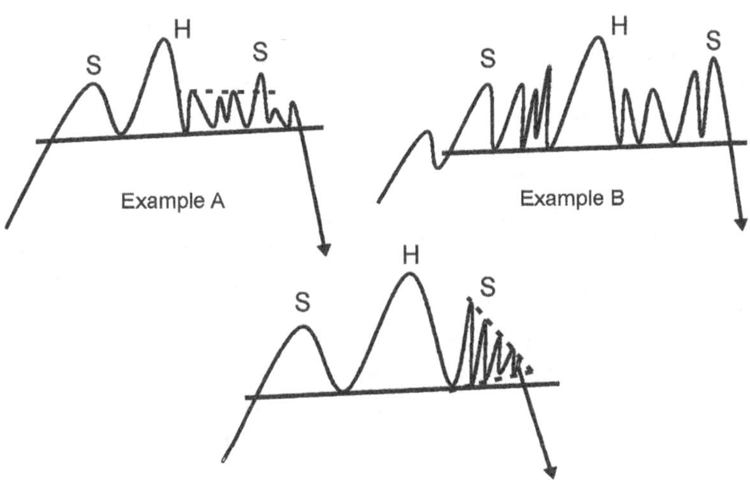

Figure 7-7 Head-and-shoulders top variations.

Chart 7-8 Anheuser Busch, daily.

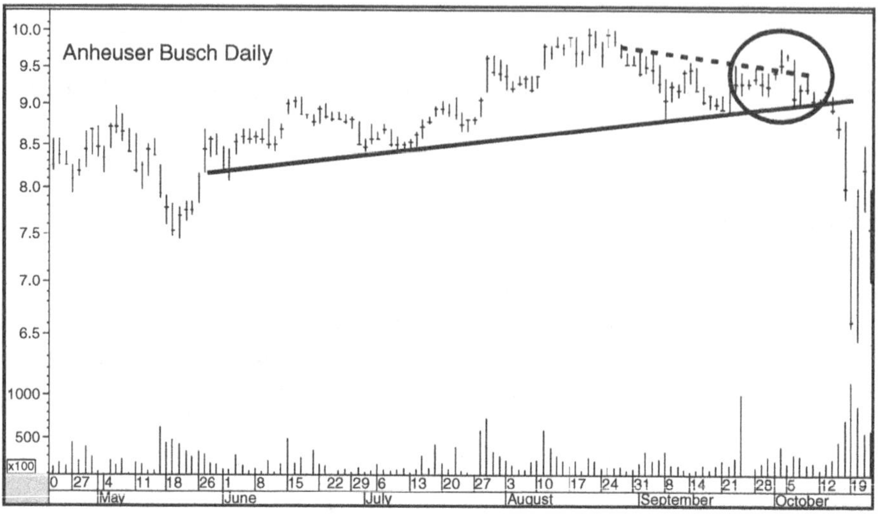

the storm. Finally the pattern is completed and the price declines precipitously.

Example B in Fig. 7-7 also portrays a substantial amount of instability, which again leads to a sharp price decline. The problem with this type of wide-ranging trading is that the breakdown is often followed by additional choppy action. Thus, while the ultimate profit achievement from taking a short position is usually well rewarded, the roller-coaster ride to get there can often be extremely nerve racking. The figure shows a pretty straightforward decline. However, Chart 7-9, for Baker Hughes, shows a more typical outcome, as the choppy early 1998 price action continually threw the validity of the breakout into doubt.

The third example in Fig. 7-7 offers a much more controlled right shoulder. In this instance, the price forms a triangle (see Chapter 9 for a full description of triangles). This offers the best of both worlds. First, you can see that the rallies are getting progressively weaker. Second, the lower trendline offers a great benchmark against which to sell or go short. Finally, if the triangle fails, there is a close point at which an intelligent stop can be placed, i.e., just above the upper trendline. Also, the converging nature of the lines indicates a fine balance between buyers and sellers. If this is resolved in favor of the sellers, the bearish overtones of the whole formation indicate a potentially sharp decline. An example featuring an upward-sloping head and shoulders is shown in Chart 7-10, for J.P. Morgan. The right shoulder itself is fairly complex. The top of the shoulder is a small head and shoulders in its own right.

Chart 7-9 Baker Hughes, 1997–1999, daily.

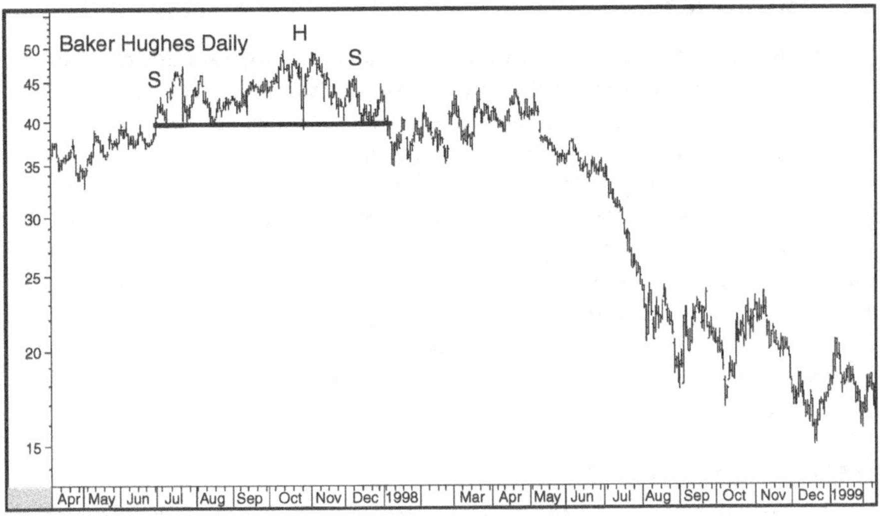

The shoulder itself is also a head and shoulders, with the April rally being the left shoulder and the triangle, contained within the two dashed lines, the right shoulder. Generally speaking, when you get a complex pattern, it is a reflection of a significant battle between buyers and sellers. In this instance, the win by the sellers resulted in a pretty dramatic decline.

Chart 7-10 J.P. Morgan, 2000–2002.

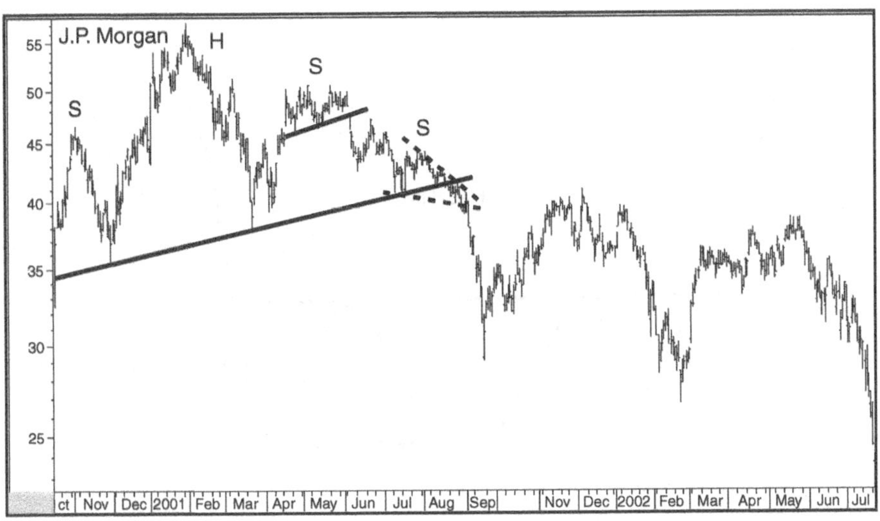

Reverse or Inverse Head and Shoulders

Head-and-shoulders patterns also form at market bottoms. Figure 7-8 shows an example. This is usually called an *inverse H&S, a reverse H&S, or an H&S bottom.* It consists of the final decline separated by two smaller ones.

Normally, volume is relatively high at the bottom of the left shoulder (Fig. 7-9) and during the formation of the head. The key volume characteristic is activity on the right shoulder, which should contract during the decline to the trough and expand substantially on the breakout. The inverse (accumulation) H&S, like the H&S distribution pattern, has a number of variations in such areas as trendline slope, number of shoulders, and so on. As with tops, the more complex the formation, the greater its significance. Some of these reverse head-and-shoulders variations are shown in Figs. 7-10 to 7-12.

Marketplace Examples

Price objectives are based on the same principle as for head-and-shoulders tops. The maximum depth is measured and then projected up from the breakout point. Chart 7-11, featuring Aetna Insurance, offers a good example of a reverse head-and-shoulders pattern. This is really a complex pattern, because if you look carefully, you can see that there are in fact two right shoulders and two left ones. Interestingly, the price objective was reached on the first rally, though the price subsequently moved up from there. The small

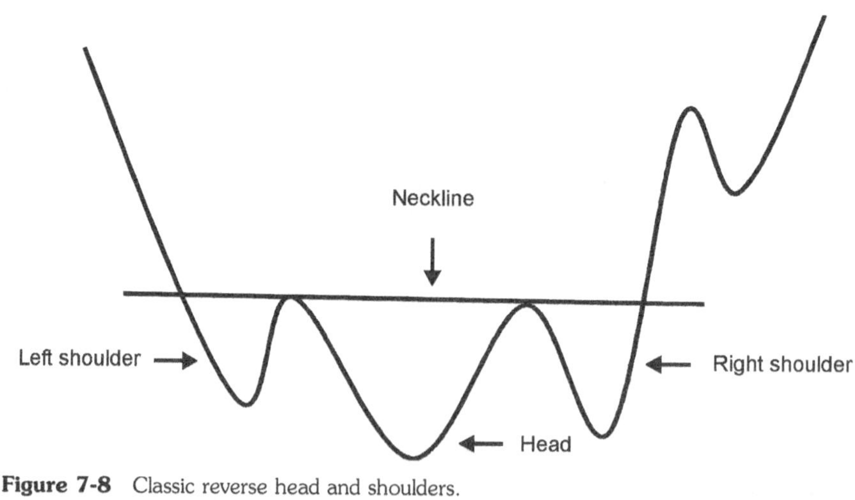

Figure 7-8 Classic reverse head and shoulders.

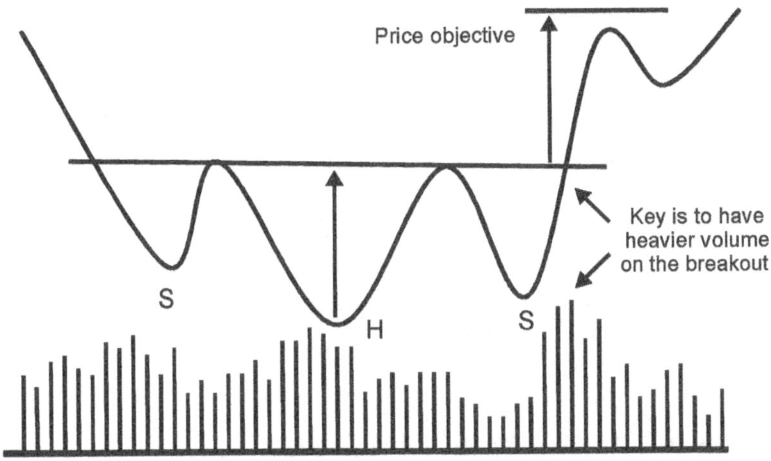

Figure 7-9 Classic reverse head and shoulders with volume.

upward-sloping dashed line, when combined with the neckline, indicates that the right shoulder was really a symmetrical triangle (see Chapter 9).

Chart 7-12, for Alcan, shows another inverse head and shoulders; this time the head, as contained within the two dashed lines, is actually a rectangle. Another rectangle develops during the formation of the right shoulder. Note how volume picks up during the rally from the final low. It contracts as the price corrects, only to expand on the breakout. Volume does not cooperate as nicely as this all the time, But when it does, it offers a higher degree

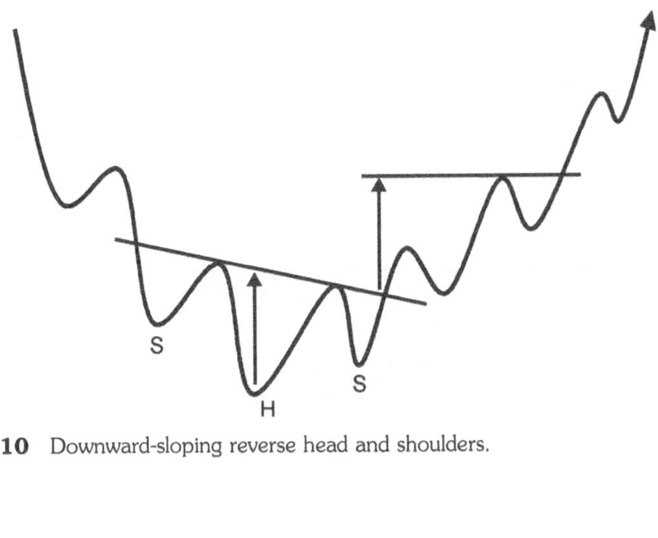

Figure 7-10 Downward-sloping reverse head and shoulders.

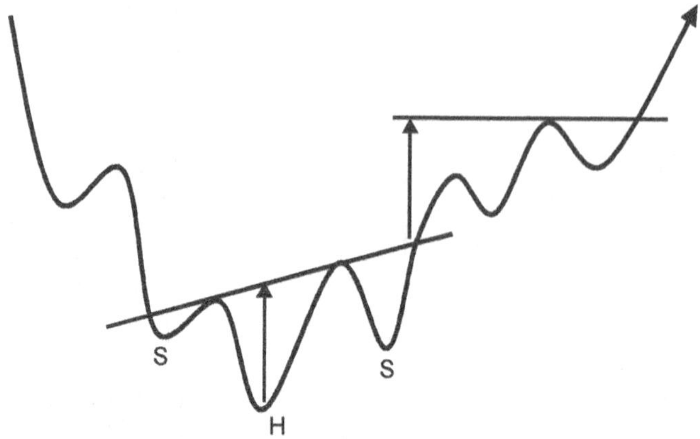

Figure 7-11 Upward-sloping reverse head and shoulders.

of probability that the pattern is valid. In this instance, the upside objective was slightly exceeded just prior to the 1987 crash.

Having said all that, it could be argued that this is not a head and shoulders at all. Note the question mark against the left shoulder. This is because the low of the shoulder is extremely close to that of the head—it's actually just a bit above the right-hand part of the head, so technically this is a reverse head-and-shoulders pattern. I bring this up because I believe *it's more important to apply common sense to price pattern construction than to apply strict rules.*

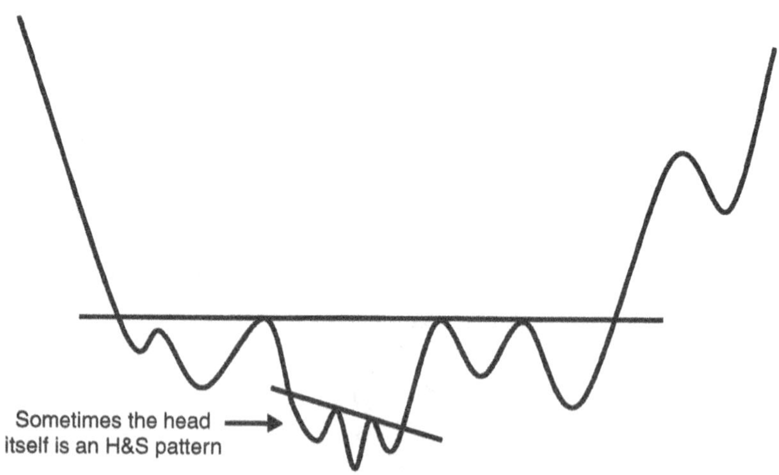

Figure 7-12 Complex reverse head and shoulders.

Chart 7-11 Aetna, 1982–1986, daily.

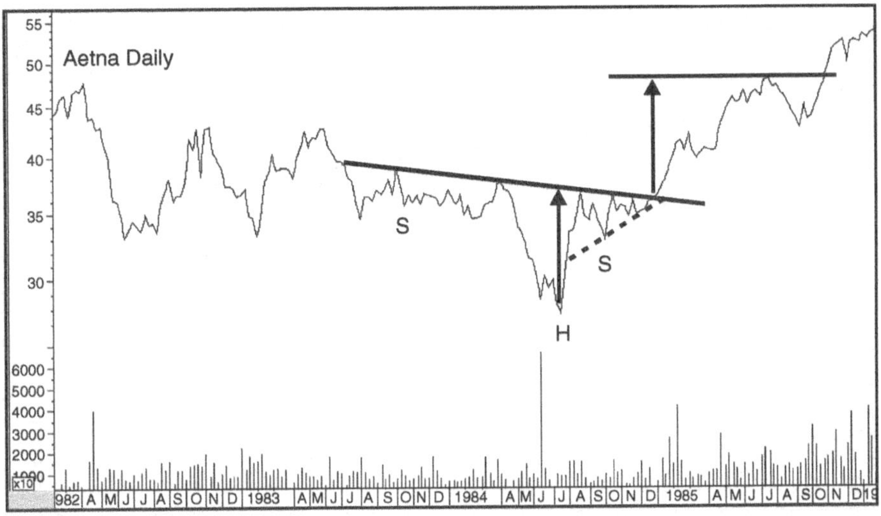

After all, we are trying to identify battlegrounds between buyers and sellers from the point of view of forecasting trend reversals. If trading action does not quite match up to the prescribed rules, it really does not matter as long as the formation works. The rules are actually guidelines for action,

Chart 7-12 Alcan, 1983–1987, weekly.

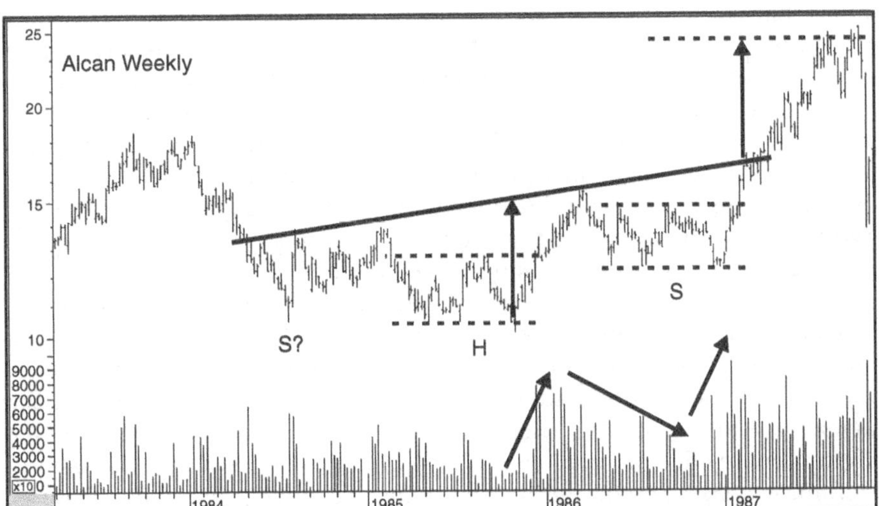

Chart 7-13 Alcan, 1981–1982, weekly.

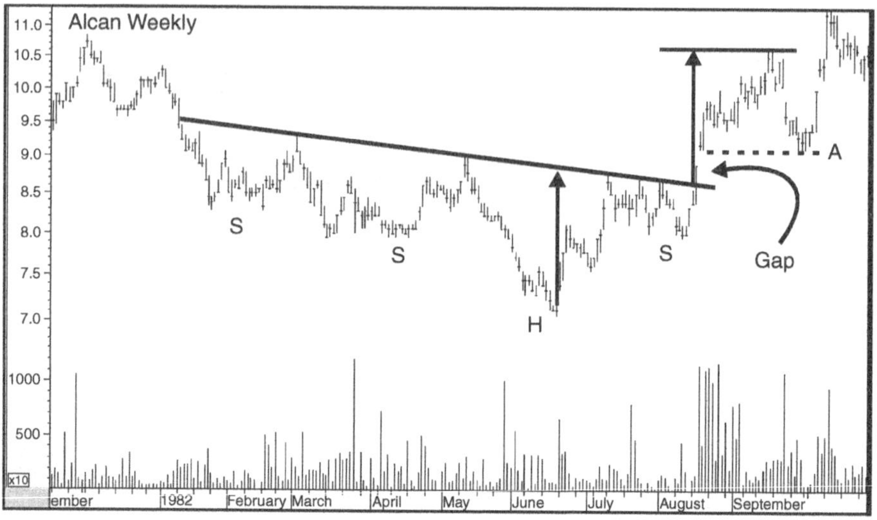

not cast in stone for every situation. Remember, it always comes down to probabilities, never certainties. Following the rules exactly implies the kind of perfection that does not exist in technical analysis.

The 1982 bottom for Alcan appears in Chart 7-13, where there is a dramatic volume increase on the breakout. This is a real treat, since it indicates extremely strong interest on the part of the buyers and signals a nice change in psychology. The market itself bottomed in August, but this stock touched its low in June. By August the right shoulder had begun to form, thereby setting up a positive divergence with the overall market. The divergence was confirmed with the completion of the reverse head-and-shoulders pattern later that month. The upside objective was reached at the initial rally peak. Note the gap that developed on the second day of the breakout. Gaps are potential support and resistance areas. See how the September correction terminated at the upper end of the gap. An attempt to close a subsequent gap was made right in the closing sessions of the chart.

The question of the degree of price activity required to justify a right or left shoulder often arises. Chart 7-14, for St. Jude Medical, indicates a horizontal reverse head and shoulders. The left shoulder is a definite rectangle and provides a good battle between buyers and sellers. The head itself is really a double-bottom formation (described in Chapter 8). However, the right-shoulder decline may be pushing the envelope as far as the pattern definition is concerned, since it did not involve much price action. Even so,

Chart 7-14 St. Jude Medical, 1983–1986, daily.

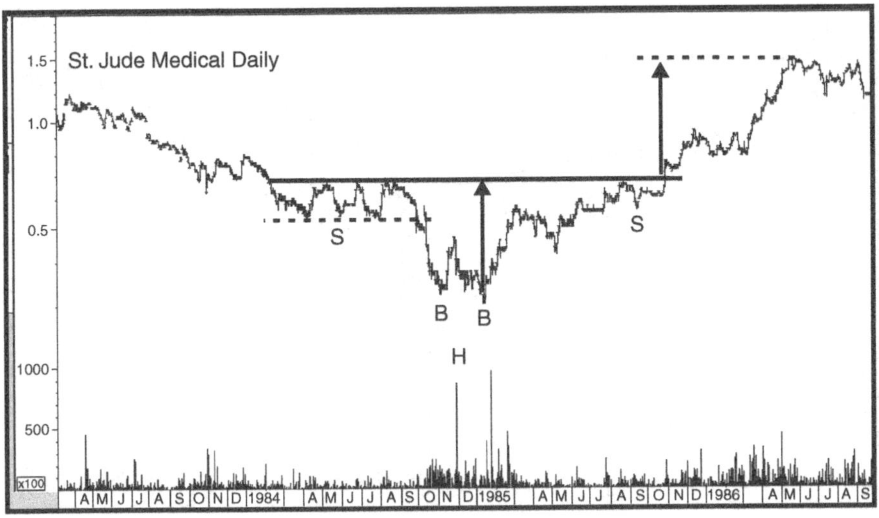

once the neckline was violated, the price had no difficulty in reaching its minimum ultimate upside objective.

They say that there is more than one way to skin a cat, and with price patterns there is often more than one way in which they can be drawn. In this spirit, Chart 7-15 features the reverse head and shoulders for St. Jude in a different way, avoiding the weak right shoulder. Note that in this instance the price more than meets the objective, but this benchmark nevertheless turns out to be a good pivotal support level for a couple of subsequent declines.

Sometimes the price action develops in such a way that it is quite difficult to decide whether it represents one pattern or another. For example, Chart 7-16, for Sysco, shows a head-and-shoulders bottom with a nice increase in volume on the breakout. Chart 7-17 shows exactly the same period, but this time I have drawn in two parallel lines, indicating that the pattern may really have been a rectangle. The price even reached a two times multiple of the indicated objective. It really doesn't matter what name we give to the price action. The essential point is that the price fell, there was a battle between buyers and sellers (the trading range), and there was a subsequent breakout to the upside on high volume. I bring this up because it is extremely easy to get hung up on names and definitions. My feeling is that you need to interpret these formations in a commonsense way, not according to strict formulas. Always try to form an understanding of the

Chart 7-15 St. Jude Medical, 1983–1986, daily.

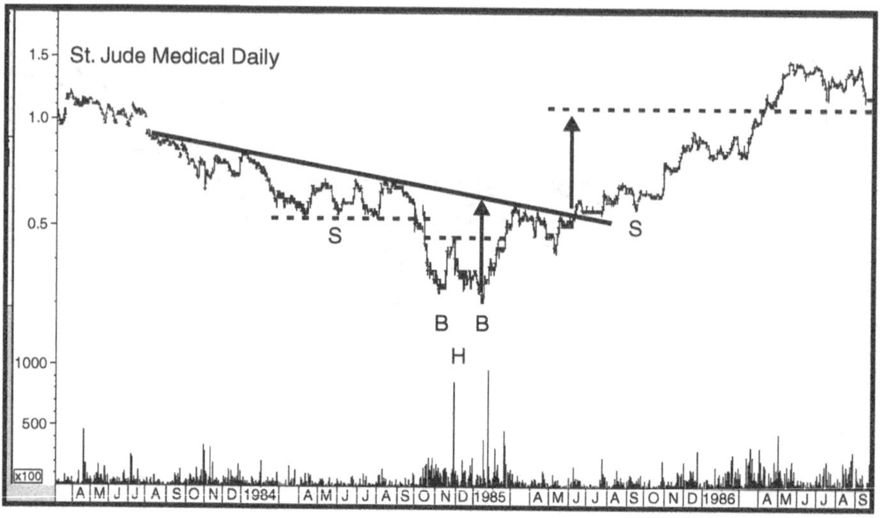

underlying psychology of any trading situation, because that's all that patterns are reflecting anyway. This means that if you can see a reversal of a peak-and-trough progression at a time when the price violates a support or resistance trendline, chances are that you have a reversal in trend. If volume

Chart 7-16 Sysco, 1981–1983, daily.

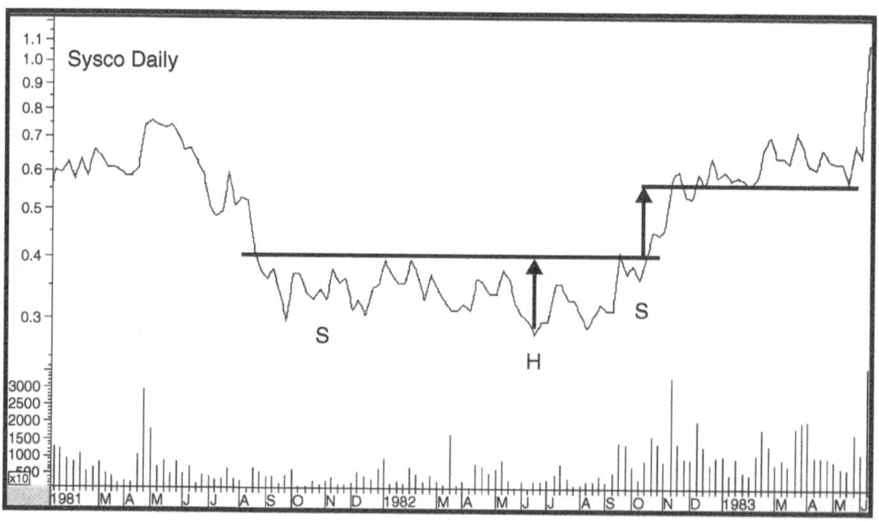

Chart 7-17 Sysco, 1981–1983, daily.

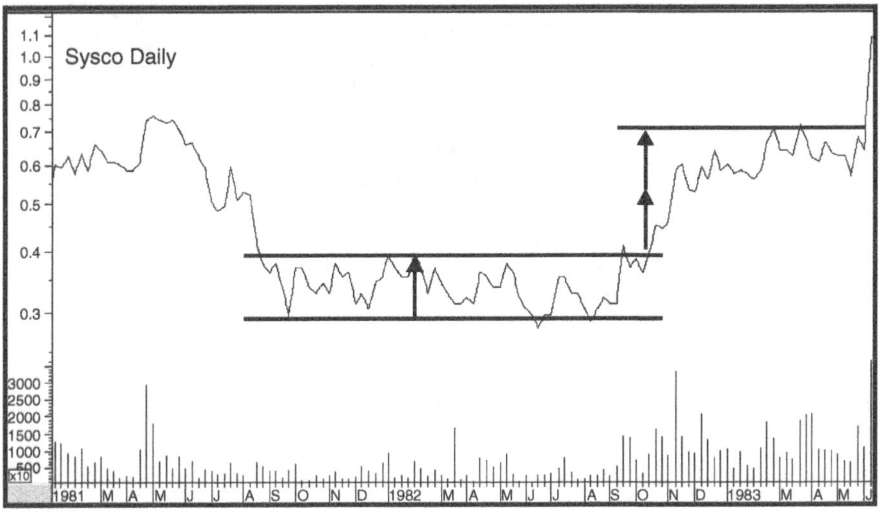

is sympathetic to your interpretation, so much the better. Remember, we give price patterns names only so that we can more easily recognize reversal phenomena.

Head-and-Shoulders Formations as Continuation Patterns

H&S and reverse H&S formations often show up on the charts as continuation patterns. The measuring implications and volume characteristics are the same as for the reversal type. The only difference is that these patterns develop *during* a trend rather than at the end. Examples are shown in Figs. 7-13 and 7-14.

Sprint PCS Group (Chart 7-18) offers a couple of good examples of consolidation head-and-shoulders tops. Notice how volume picks up noticeably at the breakout points. In a bear trend, prices can fall of their own weight, and this is normal. However, when activity picks up, it indicates that sellers are definitely motivated, and thus the danger of a sharp price decline is at its greatest. The pattern at the top of the rally, which was completed in the fall of 2000, defies definition. It is not a head and shoulders because the "right shoulder" reverses at the same level as the "head." Neither is it a true rectangle because the late 1999 and early 2000 rallies fail to reach the upper

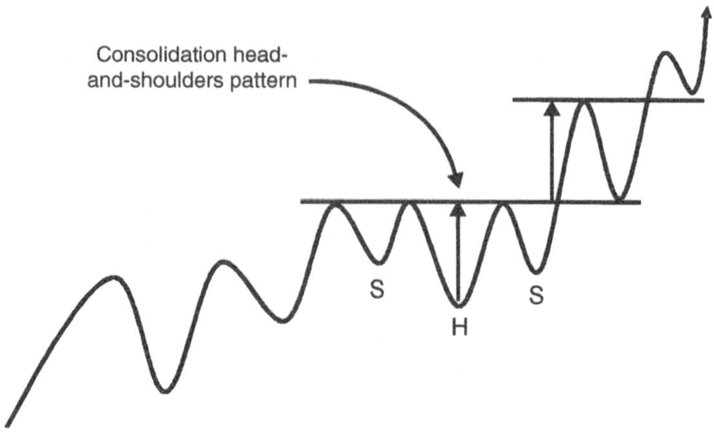

Figure 7-13 Continuation reverse head and shoulders.

trendline. It is perhaps best defined as a double top, a formation that is covered in the next chapter. As mentioned earlier, how this pattern is described is of no consequence, since an obvious trading range (battle between buyers and sellers) following a rally was violated on the downside. The day of the lower trendline penetration also saw a huge expansion in volume.

Finally, South West Airlines, Chart 7-19, offers us a massive eight-year consolidation reverse head-and-shoulders pattern. Note how the first and second multiples of the upside objective acted as support zones for subsequent

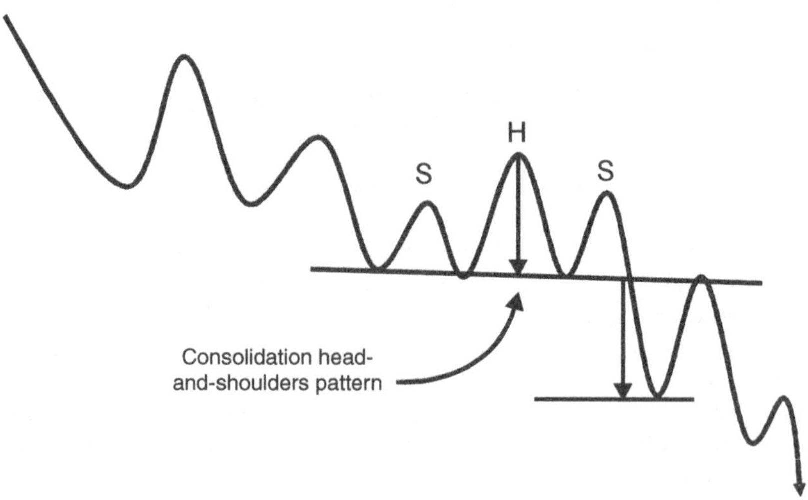

Figure 7-14 Continuation head-and-shoulders top.

Chart 7-18 Sprint PCS Group, 1999–2002, daily.

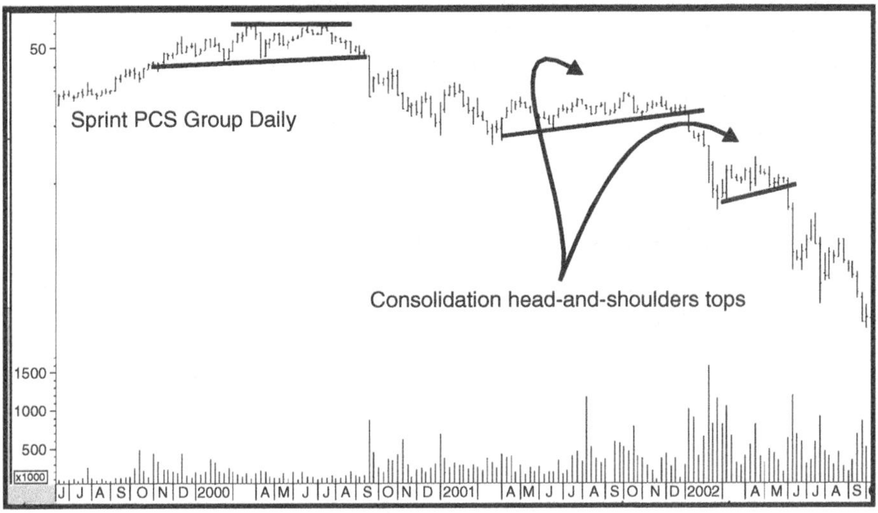

declines. The third multiple was barely reached before a new bear trend set in. One sign of a potentially bullish stock market develops when many stocks have been consolidating the way South West was in 1991. In 1982, for example, the long-term chart books were stuffed full of multiyear consolidations.

Chart 7-19 South West Air, 1980–2003, monthly.

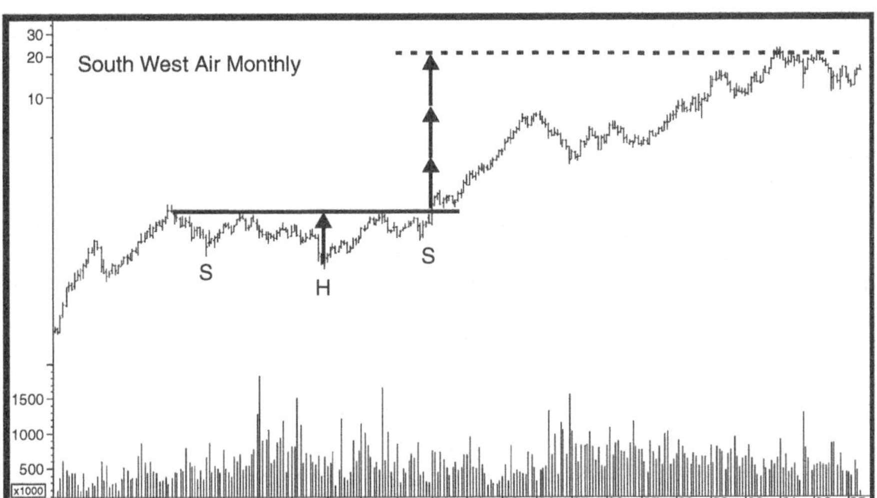

When a substantial number of stocks and groups are in such a position, they provide the foundation for a very long and sustainable bull market. This was certainly true following major breakouts in late 1982 and early 1983. The opposite would be true at a market top, where a preponderance of large head-and-shoulders tops in key stocks and industry groups would warn of impending trouble.

Head-and-Shoulders Failures

We have already established that prices are determined by crowd psychology. Individuals can and do change their minds; so can crowds, and therefore markets. As a result, what might appear to be a perfectly valid head-and-shoulders breakout one day may well turn out to be a whipsaw the next. This is generally not the case, but any trader or investor who does not recognize the ability of markets to reverse otherwise perfectly legitimate signals is in a state of delusion.

The first step is to make sure that the pattern you are following is indeed a legitimate formation. For example, the price action may exhibit all the characteristics of an H&S distribution pattern, but the price refuses to penetrate the neckline. We have already established that until the formation is completed with a decisive break below the neckline, it is not a true pattern. This is because the neckline represents a support area, and support has not been violated. In the case of a horizontal formation, failure to penetrate the neckline also means that the series of rising peaks and troughs is still intact.

Chart 7-20 features a reverse head and shoulders for Albertson's that did not work. The price rallied up to the (solid) neckline for a final time in mid-2002, but was unable to go through. The dashed trendline is there to indicate that the final part of the head and the potential inverse right shoulder actually formed a head-and-shoulders top. Often it is possible to spot these technical situations where the glass is half full or half empty. In this case it was half empty, and the price declined.

The 1992–1995 period shows two examples for Aflac in Chart 7-21. Note that the volume on the right shoulder of the first pattern on the left was particularly heavy. The second pattern's neckline was ever so slightly nicked on the downside, but the formation never really worked. One indication of the failure would have come from the penetration of the trendline joining the peaks in the right-shoulder decline. Such moderately high-volume upside breakouts are totally out of character with the normal low-volume characteristic of a right-shoulder formation and could have offered an indication that the pattern was not going to work.

Alternatively, a failure can develop after the price actually penetrates the neckline temporarily and then reverses in the opposite direction. This

Chart 7-20 Albertson's, 1998–2003, weekly.

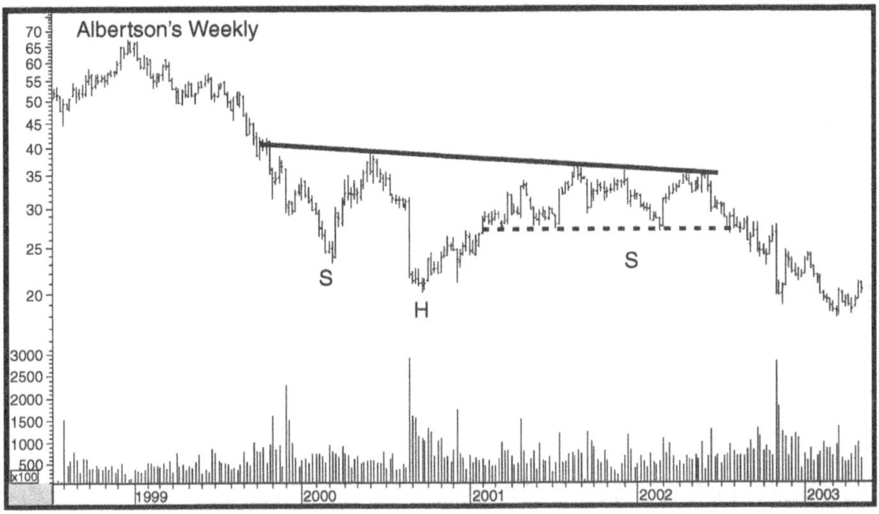

represents an H&S failure and is usually followed by an explosive rally or, in the case of a failed inverse head and shoulders, a nasty decline. Chart 7-22, for Albertson's, represents a good example of what happens after a pattern has failed to work or simply failed. In the case of a failed top, this

Chart 7-21 Aflac, 1991–1995, weekly.

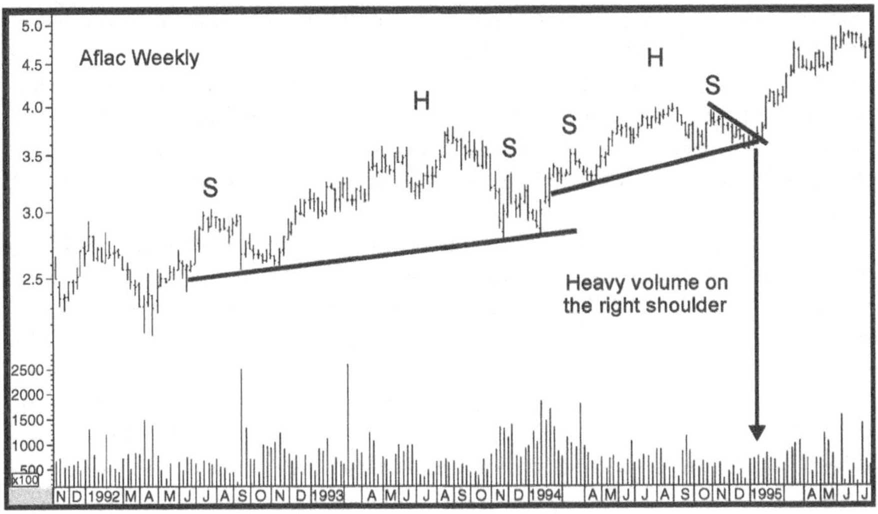

Chart 7-22 Albertson's, 1996–1999, weekly.

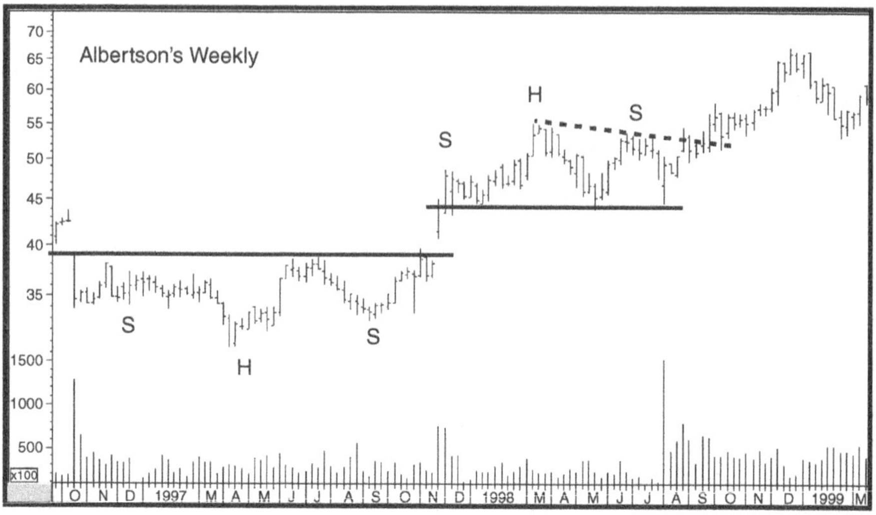

is probably the result of misplaced pessimism. Once the real fundamentals are perceived, not only do new buyers rush in, but also traders holding short positions are forced to cover. Since fear is a stronger motivator than greed, these bears bid up the price very aggressively.

Failures used to be fairly rare, but they now appear to be more common, which indicates the necessity of waiting for a decisive breakout on the downside (or the upside in the case of a reverse head and shoulders). They typically develop when the pattern suggests a break in the opposite direction to the then-prevailing trend. Obviously, if this is the actual top or bottom, the formation will be valid. However, when a head-and-shoulders top forms in a bull market and does not experience a meaningful decline, this will tend to be a countercyclical signal. In fact, the very failure of the pattern may be interpreted as a sign that the prevailing (dominant) trend probably is still in force.

There are several points in the chart where the probabilities of a valid signal sink below 50 percent and those of an outright failure start to increase. Figures 7-15 and 7-16 try to address these points. Point *A* in Fig. 7-15 represents the bottom following the break below the neckline. The next rally, which ends at *B*, is a perfectly typical development because retracements are a normal, and indeed healthy, phenomenon. The price then falls to *C* and something unexpected happens: Instead of following through on the downside, as would be expected from a head-and-shoulders top, the price rises

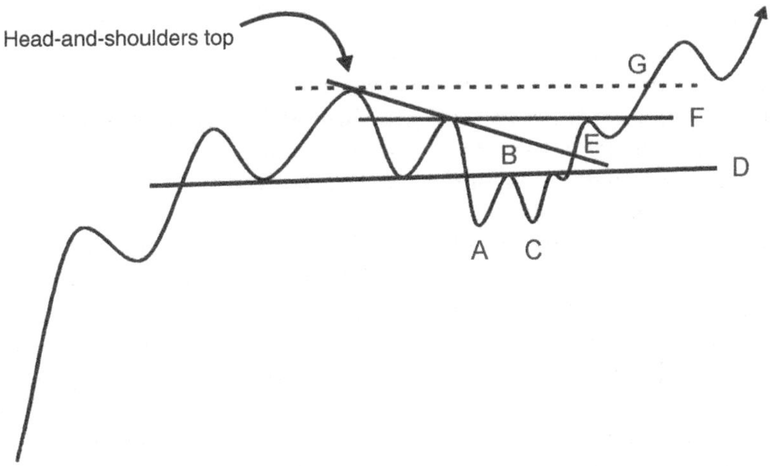

Figure 7-15 Identifying a head-and-shoulders failure.

back to the neckline again. This is the first sign that things may not work out as expected. When the price once again rallies back above the neckline (*D*), the odds of a failure increase. The balance tips more to the bullish side when the price moves above the down trendline joining the head with the right shoulder (*E*). This is probably the time to cover all shorts, since the reason for going short in the first place—i.e., the breakdown—no longer exists. The nature of the trendline will have a great deal to do with the change in probabilities. For example, if the line is steep and has been touched only twice, it will have nowhere near as much significance as it would if it were shallow

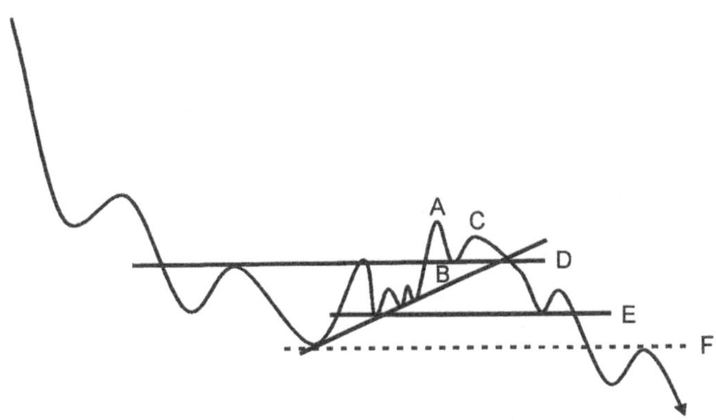

Figure 7-16 Identifying a reverse head-and-shoulders failure.

and had been touched several times. A refresher on trendline interpretation in Chapter 4 would be a good idea at this point.

The next line of defense is the right shoulder. If the price can rally above this point (*F*), then in some cases it will now be experiencing a series of rising peaks and troughs. Finally, when the price moves above the head, the pattern is cancelled beyond a reasonable doubt.

If action on the long side is contemplated, it should be taken either when the price breaks above the trendline joining the head and the right shoulder (line *E*) or when it breaks above the right shoulder (*F*) on heavy volume. Usually, such signals offer substantial profits in a very short period of time and are well worth acting on. Again, some common sense comes into play, for if the trendline joining the head and the right shoulder is unusually steep and has been touched only twice, it will not have the authority of a more shallow trendline that has been touched or approached on numerous occasions.

Inverse H&S patterns can also fail, as we see from Fig. 7-16. Again, the failure is usually followed by a fairly lengthy decline as participants who bought in anticipation of an upward breakout are flushed out when the new bearish fundamentals become more widely known. Note that the line joining the head with the right shoulder is more significant in this example than that in Fig. 7-15. This is because the line is shallower and has been touched on more occasions. The joint break with the neckline is also impressive and would greatly increase the odds of a failed pattern.

Chart 7-23 Andrew Corp., daily.

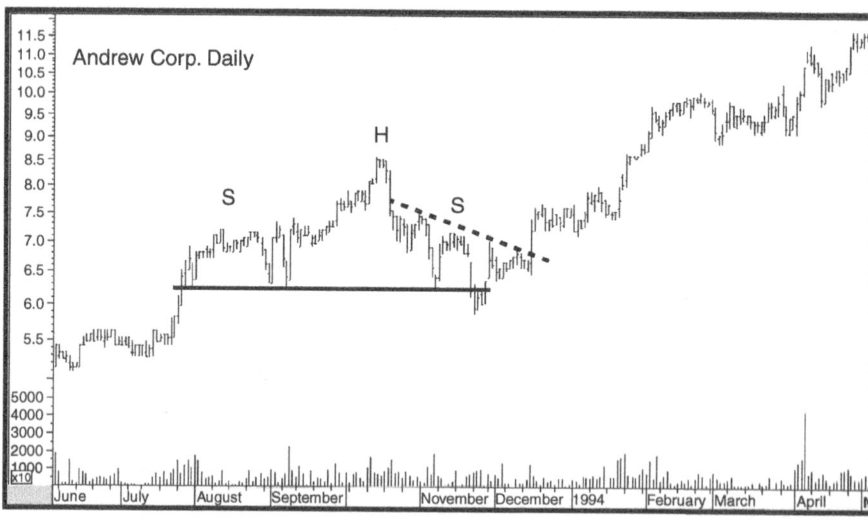

Chart 7-23 shows a failed head-and-shoulders top for Andrew Corp. This one developed during a very strong linear bull market. The first indication of failure would have been given when the price broke back above the neckline after forming a small base. The clincher developed when the dashed trendline joining several rally peaks was bettered on the upside. Failed patterns are often followed by dynamic moves in the opposite direction to that indicated by the pattern. This means that these patterns should be viewed not with fear, but as an opportunity for profits. The degree of opportunity will depend on the strength of the signal and the closeness at which a realistic stop can be placed (the perceived risk). In this case, the trendline was a very strong one and a stop could have been placed just below the low of the breakout day. Provided it was bought pretty close to the breakout point, this would have represented a very-low-risk, potentially high-reward trade.

Summary

In summary, there are several clues we can look for that suggest that a pattern will fail.

- Momentum indicators at the time of the breakout that are extremely oversold in the case of a top or overbought in the case of a bottom
- Heavy volume on the right shoulder of a potential head-and-shoulders top. Light volume on a reverse head-and-shoulders breakout
- Failure of the price to follow through in the direction of the breakout following a retracement move
- Failure of the overall market and other stocks in the industry group to act in sympathy
- The relative strength line failing to confirm the breakout

Head-and-Shoulders Top Review

- *Price characteristics:* A final rally separated by two smaller rallies at tops.
- *Volume considerations:* Very heavy volume on the left shoulder and sometimes the head. Low and shrinking volume on the right-shoulder rally. Immaterial on breakdown, but heavy volume preferred.
- *Measuring implications:* The distance from the top of the head to the neckline is projected down at the point of breakout.
- *Signs of false breakout:* The presence of a second retracement rally and failure to break the initial breakdown low. A rally above the trendline joining

the head and the right shoulder, provided it is not unduly steep and/or above the right shoulder.

Head-and-Shoulders Bottom Review

- *Price characteristics:* A final low separated by two higher lows at bottoms.
- *Volume considerations:* Heavy volume on the left shoulder and sometimes the head. Low and shrinking volume on the right-shoulder decline. Very high volume accompanying the upside breakout.
- *Measuring implications:* The distance from the bottom of the head to the neckline is projected up at the point of breakout.
- *Signs of false breakout:* Contracting volume on breakout. Price unable to hold the breakout for more than two sessions.
- *Places to unwind position in case of whipsaw breakout:* Violation of up trend-line joining head and right shoulder. Break below right shoulder, especially if accompanied by expanding volume.

8

Double Tops, Double Bottoms, and Triple Patterns

Double Tops

A double top consists of two peaks that are the culmination of a rally. They are separated by a reaction or valley in prices. The formation is completed when the price breaks below the lower level of the valley. Figure 8-1 gives an example. In *Profits and the Stock Market,* H. M. Gartley defines a double top as "representing two unsuccessful attempts to penetrate a supply area with the resultant disappointment preceding and contributing to an important subsequent decline." The principal characteristic of this formation arises from the fact that the second top is formed with distinctly less volume than the first. It is normal for both peaks to form at the same price level, but it is also possible for the second peak to slightly exceed the first or to top out just a little below it. The reaction from the first peak to the valley is usually associated with a trend of declining volume. Remember, this is not an exact science, but a commonsense interpretation of a battle between buyers and sellers.

In their book *Technical Analysis of Stock Trends,* Edwards and Magee point out that double tops are referred to by name by more traders who have a small knowledge of technical analysis than perhaps any other pattern. They go on to point out that in most cases these neophyte technicians identify these patterns *before* they have been completed, which is a definite no-no. According

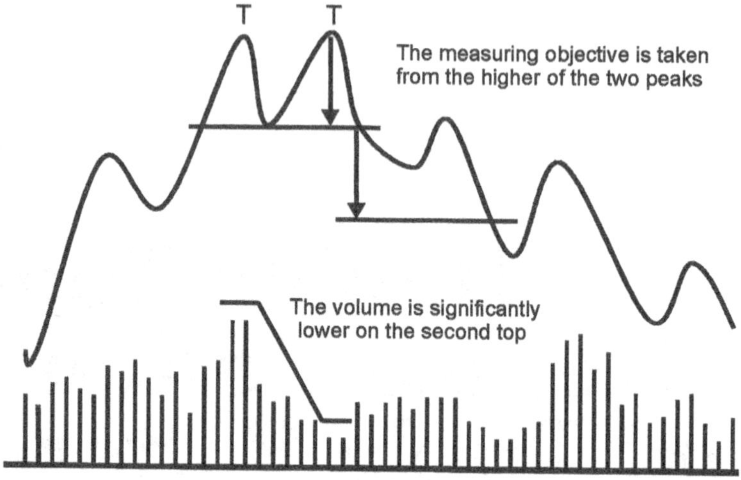

Figure 8-1 Double top.

to Edwards and Magee, double patterns are extremely rare. That certainly appears to be the case for double tops, but not for double bottoms. In doing research for this book, I ran through countless charts covering well over 10 years of data and was unable to find many examples of true double tops.

Edwards and Magee also point out that many patterns that appear to be double tops eventually transmute into other patterns that turn out to be continuation formations rather than reversals. They suggest that an important differentiating characteristic is the time separating the two peaks. If they develop on the daily charts, say at one-week intervals, this is more likely to result in a consolidation formation, such as a rectangle. Although they confess that there are no ironclad rules, their guideline for a double top is a separation greater than a month with a "valley decline" of 15 to 20 percent separating the two peaks. They admit that these rules are somewhat arbitrary, but they go on to point out that the time element is more important than the magnitude of the valley decline. Thus a two- or three-month separation between the two peaks requires less of a decline than, say, a one-month interval. These guidelines are for daily charts. To apply them to monthly or hourly charts would not, of course, make much sense because it is the relative comparison of the time frame that is important. A possibility in this case is to take the number of trading periods involved in the "one month or greater" rule and apply it to the relevant bars. Thus one week of daily trading is approximately 20 bars. Applying this to the weekly charts would imply a separation of 20-plus weeks, and applying it to an hourly chart would imply 20-plus hours. The key in all these time frames is to reflect the idea that enough time has elapsed during the valley phase that by the time the price has begun to approach the second peak, the rally is very believable, and most people are expecting a significant extension of the previous uptrend so the price will exceed the first peak by a wide margin.

Underlying Psychology

The underlying psychology might work something like this: The first top develops at the end of a substantial rally; volume is heavy, and sentiment is very positive. Then prices "unexpectedly" decline on contracting volume and disappointment sets in. This is then followed by a rally. Rising prices attract more bulls as the rally progresses, and the bullish arguments that were associated with the first peak become more believable. However, this second peak is accompanied by far lighter volume than the first. To the technician, this is a bearish factor because it indicates less enthusiasm by the buyers and suggests that prices are rallying more because of a lack of sellers than anything else. Prices subsequently decline again and break below the lower level of the valley separating the two peaks. At that time the pattern is completed, and everyone who bought during its formation is losing money and is therefore a potential seller.

Other Considerations

I mentioned earlier that the two peaks should be of roughly the same height. Edwards and Magee use a 3 percent rule for this. This is again based on daily charts. The key, though, as they rightly point out, is that buying should not push the second peak above the first by a decisive margin. This is because the second peak really signifies failure—in this case, the failure of buyers to mount a strong second rally that takes the price convincingly above the resistance indicated by the first peak. In other words, *if the second top is decisively above the first, this indicates that the series of rising peaks and troughs is still intact.* Also, when the price breaks below the valley low, a second peak that is close to the first will not cloud the interpretation that *a break below the valley low is a signal that a new series of declining peaks and troughs is underway.* What is decisive is really a matter of experience and common sense. Sometimes valuable clues can be given by other indicators. For example, you may find that there is a serious negative divergence between an oscillator and a price at the second peak. Alternatively, a smoothed oscillator may be overbought and reversing to the downside as the second peak is forming.

According to Edwards and Magee, the normal measuring objective cannot be applied to the double patterns. However, I have not found anything wrong with the normal approach. After all, if we assume that prices are determined by psychology, and if psychology often moves in proportion, why should the distance between the highest top and the valley bottom not be projected down from the breakout point? Thus, in my view, the minimum downside measuring implications for double tops should be calculated by projecting the maximum distance between the higher of the two highs and the valley low at the point of breakdown, as shown in Fig. 8-1. This suggested approach is the same as that used with rectangles and head-and-shoulders tops.

Marketplace Examples

Chart 8-1, for Jefferson Pilot, shows a double top in 1998. It's not a classic pattern in the sense that volume dries up on the second top, but it definitely has the price characteristics. There are two rallies separated by an approximately 15 percent decline and three months in time. Interestingly the decline took the price down by a little more than triple the measuring objective. If you look very carefully you can see that both tops contained small head-and-shoulders distribution patterns.

Chart 8-2 shows another double top, this time for the DJIA in the 1930s. Notice that the July–August 1937 top was associated with considerably less volume than the first peak. Prices declined substantially after the breakdown

Chart 8-1 Jefferson Pilot, 1997–1998, daily.

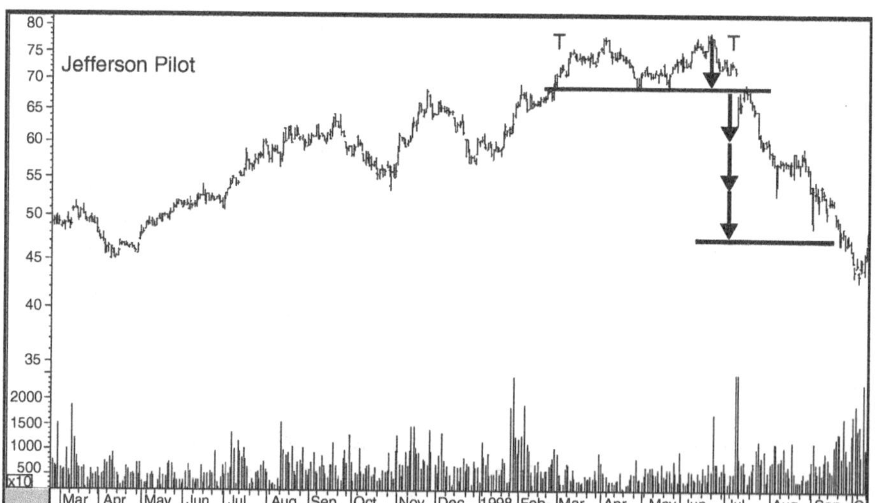

Chart 8-2 DJIA, 1936–1937, double top. Following a substantial advance from 1932, the first post-Depression bull market ended in 1937. The chart shows a classic double top. Note that the volume during the July-to-August rally was substantially below that of the January-to-March peak. (*Source: pring.com.*)

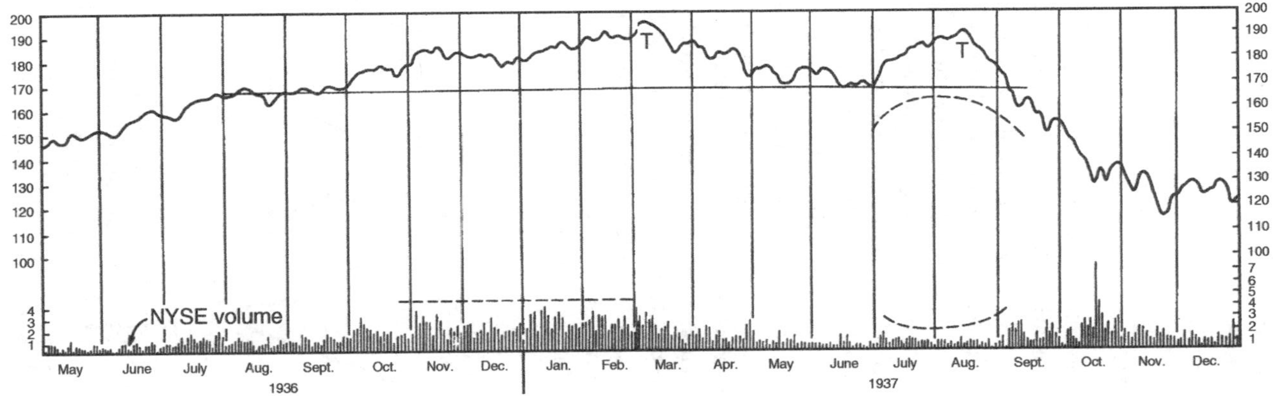

took place. Indeed, this seems to be a characteristic of "double" formations: They are either preceded or followed, or sometimes both, by a very sharp and persistent price move.

Double Bottoms

The price action of double bottoms is exactly the opposite of that of double tops. These formations are typically preceded by a very sharp price decline. An example is shown in Fig. 8-2. An initial low is formed on pretty heavy volume, often a selling climax. A subsequent price bounce retraces some of the ground that was previously lost. This advance then gives way to a decline that tests the initial low. When the price rallies above the "bounce" high, the pattern is completed. Typically, volume on the second low is extremely light, especially when compared to the initial bottom. It is a decided plus when the level of activity expands on the upside breakout. Volume in double bottoms is as easy as 1–2–3. In effect, we get high volume on the first low (1), lower volume on the second low (2), and expanding activity on the breakout (3). The volume characteristics described here are not mandatory, since many patterns that do not reflect such characteristics still appear to work. If the characteristics are present, however, the probabilities of a valid formation will be greater.

Usually the second bottom is formed above the first, but these formations are equally valid whether or not the second reaction reaches (or even *slightly* exceeds) the level of its predecessor.

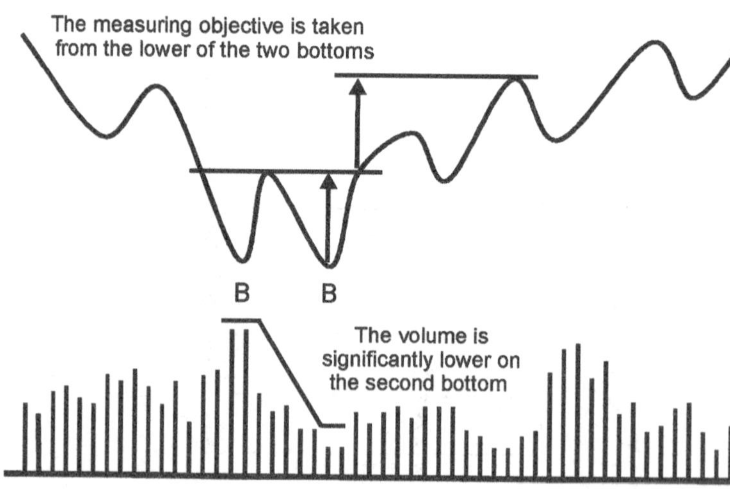

Figure 8-2 Double bottom.

Underlying Psychology

Since most double-bottom formations are preceded by a sharp decline, it's likely that the initial bounce rally, which is usually very sharp, is caused by a lack of selling pressure and a panic move by the shorts to cover their positions. The greater the volume at the initial low, the less will be the overhang from potential sellers. Once the short covering has been achieved and bargain hunters have been satisfied, prices once more begin to slip. However, since the bears have just experienced a rough ride, they are less inclined to put out more shorts. This means that selling pressure is not so intense. Another reason for a lack of selling pressure is that most of the pessimistic holders will already have sold during the initial decline, when they were highly motivated. The second price drop develops more from a lack of bids than anything else. As the price approaches the second bottom, volume often shrinks to almost nothing. This is indicative of a *sold out* as opposed to an *oversold* market. There is an old adage on Wall Street that says, "Never short a dull market." It probably applies to the second low of a double-bottom formation. This dearth of activity means that the balance between buyers and sellers is extremely closely matched, so the slightest event can have a dramatic effect on the price. At this point all the bad news has been discounted and most of the selling is out of the way, so there is only one direction in which the price can move—up.

The final break above the bounce high sets in motion a series of rising peaks and troughs as it becomes evident that the initial rally was more substantial than a dead cat bounce.

Marketplace Examples

Chart 8-3, for Lockheed Martin, shows a double bottom. Note that, as with most of the examples shown here, the pattern is preceded by a sharp and persistent decline. Also, volume at the first bottom is well above that at the second. Indeed, the second bottom is really a small inverse head and shoulders, as indicated by the dashed neckline. The contrast between the wild price movements at the November low and the more constrained and rounded low established in February is also characteristic of a double bottom.

Chart 8-4, for Nvida, is also a double bottom, since it meets the price and volume characteristics. It is preceded by a sharp decline, then there is a successful test of the initial low on lighter volume, and finally there is a break above the bounce high. Indeed, volume expands on the day that the price completes the pattern. The only missing ingredient is the time between the two lows, which is relatively small.

Chart 8-3 Lockheed Martin, 1999–2000, daily.

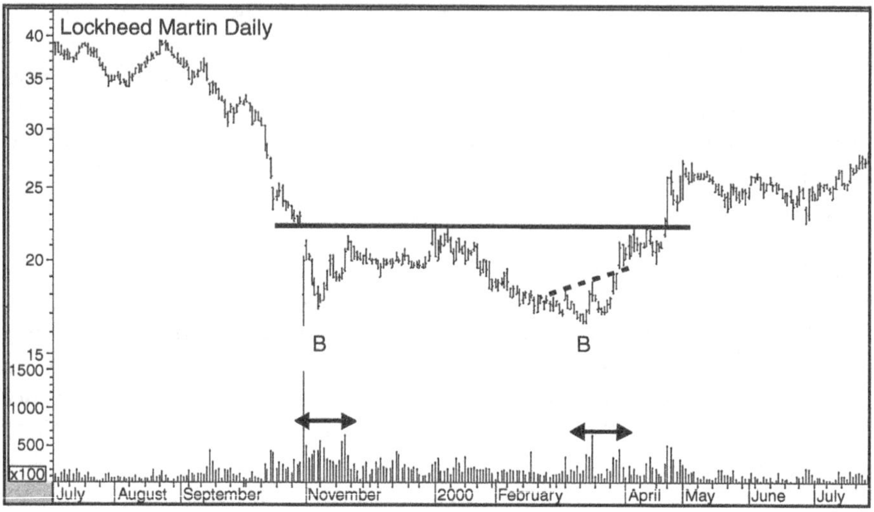

Mercury Intract, in Chart 8-5, shows a different type of double bottom. In this case, the second low is well above the first. However, the three volume characteristics are present: high volume at the initial low, lower volume on the second low, and rising volume on the breakout. Notice once again how the price barely moves during the five days that the second bottom is

Chart 8-4 Nvida, 2000–2001, daily.

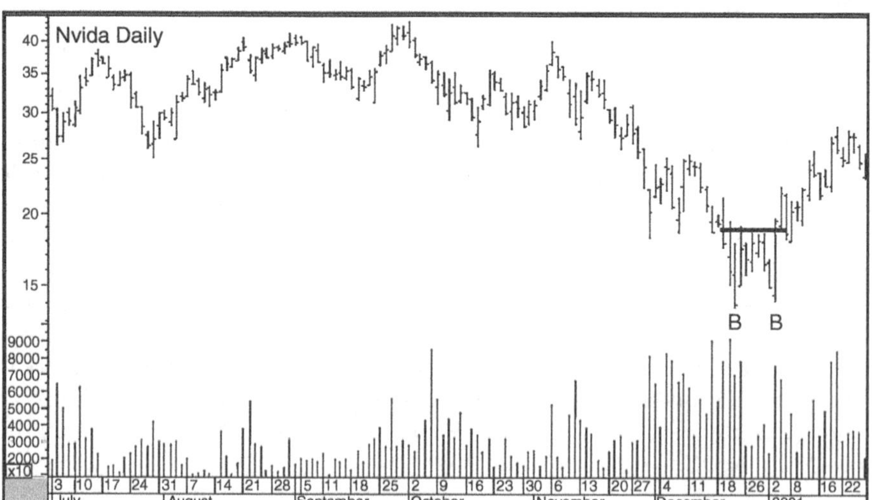

Chart 8-5 Mercury Intract, 1998–1999, daily.

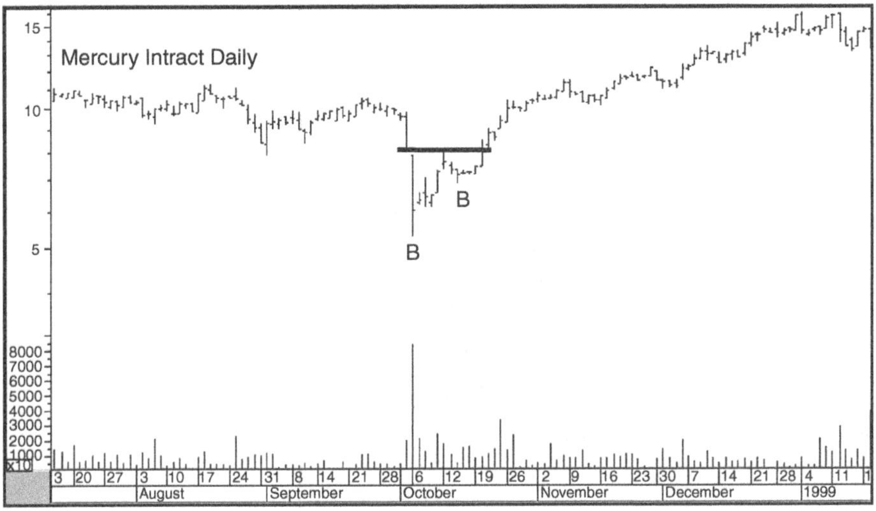

being formed. This once again indicates a close balance between buyers and sellers, so that when volume expands, the price simply explodes to the upside.

Chinese Double Bottom

If the price rallies sharply off the second bottom, buying on the breakout could involve a considerable price risk. This is because in many cases, the only viable support point under which to place a stop is the second bottom itself. Such a situation is shown in Fig. 8-3. However, during the formation of many secondary bottoms, the price declines under the constraint of a resistance trendline (Fig. 8-4). When it breaks above the line, more often than not this signals that the pattern will be completed with a break above the bounce rally high. I call these Chinese double bottoms because the retracement toward the secondary low can often be slow and very torturous to those who are long. The great advantage of these Chinese double bottoms is that they provide a potentially high-reward but low-risk buying opportunity. Generally speaking, the longer the (Chinese) torture, the more bullish the situation when the breakout finally develops. Chart 8-6, featuring UST, offers a good example. We see the 1–2–3 volume pattern along with a slow but steady decline held back by the dashed (torture) down trendline. When the price breaks above the trendline, a sharp rally is triggered. When

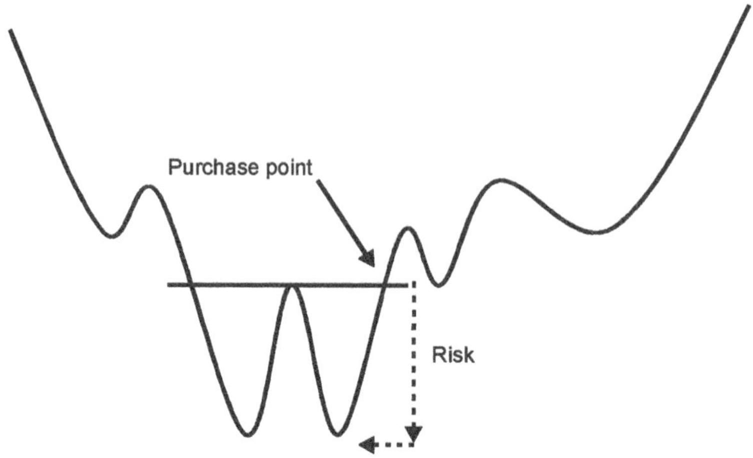

Figure 8-3 Double bottom assessing risk.

a line is fairly steep, as this one is, a powerful rally often develops. Notice the low risk, measured by the distance from an early breakout to a point just below the second bottom.

Chart 8-7, for MBNA, indicates an even longer "torture" trendline, but the trendline develops at a shallower level than that in the previous chart. Even so, a worthwhile rally with a relatively low risk develops. Generally

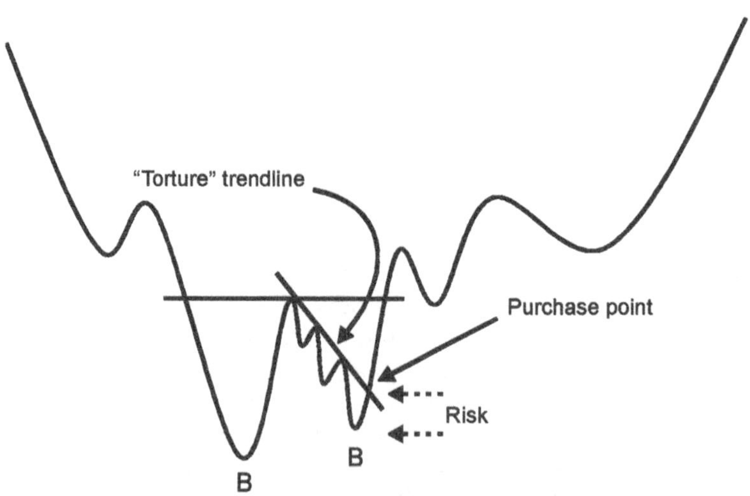

Figure 8-4 Double bottom assessing risk.

Chart 8-6 UST, 1999–2001, daily.

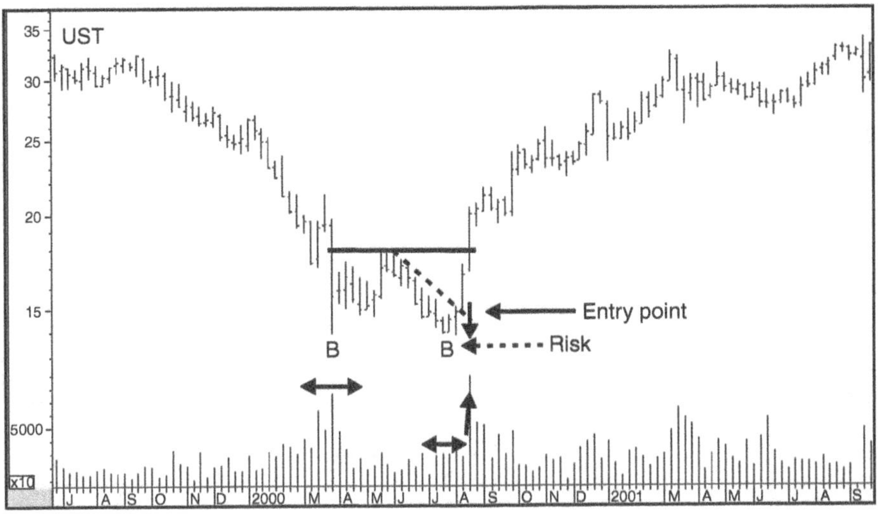

speaking, the most explosive breakouts seem to come from fairly steep torture trendlines like that in Chart 8-6. It is, however, important for them to have been touched or approached on numerous occasions.

Finally, Chart 8-8, featuring Williams, indicates another Chinese double bottom. This time the price rises quite a bit, but it does so in a more

Chart 8-7 MBNA, 1987–1988, daily.

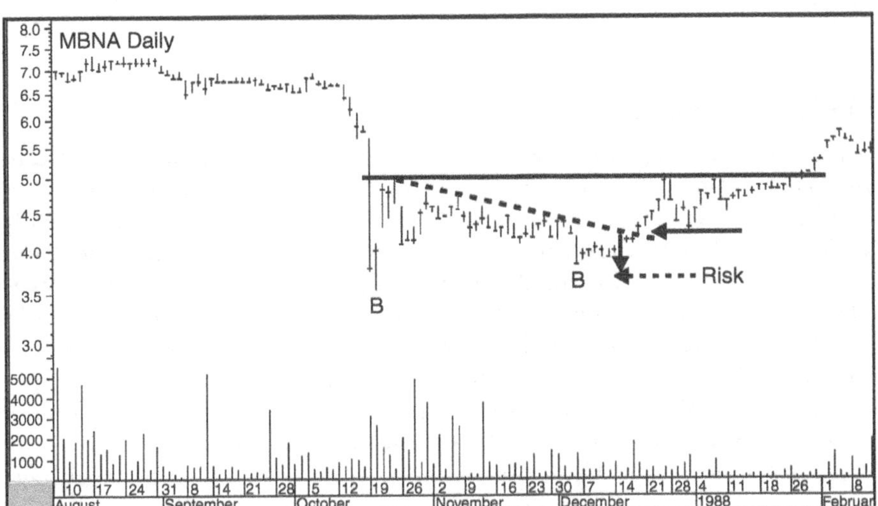

Chart 8-8 Williams, 2002–2003, weekly.

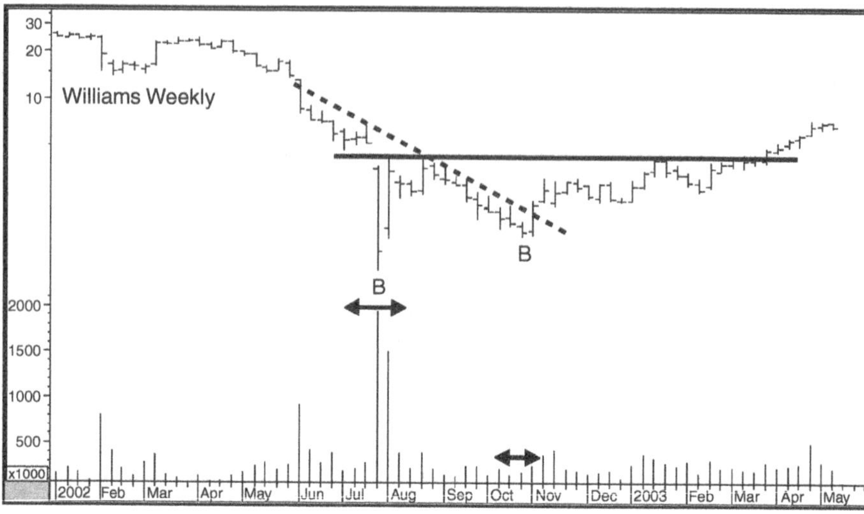

controlled manner. When the price finally rallies above the August bounce high, it has really completed a reverse head and shoulders, with the left shoulder being formed in August, the "second bottom" being the head, and the right shoulder developing in February of 2003. If a line joining the two bottoms is extended, the whole thing could be interpreted as an ascending triangle (covered in Chapter 9). It really doesn't matter what the formation is called. The important thing is that it was working as we moved into June of 2003.

Platform Double Bottom

A platform double bottom is a variation on the Chinese double bottom. In this case, the initial bottom develops after a very sharp, panic-oriented decline. The price then rallies and experiences a trading range, usually a rectangle. The trading range forms some way above the panic low and acts as a kind of platform. When a breakout above the platform takes place, the pattern is completed. An example of this concept is shown in Fig. 8-5. A marketplace example appears in Chart 8-9, featuring Sysco. Normally the stop point would be placed under support just below the bottom of the platform. In this case, a less risky minor low, set in January of 2002, could have been used. Alternatively, if a breakout above the dashed trendline had been used as an entry point, the stop could have

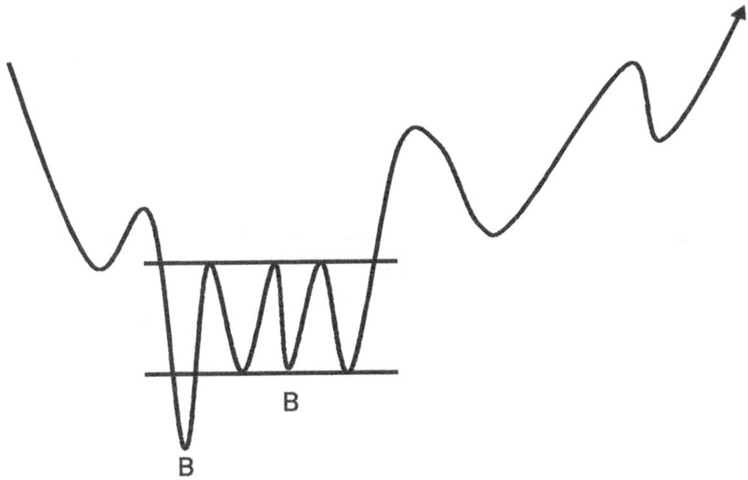

Figure 8-5 Double bottom platform.

been placed below the lower solid trendline marking the bottom of the platform. A second example, featuring Albertson's, is displayed in Chart 8-10. In this case, part of the platform could be interpreted as a consolidation reverse head and shoulders. The risk for this trade would have been about 10 percent.

Chart 8-9 Sysco, 2001–2002, daily.

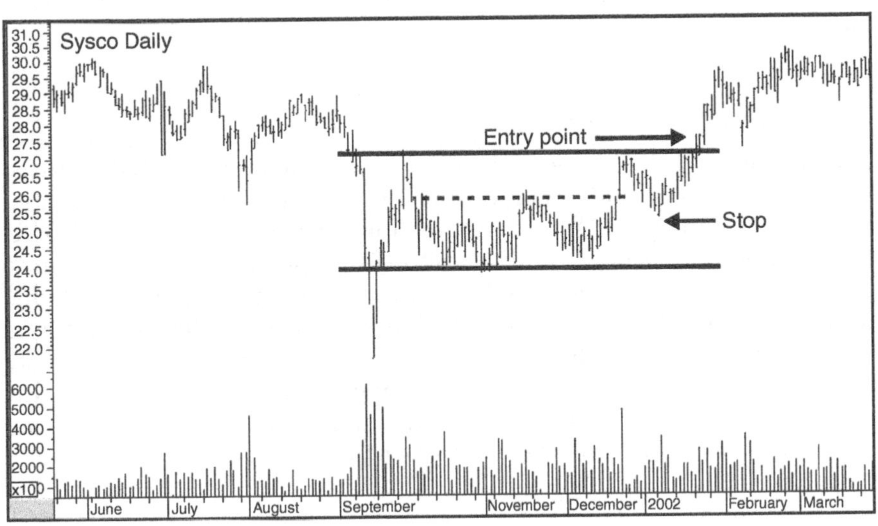

Chart 8-10 Albertson's, 1987–1988, daily.

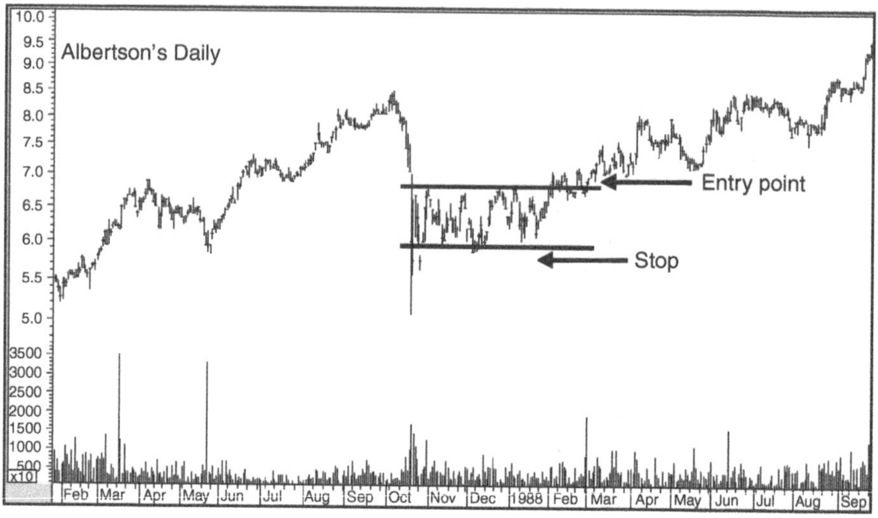

Double Bottoms as Consolidation Patterns

Occasionally a double-bottom formation will show up as a consolidation pattern. An example is shown in Chart 8-11, for Keycorp. In this situation, part of the formation turned out to be a head-and-shoulders top (the dashed trendline on the left), which was quickly canceled as the second bottom was being formed with a small reverse head and shoulders (the second dashed trendline).

Double-Bottom Failures

Like all patterns, double bottoms are occasionally subject to failed breakouts. Typically this will happen during a bear market, when the breakout is a contra-trend signal. An example is shown in Chart 8-12, for KB Home. At the time of the breakout, this looked like a perfectly normal reversal-pattern completion. The problem was that this formation developed toward the end of a bear market. In this case, a convenient failure indication was given when the price broke below the dashed support trendline. It is doubtful if this would have made a good risk/reward trade anyway. This is because the distance between the breakout point ($16) and a place just below the second low at $14 would have involved a risk of about 18 percent.

Chart 8-11 Keycorp, 1991–1992, daily.

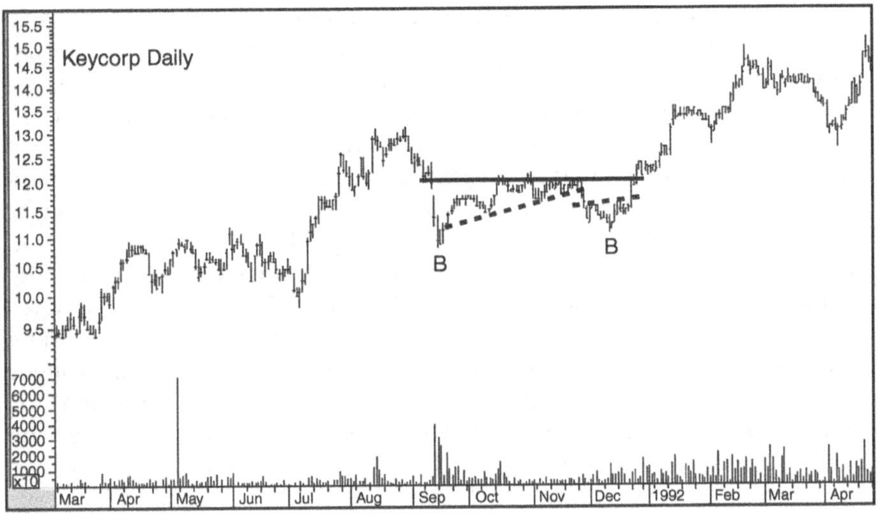

Chart 8-12 KB Home, daily.

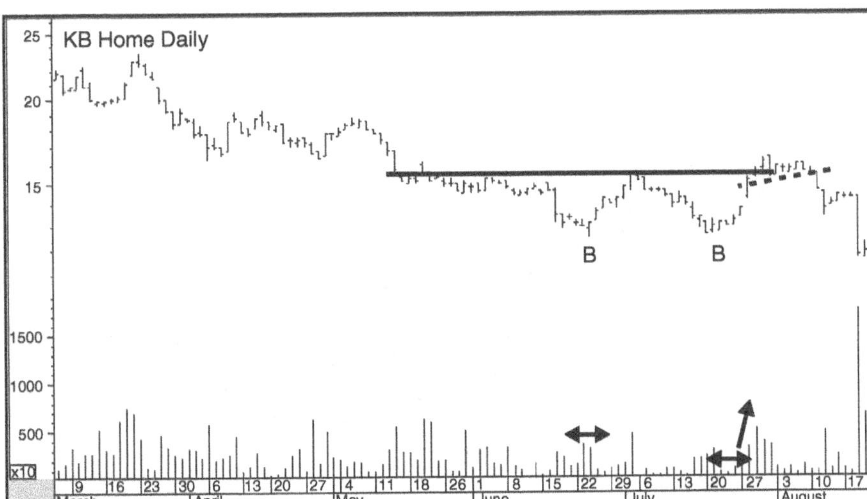

Whipsaw Double Bottom ("Lucky Seven" Double Bottom)

This is an unusual pattern that is measured in terms of waves and their relationships to previous highs and lows rather than being defined by trendlines. An example is shown in Fig. 8-6. The pattern can be divided into seven waves, hence the "Lucky Seven" title. Four waves are associated with the first bottom and three with the second. They are indicated in Fig. 8-6 by the dashed and dotted lines. The idea is that prices rally off the first bottom in a robust manner as the initial three waves of the pattern form a rising peak and trough. Then the fourth wave destroys this by breaking below the initial minor bottom. This is the whipsaw part of the equation. However, it is not a decisive signal, for at this point the rising peaks are still intact. The second three waves save the day because they result in the rising bottoms being reinstated. The pattern is completed on the seventh (lucky) wave at *X*. A second, stronger signal develops as the price rallies above the peak of the third wave at *Y*.

Often you see a pretty sharp or even explosive rally develop after the breakout. Charts 8-13, for Electronic Data, and 8-14, for Intel, show a couple of examples of this formation. The Electronic Data formation turns out to be a borderline reverse head and shoulders because the horizontal trendline almost connects with the late September high. It really doesn't matter, for anyone who had been following the Lucky Seven formula from the long side would have done quite well. The Intel chart is a more clear-cut example of a double bottom.

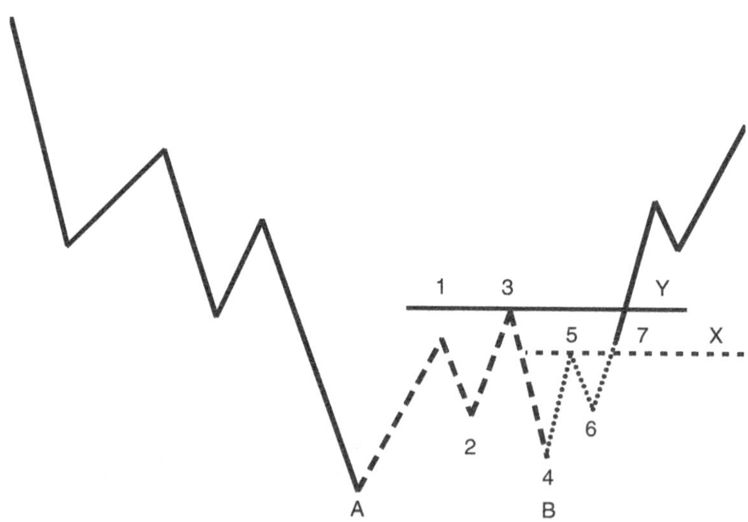

Figure 8-6 Whipsaw double bottom.

Chart 8-13 Electronic Data, 1990–1991, daily.

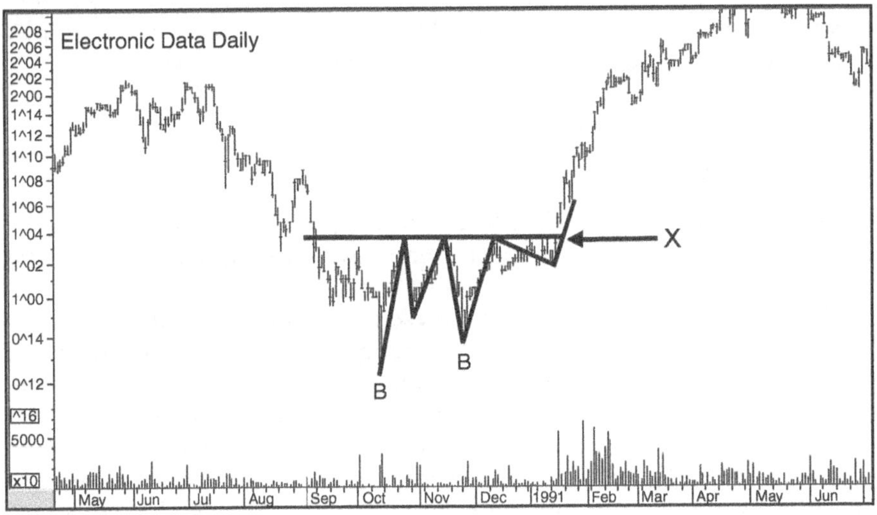

Chart 8-14 Intel, 1995–1996, daily.

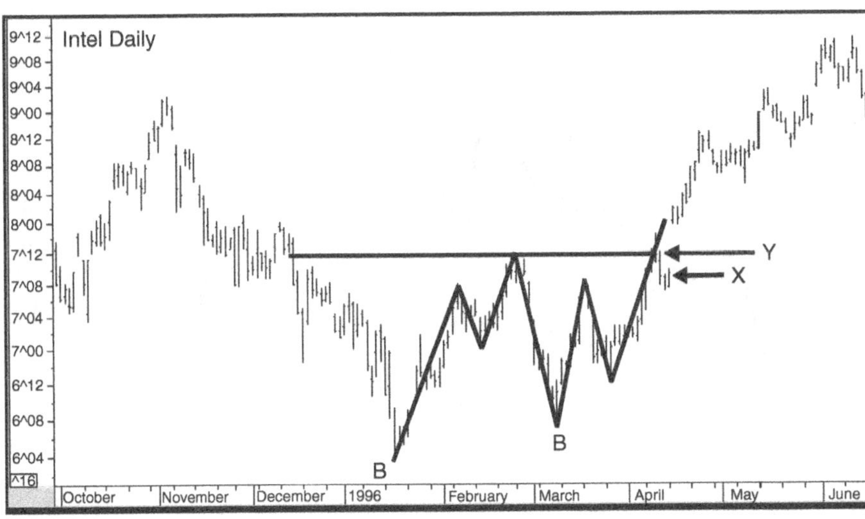

These patterns are not that common, but when you can spot them, they usually offer a good risk/reward situation. The best place to go long, referring to Fig. 8-6, is at point *X*; provided wave 7 is not too long, it is then possible to set a stop just below the bottom of wave 6.

Triple Tops

Double patterns may extend to form triple tops or bottoms, or sometimes even quadruple or other complex formations. An example of a triple top is shown in Fig. 8-7.

The measuring implication of all these patterns is determined by calculating the distance between the peak (trough) and the lower (upper) end of the pattern and projecting this distance from the neckline. It is easy to become confused between triple tops, head-and-shoulders tops, and rectangle tops. Make sure that the highest rally is not the center one; if it is, this is a head and shoulders. Also, if there is not much serious difference between the three peaks, the pattern could be a rectangle. In actual fact, all three patterns can represent a more or less horizontal trading range in which buyers and sellers battle it out. When the support line joining any of them is violated, the formation is completed. Ideally, we would want to see volume shrink on the third peak of a triple top. That's exactly what happens in Chart 8-15, for NCR. Notice also that volume expands noticeably on the downside. This indicates selling pressure, as opposed to prices falling

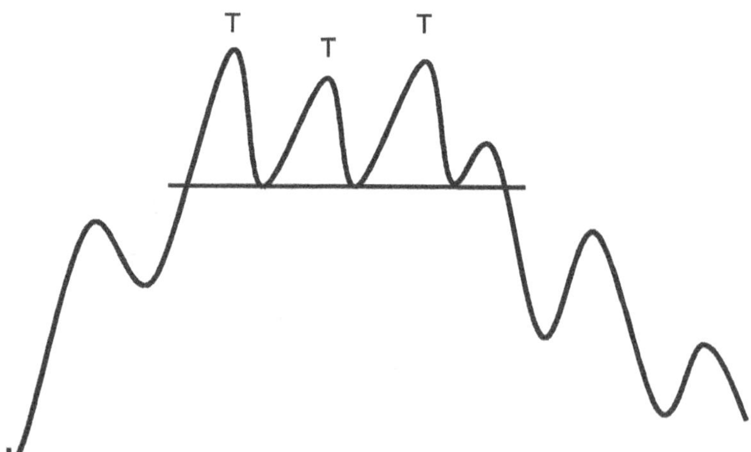

Figure 8-7 Triple top.

Chart 8-15 NCR, 1998–1999, weekly.

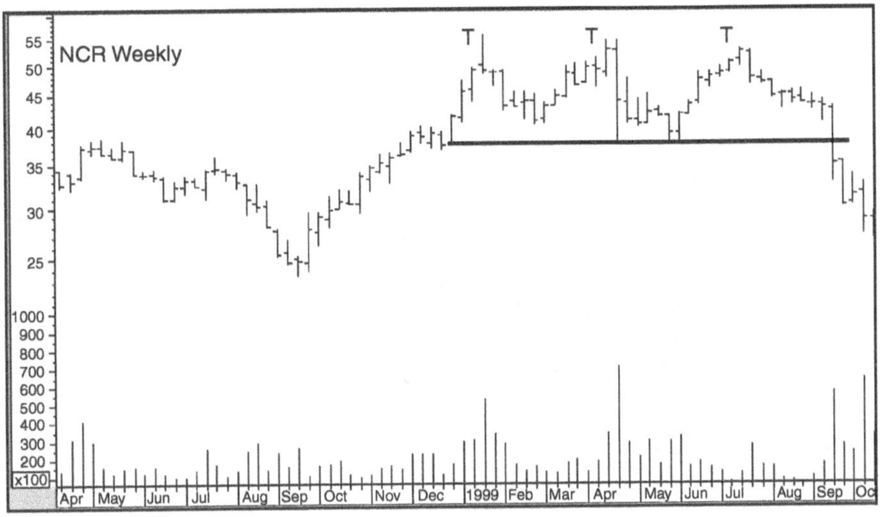

because of a lack of bids. It therefore emphasizes the bearishness of the situation.

Triple Bottoms

Like triple tops, triple bottoms experience a series of three lows (see Fig. 8-8). A line joins all the rally peaks, and the pattern is completed on the upside breakout. Volume is normally greatest at the first two bottoms, declining noticeably on the third. Mellon Financial (Chart 8-16) provides us with an example of a triple bottom. Once again volume is heavy on the August and September lows but much lighter at the October bottom.

Summary

Double-Top Review

- *Price characteristics:* Two highs following a worthwhile rally that form at approximately the same level. They are separated by a decline and a decent time interval.
- *Pattern completed:* With a decline below the valley low.

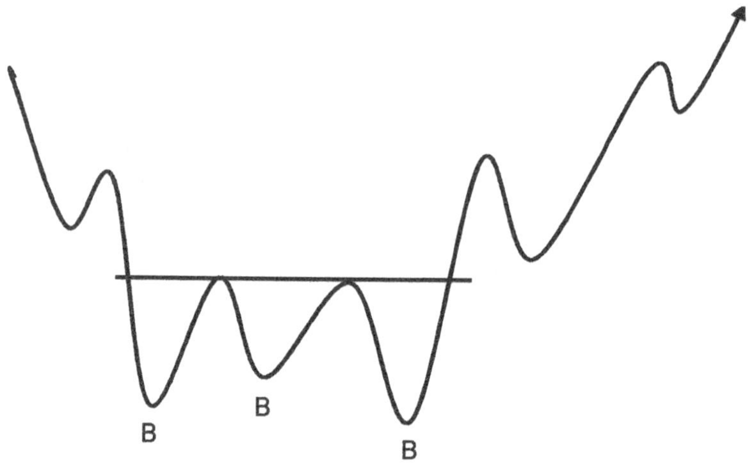

Figure 8-8 Triple bottom.

Chart 8-16 Mellon Financial, 1990–1991, daily.

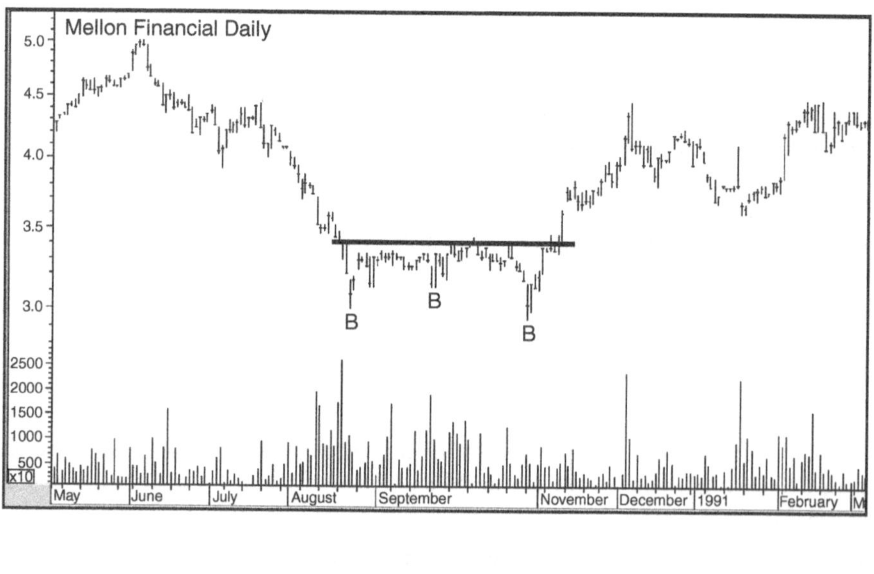

- *Volume considerations:* Heavy volume on the first top. Substantially lower volume on the second.
- *Measuring implication:* The distance between the higher of the two tops and the valley low is projected down from the breakout point.
- *Signs of false breakouts:* Retracement of 50 percent or more of the distance between the second top and the breakout point.
- *Places to unwind the position in case of a whipsaw breakout:* Retracement of 50 percent or more of the distance between the second top and the breakout point.

Double-Bottom Review

- *Price characteristics:* Two lows following a serious decline that form at approximately the same level. The two lows are separated by a rally.
- *Pattern completed:* With a move above the rally peak coming off the initial low.
- *Volume consideration:* Heavy volume on the first bottom; distinctly lower volume on the second. Very high volume should accompany the upside breakout.
- *Measuring implications:* The distance from the lower of the two bottoms is projected up from the breakout point.
- *Signs of false breakouts:* Retracement of 50 percent or more of the distance from the second low to the breakout point. Low volume accompanying the breakout.
- *Places to unwind the position in case of a whipsaw breakout:* On a decline that retraces more than 50 percent of the distance from the low to the breakout point.

Triple-Top Review

- *Price characteristics:* Following a worthwhile rally, three highs that form at approximately the same level, where the second is not higher than the other two.
- *Pattern completed:* With a decline below a more or less horizontal trendline joining the three lows.
- *Volume considerations:* Heavier volume on the first two tops; substantially lower volume on the second. These characteristics are less precise than those of other patterns.

- *Measuring implications:* The distance from the highest of the three tops is projected down from the breakout point.
- *Signs of false breakouts:* Retracement of 50 percent or more of the distance between the third top and the breakout point. Violation of a worthwhile trendline joining the third top to any minor-rally highs.
- *Places to unwind the position in case of a whipsaw breakout:* Retracement of 50 percent or more of the distance between the third top and the breakout point. Violation of a worthwhile trendline joining the third top to any minor-rally highs.

Triple-Bottom Review

- *Price characteristics:* Following a decline, three lows that form at approximately the same level, where the second is not lower than the other two.
- *Pattern completed:* With a move above an approximately horizontal trendline joining the rally peaks coming off the initial two lows.
- *Volume considerations:* Heavy volume on the first bottom; very high volume accompanying the upside breakout.
- *Measuring implication:* The distance from the lower of the three bottoms is projected up from the breakout point.
- *Signs of false breakouts:* Retracement of 50 percent or more of the rally from the third low to the breakout point.
- *Places to unwind the position in case of a whipsaw breakout:* Retracement of 50 percent or more of the distance from the final low to the breakout point. Breakout accompanied by low volume.
- Violation of any up trendline joining the final low and any higher minor lows.

9 Triangles

Triangles are the most common price pattern, but they are also one of the least reliable. They develop as both consolidation and reversal formations, and consist of an ever-narrowing trading range bounded by two *converging* trendlines. In order for a line to represent one of the boundaries, it needs to be touched on at least two occasions. This means that a triangle consists of at least four turning points, two for each line. In reality, though, such patterns are usually more reliable when one of them has been touched three or more times. Indeed, the more contact or near-contact points, the better. In Chapter 4 it was pointed out that trendlines are nothing more than dynamic levels of support and resistance. Thus, the more times a triangle boundary has been touched or approached, other things being equal, the greater the significance of that boundary as a support or resistance area, and therefore the stronger the breakout signal when it comes. There are two types of triangle, the symmetrical and the right-angled, so let's consider them in turn.

Symmetrical Triangles

A symmetrical triangle is composed of a series of two or more rallies and reactions in which each peak is lower than its predecessor and the bottom of each reaction is higher than its predecessor (see Fig. 9-1). A triangle is the opposite of a broadening formation (see Chapter 10), since the trendlines joining peaks and troughs *converge*; in broadening formations, they *diverge.*

These patterns are also known as *coils* because the fluctuation in price and volume diminishes as the pattern is completed. Finally, both price and (usually) volume react sharply, as if a coil spring had been wound tighter and tighter and then snapped free as prices broke out of the triangle. Generally speaking, triangles seem to work best when the breakout occurs somewhere between one-half and two-thirds of the distance between the widest peak

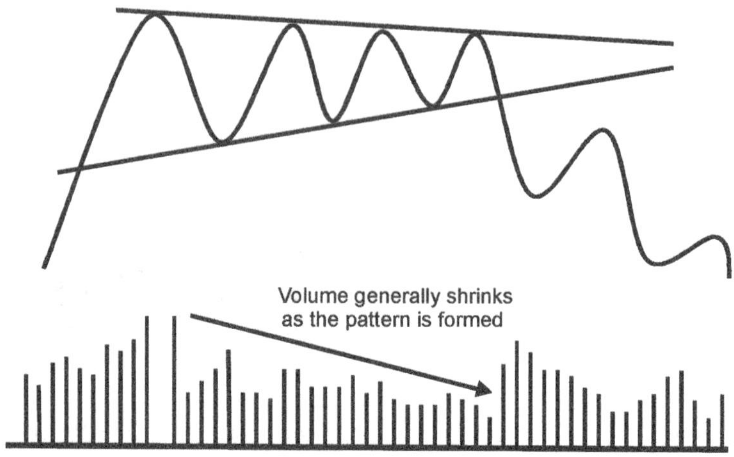

Figure 9-1 Symmetrical triangle.

and rally and the apex (as in Fig. 9-2). The volume rules used for other patterns are also appropriate for triangles. That means that activity should gradually contract as the pattern is being formed. During upside breakouts, it is important for volume to expand (see Fig. 9-3). In downside breakouts, it doesn't much matter whether volume contracts or expands, though an expansion of activity indicates selling pressure and adds a few points to the bearish case. In Fig. 9-1, for instance, volume expands on the downside

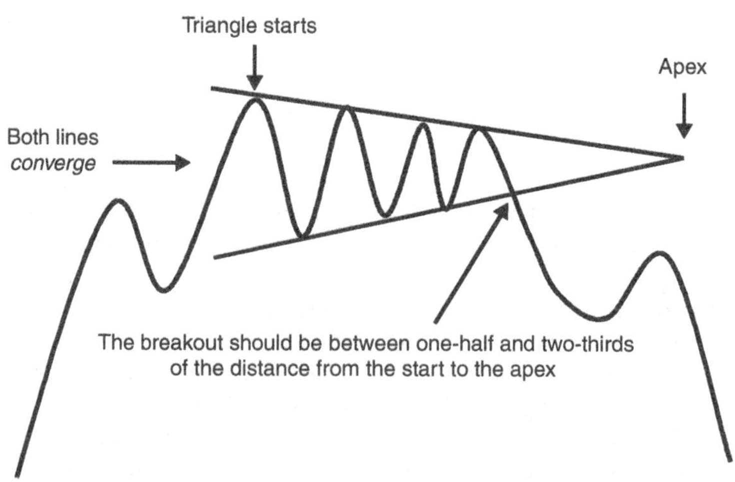

Figure 9-2 Symmetrical triangle indicating ideal breakout range.

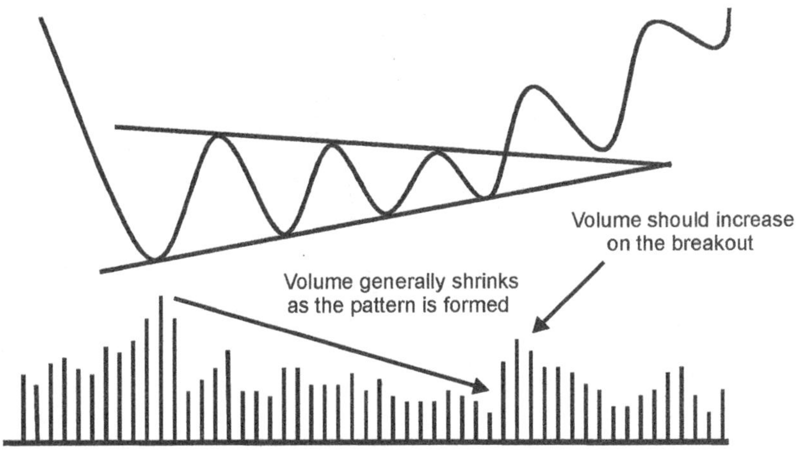

Figure 9-3 Symmetrical triangle at a bottom.

breakout, having contracted as the pattern was forming. The point here is that the battle between buyers and sellers is becoming more finely balanced as the pattern develops. Then, on the breakout, volume expands, thereby signaling from both a price and a volume point of view that control has slipped decisively to one side or the other.

Most patterns give us a clue to the direction of the ultimate breakout in the event that they are completed. The symmetrical triangle does not; it keeps us guessing. Since it should be assumed that the prevailing trend is intact until proven otherwise, it is a good idea to take it for granted that the triangle will eventually break in the direction of the prevailing trend. An example of a continuation triangle is shown in Fig. 9-4. Clues to the contrary—i.e., in favor of a reversal—would appear if the price was overextended in one direction or the other. Alternatively, it may be possible to observe that many stocks have already begun to break in a new direction. A reversal would be more likely if the pattern formed after the prevailing trend had been in place for a long time than if it had just begun. However, when taken in isolation with no other supporting evidence, the prevailing trend assumption should be applied.

The Underlying Psychology

A triangle pattern is no more than a gradually tightening battle between buyers and sellers. At the outset, the large price swings at the left-hand part of the formation indicate relative instability, showing that both sides are out of control. Prices initially rally up at the beginning of the triangle until they

Figure 9-4 Consolidation symmetrical triangle.

reach a point at which buyers become less enthusiastic and sellers quite motivated. Then the price slips back quite a ways, and those who missed the boat earlier are more inclined to buy at these lower prices. Selling is also less intense. The price then rises for a second time, but not to as great an extent before supply once again overwhelms the buyers. This could be because potential sellers, having missed out on the opportunity to sell at higher prices on the first rally, temper their greed and are prepared to settle for less profit. In any event, prices decline and buyers come in again, but each rally and reaction attracts fewer and fewer participants. The initial excitement dies down, and market participants await a resolution of the fine balance between them. As the pattern develops and the battle lines come closer and closer, neither side is able to exert as much upside or downside pressure. As a general rule, whenever price activity goes quiet, as it does close to the apex of the triangle, the slightest tip in the balance between supply and demand will result in a commensurately larger price move. Usually the more contact points, the more persistent the price move following the breakout. Another clue to the strength of the breakout is the strength of the contrast between shrinking volume as the pattern is formed and expanding activity on the breakout. The greater the contrast, the more decisive the victory and the stronger the signal.

Measuring Objectives

Traditionally, measuring objectives for triangles at market tops are obtained by drawing a line at the base of the triangle parallel to the upper trendline.

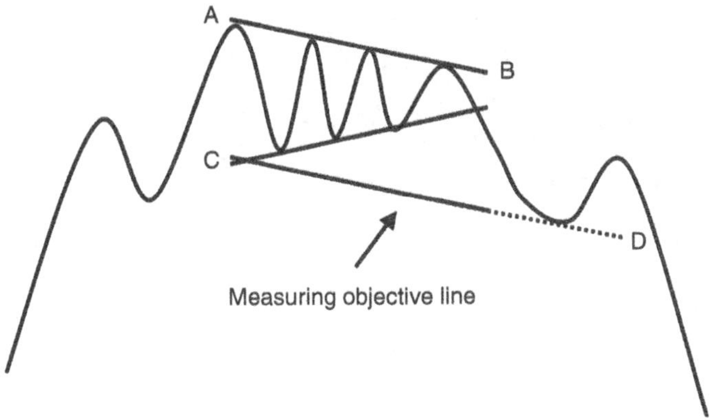

Figure 9-5 Symmetrical triangle with traditional measuring objective.

This line (*CD* in Fig. 9-5) represents the objective that prices may be expected to reach or exceed.

The reverse procedure at market bottoms is shown in Fig. 9-6. The same technique is used to project prices when triangles are of the consolidation variety.

In my own experience, I have not found this method to be particularly useful. This is because the actual price move is usually far more than the price objective. *I prefer, instead, to treat the triangle like any other pattern,*

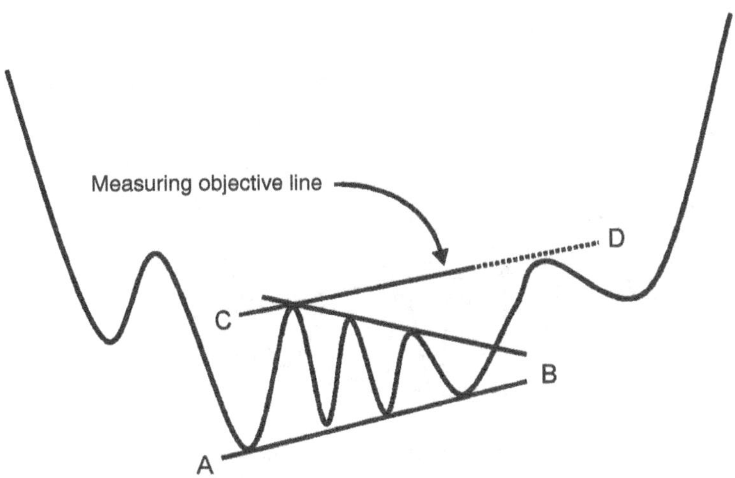

Figure 9-6 Symmetrical triangle with traditional measuring objective.

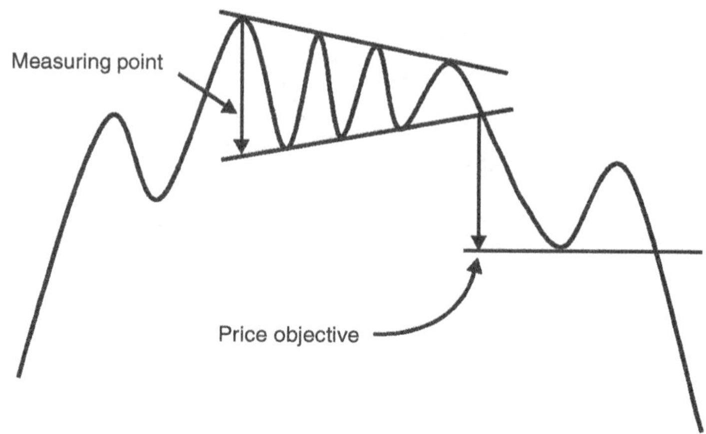

Figure 9-7 Symmetrical triangle with alternative measuring objective.

calculating its maximum depth and then projecting this distance at the breakout. Examples of this alternative method for both a top and a bottom are shown in Figs. 9-7 and 9-8. By adopting this approach, the principle of proportionality is preserved. Charts 9-1 and 9-2, featuring Yahoo, show how the two methods might work in the marketplace. The original technique takes a line parallel to the upper down trendline of the pattern and anchors it

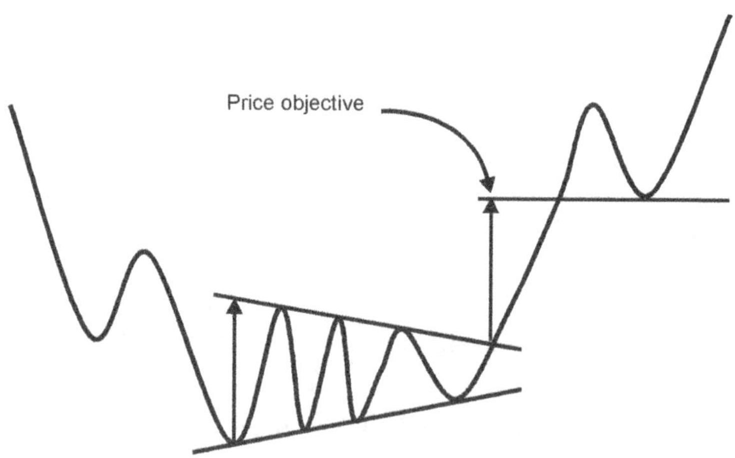

Figure 9-8 Symmetrical triangle with alternative measuring objective.

Chart 9-1 Yahoo, 2001–2002, daily.

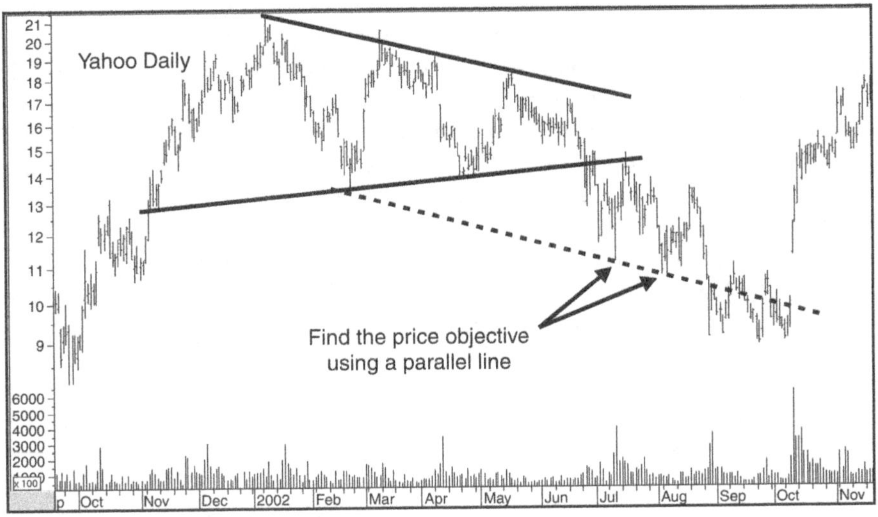

Chart 9-2 Yahoo, 2001–2002, daily.

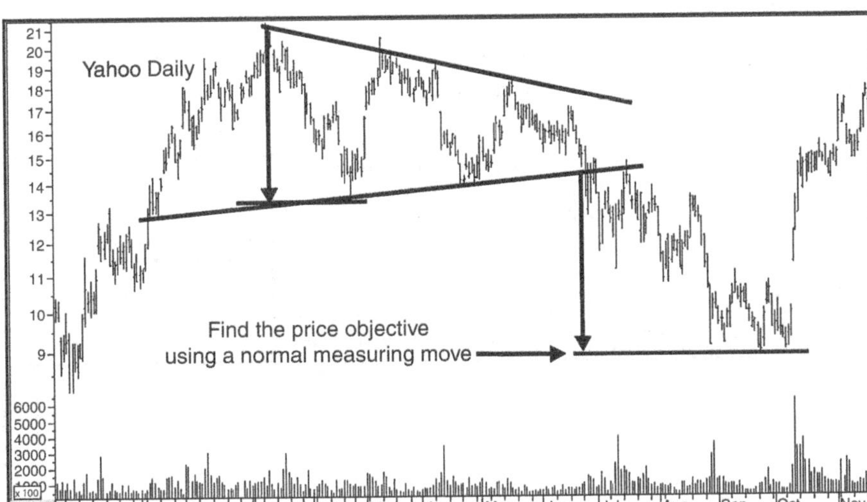

at the bottom of the initial decline. In this instance, the line becomes one of support, as it is able to reverse the July and August declines. In the second example, the distance between the peak and the initial low is measured and that distance is projected down from the breakout point. In this instance, the objective falls in line with the actual bottom. Both methods result in useful benchmarks, but the proportionate or second technique is the one that calls the final low. I have to add that even though this example was selected at random, not all price-objective moves work out this accurately.

Chart 9-3 shows another example of a symmetrical triangle at a market top, for Intel. The original measuring objective is represented by the declining dashed line. This time the price immediately breaks below this line, but the two subsequent rallies find resistance there. On the other hand, the ultimate low is made at around twice the objective called for by the proportionate method. This also represented the approximate level of the lows set in the previous June/July period. It is also worth noting that while the initial price objective was easily exceeded, this same level turned out to be resistance for the November and December rallies.

An example of a triangle bottom is shown in Chart 9-4, for Alcoa. Note how a line parallel to the lower part of the rectangle and anchored at the secondary peak at *A* provided resistance throughout the ensuing advance.

Chart 9-3 Intel, daily.

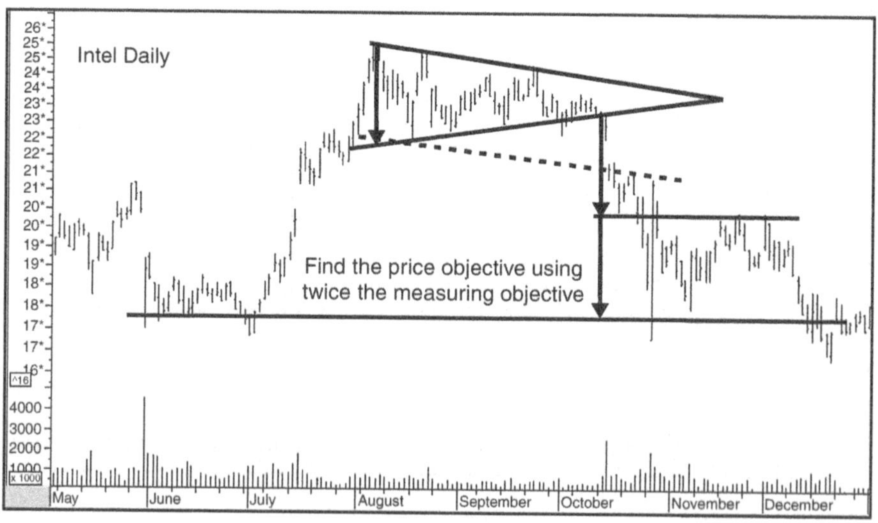

Chart 9-4 Alcoa, 1986–1989. weekly.

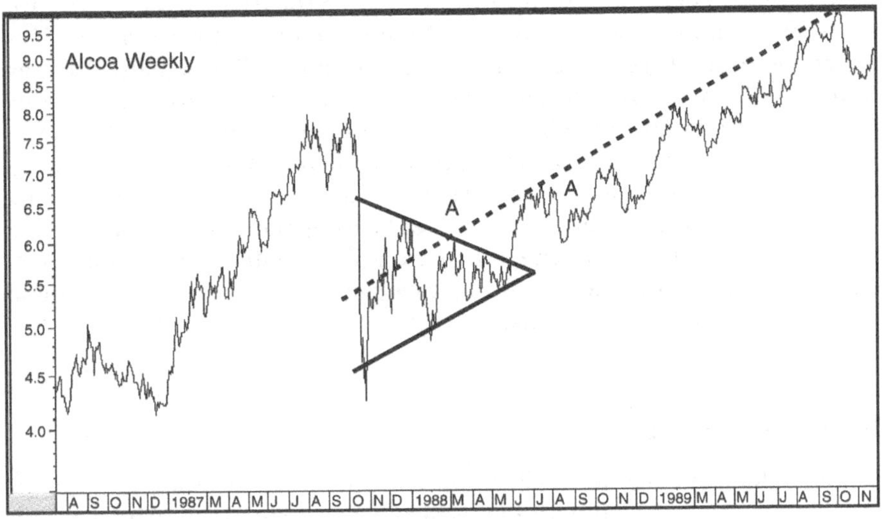

Weaving Symmetrical Triangles into Head-and-Shoulders Tops

Triangles are one of the least accurate of all the price patterns. One of the reasons is that a formation often starts out looking like a triangle, but ends up as something completely different. An example is shown in Fig. 9-9, in which a breakout develops above the dashed trendline marking the top of

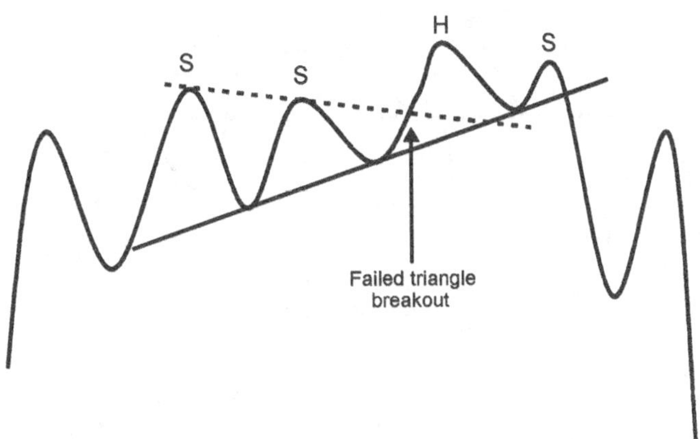

Figure 9-9 Failed symmetrical triangle.

a triangle. Later on, though, the price action unfolds into an upward sloping head-and-shoulders top. The upside breakout in the triangle therefore gave a false indication of the direction of the next significant price move. This is just one example of how a triangle can offer misleading signals. One way to reduce the probability of a whipsaw triangle breakout is to consider only formations where the price has had contact or close contact with the breakout line on more than two occasions. In fact, the more times the better, since this would reinforce the line as a resistance or support area, thereby making its penetration more likely to succeed. Bearing in mind some of the rules for determining the significance of a trendline established in Chapter 4, another filtering approach would be to exclude triangles where the angle of ascent or descent is particularly steep.

Right-Angled Triangles

Right-angled triangles are really a special form of the symmetrical type, in that one of the two boundaries is formed at an angle of 90 degrees to the vertical axis, i.e., is horizontal (Fig. 9-10). The symmetrical triangle does not give an indication of the direction in which it is ultimately likely to break. The right-angled triangle does, with its implied slanting level of support or resistance.

Like most patterns, triangles often experience retracement moves following breakouts. An example is shown in Fig. 9-11 for a right-angled ascending

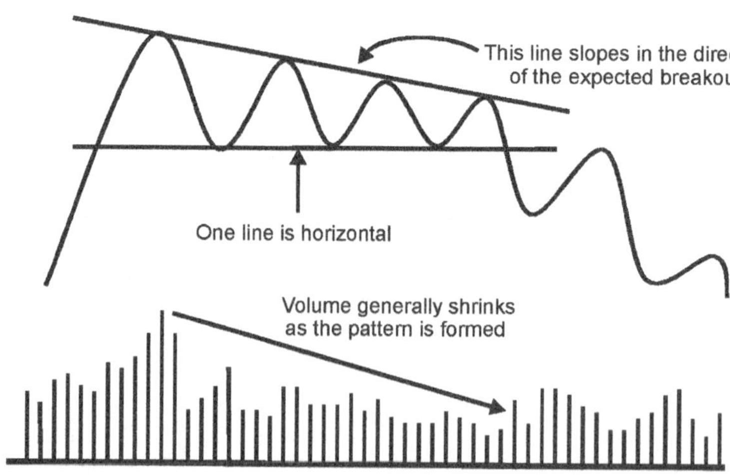

Figure 9-10 Bearish right-angled triangle.

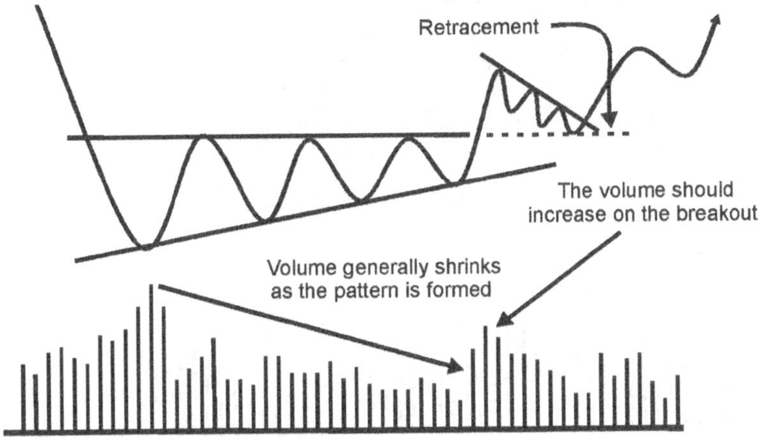

Figure 9-11 Bullish right-angled triangle with a retracement.

triangle. If an opportunity is missed on the breakout, the pullback or retracement move offers a second chance, usually under far more quiet conditions. If it is possible to construct a retracement trendline, as in Fig. 9-11, the upside penetration of the line is a good entry point, since it indicates a reassertion of the original breakout. This is especially true if the retracement move is accompanied by shrinking volume and the breakout above the retracement trendline by slightly or significantly expanding activity, as in Fig. 9-11.

Spinning Right-Angled Triangles into Rectangles

One difficulty in interpreting these formations is that many rectangles begin as right-angled triangles. Consequently, a great deal of caution should be used when evaluating these elusive patterns. An example is shown in Fig. 9-12, where a potential downward-sloping right-angled triangle develops into a rectangle.

Marketplace Examples

An example of a right-angled triangle at a bottom is shown in Chart 9-5, for Intel. If you believe that the June 1986 decline qualifies as a shoulder, it could be argued that this pattern is a reverse head and shoulders, with the horizontal trendline representing the neckline. You could also say that the "horizontal" line is not quite horizontal, and so the triangle would be more accurately called a symmetrical one. Frankly, I think we would be pushing

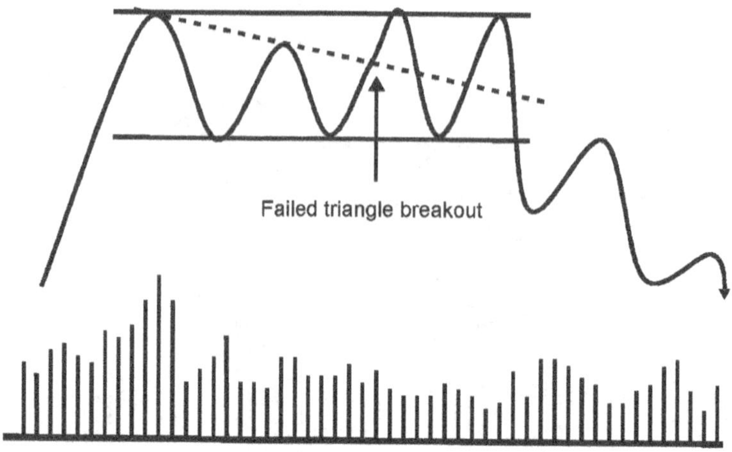

Figure 9-12 Failed bearish right-angled triangle.

the envelope on this one. It really doesn't matter what the pattern is called; the fact is that it was a clear-cut battle between buyers and sellers that was resolved in favor of the buyers, and that's ultimately what counts. Also note the substantial increase in volume as the price breaks to the upside and the fact that the lower trendline has been touched six times. If the standard for

Chart 9-5 Intel, 1986–1987, daily.

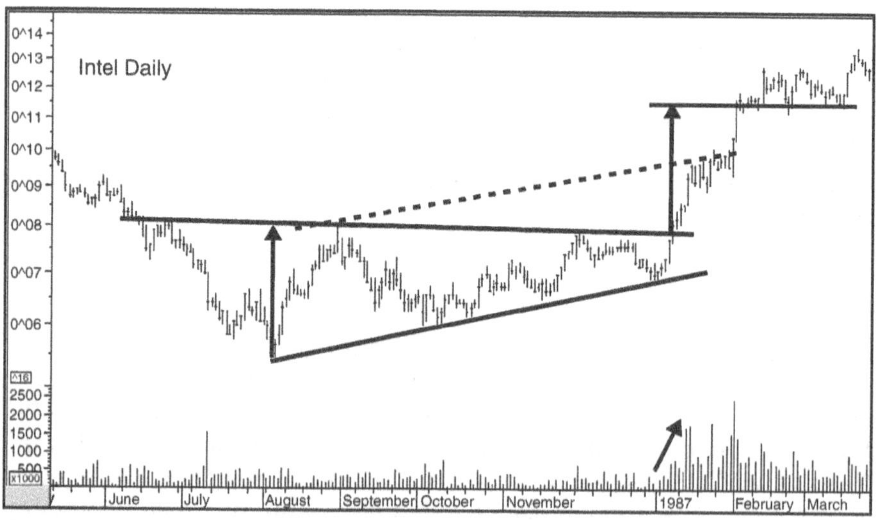

Chart 9-6 Analog Devices, 1991–1994, weekly.

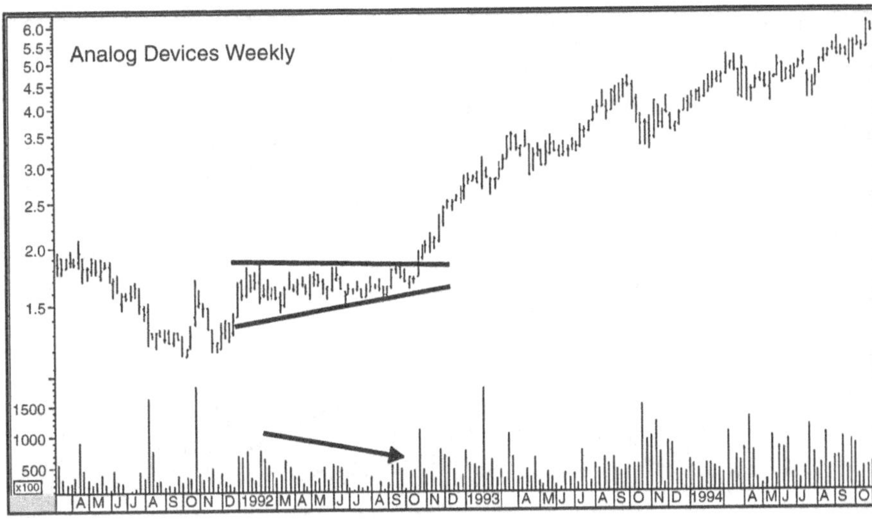

triangles is a double contact only, then this is definitely an impressive line of support. Once again I applied the two price-objective techniques. The parallel-line method caused the price to find temporary resistance in the month of January. When it finally broke above the line, a very sharp rally followed. The proportionate approach was well exceeded, but it is interesting to note that the objective level ultimately became support in the form of a neckline for a failed head-and-shoulders top formation.

Chart 9-6, for Analog Devices, shows another ascending triangle. This time it is formed above the low point for the move and is therefore a consolidation pattern. Note how volume shrinks as the pattern develops. It also expands a little on the breakout, but nothing to get excited about.

Northrop Grumman, in Chart 9-7, provides us with a fairly large descending triangle top. The original (dashed) descending line had to be redrawn because of the two 1987 rallies. It is worth noting that when the price fell through the extended dashed line for a second time, it actually experienced a pretty wide gap just prior to completing the pattern.

Right-Angled Failures

To the flexible trader or investor, a pattern failure offers great opportunity. This is probably more true of right-angled triangles than of any other formation. We saw earlier how a right-angled triangle can transform itself

Chart 9-7 Northrop Grumman, 1984–1990, weekly.

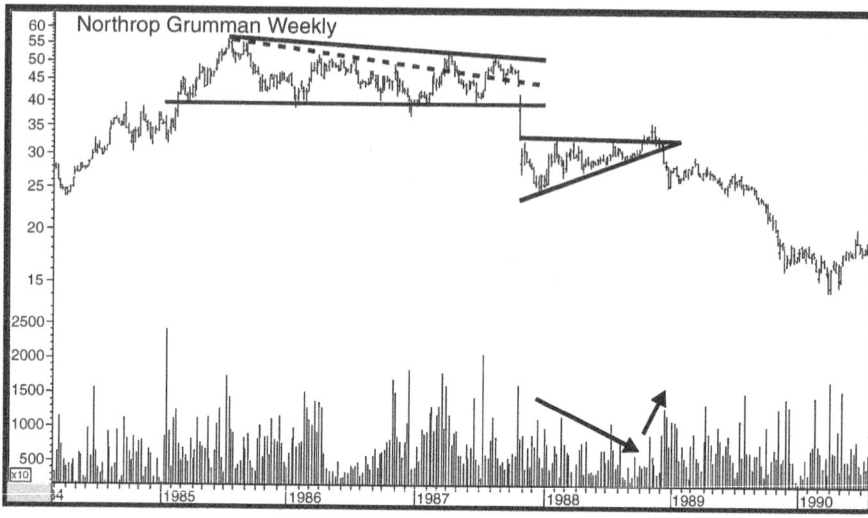

into a rectangle. However, the moves following right-angled breakdowns are usually a little more dramatic. There are two types of failure. The first develops when the price penetrates the horizontal trendline and then moves back through it. Examples for a bottom and a top are shown in Figs. 9-13 and 9-14. In Fig. 9-13, the false upside breakout develops close

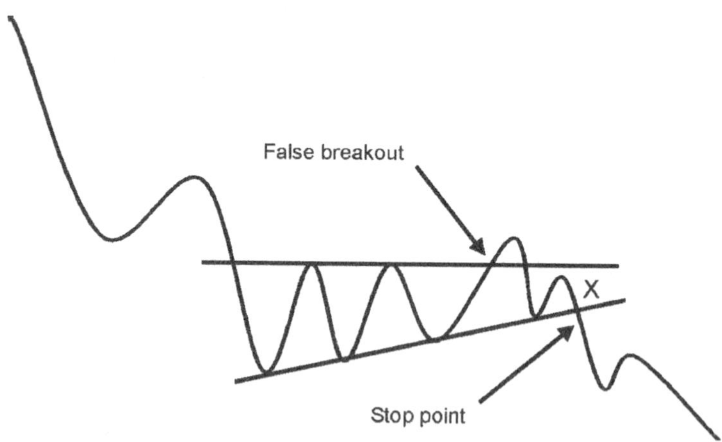

Figure 9-13 Failed bullish right-angled triangle.

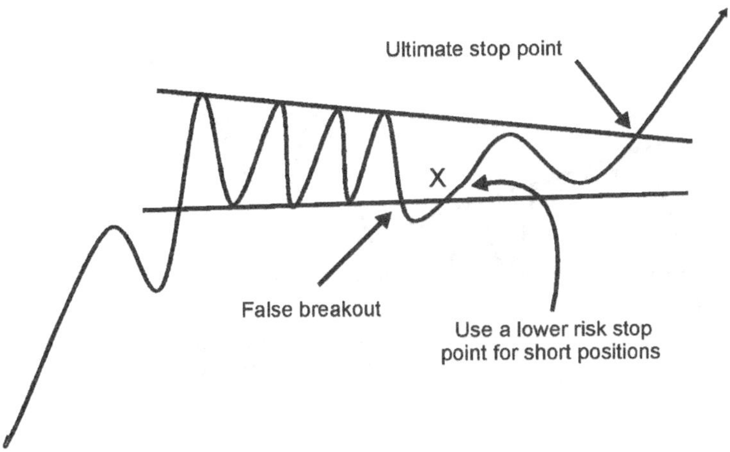

Figure 9-14 Failed bearish right-angled triangle.

to the apex, so it is possible to set a fairly close stop under the rising trendline. It would even make sense to exit the position once the price slips below the horizontal line again. However, the odds of a failure increase greatly when the rising line in a bullish pattern is penetrated. This is because this line is often a strong area of support. False breakouts often result in a strong move in the opposite direction to that expected, so it is even possible to go short on a break of the rising trendline. The buy stop would then be placed above the line at *X* and moved progressively higher until a better place is found at a lower level. Figure 9-14 shows another false break, this time from what looked like a descending pattern. The distance between the breakout point and the descending line is quite substantial, which means that any short positions, triggered from the false downside break, would be more timely covered on a rally above the horizontal trendline at *X*.

An example of an upside failure is shown in Chart 9-7, for Northrop Grumman. This 1988 failure is a classic case because the breakout developed *against* the direction of the main trend. The scene had been set earlier with a breakdown from an almost three-year right-angled triangle top. Volume for the failed pattern contracted as the pattern was developing, a normal phenomenon. However, it expanded in a very deceptive way on the breakout, thereby offering a false sense of security. Just after the price fell below the rising trendline, volume expanded rapidly. This was a clear-cut signal, since this bear market characteristic left no doubt that the sellers were now in control.

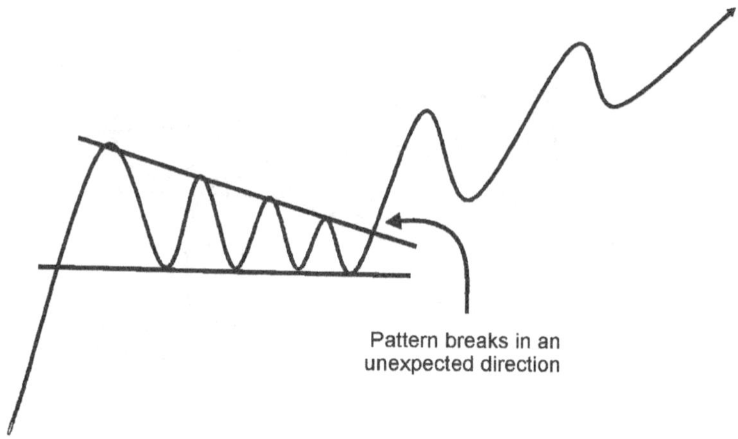

Figure 9-15 Failed bullish right-angled triangle.

The second way in which an ascending triangle can fail is when the rising or falling trendline is penetrated prior to a breakout through the horizontal line. In Fig. 9-15, buyers are gaining confidence as each decline is terminated at a higher level. Technically oriented people see this price action and buy in anticipation of a successful pattern completion. Such expectations are dashed when the price breaks below the ascending triangle; hence, there is the potential for a sharper than average decline. An example for a failed ascending triangle is shown in Fig. 9-16. If such a failure is

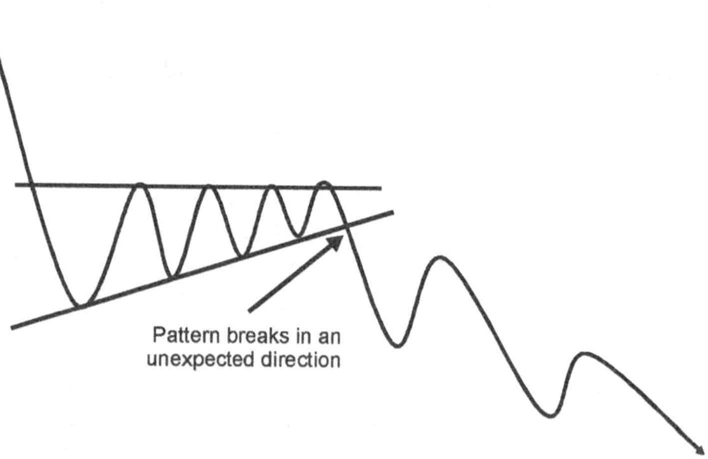

Figure 9-16 Failed bearish right-angled triangle.

accompanied by expanding volume, this really emphasizes the fact that market participants have made a mistake. The high volume indicates that a large number of people are trying to unwind their positions, while others are trying to climb on board the new trend before the train has left the station.

The Underlying Psychology of Failed Right-Angled Triangles

In the case of a failed ascending triangle, confidence rises as the price rallies to the horizontal trendline, but each decline is smaller than its predecessor. A move above the overhead resistance indicated by the horizontal line is therefore expected, and positions are taken accordingly. At the same time, sellers feel quite comfortable liquidating every time the price rises to the line. Since this happens on a number of occasions, there is no pressure to accept a lower price—that is, until the ascending line is violated. Then everybody wants out. On the one hand, the original sellers realize that it is no longer possible to attain the higher prices associated with the horizontal trendline. On the other hand, those who bought in anticipation of the upside break lose heart. Such a rationale explains why such failures are so often followed by substantial price moves.

Chart 9-8, for Linear Technology, offers a good example. In this instance, the price looked as if it were in the process of forming a descending right-angled triangle. The June–August period even took on the air of

Chart 9-8 Linear Technology, 1981–1983, daily.

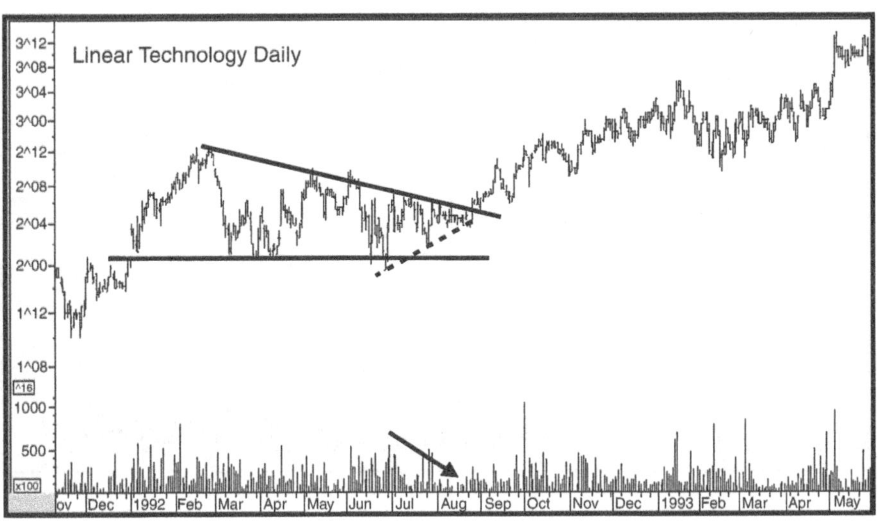

Chart 9-9 WorldCom, 1993, daily.

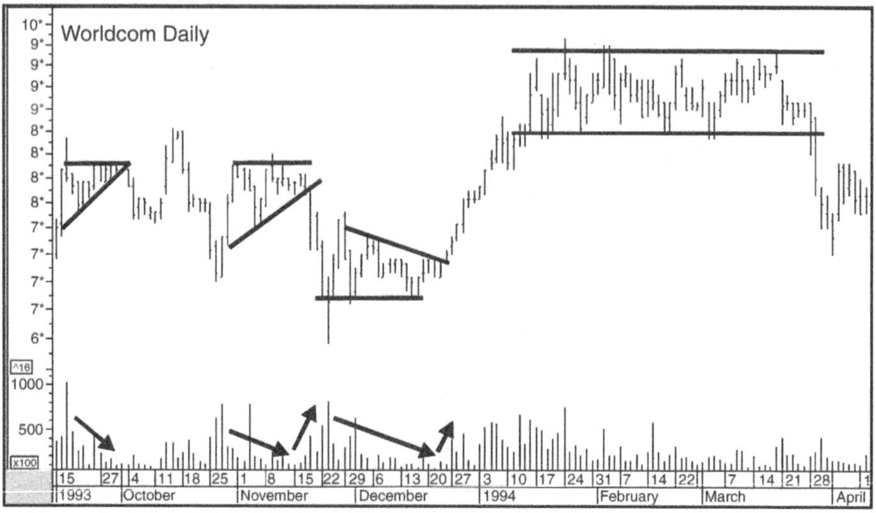

Chart 9-10 Analog Devices, 1998–2003, weekly.

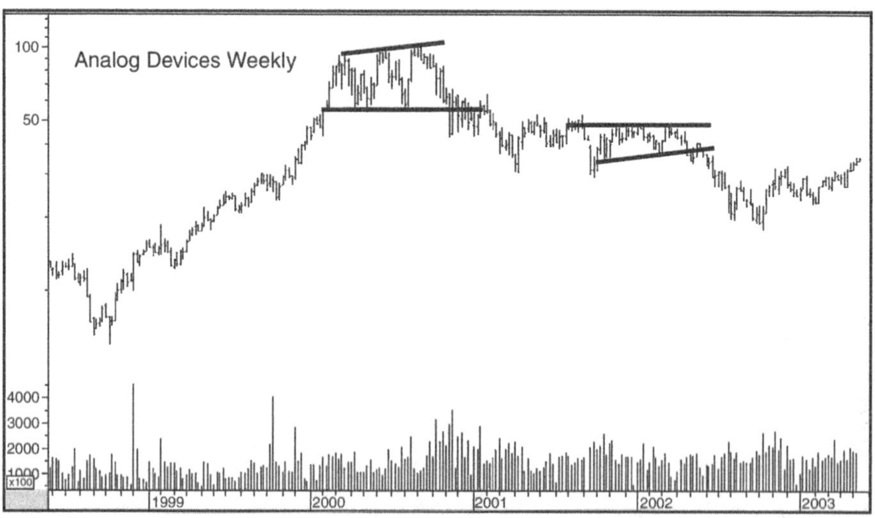

a symmetrical triangle. However, the descending triangle was never completed, and prices broke to the upside. Chart 9-9, for WorldCom, on the other hand, shows two examples of a failed ascending and one of a failed descending triangle. Notice how the volume shrinks as all three triangles are formed. It also expands as the two on the right experience false breakouts. Also featured is a large rectangle top formed in early 1994.

Finally, Analog Devices, in Chart 9-10, experienced a failed ascending pattern between late 2001 and early 2002.

Summary

Symmetrical Triangles Quick Review

- *Price characteristics:* A narrowing trading range confined between two converging trendlines moving in different directions.
- *Volume considerations:* Volume contracts as the pattern forms. Upside breakouts should be accompanied by expanding volume.
- *Measuring implications:* The maximum depth of the pattern is projected in the direction of the breakout. Alternatively, for bullish patterns, draw a line parallel to the pattern's lower trendline and anchor it at the initial rally. The extended line becomes the price objective. For bearish patterns, draw a line parallel to the pattern's upper trendline and anchor it at the initial decline. The extended line becomes the price objective.
- *Strongest breakouts:* Come from a point one-half to two-thirds of the distance between the start of the pattern and the apex.
- *Signs of false breakouts:* Weak volume accompanying an upside breakout.

Right-Angled Triangles Quick Review

- *Price characteristics:* A narrowing trading range confined between two converging trendlines, one of which is at a right angle to the vertical axis. The price is expected to break through the right-angled line in the direction of the sloping trendline.
- *Volume considerations:* Volume contracts as the pattern forms. Upside breakouts should be accompanied by expanding volume.
- *Measuring implications:* The maximum depth of the pattern is projected in the direction of the breakout. Alternatively, for bullish patterns, draw a line parallel to the pattern's lower trendline and anchor it at the initial

rally. The extended line becomes the price objective. For bearish patterns, draw a line parallel to the pattern's upper trendline and anchor it at the initial decline. The extended line becomes the price objective.

- *Strongest breakouts:* Come from a point one-half to two-thirds of the distance between the start of the pattern and the apex.
- *Signs of false breakouts:* Contracting or weak volume accompanying an upside breakout.
- *Pattern failures:* Occasionally come with a violation of the sloping trendline.

10 Broadening Formations

Broadening formations signify a very unstable technical situation and typically develop after a trend has been underway for some time. It's almost as if the battle between buyers and sellers is out of control, because these patterns exhibit wider and wider price fluctuations. They contrast well with triangles, where the trading range gradually narrows to a very balanced position prior to the breakout.

Broadening formations occur when a series of three or more price fluctuations widens out in size so that peaks and troughs can be connected with two *diverging* trendlines. Triangles come in two varieties, and so do broadening formations. These variations are called *orthodox* and *right-angled.* The right-angled type is sometimes referred to as a *broadening formation with a flat top* (the accumulation version) or a *flat bottom* (the distribution variety). Let's start with the classic or orthodox pattern.

Orthodox Broadening Formations

An example of an *orthodox broadening top* is shown in Fig. 10-1. It comprises three rallies, with each succeeding peak being higher than its predecessor. The three peaks are separated by two bottoms, with the second bottom being lower than the first. Orthodox broadening formations are associated with market peaks rather than troughs, although some of the textbooks tell us that they can develop at the end of bear trends. Orthodox broadening formations are sometimes called reverse triangles, because that is essentially what they are. On those rare occasions when they appear at market bottoms,

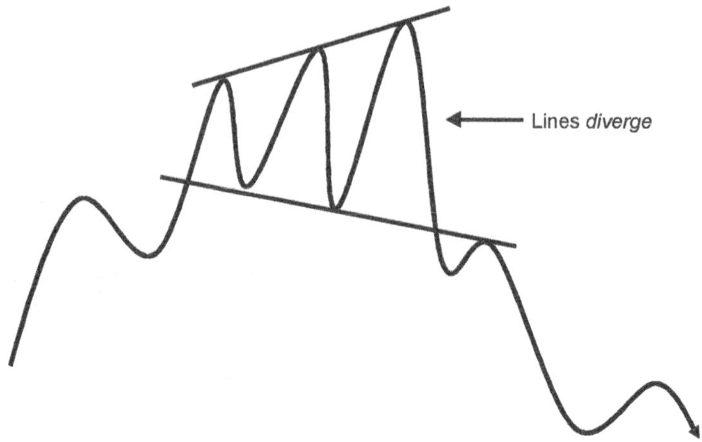

Figure 10-1 Orthodox broadening formation.

they are sometimes called *megaphone* bottoms because their appearance is similar to that of a megaphone.

Some patterns are ideal for trading because they offer clear demarcation lines for entry and convenient low-risk stop points in case things go wrong. A right-angled triangle that breaks out close to the apex is a good example. Unfortunately, this is not the case with the orthodox broadening formation, since these patterns are extremely difficult to detect until some time after the final top has been formed. Also, there is no clearly definable level of support, the violation of which serves as a convenient benchmark. The violent and emotional nature of both price and volume swings further compounds the confusion and increases the complexity of defining these situations. Obviously, a breakout is difficult to pinpoint under such conditions, but if the formation is reasonably symmetrical, a decisive move below the descending trendline joining the two bottoms, or even a decisive move below the second bottom, usually serves as a timely warning that an even greater decline is in store.

Measuring implications are similarly difficult to determine, but normally the volatile character of a broadening top formation implies the completion of a substantial amount of distribution. Consequently, price declines of considerable proportion usually follow the successful completion of such patterns.

The problem is that the breakdown point from such formations develops well after the final turning point of the previous move, so if you are long, you will probably say to yourself, "I can't sell here; it's declined far too much. I'll wait for a bounce." Unfortunately, this is not a good strategy, since the completion point of such formations is often just the tip of the iceberg. The reason lies in the fact that the orthodox pattern usually develops after a very lengthy bull move, when prices have increased substantially from the previous bear market low. Consequently, there is no shortage of sellers who are able to cash in on their profits. The volatility due to the diverging nature of the formation also adds to the feeling of instability. When prices are unstable, holders who would otherwise be reasonably calm and controlled have a greater tendency to panic. It is not unlike the idea that people living in a violent-crime-ridden neighborhood will have a greater tendency to resort to violent solutions than someone living in a quiet suburb.

Having spent a page or two describing the orthodox broadening formation, it must be pointed out that two classic texts, Edwards and Magee and H. M. Gartley, both agree that apart from the 1929 top, when such patterns were rampant, there is not much evidence of this formation's existence. Indeed, after looking through 20 years of data on the Nasdaq 100 and most of the S&P 500, I failed to come up with what I would regard as either useful examples or situations in which where the risk/reward was favorable. It would appear, therefore, that this formation is pretty well extinct. Certainly the lack of good examples makes it impracticable. What is not impracticable is the right-angled broadening variety, which is covered next.

Right-Angled Broadening Formations

The easiest types of broadening formations to detect are those with a "flattened" bottom or top, as shown in Figs. 10-2 and 10-3.

These patterns are sometimes referred to as *right-angled broadening formations.* Since the whole concept of widening price swings suggests highly emotional activity, volume patterns are difficult to characterize, although at market tops, activity is usually heavy during the rally phases. The patterns at both bottoms and tops are similar to head-and-shoulders patterns except that the "head" in the broadening formation is always the *last* part of the pattern to be formed. A bear signal comes with a decisive downside breakout. Volume can be heavy or light, but if activity expands at this point, this is an additional bearish factor.

Since a broadening formation with a flattened top is an accumulation pattern, volume expansion on the breakout is an important requirement, as

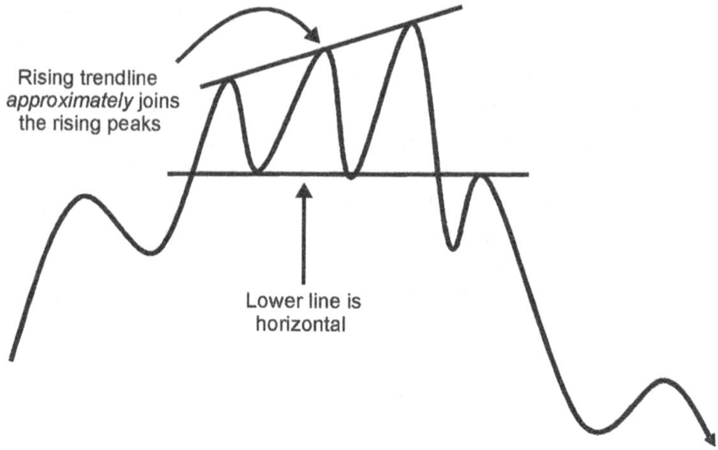

Figure 10-2 Right-angled broadening top formation.

shown in Fig. 10-4. In my experience, these formations pack a punch far greater than their size would suggest. They are really head-and-shoulders tops (bottoms) where the situation is so bearish (bullish) that the price does not have any time to trace out a right shoulder.

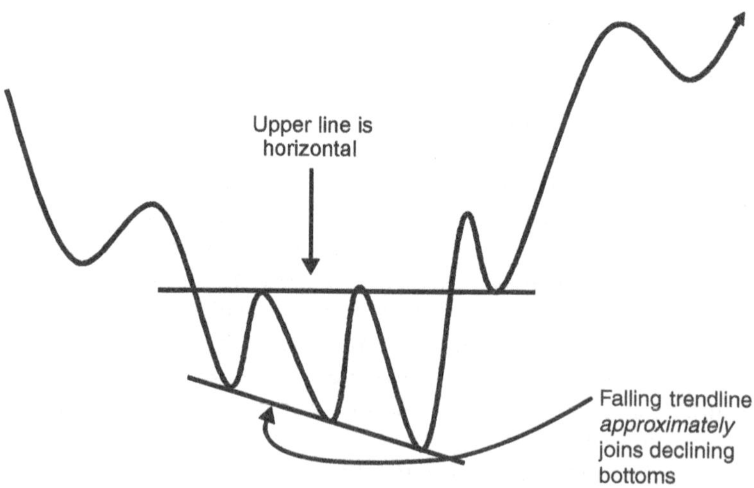

Figure 10-3 Right-angled broadening bottom formation.

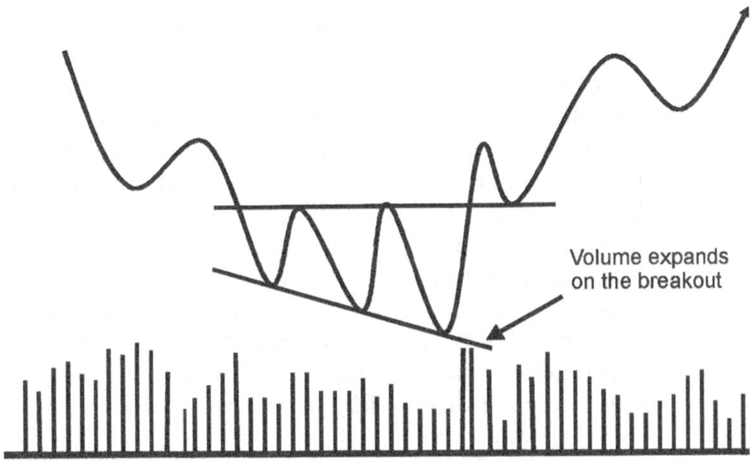

Figure 10-4 Right-angled broadening bottom formation.

The Underlying Psychology

Broadening formations with a flat top usually appear as the culmination of a persistent downtrend. At the start of the formation, bearish sentiment is typically quite excessive. The price initially sells off, then subsequently rallies to the horizontal level of resistance. When the bears see that the resistance has held, they are emboldened to put out more shorts, and a decline sets in. The price then rallies again and finds resistance in the area at the top of the pattern, but the advance from the second low is not sufficient to cause the shorts to cover. Indeed, when the price fails to rally through the resistance, the bears are even more emboldened to put out even more shorts.

As the price falls below the previous low, latecomers are attracted to the short side. After all, they can see that in the past few weeks and months, there was easy money to be made from shorting, especially as the news background is so negative that prices are "sure" to go down a lot more. This is enough to panic weak holders, who experience the give-up phase and liquidate to anyone "kind" enough to take the security off their hands. If bearish sentiment was widespread coming into the pattern, it is now universal, as virtually everyone is a believer in the bear trend. Those who are left are either strong holders with a positive long-term belief in the eventual outcome or short sellers. The bottom line is that there is little or no selling pressure but lots of potential buying pressure from the mercurial shorts.

The gasoline is on the fire. All that is needed is a match. That could be provided by unexpected good news, a change in the direction of the overall market, or some other reason. Perhaps the news is particularly bad and the price does not decline. This type of action will spook the shorts, who argue that if bad news won't cause a further decline, nothing will. The reason is immaterial. What matters is that the price starts to rise, and rise quickly, fueled by some short covering and bargain hunting. It then explodes through the resistance represented by the horizontal trendline, and the pattern is completed. Buyers are reluctant to enter at this level because the price has already risen substantially from the low. However, those with a long-term conviction are not deterred. Also, traders who are still struggling to cover their short positions continue to buy. Remember, those who are short are not thinking about the downside risk; they are worried about the unlimited upside catastrophe that will occur if prices continue to rally. Virtually everyone who shorts has a relatively brief time horizon, so the rally coming off a broadening low has the feel of a huge unexpected bull market. There is only one solution: Cover before prices go any higher!

The reason why the rally extends probably arises from the utterly and completely bearish environment at the low. Anyone who was previously long and wanted to get out has already done so. As a result, the security in question is held either by long-term believers or by shorts. One isn't going to sell, and the other literally has to buy.

The psychology at tops is exactly the opposite. Here, the formation starts after a persistent advance, which encourages widespread optimism as the price makes successive new highs during the development of the broadening part of the pattern. Naturally, these progressively higher rallies discourage the shorts. They probably place stops just above resistance, which they judge to be at the previous high. After a couple of attempts at this, they give up. This means that at the final top, there is a very small short position. Large short positions act as support for declines; small ones do not.

Since the pattern develops after a fairly lengthy advance, new buyers are attracted every time the price rises to a new high because there is no feeling of downside risk. Unfortunately, these new players are of much poorer quality than, for example, the type of person who held on through the final throes of a broadening bottom. These participants are attracted by the good news and attractive prospects being painted by the media, brokers, and others. The progressively stronger rallies associated with this pattern also result in careless decisions, since rising prices bail out the greedy and inexperienced buyers who become accustomed to a one-way street. These are indeed LIFO buyers—last in, first out. Consequently, when the price reaches its final peak, holdings are concentrated among uninformed and weak holders. To make matters worse, there is very little cushion in the form of short positions. Prices then begin to decline rather rapidly. Since a quick sell-off of this nature is unexpected, few are able to get out at the beginning. As the price falls through the support at the horizontal trendline, it attracts more selling, but any short covering that would normally have taken place at the support trendline is not available as a result of previous short squeezes. Therefore, prices continue to fall. The ensuing decline is fairly persistent because it takes a long time to liquidate the weak holders who bought the security in the heady days when the top was forming.

Measuring Implications

The measuring objectives for these patterns are taken from the maximum distance between the peak (or the bottom, in the case of accumulation) of the formation and the horizontal line. The distance is then projected from the breakout point in the direction of the breakout.

Right-angled broadening formations can experience retracement or pullback moves just like other patterns. Because they are fairly violent and unstable, these retracements can be extremely sharp und unnerving. Fortunately, they are normally short-lived.

Chart 10-1 shows a right-angled broadening top for Intel. In this case, the downside objective was reached during the breakout move. It is unusual to

Chart 10-1 Intel, daily.

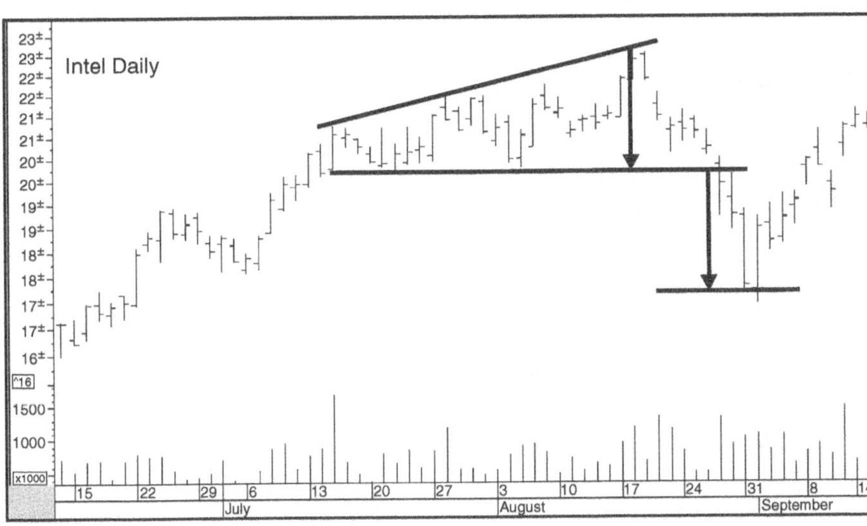

Chart 10-2 Ericsson, daily.

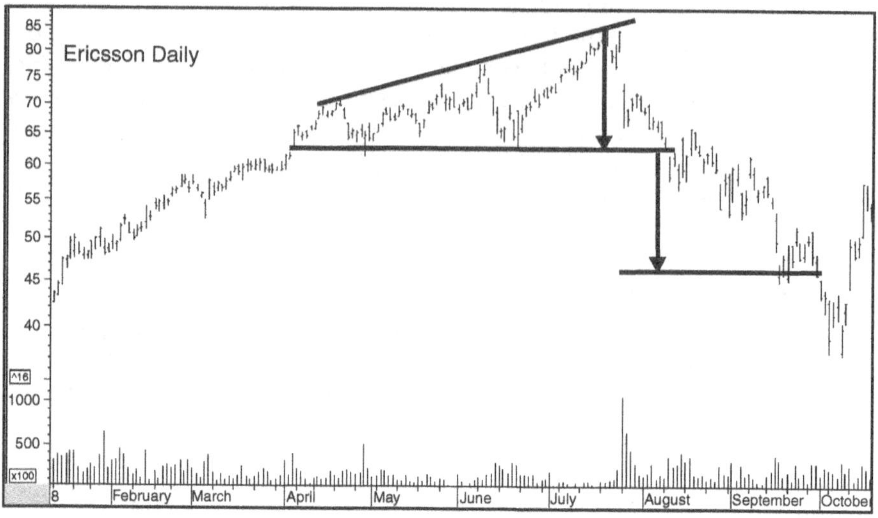

see such a quick reversal after this pattern has been completed, since prices normally drop or rally far more than the indicated objective. In this respect, the top in Ericsson in Chart 10-2 is a more typical example. Note also the retracement move that developed right after the breakdown. This would

Chart 10-3 Aetna, daily.

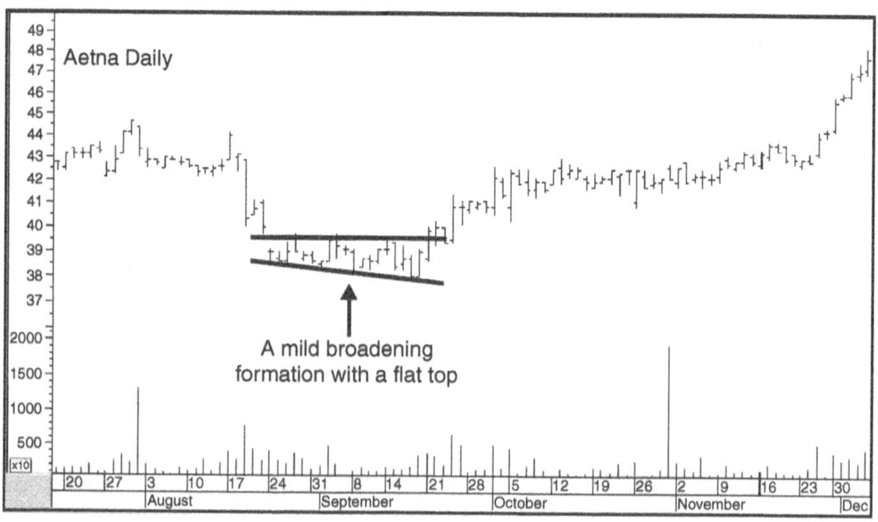

Chart 10-4 U.S. Dollar Index, 1975–1983, monthly.

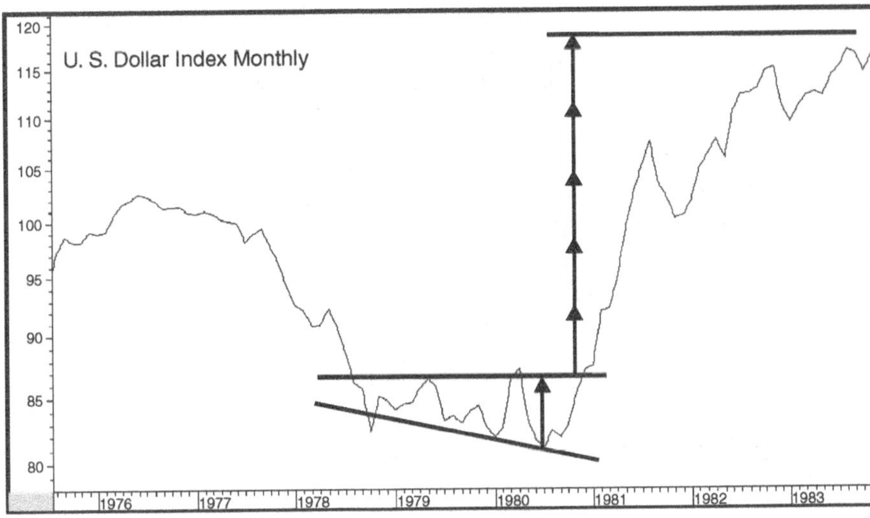

have been quite unnerving to anyone who had gone short on the breakout, since there was no logical *low-risk* resistance level above which to place a stop.

Another example of a right-angled broadening bottom appears in Chart 10-3, for Aetna. This time the broadening or diverging part of the formation is more controlled and not that deep. The breakout and subsequent move are also more constrained.

Generally speaking, the broadening variations pack a great deal more punch than an equivalent-sized head-and-shoulders pattern. Just take a look at Chart 10-4, featuring a monthly close of the Dollar Index. In this instance, the price rallied very quickly to five times the objective.

Where to Draw the Lines

A lot of the time, it is necessary to use a little poetic license when constructing these patterns. Let's consider the accumulation variety in this explanation. What we are really trying to construct is a reverse right-angled triangle, as shown in Fig. 10-5. Note that because of the jagged nature of the price action, it is not possible to join all the rallies and reactions exactly. Often we have to compromise on an approximate area of resistance for the horizontal part of the formation, for example. If you think of the underlying psychology of the pattern as described earlier, everything still fits. The unfortunate thing is that there are rough approximation points rather than black-and-white signals that give us greater confidence in the completion of these patterns.

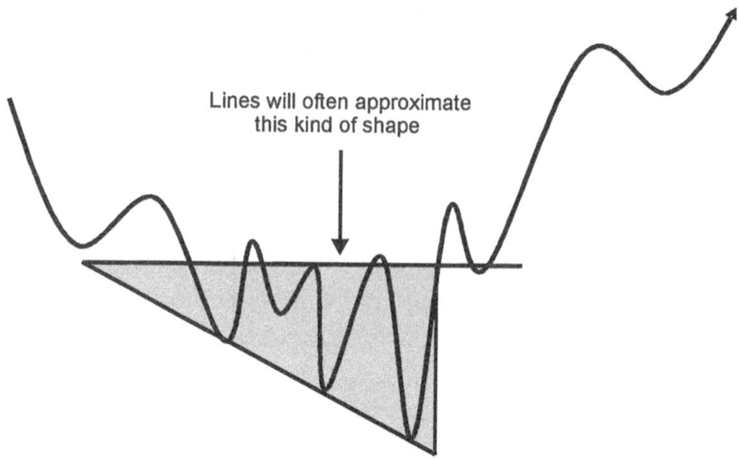

Figure 10-5 Right-angled broadening bottom formation featuring shape.

Charts 10-5 and 10-6 both feature bottoms for the Philadelphia Gold and Silver Share Index. In Chart 10-5, each of the lines is temporarily breached once, but there is no doubt that the formation reflects the broadening concept with a flat top. The initial rally (*A*) in Chart 10-6, on the other hand, presents us with a bit more of a challenge; however, if the angled line is

Chart 10-5 Philadelphia Gold and Silver Share Index, daily.

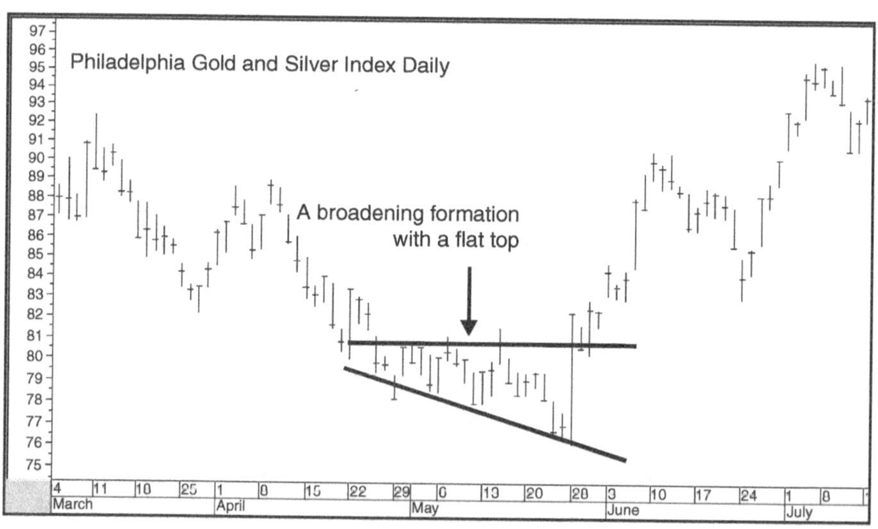

Chart 10-6 Philadelphia Gold and Silver Share Index, daily.

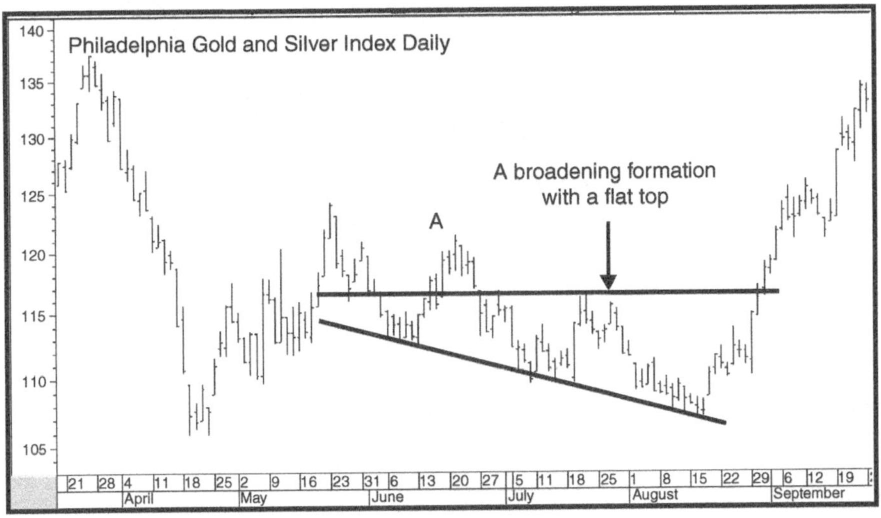

brought back to the apex, it is evident that it forms part of the pattern. Note that the angled or diverging line was approached or touched on numerous occasions and therefore represented substantial support. It also gave the pattern more credibility, so when the breakout through the horizontal trendline did take place, it was followed by a very worthwhile move.

The multiyear bottom in the Dollar Index (Chart 10-4) also presented a small challenge in construction, since both lines were exceeded once. However, there can be no denying the exceptionally strong rally that followed.

Right-Angled Broadening Formations as Consolidation Patterns

These broadening formations can also develop as consolidation patterns, as shown in Fig. 10-6 for an uptrend. Chart 10-7, for the copper price, shows a consolidation right-angled top. The achievement of triple the downside objective indicates that these formations should be respected as much as the tops and bottoms. Note the broadening bottom that formed at the end of the decline. The angle of descent was quite sharp. If you look at the examples in this chapter, you will see that there is a very rough correlation between the angle of the broadening part and the speed of the ensuing move. Thus, the sharper the angle (the greater the volatility), the more likely it is that a precipitous decline or explosive rally will follow.

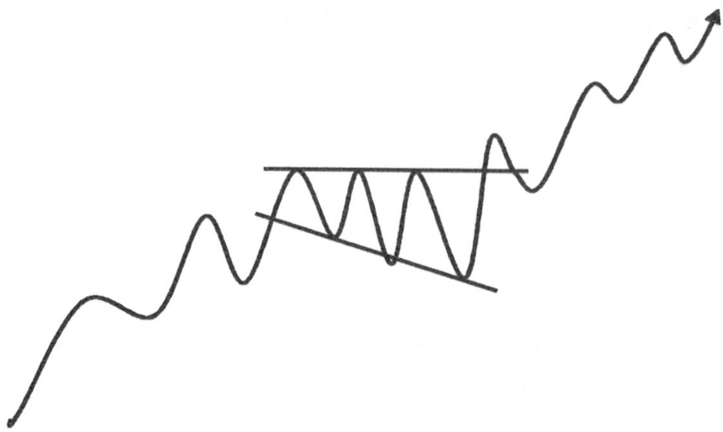

Figure 10-6 Consolidation right-angled broadening bottom formation.

Failed Broadening Formations

Broadening formations occasionally fail to work. Possibilities are shown in Fig. 10-7 and 10-8. Unfortunately, there does not appear to be a reliable or timely point beyond which it is safe to say that the pattern has failed to operate unless a minor peak or trough develops during the breakout

Chart 10-7 Copper, 2000–2002, weekly.

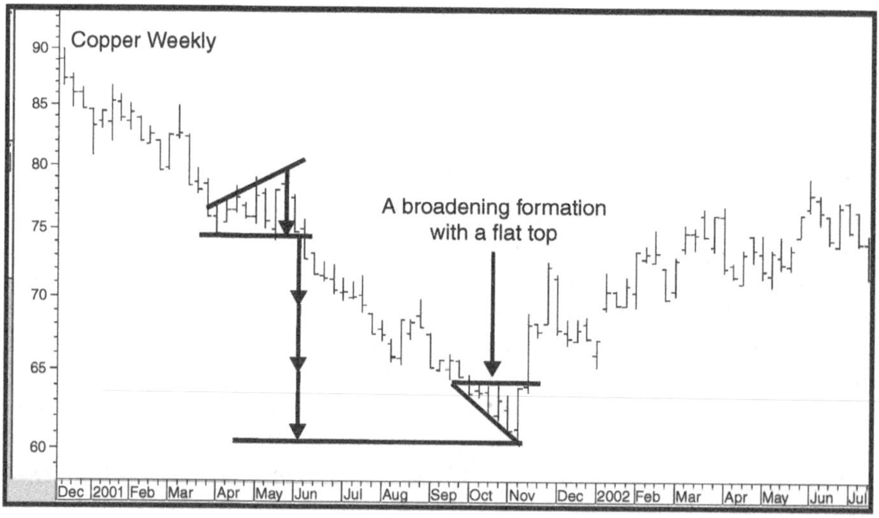

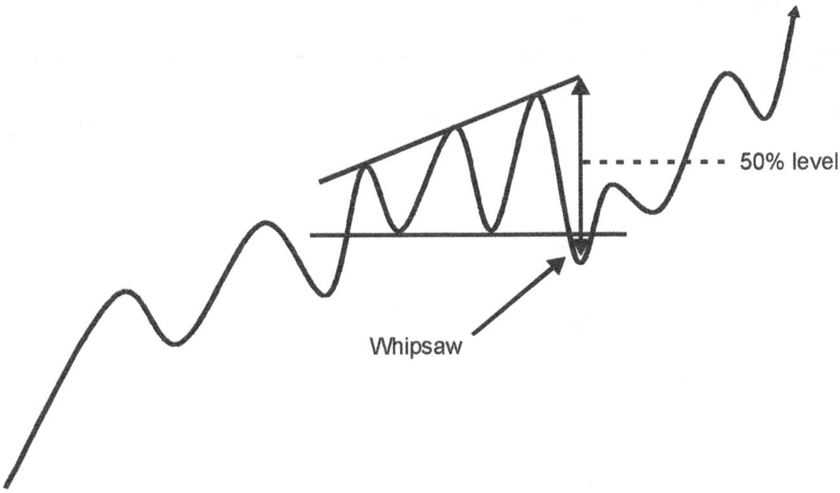

Figure 10-7 Failed right-angled broadening top formation.

decline or rally. The best defense in such cases is to adopt the 50 percent rule, in which the halfway mark of the final reaction (Fig. 10-7) or rally (Fig. 10-8)—i.e., the dashed lines—is used as the give-up point. Some patterns may still work out after the 50 percent plus retracement has taken place, but generally speaking, a breakout that is followed by such a strong

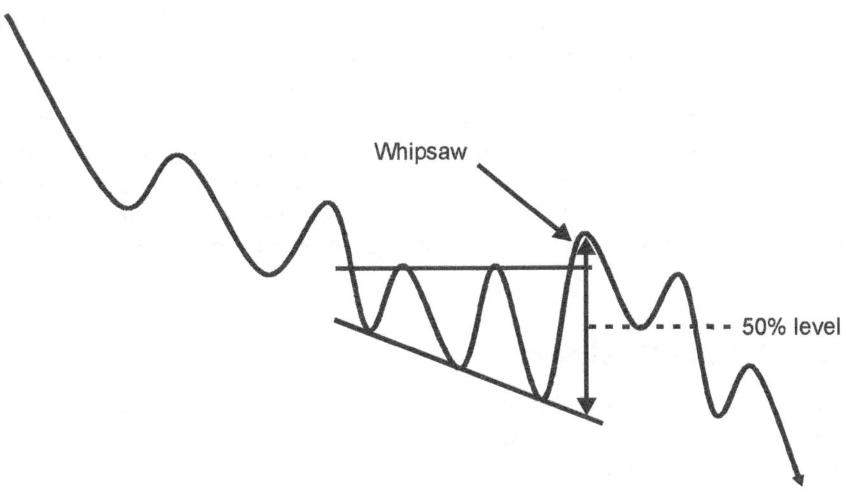

Figure 10-8 Failed right-angled broadening bottom formation.

Chart 10-8 Avery Dennison, 1980–2003, monthly.

countermove is not really in the spirit of the formation and should be treated accordingly.

Chart 10-8, for Avery Dennison, shows a failed orthodox broadening formation. Up to the end of 1990, it looked like a large top. However, by the beginning of 1991, the stock had experienced a sharp rally. Since the end of 1990 also marked a low for the overall market, it is evident that the stock rallied in sympathy with the rest of the list. Generally speaking, it is very difficult for a stock to complete a major top such as this one if the overall market is turning at the same time. Of course, it usually is not possible to gauge a market turn until well after the fact. However, if you can, be wary of patterns that forecast prices continuing to move in the direction of the previous prevailing trend. In this case, it was not until the price experienced a series of rising peaks and troughs as it broke above the dashed trendline that the balance of evidence, as far as this pattern was concerned, moved to the bullish side.

Broadening Wedges

Sometimes the horizontal line in the "right-angled" broadening formation is set at a slight angle, as shown in Figs. 10-9 and 10-10. Note that both lines are actually moving in the same direction. The principles of interpretation for these patterns are the same as for the right-angled variety. The breakout

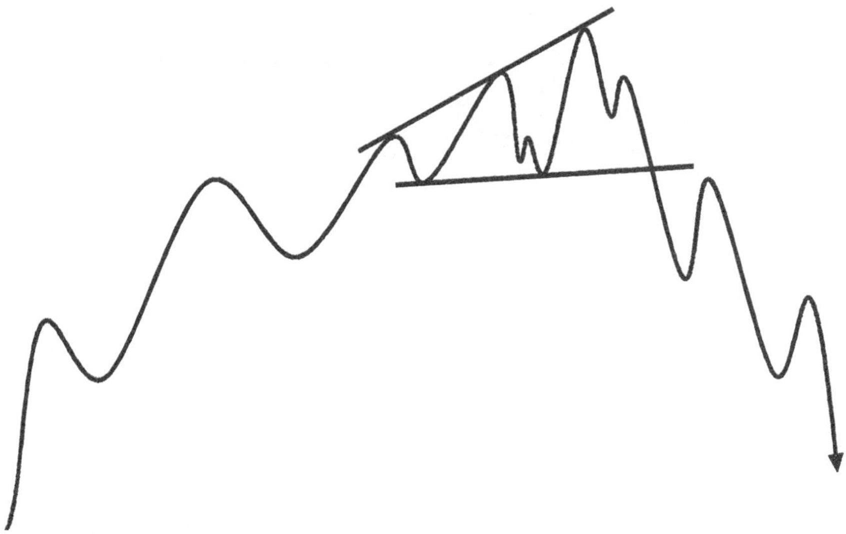

Figure 10-9 Broadening wedge.

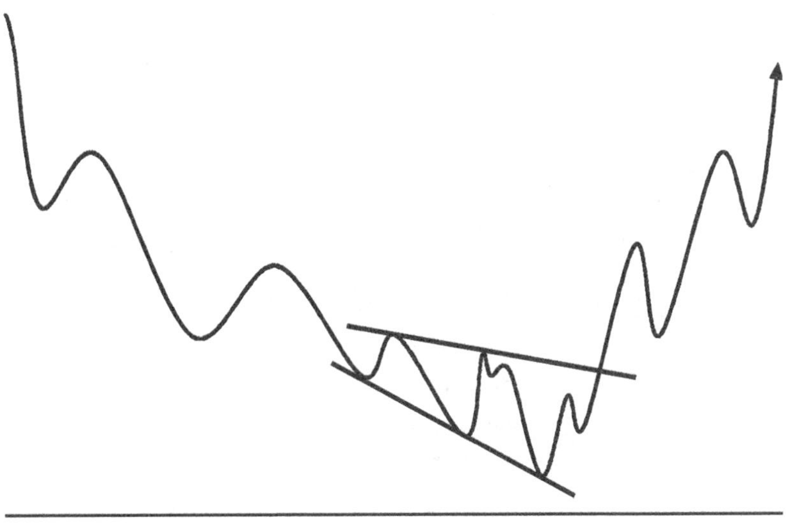

Figure 10-10 Broadening wedge.

Chart 10-9 Advanced Micro, 1987–1988, daily.

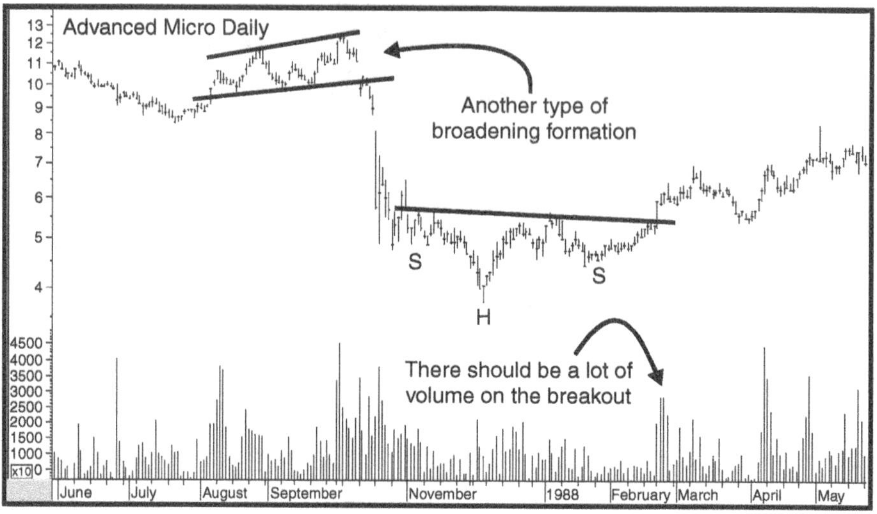

Chart 10-10 Amerisour Bergn, daily.

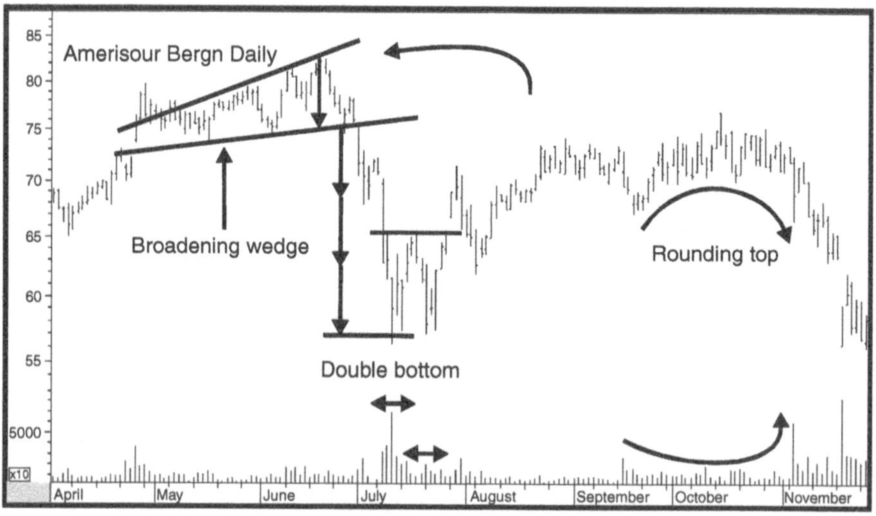

Chart 10-11 ADC, 1980–1990, weekly.

implications are similar in that broadening wedges continue to pack a substantial punch when they are completed.

An example of a top is shown in Chart 10-9, for Advanced Micro. Note the sharp drop that follows the breakdown. Another example is shown in Chart 10-10, for Amerisour Bergn. This time the decline stops at approximately three times the price-objective multiple. Note that there is also a nice double bottom, the completion of which tells us that the decline is over. Finally, a rounding top (see Chapter 11) forms at the very right-hand side of the chart.

The last chart in this chapter, Chart 10-11, shows a broadening wedge for ADC. In this instance, the full potential of a very bearish-looking pattern was not realized. An indication of the abbreviated decline was given when the price held above its secular bull market trendline and broke out from an almost one-year rectangle.

Summary

Orthodox Broadening Tops Quick Review

- *Price characteristics:* A trading range following a substantial bull market that is bounded by two diverging trendlines. Each line should be touched on at least two occasions.
- *Frequency:* Very rare pattern.

Right-Angled Broadening Tops Quick Review

- *Price characteristics:* A trading range following a rally, bounded by two diverging trendlines. The lower line is at or near a right angle to the vertical axis. Each line should be touched on at least two occasions. Poetic license is often required in constructing these lines, since they are not always touched exactly, as is the case with most other patterns.
- *Volume considerations:* Volume is usually higher on the first two peaks. Expanding activity on the downside breakout is particularly bearish.
- *Measuring implications:* The maximum depth of the pattern is projected in the direction of the breakout. This is usually well exceeded by these very bearish formations.
- *Retracement moves:* Since these are very dynamic patterns that are fraught with volatility, retracements are typically short but very sharp.
- *Signs of false breakouts:* Very difficult to spot. A rally above a previous minor high or a retracement in excess of 50 percent of the breakout decline can be used.

Right-Angled Broadening Bottoms Quick Review

- *Price characteristics:* A trading range following a long decline, bounded by two diverging trendlines. The upper line is at or near a right angle to the vertical axis. Each line should be touched on at least two occasions. Poetic license is often required in constructing these lines, since they are not always touched exactly, as in the case with most other patterns.
- *Volume consideration:* Upside breakout is particularly bullish.
- *Measuring implications:* The maximum depth of the pattern is projected in the direction of the breakout. This is usually well exceeded by these very bullish formations.
- *Retracement moves:* Since these are very dynamic patterns that are fraught with volatility, retracements are typically short but very sharp.
- *Signs of false breakouts:* Very difficult to spot. A decline below a previous minor low or a retracement in excess of 50 percent of the breakout rally can be used.

Broadening Wedges Quick Review

- *Price characteristics:* Similar to those of right-angled broadening formations, except that the right-angled line experiences a slight slope and is not drawn at 90 degrees.
- All other characteristics are similar.

11 Miscellaneous Patterns

Diamonds

Diamond patterns really consist of a small orthodox broadening formation preceding a symmetrical triangle. An example is shown in Fig. 11-1. Edwards and Magee describe a diamond as a head and shoulders with a V-shaped neckline, which is what it really is. Figure 11-2 shows the same example as Fig. 11-1, but this time with a head and shoulders type of interpretation. Diamonds tend to develop more at tops than at bottoms and usually require some poetic license to construct. This is because the rally highs and decline lows do not usually match up exactly with the two diverging and converging sets of lines required to construct an idealized pattern. Sometimes they do, but in most cases they do not.

Rectangles, with their two parallel lines of support and resistance, are pretty easy to define. Diamonds, on the other hand, often involve some creativity in their construction. Unless you are careful, this inability to be more specific can lead to problems. To put it another way, it is easy for the novice to visualize a diamond formation that is not actually there.

The measuring requirement works on the same principle as that for other formations. Figure 11-1 shows this principle in action. Chart 11-1, featuring BMC Software, offers an example of a diamond formation that turned out to be a consolidation during an uptrend. Chart 11-2, for the same company, shows another possibility, this time for a top. The dashed line is there to point out the similarities between a diamond and a head-and-shoulders top. This is because the dashed line is really the neckline of a head and shoulders.

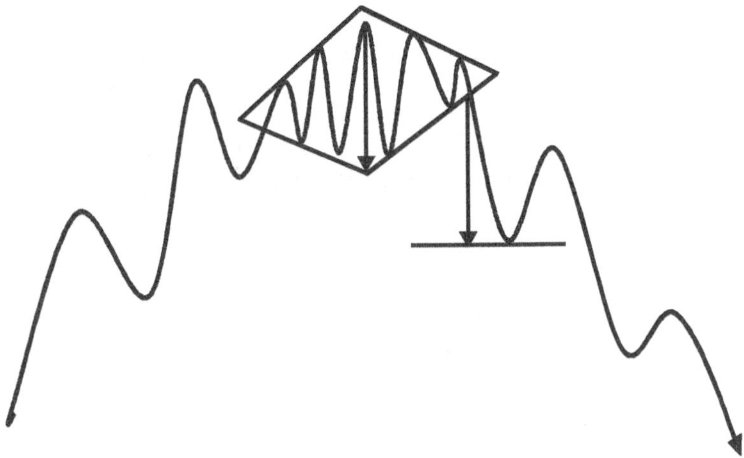

Figure 11-1 Diamond top.

Note that the downside objective from the diamond was achieved on the initial decline.

Generally speaking, diamonds are not a very useful type of pattern. First, they are quite rare—certainly less common than, say, head-and-shoulders formations. Second, a valid diamond formation is very difficult to identify and therefore can result in misleading conclusions.

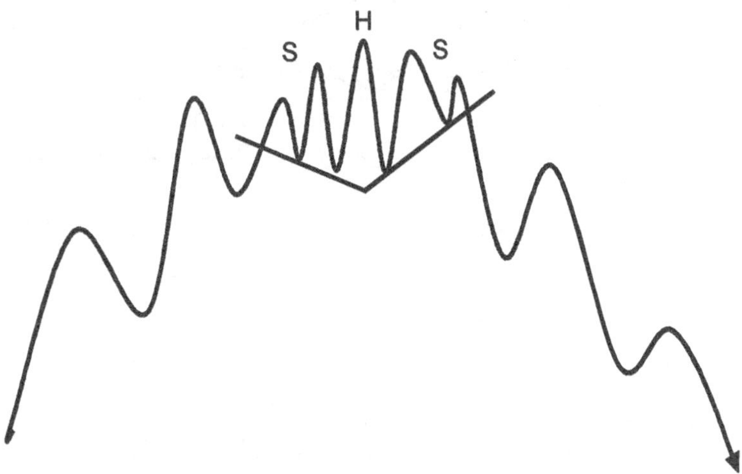

Figure 11-2 Diamond top with "butterfly" head and shoulders.

Chart 11-1 BMC Software, 1995–1996, daily.

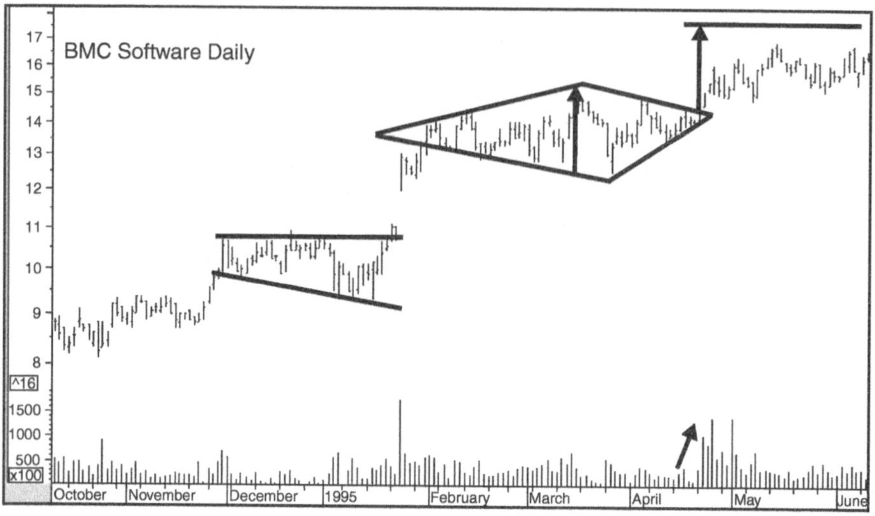

Chart 11-2 BMC Software, 1993–1994, daily.

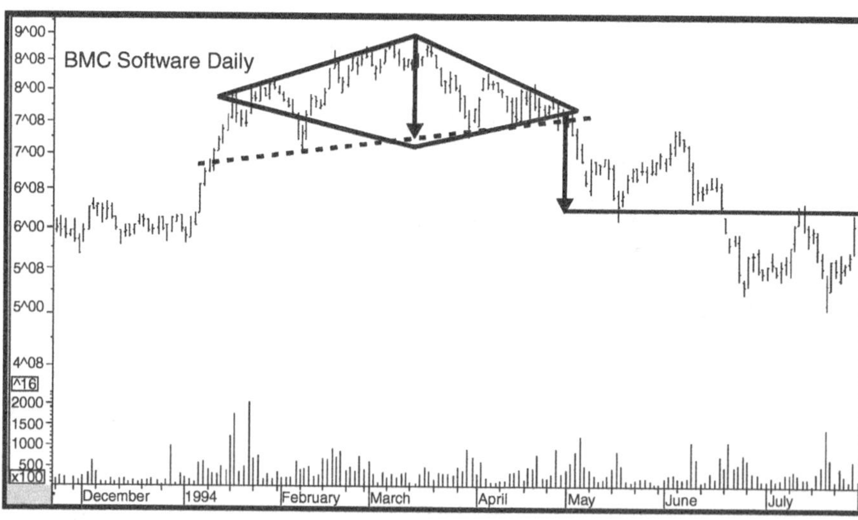

Giant Wedges

The subject of wedges is covered in Chapter 12, on smaller price patterns. These formations generally develop as short-term contra-trend consolidation patterns during the course of an ongoing trend. The giant wedges described here are typically much larger and tend to develop at the end of a trend. Occasionally they encompass the whole trend. Compared to, say, head-and-shoulders formations or triangles, these formations are more of a collector's item. However, when they can be correctly identified, they are often followed by very sharp reversals. A giant wedge consists of two trendlines that converge in the direction of the prevailing trend. They differ from symmetrical triangles in that the trendlines from which a giant wedge is constructed move in the *same* direction. Symmetrical triangles, on the other hand, consist of one rising and one falling line. Examples of giant wedges for both tops and bottoms are featured in Figs. 11-3 and 11-4.

The angle of convergence between the two lines is sometimes very slight. In such situations, there is only a marginal difference between a wedge and a trend channel, where the two lines are approximately parallel. The distinction between these two concepts is not important because a break below the lower line or a rally above the upper one has essentially the same implications in both formations. As a general rule, though, we may observe that the closer the two lines are at the breakout point *relative* to where they were at the start of the pattern, the stronger the signal. This is because the narrowing of the pattern reflects a finer balance between buyers and sellers.

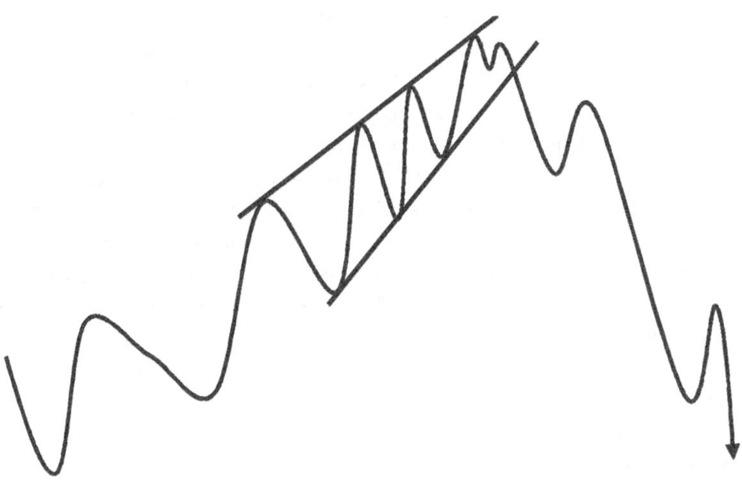

Figure 11-3 Giant wedge top.

Figure 11-4 Giant wedge bottom.

Consequently, the breakout, when it comes, indicates a more decisive victory.

Psychological Rationale

When you think about it, a giant wedge starts off with extremely wide price fluctuations, then gradually reflects a greater balance between buyers and sellers. When the breakout from a falling giant wedge comes, the balance is broken in favor of the previous losers, i.e., the buyers. Short positions have to be quickly unwound simultaneously with new money coming in. As a result, an explosive advance develops. This process is reinforced by the fact that participants become progressively more bearish as the wedge is formed, since they are used to a series of declining peaks and troughs. As the wedge narrows, a sense of calm sets in as the bears anticipate a downside breakout. The lack of volatility therefore lures them into a sense of false security. For technically oriented traders, it is possible to qualify any upside risk by using a break above the upper trendline of the wedge as a stop loss point. Consequently, when the break does come, everybody is a buyer, and this often results in an above-average rally. The same rationale in reverse could be applied to a bearish rising giant wedge in that a break to the downside catches market participants completely by surprise. In many instances the psychology associated with breakouts from these giant patterns resembles that associated with failures of right-angled triangles, discussed in Chapter 9.

Marketplace Examples

Chart 11-3, for KLA Technology, features two giant wedges, both of which embrace complete bear markets. Each primary decline has five waves and ends with an explosive move to the upside. Notice also that the lower lines do not exactly touch the lows. This indicates that it is more imperative to identify the "flavor" of the price action than to try to capture precise turning points. Having said that, we really want the price to touch or come very close to the upper line, since that will be the one that signals a reversal in trend when it has been successfully penetrated. If this line is constructed in a loose manner, it will be necessary to give the price more room during the breakout, since the demarcation point will be less precise. This could lead to unacceptable risk in the event of a false breakout. The example on the left in Chart 11-3 shows that the upper line is penetrated at approximately the same point as the peak of the rally coming off the bottom. Thus we get a giant wedge signal that develops simultaneously with a reversal in the downward peak-and-trough progression. The minimum ultimate price objectives have also been calculated using the classic maximum depth technique. In the case of the example on the left, the projection was pretty accurate so far as the initial rally was concerned.

Chart 11-4 shows a rising giant wedge for Intel. This one took just under six months to form. Note how the ultimate low following the breakdown developed at approximately four times the minimum downside objective.

Chart 11-3 KLA Technology, 1994–1999, daily.

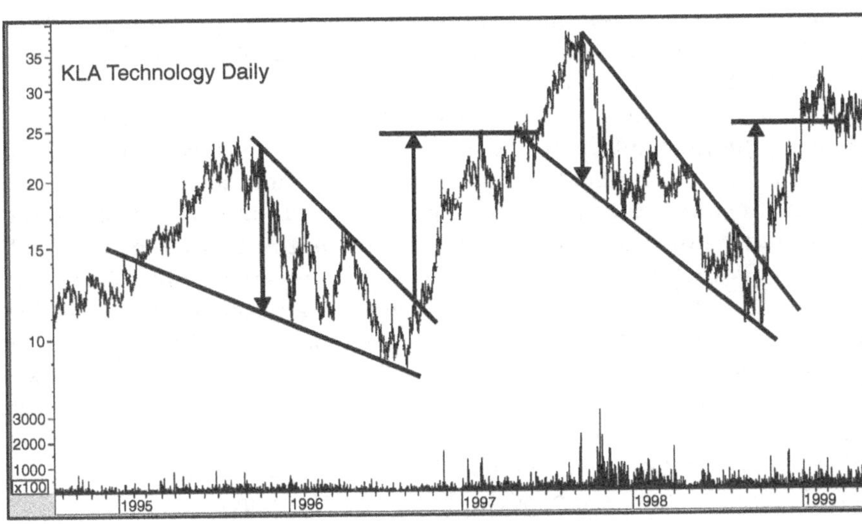

Chart 11-4 Intel, daily.

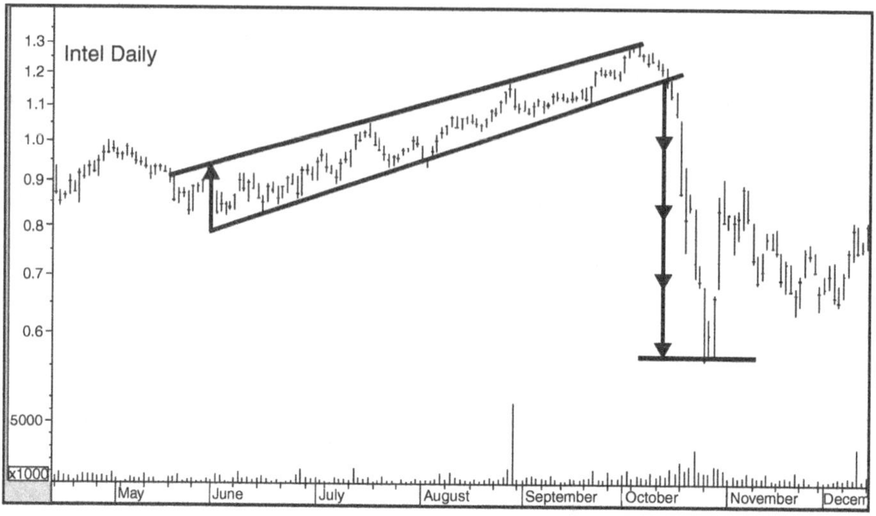

The downside breakout was followed by a pretty sharp decline. This formation is very close to a channel, since the two lines do not converge that much. It also represents an exception to the rule stated earlier that the narrower the lines at the breakout point, the sharper the ensuing decline is likely to be, thereby underlining the fact that technical analysis deals in probabilities rather than certainties.

Biomet, in Chart 11-5, shows another bullish falling giant wedge. In this case, volume picks up noticeably on the upside breakout. Note also that the breakout rally is a reasonably sharp one.

Chart 11-6, also for Biomet, shows an example of a consolidation giant wedge. If the June bottom was interpreted as a head, you could call part of this formation a consolidation inverse head and shoulders. I don't think it really matters what the pattern is called. The fact is, the price broke to the upside and represented a valid signal that the uptrend was to be resumed.

Finally, Sterling Bancorp, in Chart 11-7, provides an example of a bullish giant wedge, where both the single and double multiples of the projection proved to be strong resistance points. If you look very carefully, you can see that the price action between the end of 1999 and the breakout point was really a downward-sloping head-and-shoulders bottom. The upper line forming the wedge represented the neckline. The breakout therefore offered a triple signal: completion of the pattern, a rising series of peaks and troughs, and, of course, a breakout from a giant wedge.

Chart 11-5 Biomet, 1982–1985, daily.

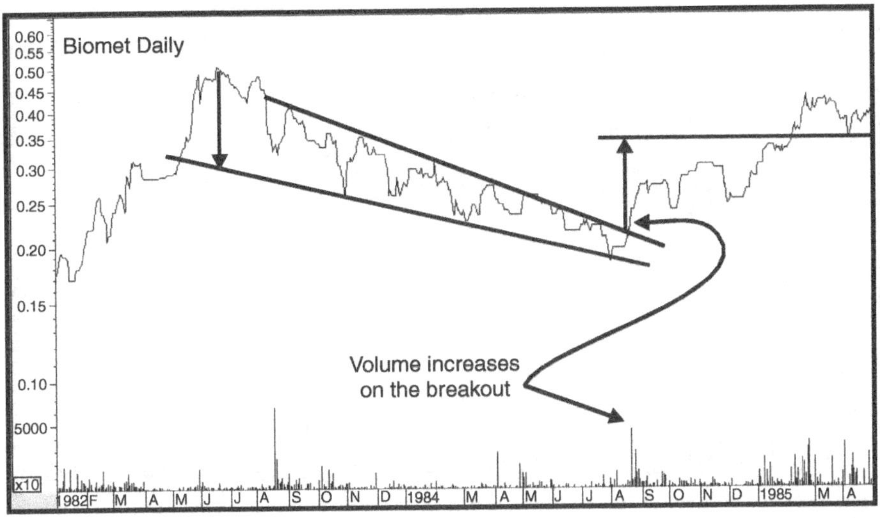

Chart 11-6 Biomet, daily.

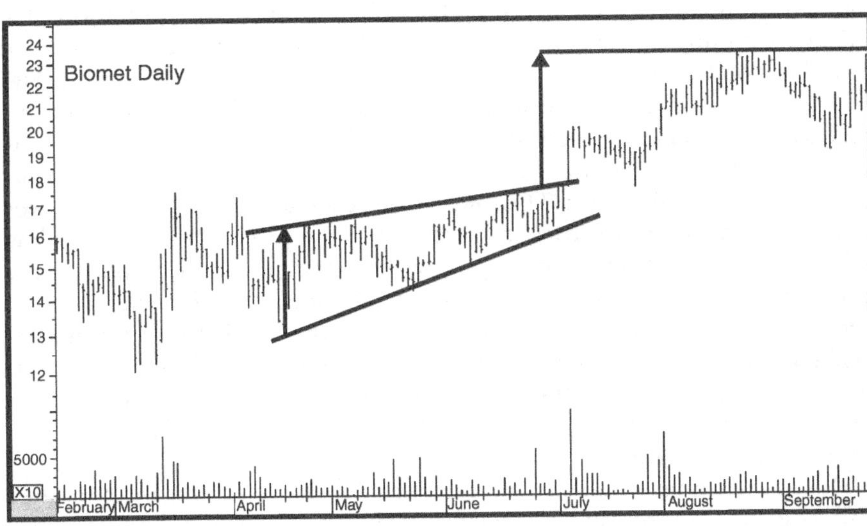

Chart 11-7 Sterling Bancorp, 1996–2001, weekly.

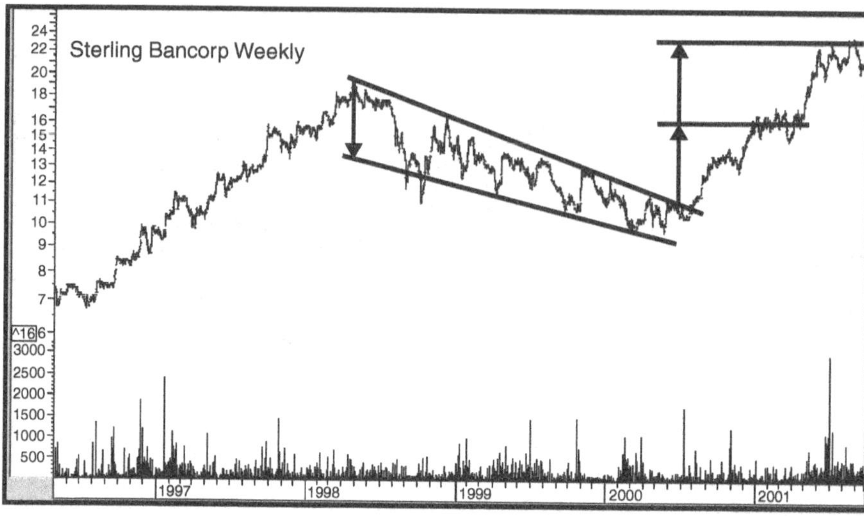

Rounding Bottoms (Saucers) and Tops

Most patterns offer clearly definable breakout points, but rounding patterns do not. When plotted on a chart, they look interesting, but from a practical point of view they are not very useful because they are usually identifiable only well after the fact. Figures 11-5 and 11-6 show the formation of a saucer (rounding bottom) and a rounding top. A saucer pattern occurs at a market bottom, while a rounding top develops at a market peak. A classic saucer is constructed by drawing a circular line, which roughly approximates an elongated or saucer-shaped letter U, under the lows. As the price drifts toward the low point of the saucer, investors lose interest and downward momentum dissipates. This lack of interest is also reflected by the level of activity, which almost dries up at the time the price is reaching its low point. As the formation is completed, both price and volume experience a rapid acceleration to the upside. Occasionally they experience a sideways trading range at higher levels. If that happens, the breakout from this consolidation offers a timely buy signal. Risk can be controlled by placing a stop below the lower level of the trading range. According to Edwards and Magee, rounding bottoms have a tendency to develop in low-cap stocks, where they take many months to complete.

The price action of the rounded top (or *inverted bowl*, as it is sometimes called) is exactly opposite to that of the saucer pattern, but the volume

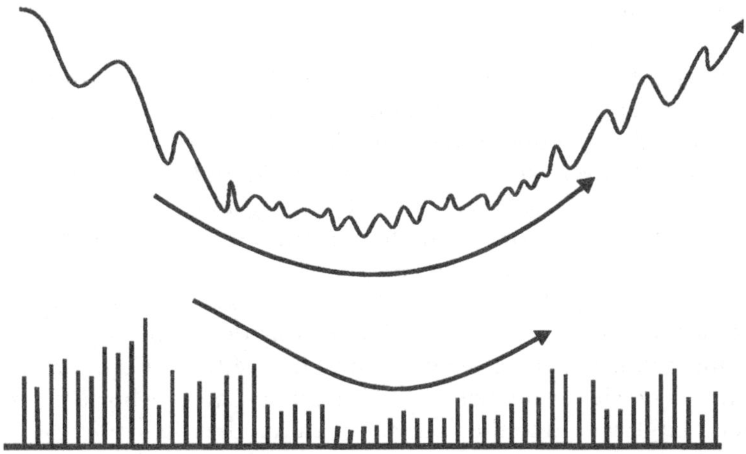

Figure 11-5 Rounding (saucer) bottom.

characteristics are the same. This means that if volume is plotted below the price, it is almost possible to draw a complete circle, as shown in Fig. 11-6. The tip-off about the bearish implications of the rounded top is the fact that volume shrinks as prices reach their highest levels, then expands as they fall. Both these volume characteristics are bearish and are discussed in greater detail in Chapter 5.

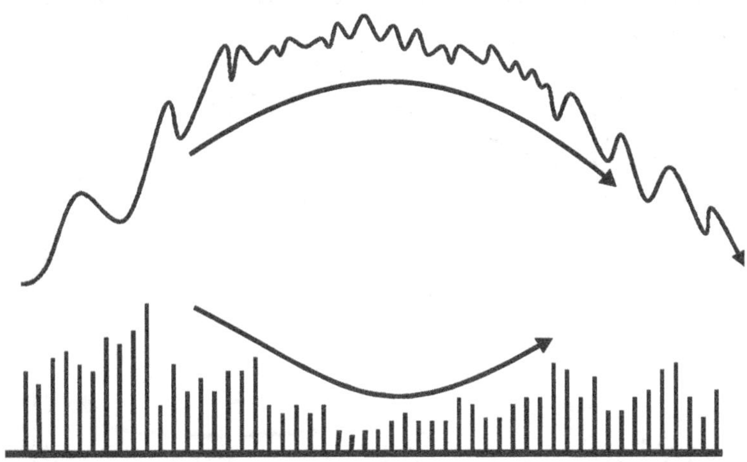

Figure 11-6 Rounding top.

Rounding tops and bottoms are fine examples of a gradual changeover in the demand/supply balance that slowly picks up momentum in the direction opposite to that of the previous trend. Quite clearly, it is difficult to obtain breakout points for these patterns, since they develop slowly and do not offer any clear support or resistance levels on which to establish a potential benchmark. Even so, it is worth trying to identify them, since they are usually followed by substantial moves. Rounding and saucer formations can also be observed as consolidation phenomena and can take as little as three weeks or as much as several years to complete.

Chart 11-8, for Bed Bath & Beyond, shows a classic rounding top. Volume shrinks as the high is being reached and expands greatly as prices accelerate on the downside. Once again, the problem with a pattern such as this is that there is no clearly definable benchmark beyond which you can say that the trend has reversed to the downside, or even that the pattern is invalid.

Chart 11-9, for German American, shows another rounding top. This time the volume configuration is not consistent, but the pattern works anyway. The price tried to trace out a small rounding bottom but failed. This was fairly obvious once it had slipped below the support trendline.

Synovus Financial (Chart 11-10) traces out a sort of consolidation saucer pattern between September 1993 and April 1995. The two converging lines show that the pattern could also be categorized as a right-angled triangle. Once again, it does not matter what the pattern is called. It's the fact that it worked that's important. As you can see, the battle between buyers and

Chart 11-8 Bed Bath & Beyond, daily.

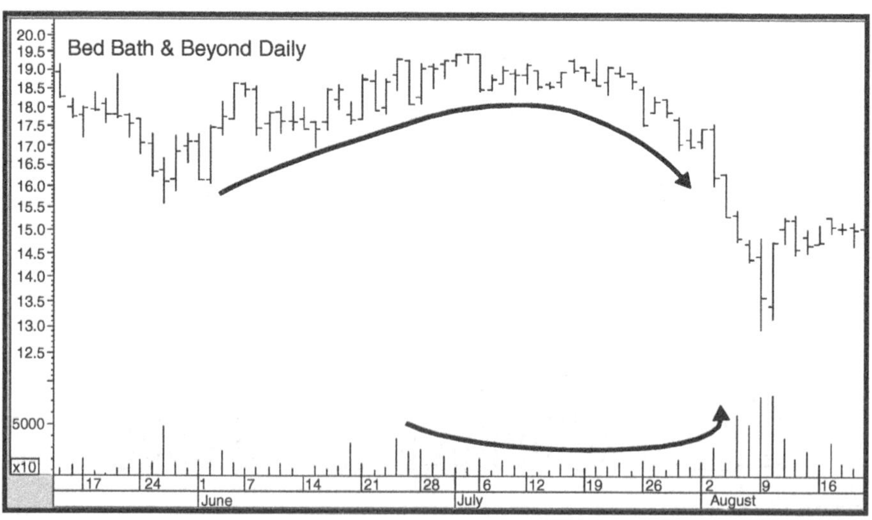

Chart 11-9 German American, 1995–1999, weekly.

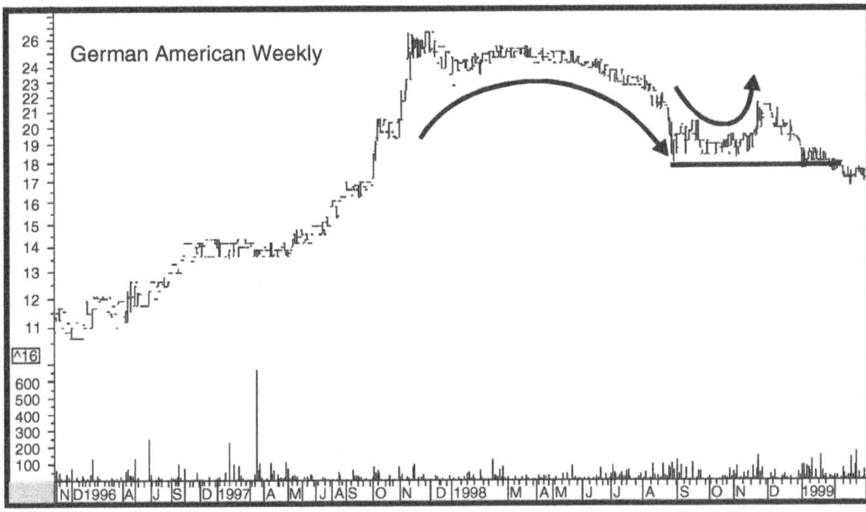

sellers gradually moved in favor of the buyers as prices moved higher. This idea of a saucer bottom being a consolidation formation is an important one, since it reflects a long period of controlled profit taking as buyers gradually gain sufficient confidence to enable them to push prices higher.

Chart 11-10 Synovus Financial, 1992–1995, weekly.

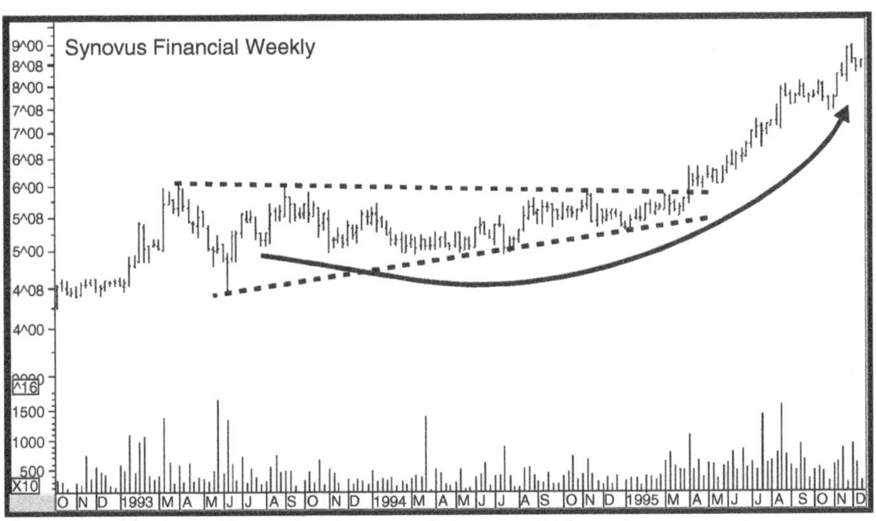

Chart 11-11 Sterling Financial, 1994–1998, weekly.

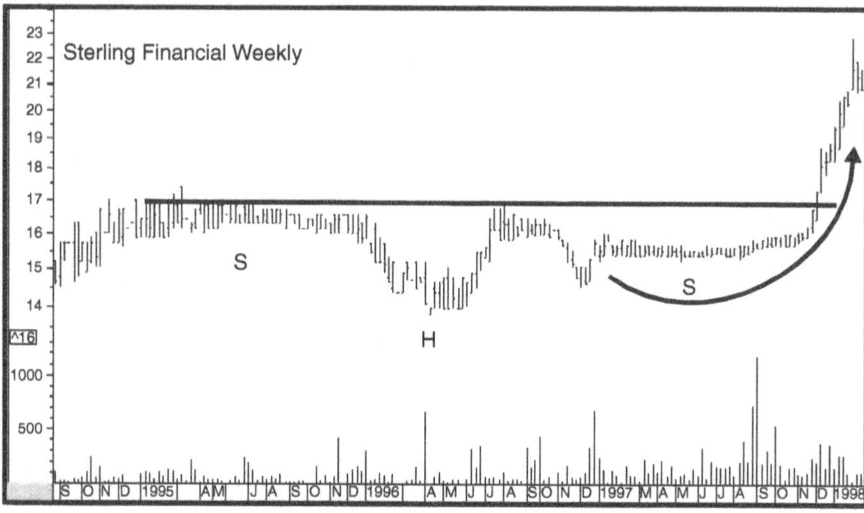

Sterling Financial (Chart 11-11) also offers an example of a consolidation rounding bottom. In this case, the saucerlike pattern is really the right shoulder of a consolidation reverse head-and-shoulders formation.

Chart 11-12, for Wachovia, really features a consolidation reverse head and shoulders. However, the rounding nature of the pattern cannot be

Chart 11-12 Wachovia, 1992–1995, weekly.

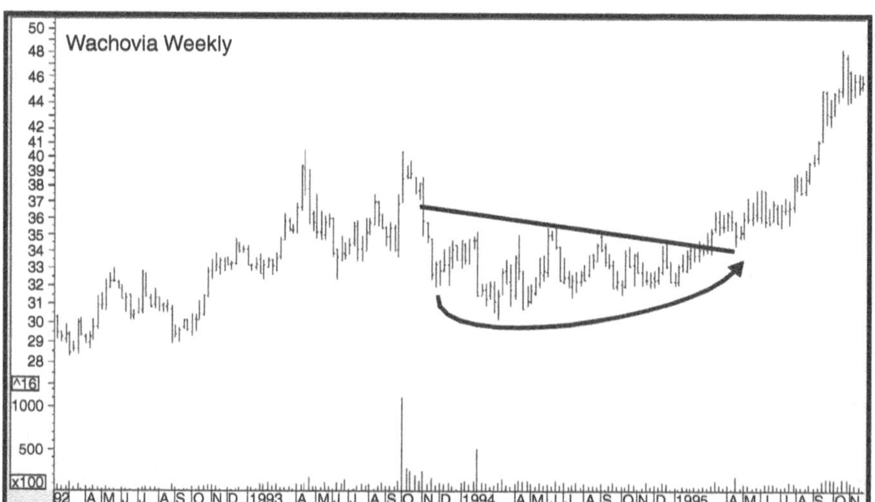

denied. Thus it is possible to extend the idea of a saucer bottom or rounding top to embrace a circular line that reflects a series of gradually rising bottoms or peaks, depending on the nature of the situation. The concept of a gradual reversal in which buyers gain the upper hand is still the same.

Cup with a Handle

This pattern has been made famous by William O'Neil and is described in his *How to Make Money in Stocks* (McGraw-Hill, 1995). The pattern develops as a bullish one, usually in a continuation format. Figure 11-7 shows that it takes the form of a big U (the cup), followed by a rally and a small rounding platform (the handle). The left-hand part of the cup usually marks the culmination of a strong rally and is often associated with heavy volume. The bottom of the cup can take the form of a rounding bottom, as in Fig. 11-7, or some ranging action, as in Fig. 11-8. The next step in the development of this pattern is a rally on expanding volume, followed by a period of profit taking in which both volume and price go quiet. Finally, the handle is completed and prices explode to the upside.

If this pattern is going to fail, the signal to look for is a break below the lower part of the handle. If the price eventually breaks above the upper level of the handle, the situation will again become bullish. Any breakouts that develop with shrinking volume, though, should be regarded with suspicion.

Chart 11-13 shows a cup with a handle formation for ADC Telecom. The breakout above the handle is not accompanied by much of an expansion

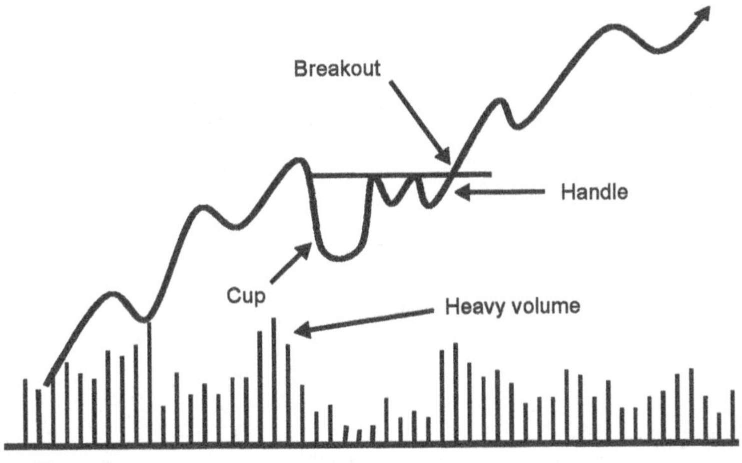

Figure 11-7 Cup with a handle.

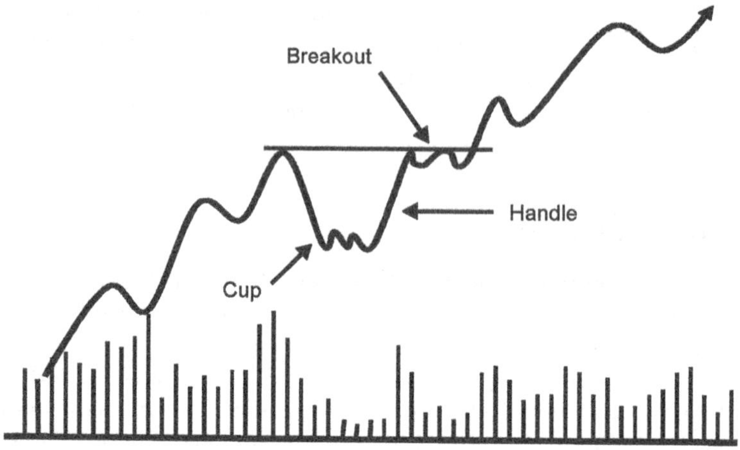

Figure 11-8 Cup with a handle.

in volume, but the price certainly doesn't suffer. The cup in Chart 11-14, for Adelphia, is more of a V formation. William O'Neil clearly states that the cup should be rounded, so that a good solid base can be formed for later price advances. In this case the base is really formed during the handle

Chart 11-13 ADC Telecom, 1990–1991, daily.

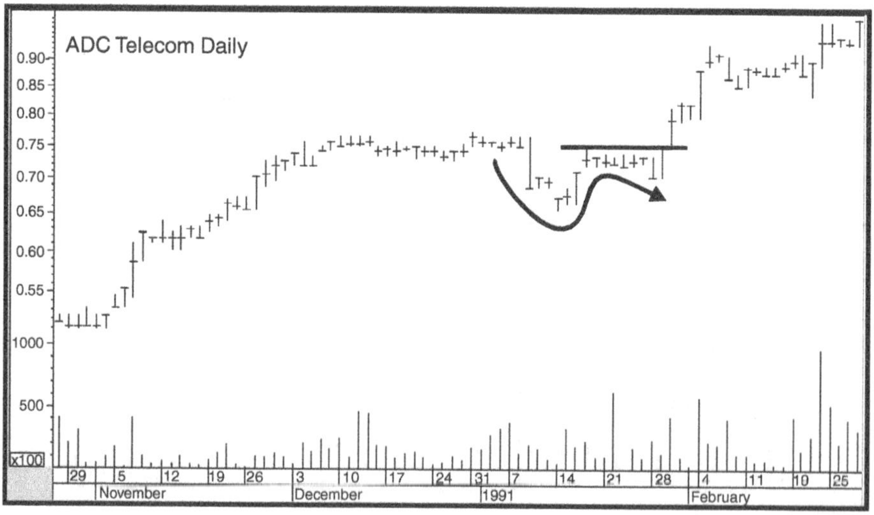

Chart 11-14 Adelphia, daily.

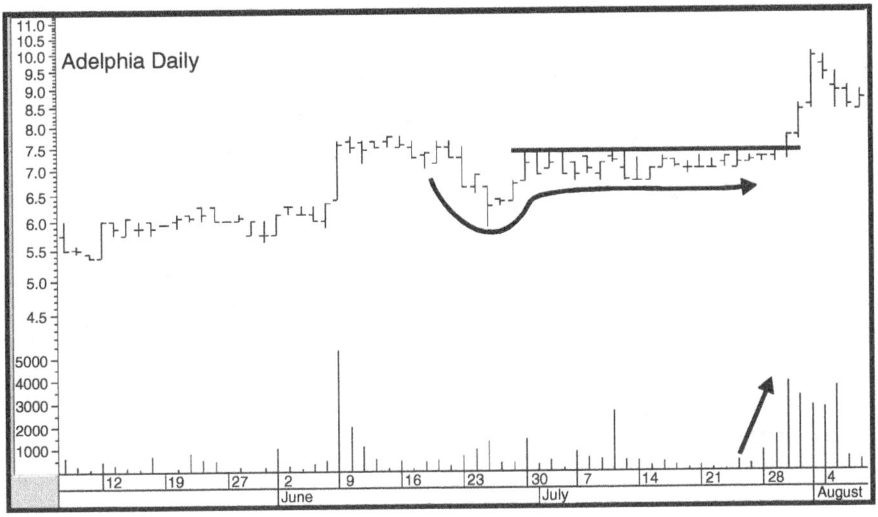

stage on very quiet action. When this extended period of profit taking is completed, both price and volume explode to the upside.

Shakeout Tops and Bottoms

A shakeout pattern is really a variation of other patterns. At tops, it represents a consolidation following a strong rally and a subsequent sharp reaction. I call these patterns shakeouts because the price is shaken out of the consolidation on its way to its bear market low. Since these formations are really part of a much larger reversal process, they are typically followed by an eventual decline that is greater than would be suggested by the size or depth of the pattern. Figure 11-9 shows an example in which a head-and-shoulders consolidation is the straw that breaks the camel's back. In Fig. 11-10, the shakeout pattern is a rectangle. These formations also appear at bottoms, for which an example is shown in Fig. 11-11. Here we can see that an abrupt reversal is subsequently followed by a trading range. The ranging action in this example is a rectangle, but it could just as easily have been a reverse head and shoulders or a triangle. Like tops, these bottoming formations are often followed by advances that last much longer and take prices much further than would be expected from their size and depth. Examples of these patterns in action are shown in Charts 11-15 and 11-16. Note also in

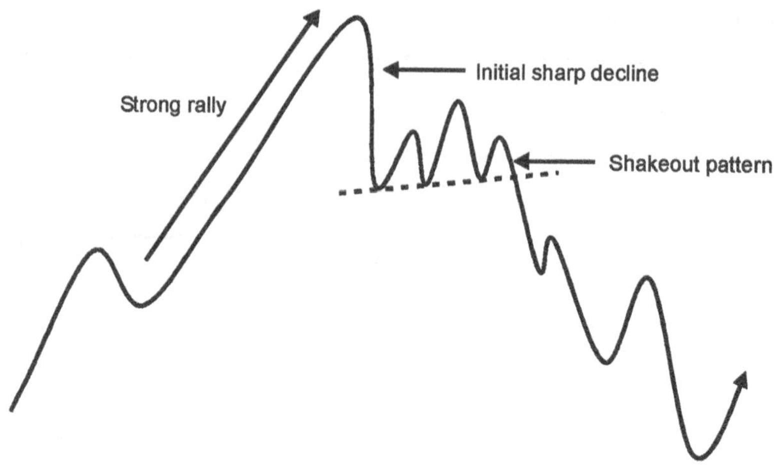

Figure 11-9 Shakeout top.

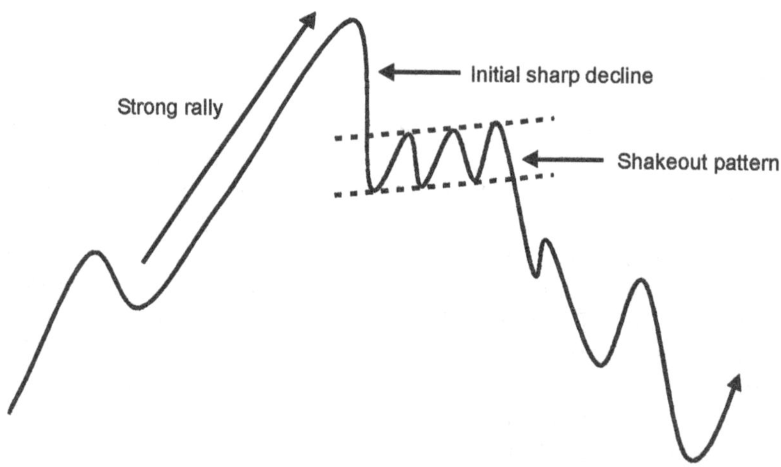

Figure 11-10 Shakeout top.

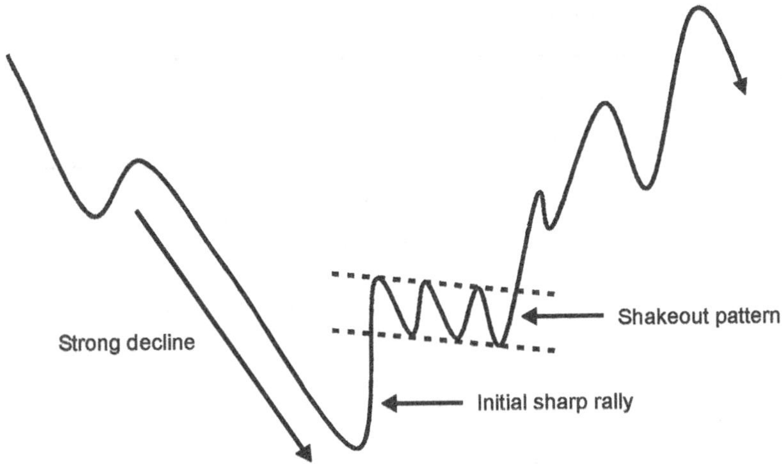

Figure 11-11 Shakeout bottom.

Chart 11-15 AMR, 1996–2002, weekly.

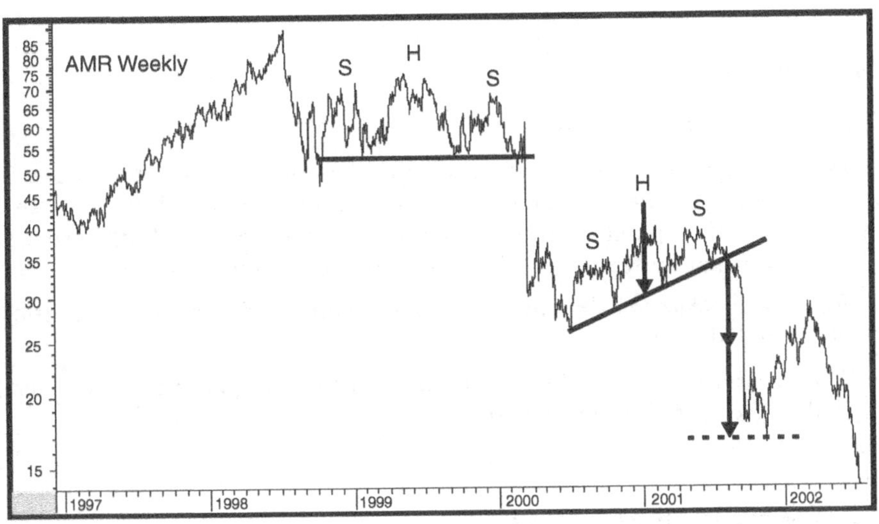

Chart 11-16 Yahoo, 1998–1999, daily.

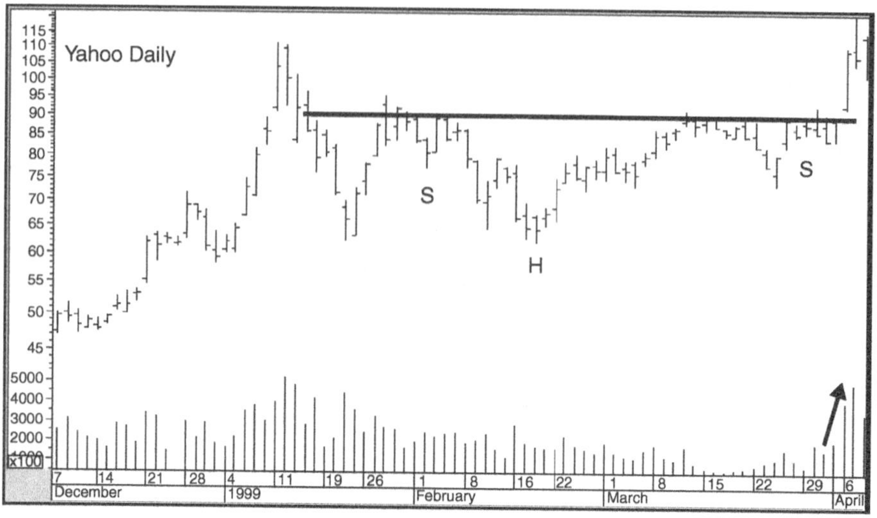

Chart 11-15 the completion of an upward sloping consolidation head and shoulders, where the initial low developed at exactly twice the measuring objective.

Summary

Diamonds Quick Review

- *Price characteristics:* A pattern that consists of an orthodox broadening formation followed by a symmetrical triangle; when combined, the two patterns have the appearance of a diamond. They develop as both reversal and continuation formations but are difficult to identify correctly.
- *Volume considerations:* Expanding volume on an upside breakout is particularly bullish.
- *Measuring implications:* The maximum depth of the pattern is projected in the direction of the breakout.

Giant Wedges Quick Review

- *Price characteristics:* Price action bounded by two converging trendlines moving in the same direction. These are large formations that take at least four to six months to form. Occasionally they envelop a complete primary trend.

- *Measuring implications:* The maximum depth of the pattern is projected in the direction of the breakout.
- *Special characteristics:* Giant wedges are unusual, but when they are completed, they are often followed by explosive long-term moves.

Rounding Tops and Bottoms Quick Review

- *Price characteristics:* Rounding bottoms consist of a saucerlike pattern, where the price slowly but surely gathers substantial upside momentum. Tops consist of a slow rounding process that gradually picks up momentum on the downside.
- *Volume characteristics:* Both tops and bottoms are accompanied by a saucerlike pattern in volume.
- *Special characteristics:* Because of the rounding nature of these patterns, there are no definable benchmarks beyond which a clear-cut breakout can be identified.

Cup with a Handle Quick Review

- *Price characteristics:* A cup-shaped consolidation pattern that forms after a rally. The handle forms part of the way up the right-hand side of the cup and is a period of profit taking. The pattern is completed with a break above the handle.
- *Volume considerations:* The two key ingredients are low volume during the formation of the handle and expanding volume on the upside breakout.
- *How to recognize failures:* Shrinking volume on the breakout or a price pullback below the lower level of the handle.

PART III
Short-Term Patterns

12 Smaller Patterns and Gaps

Most of the patterns discussed in this chapter are relatively small and are of the continuation variety. They reflect controlled profit taking during an advance and controlled digestion of losses during a decline. Flags, pennants, and wedges all consist of a trading range bounded by two trendlines sloping in a similar direction. Typically the slope develops in a countercyclical way. This means that bullish patterns will slope in a downward direction and develop in a bull market. Similarly, bearish patterns will slope in an upward direction and form during primary bear moves.

Flags

A *flag* is a quiet parallel trading range accompanied by a trend of declining volume. Such formations usually interrupt a sharp, almost vertical price rise or decline. As the name implies, this formation looks like a flag on the chart. Since they are continuation patterns, flag completions involve a breakout in the same direction as the previous trend. Examples for both an up and a down market are shown in Fig. 12-1. Essentially, flags take the form of a narrow trading range in which the rally peaks and reaction lows can be connected by two parallel lines. The lines move in a countercyclical direction. In the case of a rising market, the flag is usually formed with a slight downtrend, but in a falling market it has a slight upward bias. Flags may also be horizontal, in which case they are really a special form of rectangle.

The classic texts tell us that in a rising market, an idealized pattern usually separates two halves of an almost vertical rise. Volume is normally

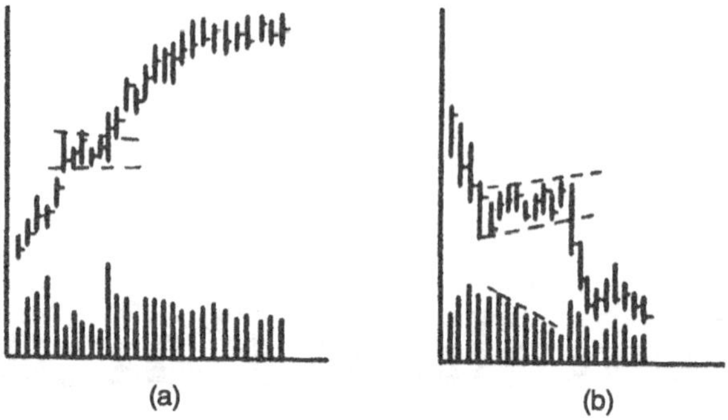

Figure 12-1 Flags.

extremely heavy just before the point at which the flag formation begins. As the formation develops, activity gradually contracts to almost nothing. It then explodes as the price works its way out of the completed formation. On the daily charts, flags can form in a period as short as five days or take as long as three to five weeks. It is also true to say that flags are starting to become an endangered species. Searching for examples for this book, especially a pause within a vertical rise or fall, became quite a challenge. Whenever a concept becomes this difficult to demonstrate with real-live examples, I start to question its usefulness.

The formation of the flag in a downtrend is also accompanied by declining volume. This type of flag represents a trading range with an upward bias in price, so the volume implication is bearish in nature, i.e., rising price with declining volume. When the price violates the lower part of the flag, the sharp slide continues and volume tends to pick up. However, it need not be explosive, because prices can just as easily fall due to a lack of bids as they can because of strong selling pressure. Only upside breakouts in bull markets require heavy volume.

It is important to make sure that the price and volume characteristics agree. For example, in a bull trend, the price may consolidate following a sharp rise, in what *appears* to be a flag formation, but volume may fail to contract appreciably. In such cases, great care should be taken before coming to a bullish conclusion, since the price may well react on the downside. A flag that takes more than four weeks to develop should also be treated with caution. This is because these formations are, by definition, temporary interruptions of a sharp uptrend. A period in excess of four weeks represents an unduly long time for profit taking, and therefore has a lower probability of being a true flag.

Flags are usually reliable patterns from a forecasting point of view. Not only is the direction of the ultimate breakout indicated, but the ensuing move is usually well worthwhile from a trading point of view. More to the point, it is usually pretty fast.

Measuring Implications

Technical folklore has it that flags form at the halfway point of a move. Once the breakout has taken place, a useful method for setting a price objective is to estimate the size of the move in the period immediately before the flag formation began. This distance is then projected in the direction of the breakout from the breakout point. In technical jargon, flags are said to fly at half-mast, i.e., they are halfway up the move. Since they take a relatively short period to develop, flags do not show up on weekly or monthly charts.

Chart 12-1, for American Electric Power, features a bearish flag that developed during a major down move. Note that the volume level shrank to almost nothing as the flag was being formed. It then exploded on the day of the breakout. Unfortunately, there was no easy way to get out because of the huge gap. Normally we would expect to see at least some trading within the flag trading range on the day of the breakout.

Chart 12-2, for Adelphia, shows two flags. The first, on the left, took barely a week to form. Volume started to pick up on the day of the breakout, and by the second day expanded to a very heavy level. The second one developed in a period of slightly more than three weeks. In this case, the volume

Chart 12-1 American Electric Power, 1995–1996, daily.

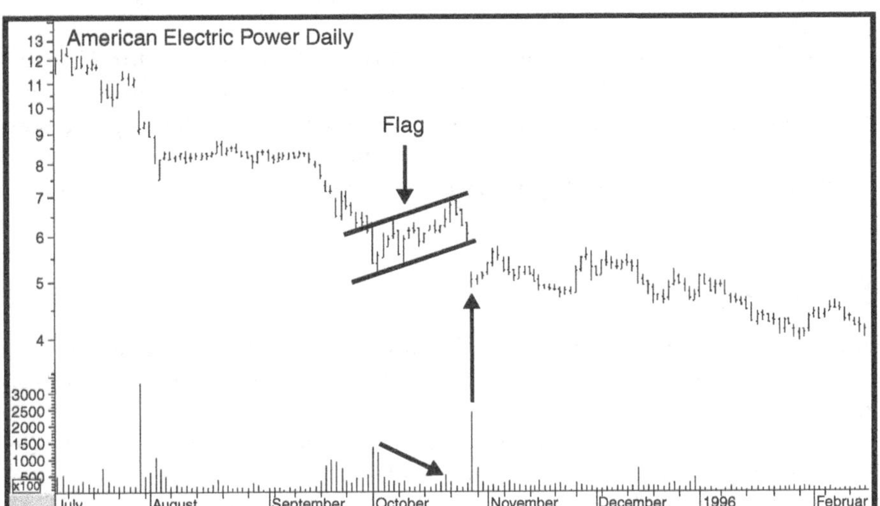

Chart 12-2 Adelphia, daily.

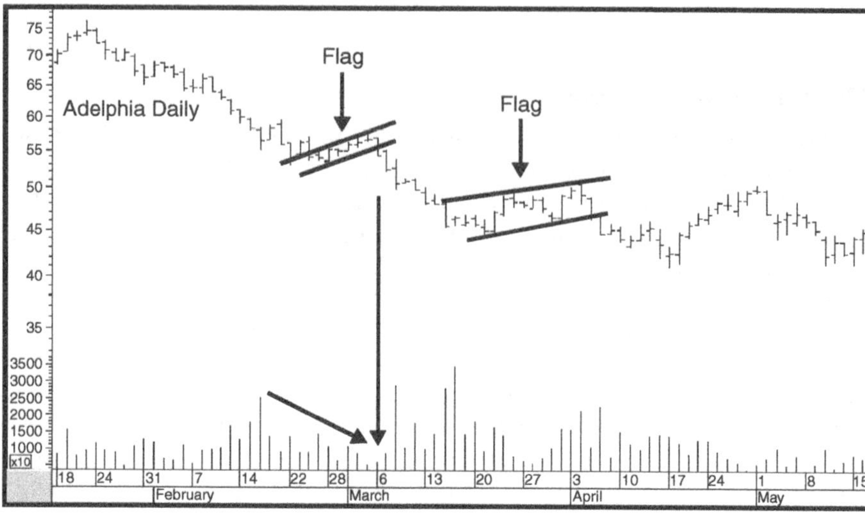

pattern differed from the classic pattern, since it expanded during the formation of the late March–early April rally. Normally we expect activity to gradually shrink as the pattern is being formed. Only on the breakout is it expected to expand.

Chart 12-3, for Adaptec, features a bullish flag. Once again volume increased substantially on the upside breakout but did not experience the normal noticeable profit-taking shrinkage during the formation of the pattern.

Finally, Chart 12-4 shows another example of a bullish flag for Adaptec. Here there is a very definite contrast between the shrinking volume during the flag's formation and the expanding activity at its completion. Note also that while the measuring implication was more than achieved, the actual level of the projection did serve as a resistance level for a few sessions.

Pennants

A pennant develops under exactly the same circumstances as a flag and has similar characteristics. The difference is that this type of consolidation formation is constructed from two converging trendlines, as shown in Fig. 12-2. In a sense, the flag corresponds to a rectangle and the pennant to a triangle, because a pennant is, in effect, a very *small* triangle. The difference between the two formations is that a triangle consists of a trading range bound by

Chart 12-3 Adaptec, daily.

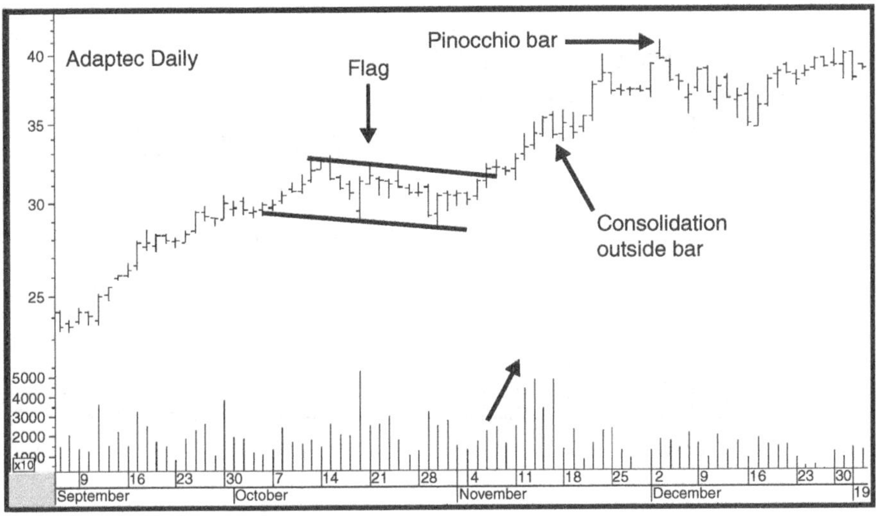

two converging trendlines that point in *different* directions. In the case of a pennant, the two trendlines both move in the *same* direction. If anything, *volume* tends to contract even more during the formation of a pennant than during that of a flag. In every other way, however, pennants are identical to

Chart 12-4 Adaptec, daily.

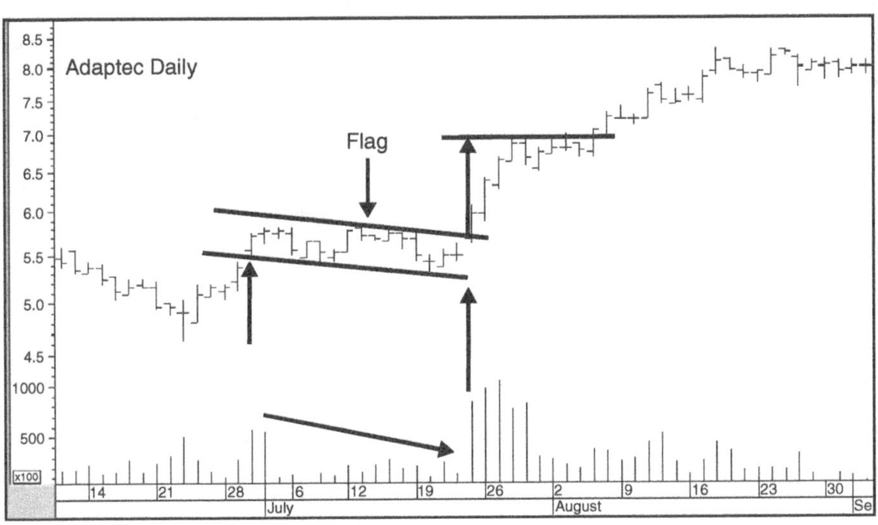

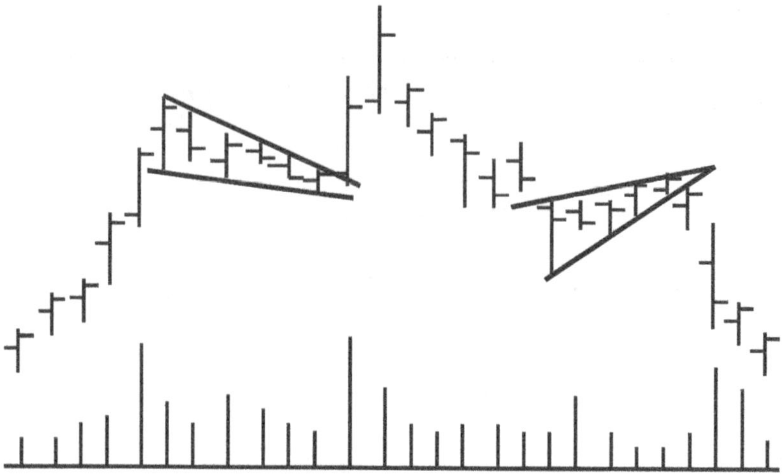

Figure 12-2 Pennants.

flags: measuring implication, time taken to develop, volume characteristics, and so on.

Chart 12-5, featuring Adobe, displays a two-week pennant. In this case, the trading range is extremely tight and volume contracts until the breakout.

Chart 12-5 Adobe, daily.

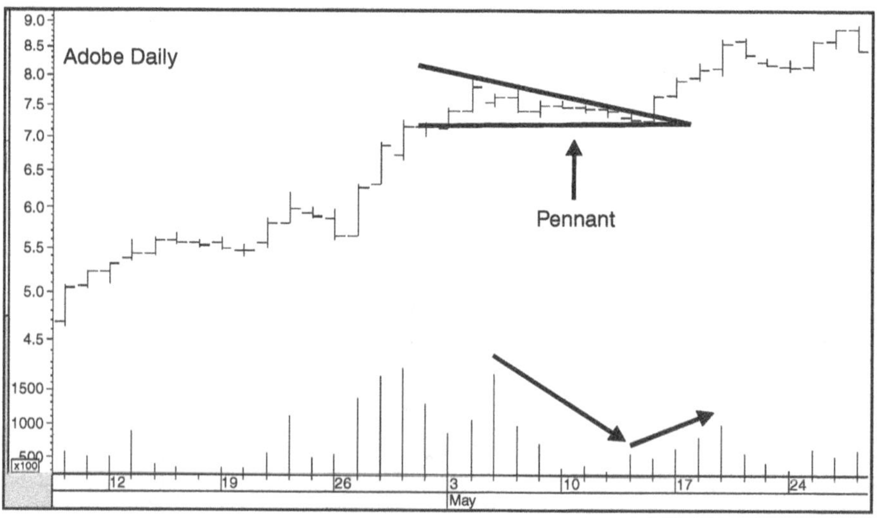

Chart 12-6 Vitesse, daily.

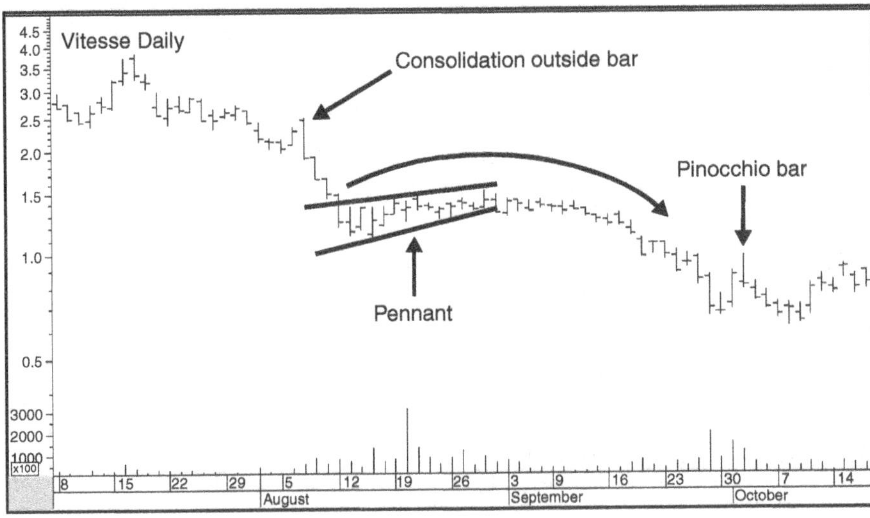

The next example of a pennant is provided by Vitesse in Chart 12-6. It forms part of a rounding top consolidation formation. In this instance, volume contracts during the formation of the pennant but does not expand on the gentle downside breakout.

Chart 12-7, for Veritas Software, shows a different type of formation. In this case we see a triangle formation with converging lines moving in the same direction. However, the two converging lines in a classic pennant should be moving in a *contra-trend* direction, but in this instance, they are both rising during an ongoing rising trend instead of falling. The underlying psychology, though, is still the same, since the battle between buyers and sellers gradually becomes more balanced as the trading range and accompanying activity contract. Finally one side scores a decisive victory as prices break to the upside on very heavy volume. There is also a flag that developed in the May–June period.

Chart 12-8, also for Veritas, shows a more classic bullish pennant. Note how the price explodes during the breakout. Later on we see a flag, and finally a consolidation triangle. The contrast between the pennant, with its two trendlines pointing in the same direction, and the triangle, where the trendlines point in different directions, is also apparent from this chart.

USA Networks (Chart 12-9) presents us with another flag. It also features a pennant; once again the two lines slope in the same direction as the main trend, as in Chart 12-7. In this case the "pennant" has a slight upward slope, so it is not a classic example, which should, of course, point in a contra-trend

Chart 12-7 Veritas Software, daily.

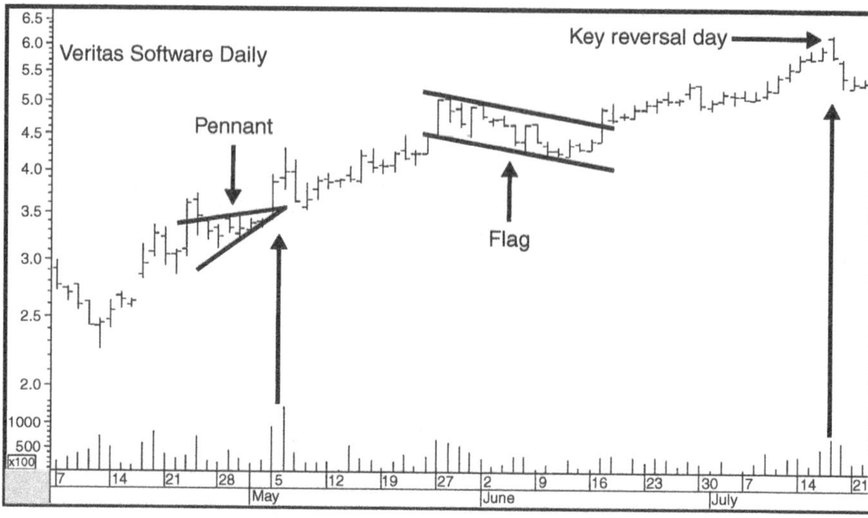

Chart 12-8 Veritas Software, 1994–1995, daily.

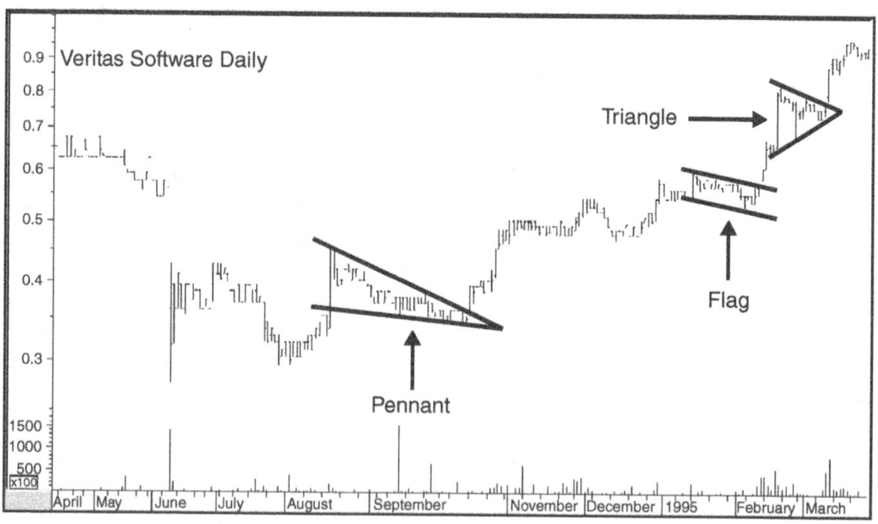

Chart 12-9 USA Networks, daily.

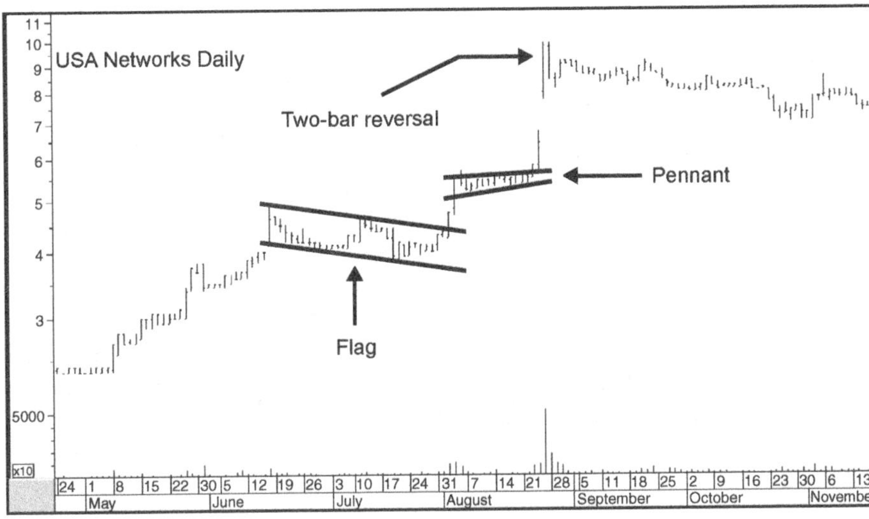

direction. However, whenever we see this kind of a situation in which a very tight and narrowing balance between buyers and sellers edges up, the upside breakout is often explosive. This example was no exception to that rule. Volume explodes on the breakout, and the rally is capped with a two-bar reversal (see Chapter 16 for an explanation).

Wedges

A wedge is very similar to a triangle in that two converging lines can be constructed from a series of peaks and troughs, as shown in Fig. 12-3, but, whereas a triangle consists of one rising and one falling line, or one rising or falling line and one horizontal line, the converging lines in a wedge both move in the *same* direction, as for a pennant. A falling wedge represents a temporary interruption of a rising trend, and a rising wedge is a temporary interruption of a falling trend. It is normal for volume to contract during the formation of both types of wedge. Since they can take anywhere from two to eight weeks to complete, wedges sometimes occur on weekly charts, but they are too brief to appear on monthly charts unless they are giant wedges, as described in Chapter 11.

Rising wedges are fairly common as bear market rallies. Following their completion, prices usually break very sharply, especially if volume picks up noticeably on the downside.

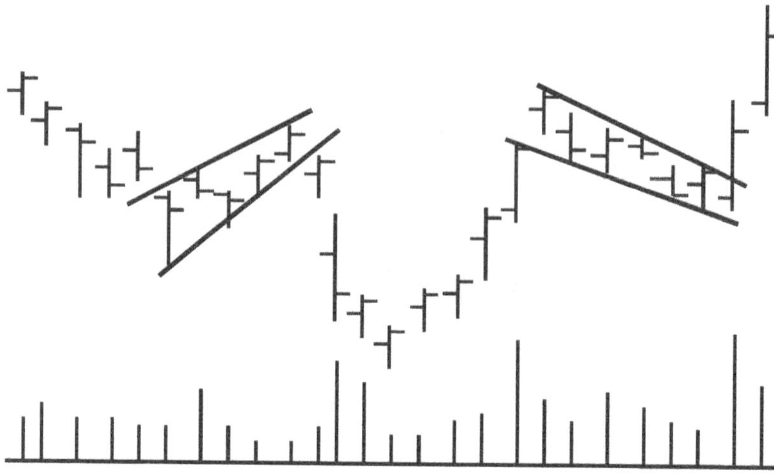

Figure 12-3 Wedges.

The wedge and the pennant are very similar, since they both consist of converging trendlines that move in a contra-trend direction. The difference is that the breakout point of a pennant forms very close to or even right at the apex. The two projected lines for the wedge, on the other hand, would meet way in the future—in many instances, literally off the charts. Figure 12-4 puts

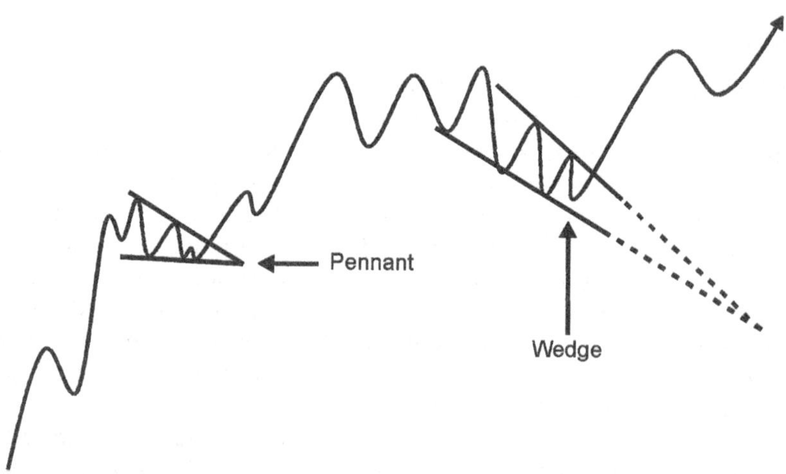

Figure 12-4 A pennant vs. a wedge.

Chart 12-10 Yahoo, daily.

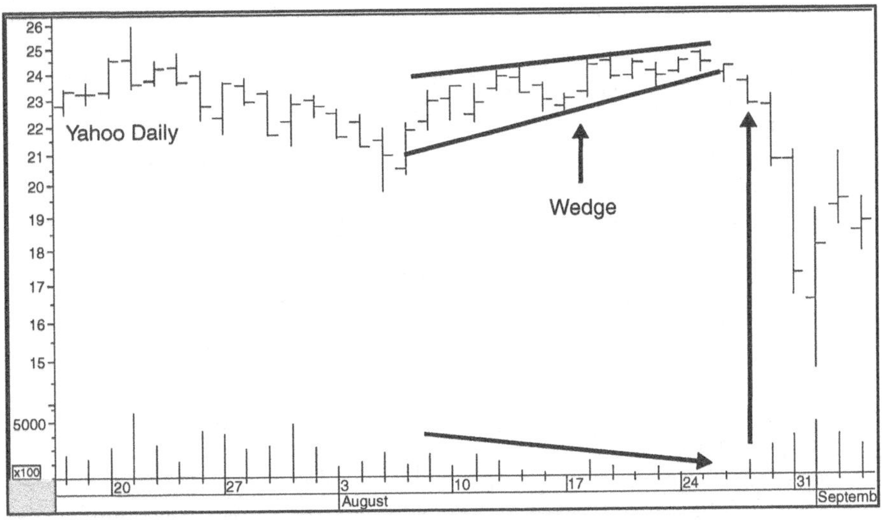

us straight on this one, as you can see that the projected dashed lines for the wedge meet well after the breakout point. Compare this to the pennant, which is much more akin to a triangle. Sometimes the difference between these two formations is hard to judge. For example, the pattern in Chart 12-6 was called a pennant, but it could arguably have been called a wedge. If anything, wedges generally appear to take longer to form than pennants.

Chart 12-10, for Yahoo, shows a rising wedge that develops after the first decline. You can see that the lines are not even close to a meeting point as the breakout develops. Note also that volume picks up the day of the breakout. During a bear trend, it is possible for prices to fall of their own weight. However, when activity picks up, it indicates that the sellers are motivated and makes the whole situation that much more bearish.

Chart 12-11, featuring Vitesse, offers a good example of a small rising wedge in terms of price action. Volume characteristics, though, are not typical, since there is no contraction as the wedge is forming and no expansion on the breakout. This example shows that it is possible for wedges, like other formations, to develop without the classic volume configuration. In most situations, though, the gradual shrinking of activity as the pattern forms and the explosion on the breakout usually result in a more powerful move. Also, when volume contracts during the formative period, it offers a valuable clue that the pattern will turn out to be valid.

Chart 12-11 Vitesse, daily.

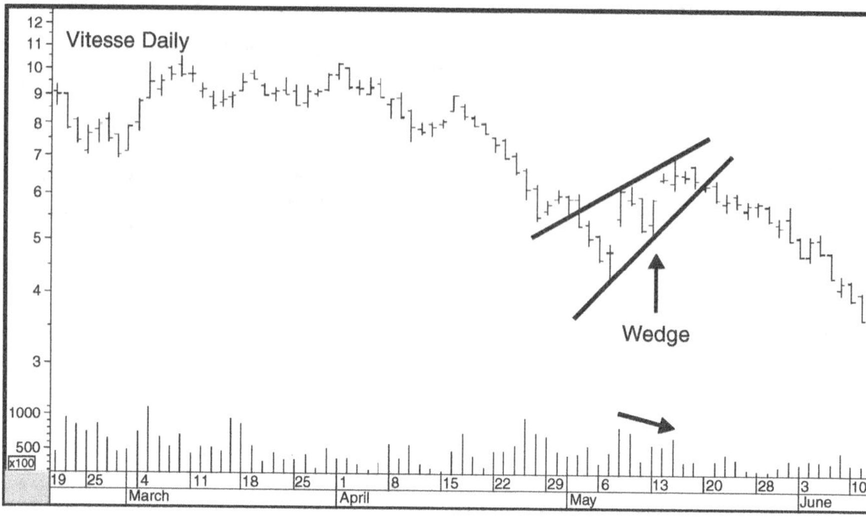

Gaps

A gap occurs when the lowest price in a specific trading period is above the highest level in the previous trading period or when the highest price in a specific trading period is below the lowest price in the previous trading period (Fig. 12-5). On a daily bar chart, the trading period would be a day; on a weekly chart, a week; and so forth.

Gaps do not appear on line or close-only charts, but are confined to bar charts. They are represented by an empty vertical space between one trading period and another, and they reflect highly emotional periods. They most commonly form in overnight trading as good or bad news is digested by the market. Daily gaps are far more common than weekly ones because a gap on a weekly chart can occur only between Friday's and Monday's price range; i.e., it has a 1-in-5 chance relative to a daily chart. Monthly gaps are even rarer, since such "holes" on the chart can develop only between monthly price ranges. The most typical place to find gaps on intraday charts is at the open. I will have more to say on that point later.

The Importance of Gaps as Emotional Points

The places where gaps start and terminate are potential pivotal points on a chart because they represent high emotion. If you have an argument with

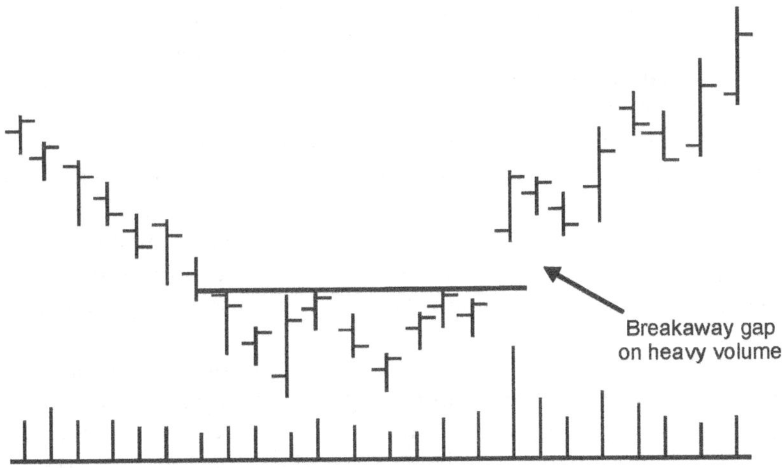

Figure 12-5 Breakaway gap.

a friend and one of you shouts really loudly at one point, you will both tend to remember that particular moment because it represents an emotional extreme. The same principle can be applied to technical analysis, since charts are really a reflection of psychological attitudes. This means that when the price returns to the area of previous gaps, the upper and lower points of those gaps have the potential to become important support and resistance levels where short-term trends may be temporarily reversed.

The Psychological Rationale for Why Most Gaps Are Eventually Filled

A gap is said to be closed, or "filled," when the price reverses and retraces the whole range of the gap. On daily charts this process sometimes takes a few days, and at other times takes a few weeks or months. In some rare instances the process is *never* completed.

There is an old saying that the market abhors a vacuum, which means that most gaps are eventually filled. It is certainly true that almost all eventually are, but exceptions definitely occur. The underlying psychology is akin to, say, a husband and wife having a spirited disagreement. Tempers on both sides rise to a pretty high level as accusations and counteraccusations escalate. Then, almost invariably, after some time has elapsed and as one or both parties put pride aside and see the error of their ways, the relationship returns to normal, and an attempt is made to close the emotional gap in the relationship.

Since it can take months or even years to fill a gap, trading strategies should not be implemented solely on the assumption that a gap will be filled in the immediate future. *In the majority of cases, some attempt is made to fill the gap*, but quite often a partial filling on a subsequent test is sufficient. Most gaps are closed because they are emotional affairs and reflect strong psychological motivation on the part of traders—we could say excess fear or greed, depending on the direction of the trend. Decisions to buy or sell *at any cost* are not objective ones. This means that people are likely to have second thoughts when things have cooled down. The second thoughts, in this case, are represented by the closing of the gap, or at least a good attempt at closing it.

Gaps should be treated with respect, but their importance should not be overemphasized. Those that occur during the formation of a price pattern, known as *common gaps* or *area gaps*, are usually closed fairly quickly and do not have much technical significance. Another insignificant type of gap results from a stock's going ex-dividend.

There are three other types of gaps that we need to examine. These are breakaway, runaway, and exhaustion gaps.

Breakaway Gaps

A breakaway gap is created when a price breaks out of a price pattern or some other trading range configuration. An example of an upside breakaway gap is shown in Fig. 12-5. Generally speaking, the presence of the gap emphasizes the bullishness or bearishness of the breakout, depending on which direction it takes. Even so, it is still important for an upside breakout to be accompanied by a relatively high level of volume. Gap breakouts that occur on the downside are not required to be accompanied by heavy volume.

It should not be concluded that every gap breakout will be legitimate because the "sure things" do not exist in technical analysis. However, a gap that is associated with a breakout is more likely to be valid than one that is not so associated. If a gap does turn out to be a whipsaw, then this will usually be signaled sooner rather than later. Since most gaps are filled, and there is rarely a reason why you *have* to buy, it could be argued that it is better to wait for the price to at least attempt to fill the gap before committing money. After all, if you miss out because the price does not experience a retracement, all you have lost is an opportunity. Certainly you will experience some frustration, but at least you will not have lost any capital. With markets there is *always* another opportunity. If you have the patience and the discipline to wait for that opportunity, you will be much better off in the long run. The problem, especially in this day and age of shrinking time spans, is that most of us are not blessed with the patience and discipline that we so badly require for successful trading and investing.

The danger of buying on a gap breakout is that you will get caught up in the emotions of the crowd. This buy-at-any-cost mentality is likely to result in discouragement when the price inevitably retraces to the downside as emotions calm down. The advice is not that you should never buy a gap breakout, but that you should think very carefully and mentally prepare yourself for the high probability that the price will correct, thereby placing your position temporarily under water.

Breakaway gaps that develop during the early stages of a primary bull market are more likely to be valid than those that develop after a long price advance. This is because young bull markets have a tremendous amount of upside momentum. This means that there is less likelihood of indecisiveness being reflected in the charts in the form of retracement moves and trading ranges. On the other hand, breakaway gaps that develop at the end of a bull move are more likely to indicate emotional exhaustion as the sold out bulls literally give up on any possibility of being able to buy again at lower prices. The same principle in reverse applies to bear trends.

In *Technical Analysis of Stock Trends*, Edwards and Magee have a slightly different take. Their advice about whether to buy a breakaway gap rests on the volume configuration. They state that if volume is high just prior to the gap and shrinks as the price moves away from the upper part of the gap, then there is a 50–50 chance of a retracement. On the other hand, if volume expands at the upper part of the gap as prices move away from it, then the odds of a retracement or gap-closing effort are substantially less. Such characteristics, they imply, should be bought into.

I think this can be taken a little further by setting a three-step rule for buying breakout gaps. A theoretical example is shown in Fig. 12-6. First, it's important for the gap to develop at the beginning of a move, which implies that it should be preceded by at least an intermediate decline. In other words, if a gap is to represent a sustainable change in psychology, it must have some pretty bearish psychology (as witnessed by the preceding decline) to reverse. Second, the gap day should be accompanied by exceptionally heavy volume. This again reflects a change in psychology because the bulls are very much in control. Third, an attempt to close the gap should be made within two to four days, and the price should take out the high of the day of the gap. If an attempt to close the gap fails, so much the better. The idea of the test is that market participants have had a chance to change their (bullish) minds and did not. The part of the rule about the new high is really a way of determining whether the market confirms the gap following the successful test.

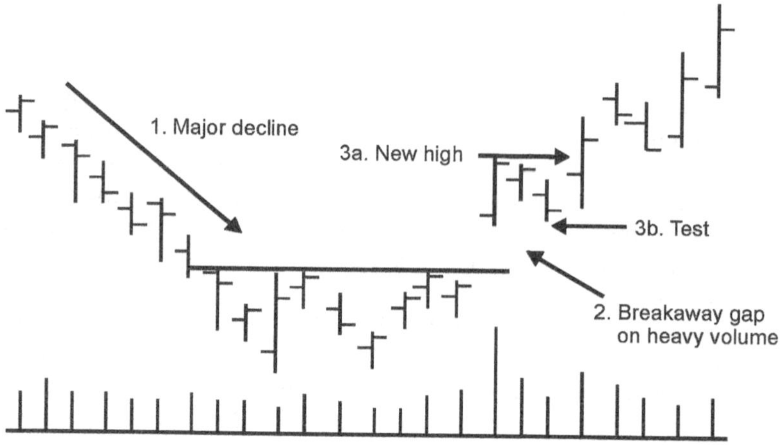

Figure 12-6 Three-step rule for buying breakaway gaps.

Chart 12-12, for Yahoo, shows a nice breakaway gap at the start of a major market move. Volume on the day of the gap was exceptionally heavy. In this case, the momentum was so powerful that there was no retracement move whatsoever. This gap had two things going for it: the heavy volume and the fact that the market itself was just coming off a major low.

Chart 12-12 Yahoo, 2002–2003, daily.

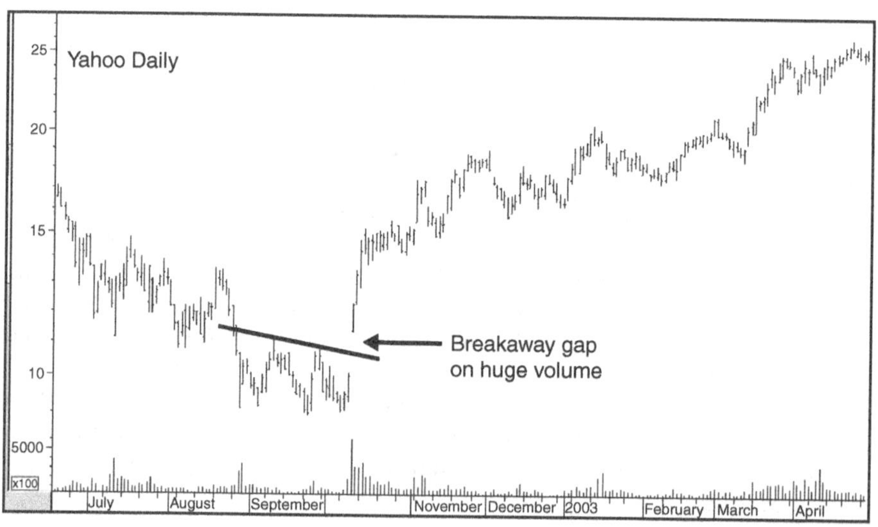

Breakaway gaps are often followed by worthwhile moves, but there do not appear to be any useful measuring yardsticks that can be applied. Perhaps this is because these gaps develop very early, as the new trend is just getting underway. As a result, all measuring objectives would be quickly attained and exceeded. In such cases, the measuring objective is usually better obtained from the pattern or other entity from which the breakaway gap develops.

Chart 12-13, for Amazon, shows a breakaway gap in early 2003. In this instance, the gap was preceded by a small decline. Rules 2 (exceptionally heavy volume) and 3 (test of the upper area of the gap, followed by a post-gap-day high on the fifth day following the day of the gap) were also in force. Note that in this case, the breakout does not come from a price pattern, but from a down trendline.

In Chart 12-14, featuring Apple, rule 1 was satisfied, although the previous decline, in which the stock had come down from $30, is not shown. Rules 2 (heavy volume) and 3 (test of the gap followed by a new high) are met inside the ellipse. There was also a subsequent attempt to fill the gap in December 1993. Note how its upper area became a great support zone that halted the decline. We see another gap develop in early 1994 on very heavy volume and a subsequent test of its upper area. What is striking is that the confirmation is a kind of a double signal because it simultaneously takes out the gap day's high and the high for the previous move. It would be nice to say that the price went on to double after this, but that was not the case;

Chart 12-13 Amazon, daily.

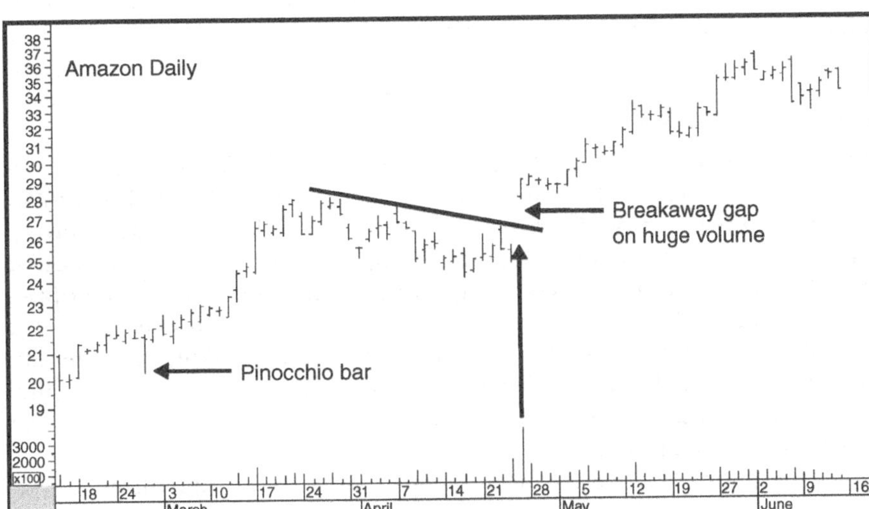

Chart 12-14 Apple, 1993–1994, daily.

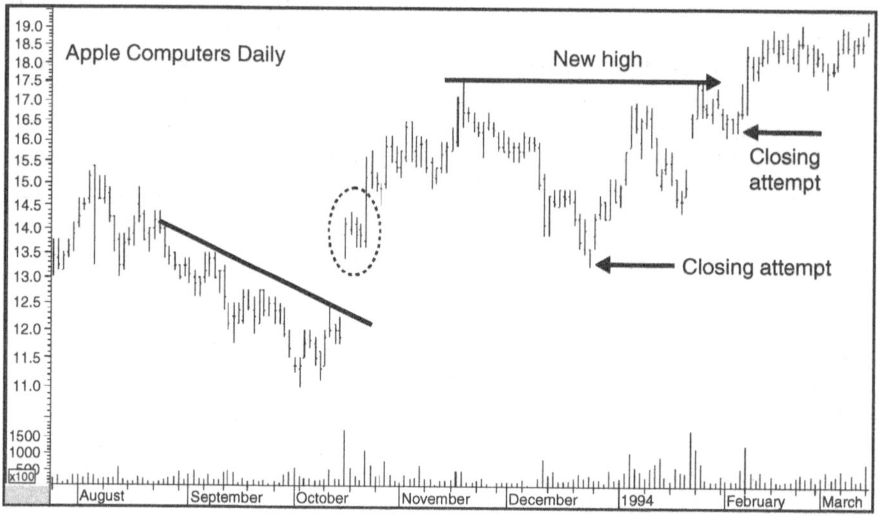

it barely made the $19 level before declining to the lower level of the initial gap (on the left), or just over $12.

A downside breakaway gap appears in Chart 12-15, for Amazon. This breakout developed at the end of a bear market rally. In this case the gap day was associated with exceptionally heavy volume and closed near its low. A weak attempt to close the gap developed out of a small rounding top. Eventually the level of the post gap low was taken out. This would have been the signal for any diehards to liquidate.

Continuation, or Runaway, Gaps

Runaway gaps occur during a straight-line advance or decline, when price quotations are moving rapidly and emotions are running high (see Fig. 12-7*a*). Sometimes they are closed very quickly, e.g., within a day or so. Alternatively, they may tend to remain open for much longer periods and generally not be closed until the market makes a major or intermediate swing in the opposite direction to the price movement that was responsible for the gap. This type of gap often occurs halfway between a previous breakout and the ultimate duration of the move. For this reason, continuation gaps are sometimes called *measuring gaps*. Occasionally more than one continuation gap develops during a price move.

Continuation gaps are far more likely to show up in thinly traded markets or stocks than in well-seasoned issues. This is probably because the door

Chart 12-15 Amazon, daily.

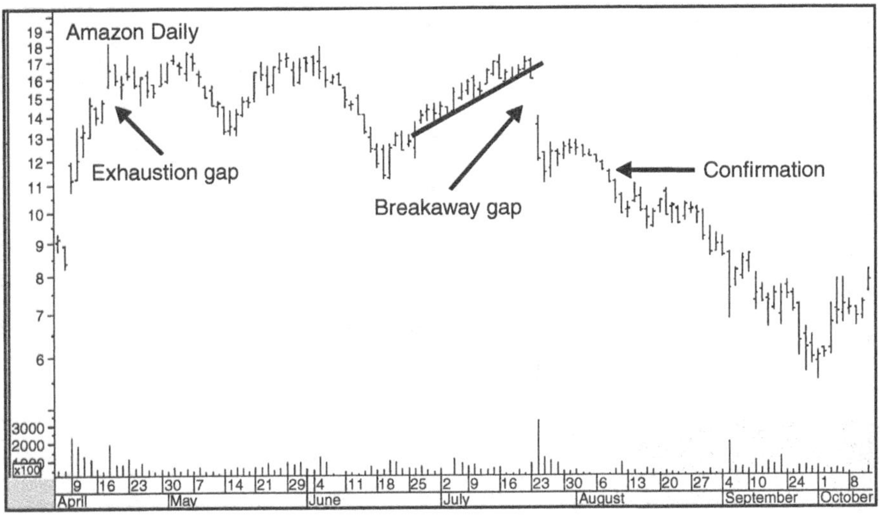

of opportunity is much narrower, and if everyone is trying to get in or out at the same time, there are fewer people who can be accommodated at the desired price. Consequently, their buying (selling) demands can be accommodated only at much higher (lower) prices.

Chart 12-16, featuring Yahoo, shows a runaway or measuring gap in September. Note how it develops about halfway up the move, as indicated by the arrows. As soon as the objective was obtained, the price quickly reversed and returned to the upper area of the gap. The chart also features a breakaway gap that was retraced about 20 trading days later. Then the price exploded to the upside.

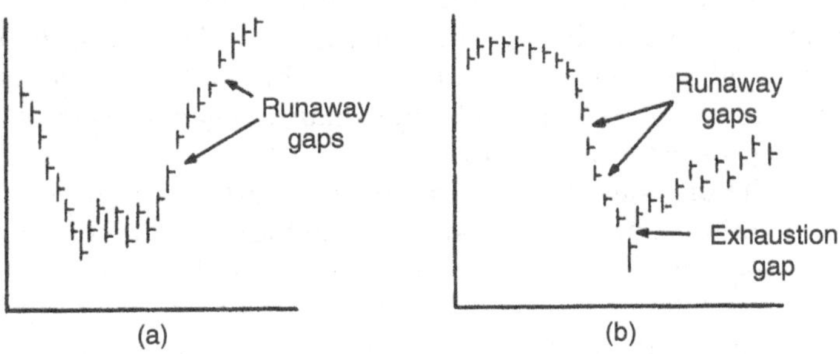

Figure 12-7 Runaway and exhaustion gaps.

Chart 12-16 Yahoo, daily.

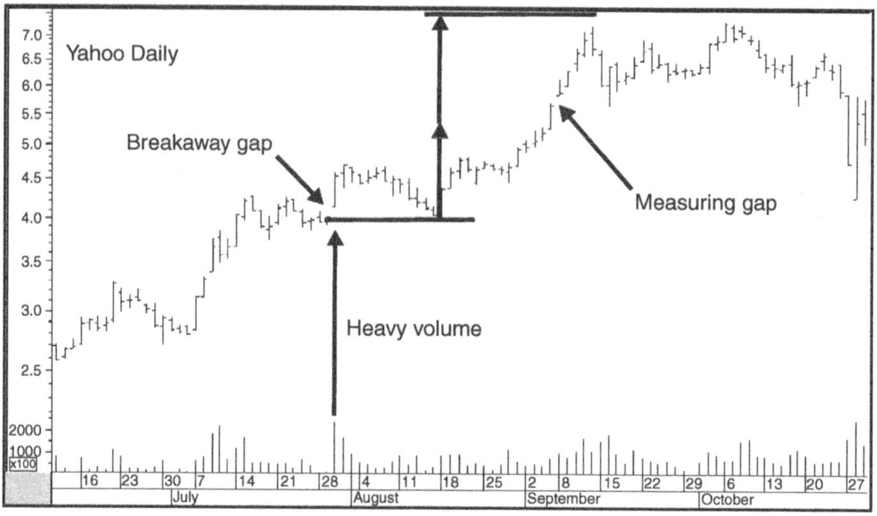

Chart 12-17 also features Yahoo. Here we can see that the runaway gap in January launched a rally that eventually topped out at four times the measuring objective. The initial objective also worked, since it halted the rally for a couple of days. Note also the two breakaway gaps that started the move and the failed attempt to completely close the first of these.

Exhaustion Gaps

When a price move contains more than one runaway gap, this indicates that a very powerful trend is in force. The presence of a second or third gap should also alert the technician to the fact that the move is rapidly maturing. Hence, there is a possibility that a second or third runaway gap will be the final one. An exhaustion gap is, therefore, associated with the terminal phase of a rapid advance or decline and can be the last in a series of runaway gaps (Fig. 12-7*b*). Alternatively, an exhaustion gap may merely develop after a long, protracted price move.

In effect, the breakaway gap represents the start of a move, the runaway gap is in the middle, and the exhaustion gap indicates the terminal phase. Exhaustion gaps are therefore associated with rapid and protracted price moves and signal the beginning of the giving up phase, as buyers convince themselves that a buying opportunity on a correction will never develop.

Chart 12-17 Yahoo, daily.

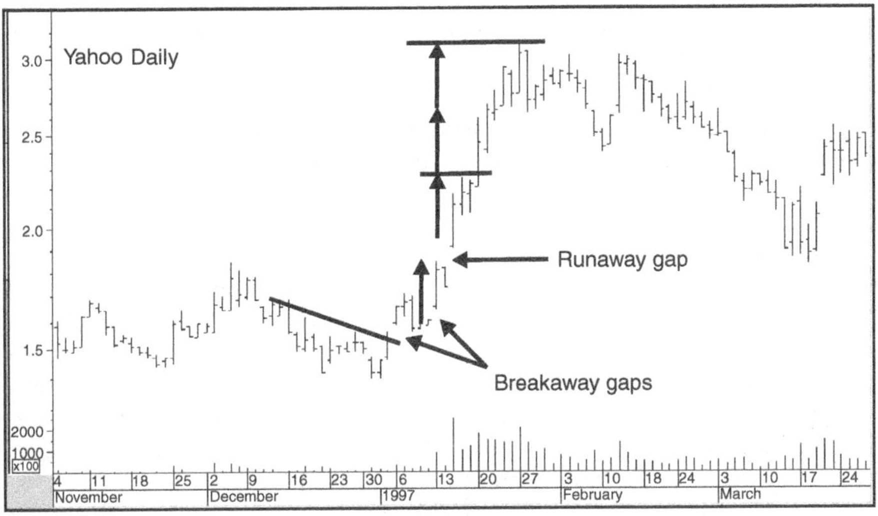

In a downtrend, sellers persuade themselves that a relief rally will never allow them to get out with a smaller loss. Indeed, in *Profits in the Stock Market*, H. M. Gartley argues that downside exhaustion gaps often develop between one and three days prior to a selling climax session.

Spotting exhaustion gaps is not easy, for how do you know at the time that the gap is not a runaway gap? First of all, if the gap develops close to the beginning of a move, it is more likely to be a breakaway type, so the probability of its being an exhaustion gap can be more or less ruled out. The odds are even greater if the objective called for by a price pattern or trendline breakout has not yet been achieved.

One clue that an exhaustion gap may be forming is an unusually heavy level of volume in relation to the price change for that day. In such a case, volume usually works up to a crescendo, well above previous levels. Sometimes the price closes near the vacuum (or gap) and well away from its extreme reading. If the next day's trading creates an "island," with the gap day being completely isolated from the previous day's trading by a vacuum, this is usually an excellent sign that the gap day was in fact *the* turning point. This indicates only temporary exhaustion, but it should be a red flag to highly leveraged traders that they should liquidate or cover their positions.

Alternatively, the day of the gap or one of the subsequent sessions may develop into a one-day price pattern, such as those described in subsequent chapters. In that event, the gap and the price action will reinforce each other, thereby increasing the probabilities of a near-term reversal. In any event, an exhaustion gap should not be regarded as a sign of a major reversal, but merely as an indication that, at the very least, some form of consolidation should be expected.

If you are monitoring an oscillator that is overbought (or oversold, in the case of a decline) or has experienced a divergence or two with the price, this indicates an overextended price trend. Such a combination is more likely to be associated with an exhaustion gap than an oscillator that is at a neutral reading.

Edwards and Magee point out that runaway gaps are usually left open for some time and typically require an intermediate or even primary trend in the opposite direction to the gap before they are closed. On the other hand, since an exhaustion gap is indicative of the terminal phase of a trend, it is usually closed within a few sessions. Such action provides strong evidence that the gap is not of the measuring or continuation variety. Even then, however, it should be appreciated that such gaps in and of themselves indicate only a pause in the current trend or a short-term reversal. They are not signals of a major trend reversal. It's possible that an exhaustion gap will appear at a major turning point, but that is likely to be more of a coincidence. Other tools, such as long-term momentum, should be used for the identification of a major trend reversal.

Finally, exhaustion gaps are occasionally referred to as *wide* gaps. This is because they tend to be wider than runaway gaps. In this sense, like heavy or light volume, the term *wide* is a relative one. A "wide" bar can be recognized only in relation to previous chart action and is therefore a matter of personal judgment and experience.

Chart 12-18, for Apple, shows an extremely wide gap in early August. Note the incredible expansion of volume. The next day the price experienced a very small gap, which was immediately closed. After a long run like this, the quick gap closing is the first sign of exhaustion. Within a couple of sessions the wide gap below it was also closed, an even stronger sign of fatigue.

Chart 12-19, for Adobe, shows two types of gap. The rally begins with a breakaway gap on good volume. An attempt is made to close the gap, and when that fails, a confirmation develops as the price makes a new high. The measuring implication for the runaway gap is reached in a fairly precise manner, but not before we see another gap. The tip-off that this was an exhaustion gap came when the gap was quickly closed during the next session. This particular gap-closing day was an outside bar, which is discussed as a reversal phenomenon in Chapter 13.

A second exhaustion gap develops at the extreme right-hand part of the chart. Note the confirmation as the price breaks above a small base and closes the complete gap within a few sessions.

Chart 12-18 Apple, daily.

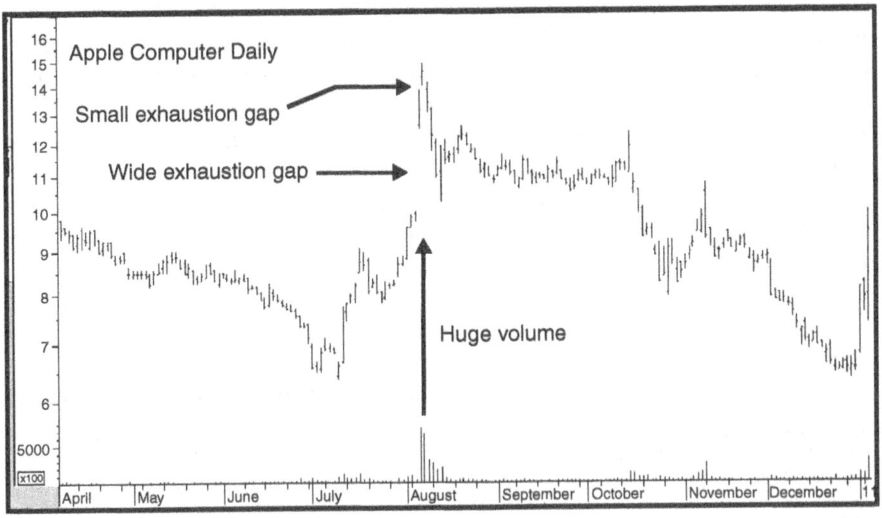

Chart 12-19 Adobe, 1997–1998, daily.

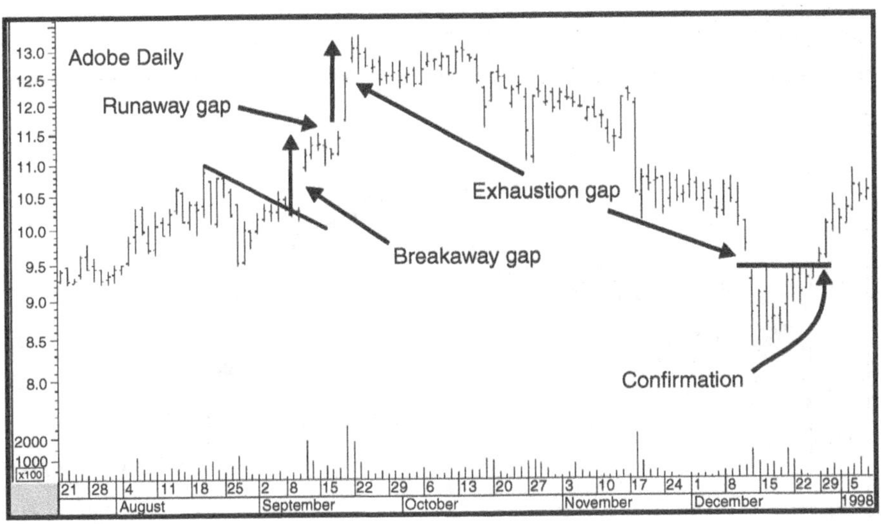

Intraday Gaps

There are really two types of *opening* gap in intraday charts. The first develops as prices open beyond the trading parameters of the previous session, as in Chart 12-20. I'll call these *classic gaps*, since these are the ones that also appear on the daily charts.

The second, more common type of gap develops *only* on intraday charts as the opening price of a new day gaps well away from the previous session's closing bar. I'll call these gaps *intrabar gaps* because they fall between two bars calculated on an intraday time frame. For example, in Chart 12-21, the price opened up higher and created a gap. However, if you look back, you will see that the trading range of the previous day (contained within the box on the left) was not exceeded at the opening price, and thus on a daily chart there would have been no gap.

If you are a trader with a two- to three-week time horizon who is using intraday charts, you should approach gaps in a different way from someone with a one- or two-day time horizon.

People in the first category should try to avoid initiating trades at the time the gap is created. This is because almost all gaps are eventually closed. Sometimes this happens within a couple of hours, and at other times it can take two or three weeks. Consequently, if you buy on an opening gap on the upside, as in Chart 12-21, you run the risk that the gap will soon be closed.

Chart 12-20 March 1997 bonds 15-minute bar. (*Source: pring.com.*)

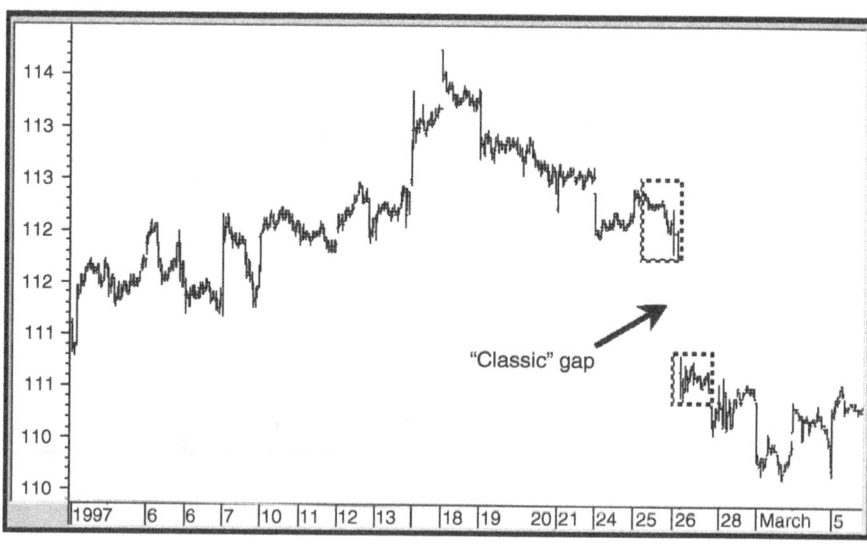

Chart 12-21 March 1997 bonds 15-minute bar. (*Source: pring.com.*)

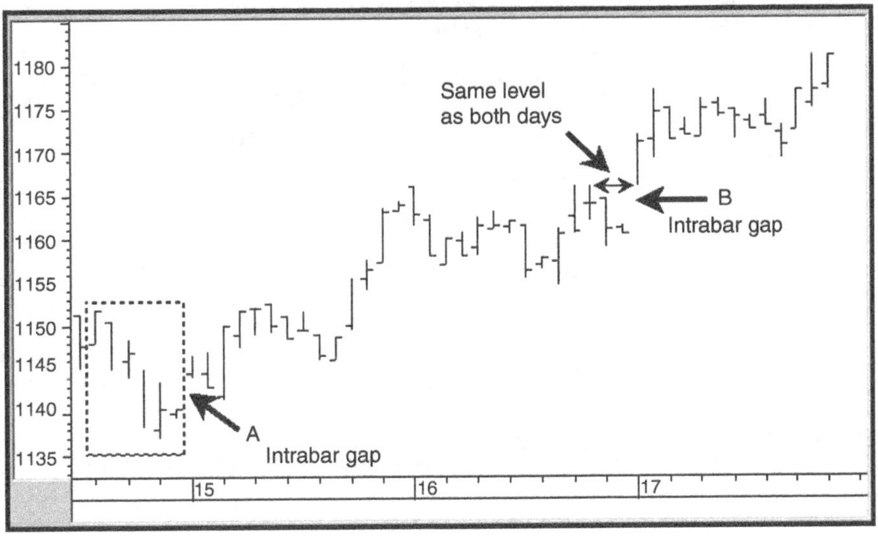

The problem is, you do not know whether it will be closed in two days or four weeks.

Intraday traders are also advised to step aside when the market opens sharply higher or lower. In the case of stocks, this is caused by an order imbalance. That means that the market makers are forced to go short so that they can satisfy the unfilled demand. They naturally try to get the price a little higher at the opening so that it will come down a little, enabling them to cover all or part of the short position. The process will be reversed in the case of a lower opening. The key, then, is to watch what happens to the price *after* the opening range. Normally, if prices work their way higher after an upside gap and opening trading range, this sets the tone of the market for at least the next few hours, and often longer.

On the other hand, if the price starts to close the gap after a few bars, then the tone becomes a negative one. In Chart 12-22, featuring Merrill Lynch, there is an opening gap on the Wednesday. After a bit of backing and filling, the price gradually worked its way lower throughout the day. The signal that the opening could be an aberration developed after the price slipped below the trendline. Note how the trendline became resistance for the rest of the session. Thursday saw another opening gap, but this time there was very little in the way of a trading range, since the price continued to climb. Again the rally away from the opening bar set the tone for the rest of the day. On Friday another gap appears, but this time the opening trading

Chart 12-22 Merrill Lynch 7.5-minute bar. (*Source: pring.com.*)

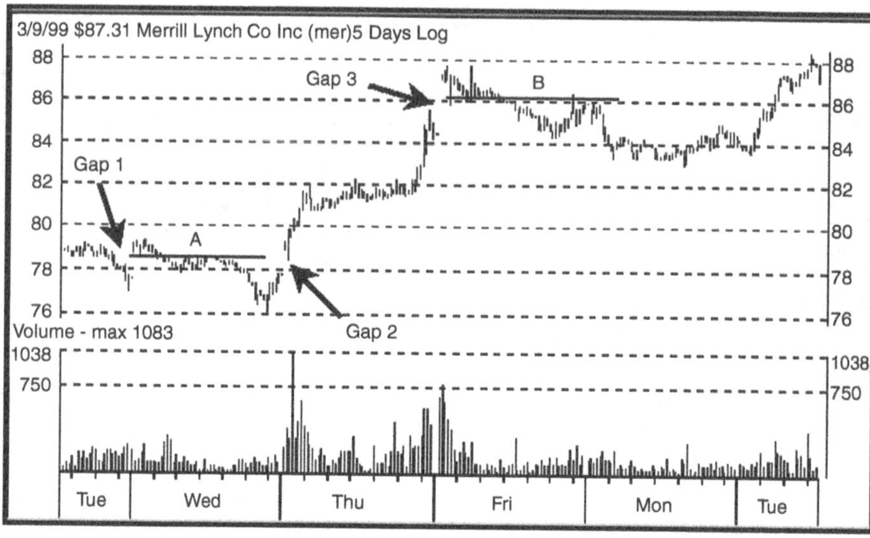

range is resolved on the downside as the price breaks below the $86 level. Once again this proves to be resistance for the rest of the day.

Island Reversals

An island reversal is a compact trading range created at the end of a sustained move and isolated from previous price behavior by an exhaustion gap and a breakaway gap. A typical island reversal is shown in Fig. 12-8. However, it should be stated at the outset that islands are a pretty rare phenomenon in the charts and are in and of themselves short-term phenomena. They can appear, though, at the end of an intermediate or even a major move and form part of an overall price pattern, such as the top (or bottom) of a head-and-shoulders formation (or an inverse head-and-shoulders pattern). Islands occasionally occur as one-day phenomena.

Chart 12-23, featuring Apple Computer, shows an island bottom. However, since it developed within the confines of a bear market, the island failed. Initial confirmation of this developed when the second island was completed with a downside gap right at the end of April. Final confirmation occurred when the price broke below the dashed trendline, which was in fact the neckline of a consolidation head and shoulders. In this case, the second island represented the bulk of the head. This emphasizes that a large number of islands are really patterns within patterns.

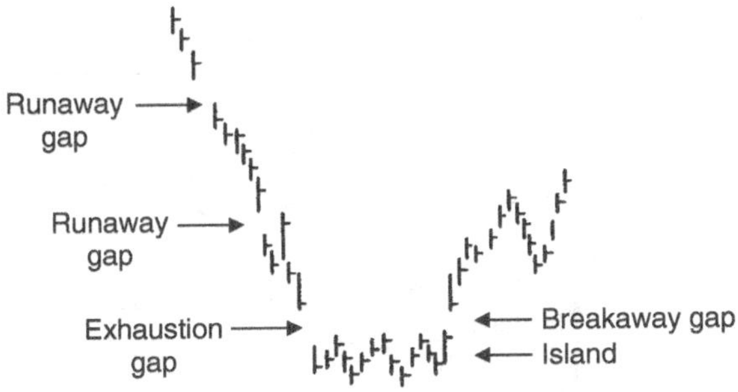

Figure 12-8 Island reversal.

One-Day Island

A one-day or one-bar island has the same characteristics as the island reversal just described. However, this particular pattern, as its name implies, consists of only one isolated and lonely bar.

A one-day island for Altera is featured in Chart 12-24. Note the very large volume on the day of the island and the fact that the price closed very near the low for the day. Also, volume on the second day was even heavier. An expansion of volume on the downside is usually bearish, but such an expansion the day after a one-day island was the kiss of death.

Chart 12-23 Apple, 1996–1997, daily.

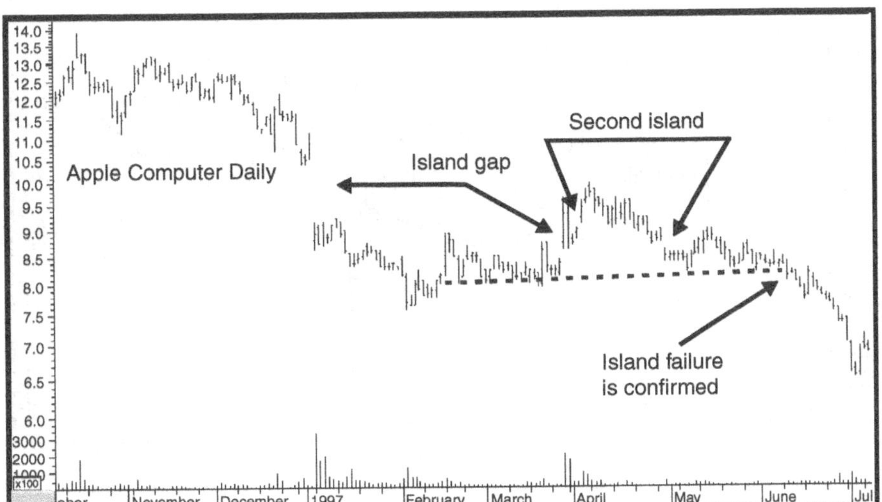

Chart 12-24 Altera, daily.

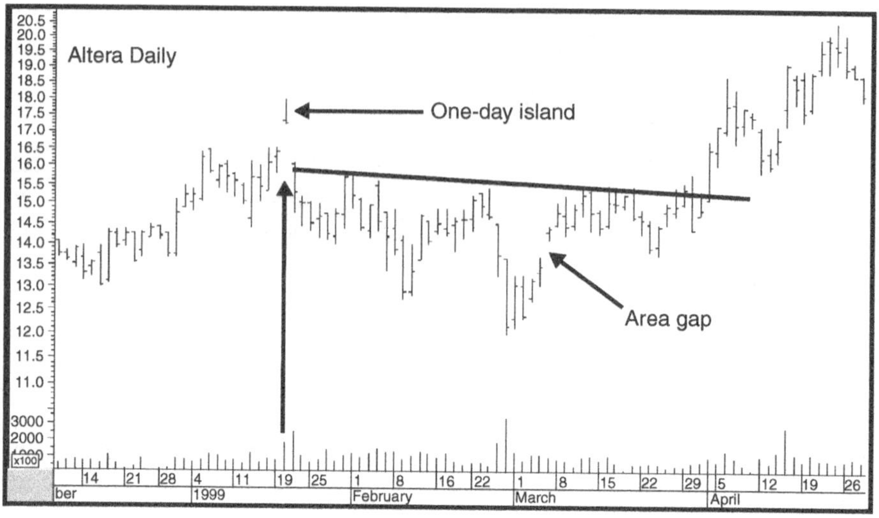

Chart 12-25 Yahoo, daily.

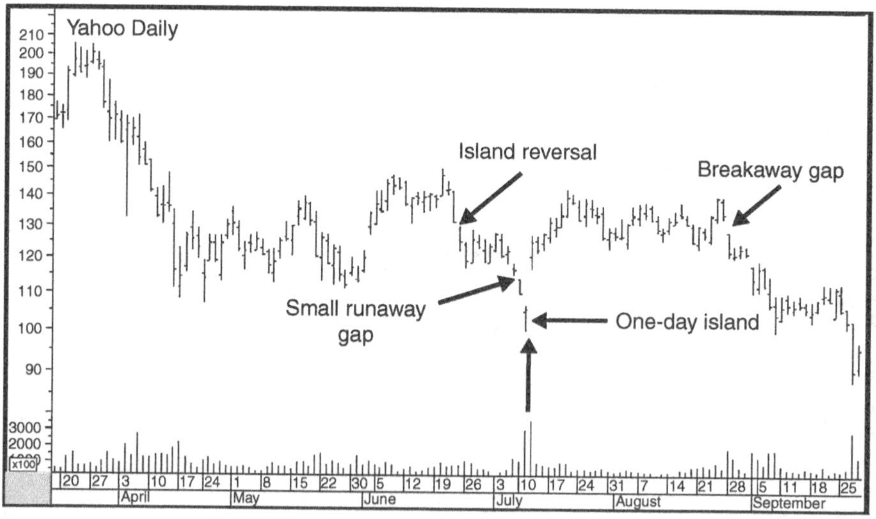

Finally, Chart 12-25, for Yahoo, shows a small, bearish island top. Later on we see a runaway gap followed by a one-day island. You can see how the gap day closed on its high and was accompanied by exceptionally heavy volume. The day following the one-day island experienced even greater volume. The extreme right-hand part of the chart shows a two-bar reversal followed by a breakaway gap to the downside. (For an explanation of two-bar reversals, please see Chapter 16.)

Summary

Flags Quick Review

- *Price characteristics:* A small trading range bounded by two parallel lines that slope in the opposite direction to the prevailing trend.
- *Volume configuration:* Volume shrinks as the pattern is being formed and expands in the case of an upside breakout. Expansion in volume is not a requirement for a downside break but will enhance the validity of such a break.
- *Type:* Appears as a continuation pattern.
- *Measuring implication:* The flag often appears halfway up or down a price trend.

Pennants Quick Review

- *Price characteristics:* A small trading range bounded by converging trendlines sloping in the *same* direction, which should be opposite to the direction of the main trend.
- *Volume configuration:* Volume shrinks as the pattern is being formed and expands in the case of an upside breakout. Expansion in volume is not a requirement for a downside break but will enhance the validity of such a break.
- *Type:* Appears as a continuation pattern.
- *Measuring implication:* The pennant often appears halfway up or down a price trend.

Wedges Quick Review

- *Price characteristics:* A small trading range bounded by two converging lines that slope in the opposite direction to the prevailing trend. Wedges differ from pennants in that they usually take longer to form and their theoretical apex is a long way from the breakout point.

- *Volume configuration:* Volume shrinks as the pattern is being formed and expands in the case of an upside breakout. Expansion in volume is not a requirement for a downside break but will enhance the validity of such a break. Breakouts are often followed by very sharp moves.
- *Type:* Appears as a continuation pattern.
- *Measuring implication:* The maximum distance between the two converging lines is projected in the direction of the breakout.

Gaps Quick Review

- *Price characteristics:* A vacuum or hole in the chart that develops because of high emotion. Gaps are usually closed and represent potential support and resistance areas.
- *Volume configuration:* High volume on a gap increases its potential significance.
- *Type:* Breakaway gaps develop at the beginning of a move, runaway gaps in the middle of a move, and exhaustion gaps at the end of a move. Island reversals are small price patterns (or one bar, in the case of a one-bar island) that are isolated from the main price trend by two gaps. They often signal the termination of an intermediate move. Ex-dividend and area gaps have little significance.

13
Outside Bars

Introduction to One- and Two-Bar Patterns

The price patterns covered in earlier chapters take some time to complete—usually at least 15 bars. They all reflect changes in the relationship between buyers and sellers, indicating that there has been a change in the underlying sentiment.

This and subsequent chapters describe much smaller patterns that are confined to one or two bars. These formations can be extremely useful because they trigger signals at a relatively early stage in the development of a new trend and usually offer very practical benchmarks, above or below which it is possible to place low-risk stops.

Historically, the patterns described in Chapters 13 to 16 have been called one- and two-day patterns or one- and two-week patterns. With the advent of intraday charts, these titles no longer encompass the majority of these patterns. Therefore we will use the term *bar* rather than *day* to describe them.

A key factor determining the significance of any pattern is the pattern's size. These one- and two-bar patterns do not take very long to form, so they only have a short-term influence on prices. For example, a pattern consisting of a one-day bar would be expected, under normal circumstances, to affect the price over, say, a 5- to 10-day period. A two-bar pattern created from 10-minute bars would influence the trend over the course of the next 50 minutes to an hour or so. Even though this is a relatively short period, the more I study these patterns, the more impressed I become with their ability to signal short-term trend reversals reliably.

When a trend has reached maturity and the long-term technical picture is consistent with a turn, these one- and two-bar patterns often develop literally at the final turning point of the move. In a sense, the one- and two-bar patterns become dominoes or reverse dominoes as they become the final straw that tips the long-term technical balance in a new direction; but more on that later.

Not All Patterns Are Created Equal

We tend to think of the signals from these patterns as being either buy or sell indications, and that is fine as far as it goes. However, it's equally important that we attempt to judge their quality, since not all patterns are created equal. This means that we should consider these signals in terms of stars or shades of gray. For example, pattern A might contain the characteristics of a specific formation, but pattern B could reflect them in a stronger way. Thus A could be a two-star pattern, but B might be classified as five-star. Technical analysis deals in probabilities, so a five-star signal would offer higher odds of a valid trend reversal than, say, a two-star signal, and so forth. Just as there are no guarantees in technical analysis, there are no guarantees that a five-star signal will always be valid, or that a one-star signal will be followed by a weak move; it's merely that the odds favor this.

What we are doing is hunting for clues to the strength and significance of a change in sentiment that is being signaled by a particular reversal phenomenon. I could *say* the word *help*, for example, but if I *shout it* from the rooftop, you will get the message that I need help far more clearly. The same principle operates in the marketplace. Consequently, one- and two-bar patterns should be interpreted as shades of gray rather than as black or white because some patterns offer stronger signs of exhaustion than others.

General Interpretive Principles

There are several interpretive ground rules that apply to all these one- and two-bar formations:

1. In order for these formations to be effective, there must be something for them to reverse. This means that top reversals should be preceded by a meaningful rally, and bottom formations should be preceded by a sharp sell-off. As a general rule, the stronger the preceding trend, the more powerful the effect of the one- and two-bar price pattern.
2. These formations generally reflect an exhaustion point. In the case of an uptrend, such patterns develop when buyers have temporarily pushed prices up too far and need a rest. In the case of a downtrend, there is little, if any, supply, because sellers have completed their liquidation. Such

patterns are almost always associated with a reversal in the prevailing trend.

3. Not all patterns are created equal. Some show all of the characteristics described later in a very strong way. Others reflect just a few of these characteristics in a mild way. What we might call a five-star pattern, with all the characteristics, is more likely to result in a strong reversal than, say, a two-star pattern that has mild characteristics. It is therefore necessary to apply a certain degree of common sense to interpretation of these patterns, rather than jumping to the immediate conclusion that the presence of one of them guarantees a quick, profitable price reversal.
4. Occasionally, it is possible to observe some form of confirmation closely following or even during the development of a one- or two-bar pattern. Examples would include the completion of a larger pattern or, more likely, the violation of a trendline. Such events not only add significance to the pattern but also increase the odds on this being a valid signal.

One- and Two-Bar Western Patterns Compared to Japanese Candlesticks

Before we move on to a more specific study of the individual patterns, it is important to understand that many of them bear a close resemblance to Japanese candlesticks. I say "close" because candlestick interpretation places great emphasis on the opening and closing prices. Many Japanese patterns are determined by these two points relative to the opening and closing prices of the previous candle. Opening and closing prices are also important in bar chart interpretation, but so is the entire trading range, since it captures the complete emotional makeup of the bar. A comparison between the two methods of charting, where appropriate, will be made in this and the following three chapters. First, though, a very quick heads-up on candles. For a review of the subject in more depth, please see my *Introduction to Candlestick Charting* (workbook and CD-ROM tutorial) or the classic work on the subject, Steve Nison's *Introduction to Candlesticks.*

Overview of Candlesticks

An individual candlestick consists of a rectangle with two protruding lines, one above the rectangle and the other below it. The rectangle is called the *real body* and reflects the opening and closing prices. The two vertical lines are called *wicks* and represent the trading between the open/close and the

Chart 13-1 A black candlestick.

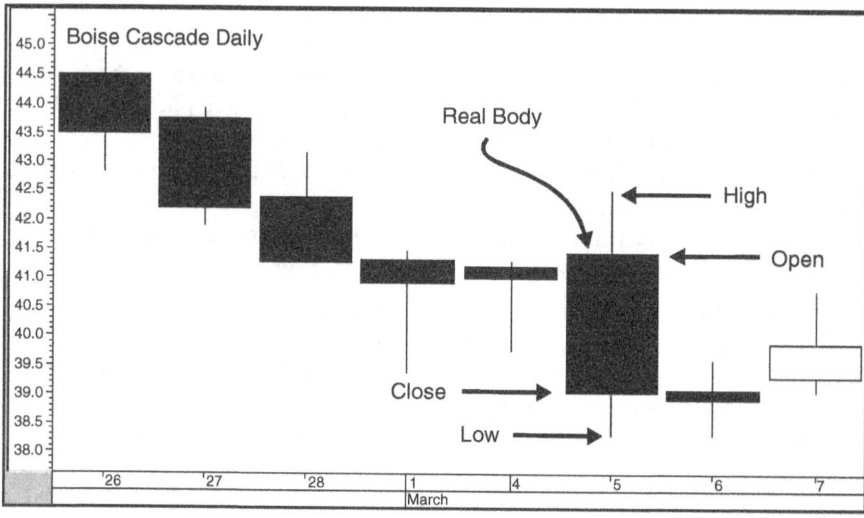

high and low. Candlesticks come in two colors, black and white. The color that is plotted is determined by the relationship between the open and the close. If the open is higher than the close, the rectangle is colored black, as in Chart 13-1. If the close is higher than the open, the real body is colored white, as shown in Chart 13-2. In a very general sense, white candles are considered bullish and black ones bearish. That is a very simplistic statement, however, and needs to be qualified by the circumstances in which they develop. Since candlesticks and bar charts display identical information, there is nothing in a candlestick pattern that cannot be found in a bar chart, and vice versa. The principal difference is that candlesticks exhibit certain charting phenomena in a simpler way than bars do. They also place greater emphasis on the opening and closing levels. So, you may ask, why use bars? The answer is that several other phenomena can be recognized more easily on a bar chart. Also, because bars are thinner, more data can be readably displayed on a chart. Because psychology is the prime determinant of prices in any freely traded market, highs and lows need to be taken into account. They are not ignored in candles, but they are easier to spot in the bars.

Outside Bars

An outside bar is a bar whose trading range totally encompasses that of its predecessor. These patterns develop after both down- and uptrends and

Chart 13-2 A white candlestick.

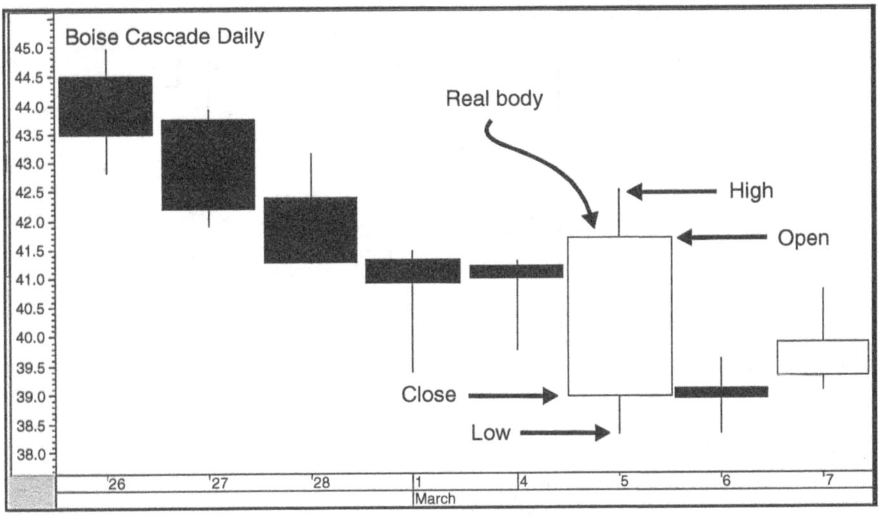

represent exhaustion. An example of a top reversal is shown in Fig. 13-1 and an example of a bottom in Fig. 13-2.

Determining Their Significance

The guidelines for deciding on the potential significance of an outside bar are as follows:

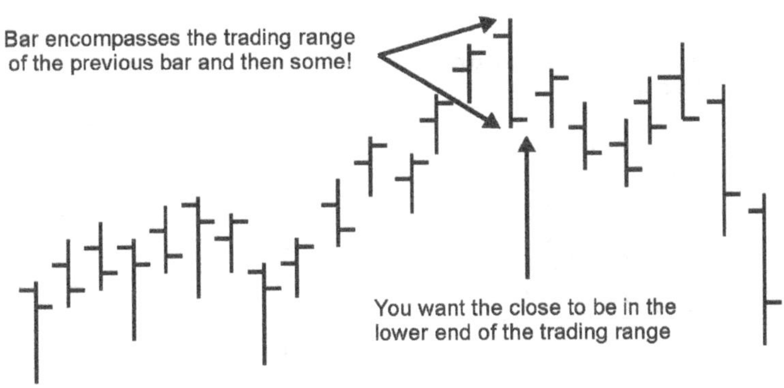

Figure 13-1 Outside bar at a top.

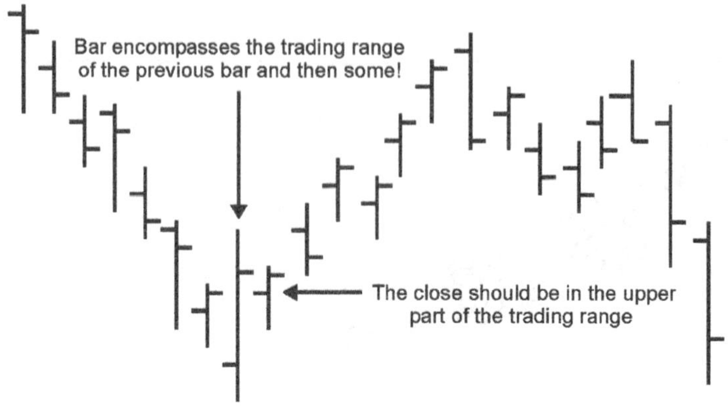

Figure 13-2 Outside bar at a bottom.

1. *The wider the outside bar relative to the preceding ones, the stronger the signal.* This arises from the fact that the outside bar is supposed to reflect a change in the balance between buyers and sellers. In the upper part of Fig. 13-3, the buyers have had the upper hand until the period of the outside bar. They come into the bar expecting more of the same, but by the close sellers have managed to take the price below the previous

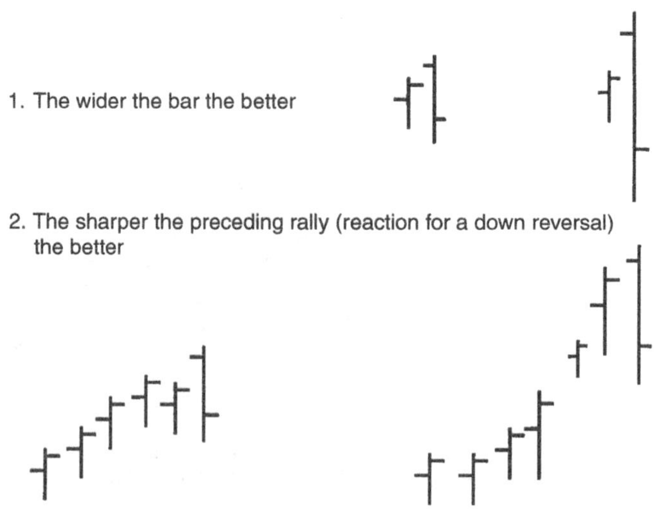

Figure 13-3 Measuring the significance of outside bars.

period's low. Thus a subtle change in the strength or inclination of buyers and sellers has taken place. No longer are buyers willing or able to push prices higher.

2. *The sharper the rally (reaction) preceding the outside bar, the more significant the bar.* It stands to reason that if a change in sentiment is going to take place, there must be something to change. Therefore, the stronger the trend preceding the outside bar, the stronger the implied sentiment dominating that trend. When opinions move to an extreme, they are very vulnerable to change. In other words, if the preceding trend is strongly positive, all the bullish arguments will be fully discounted. Thus, at some point, buyers will become exhausted and the market will be vulnerable to profit taking. This subtle change is reflected in the outside day. An example is shown in the lower part of Fig. 13-3.
3. *The more bars encompassed, the better the signal.* In most situations, the outside bar will encompass only one other bar. However, when it encompasses several bars, the signal that the balance has shifted from buyers to sellers at a top or from sellers to buyers at a bottom becomes that much stronger. The encompassed bars become a small price pattern in themselves. An example is shown in Fig. 13-4.
4. *The greater the volume accompanying the outside bar relative to previous bars, the stronger the signal.* This again goes back to the idea that the trend preceding this pattern has been dominated by one side or the other. The bar itself indicates that this domination is no longer in force. If volume is particularly heavy, then more market participants are voicing their views.

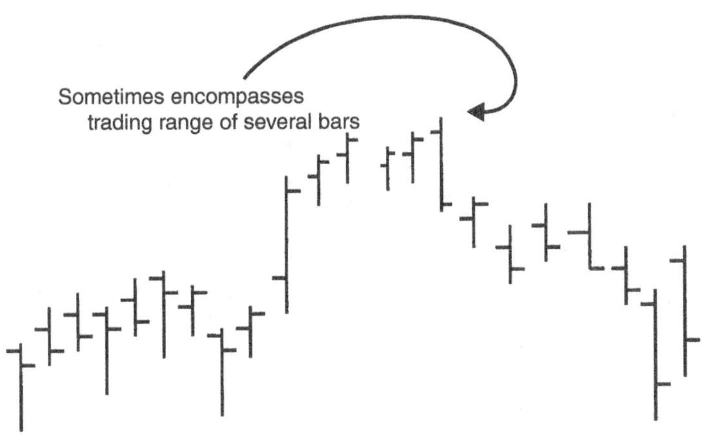

Figure 13-4 Outside bar encompassing several bars.

Strength in numbers, as reflected by the increased activity, increases the significance of the outside bar.

5. *The nearer the price closes to the extreme point of the bar that is away from the direction of the previous trend, the better.* For example, if the previous trend was down and the price closes very near the high, this is more favorable than if it closes near the low, and vice versa. This arises because the outside bar is supposed to signal a reversal in sentiment and a change in trend. The fact that the closing in this example develops near the high merely emphasizes the strength of the buyers, thereby adding to the validity of the signal.

If the close develops near the high in a rising trend or near the low in a falling trend, then the outside bar is not consistent with a change in psychology. In this case, the outside bar will become a consolidation, not a reversal pattern. An example is shown in Fig. 13-5, where the outside bar appears after a small consolidation, but the close takes place near the high of the bar. In this instance, the sellers tried hard to push the price lower and extend the correction. By the end of the period, though, the buyers had taken over and were able to close the price very near to its high.

When considering outside bars or any of the other one- and two-bar price patterns, it is important to ask yourself the question, "What is the price action of this bar telling me about the underlying psychology?" Wide bars, sharp preceding rallies or reactions, and high volume all suggest a change in the previous trend of sentiment.

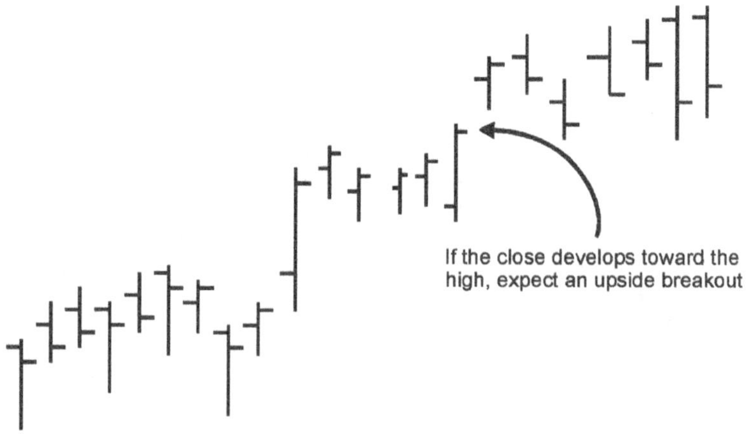

Figure 13-5 Consolidation outside bar.

Not all one- and two-bar patterns are followed by a *reversal* in trend. Some, for example may be followed by a *change* in trend, as prices consolidate after an up or down move.

Marketplace Examples

Chart 13-3 features an example of an outside bar for Merrill Lynch. It's really a five-star signal, since it has pretty well all of the characteristics of a strong reversal.

The price was in a persistent downtrend during the afternoon of the twenty-first. Then a strong bar, totally encompassing the trading range of the bar that traced out the low point for the move, developed. This was a pretty strong statement because the bar opened near its low and closed almost at its high. Note also the very high volume that accompanied this formation.

One- and two-bar patterns are not always followed by an immediate reversal in price. Indeed, they are often subject to some retracing or waffling action prior to the onset of a strong reversal. This type of action is, of course, consistent with other price patterns. This chart shows an example of this, as the price experiences a two-bar correction prior to taking off on the upside. This can be a good thing if you are thinking of taking a long position. Remember, the stop should be placed below support, which in this case is

Chart 13-3 Merrill Lynch 10-minute bar.

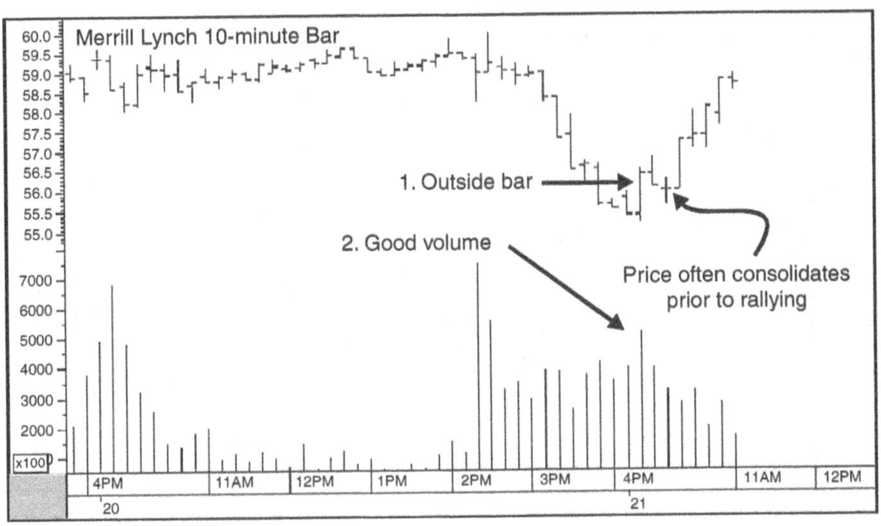

the extreme low of the outside bar. The retracement allows you to enter the trade with a lower risk, but with the same potential reward. Generally speaking, though, I would prefer to see a small correction, for often the more ground that is retraced, the weaker the signal. Even so, we cannot say that the outside bar has been cancelled until the price actually moves beyond its extreme point, though anything greater than a 50 percent retracement is cause for concern.

Several outside bars are apparent in Chart 13-4. Example *A* is a good one because it is preceded by a relatively strong rally and is reasonably wide. Example *B* fails completely. The reasons lie in the fact that the close is right on the low, the bar is not much larger than the previous one, and the bar is not preceded by much of a decline. While in a strict technical sense this is an outside bar, it is not signaling much in the way of a change in sentiment.

Even though the price rallied for a very short period, example *C* was not really successful either. It's true that it was preceded by a decline, was a reasonable size, and closed at its high. However, I purposely put in this example to show that even when a substantial number of the requirements are present, this does not guarantee the success of a pattern.

Chart 13-5 shows two more examples of outside bars for the DJIA in March of 2001. The first represents a reversal from a downtrend to an uptrend. It's always nice when we can see a one- or two-bar pattern confirmed by additional

Chart 13-4 S&P Composite 5-minute bar.

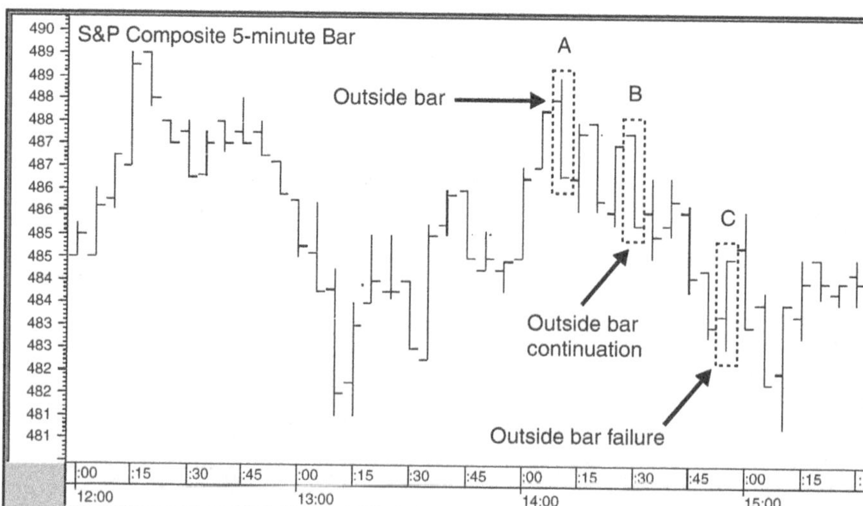

Chart 13-5 DJIA 60-minute bar.

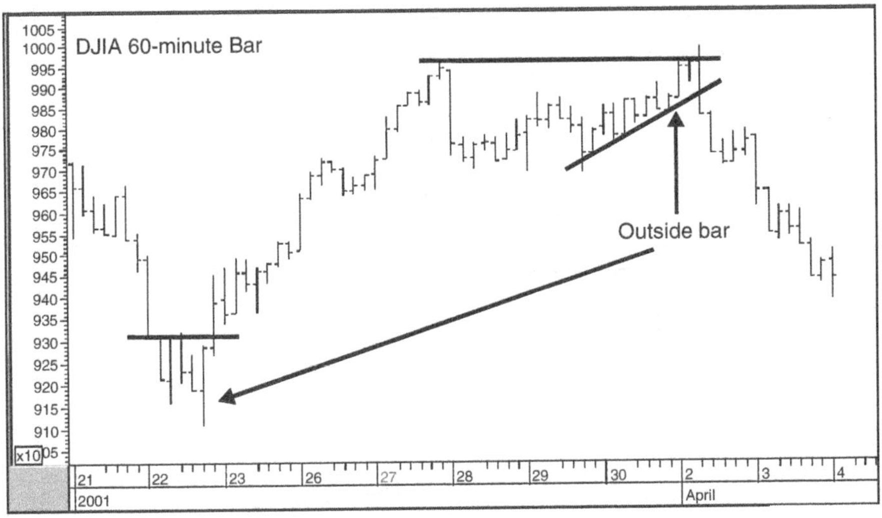

evidence pointing to a trend reversal. In this case, the price breaks out from a small base just after the outside bar. The second example on the chart, which developed in April, marks the top of a very sharp rally. Note that the outside bar is very wide, encompasses the three previous bars, and also violates a good up trendline. Add to this the fact that it also experienced a whipsaw break above the horizontal trendline and you have all the ingredients of a dramatic change in sentiment.

Chart 13-6 is a daily chart of the Nasdaq 100. The outside bar on the left has a lot of the ingredients of a valid pattern. It is preceded by a good rally, and the bar itself is wide and encompasses several other bars. It also opened in the direction of the then-prevailing trend and closed on its low. The question naturally arises as to why it failed. One explanation is that in really strong up- or downtrends, one- and two-bar pattern reversals represent contra-trend signals, and contra-trend signals often result in whipsaws. Note that in this case, the outside bar was the market's attempt to close a gap that had opened up several trading days earlier. The lower part of the bar therefore reached a support area.

In addition, it's important to remember that we are dealing in probabilities, not certainties, in technical analysis. Failures can and do exist. That's why it is always necessary to look over your shoulder and mentally rehearse where you are going to get out should the low-probability losing scenario develop. In this case, the stop would be placed above the upper point of the outside day.

Chart 13-6 Nasdaq 100, daily.

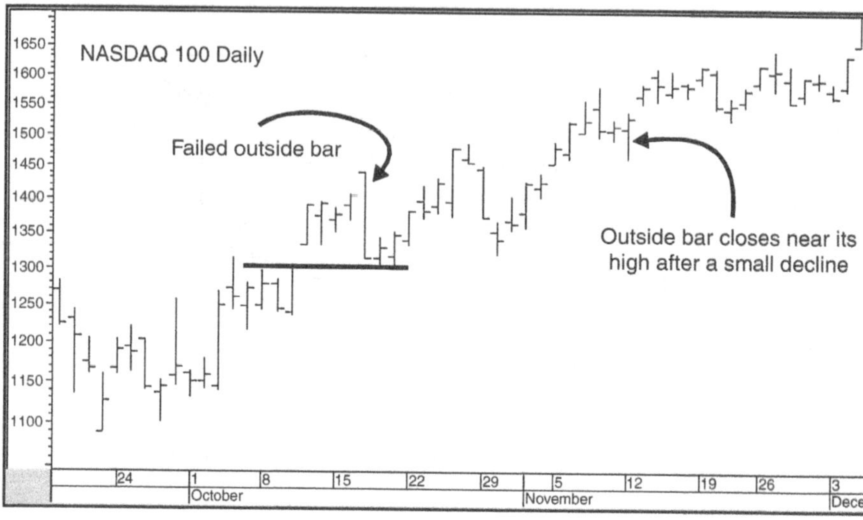

The second outside bar canceled out a bearish outside bar that had formed two days earlier. Usually cancellations are followed by a pretty strong move, and this example was no exception.

Chart 13-7, for cocoa, shows two outside bars. The first should have been expected to reverse to the upside, but a couple of factors got in the way. First, the bar whipsawed above a down trendline. Second, the close was near the low for the week, instead of the high. While this was technically an outside bar, and it was preceded by a sharp downtrend, these other factors more than canceled out its bullish aspects.

The second outside bar developed at the low for the decline. Here we see a reversal of the factors that had caused the earlier failure. The price closed above the down trendline almost at the high for the week, for a classic reversal.

Chart 13-8 features another weekly example for cocoa. This time the outside bar is the third in a series of three outside bars. The effect is that they reinforce each other, for a very strong signal. In addition, notice that the final outside bar also closes above the resistance trendline joining several lows. This indicates that the break was a whipsaw, which added even more icing to the bullish cake.

Finally, Chart 13-9 shows the very significant October 2002 bear market low in the U.S. stock market, where an outside bar was accompanied by very heavy volume.

Chart 13-7 Cocoa, 1991–1992, weekly.

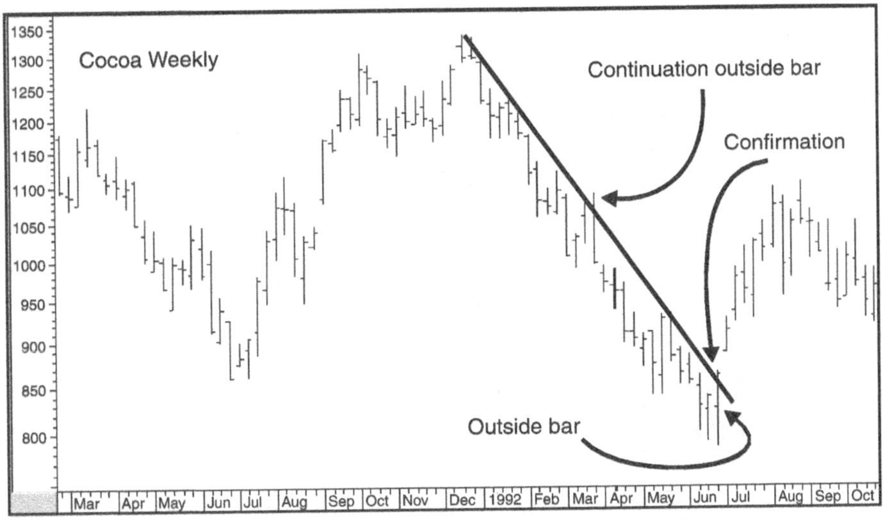

Chart 13-8 Cocoa, 1999–2001, weekly.

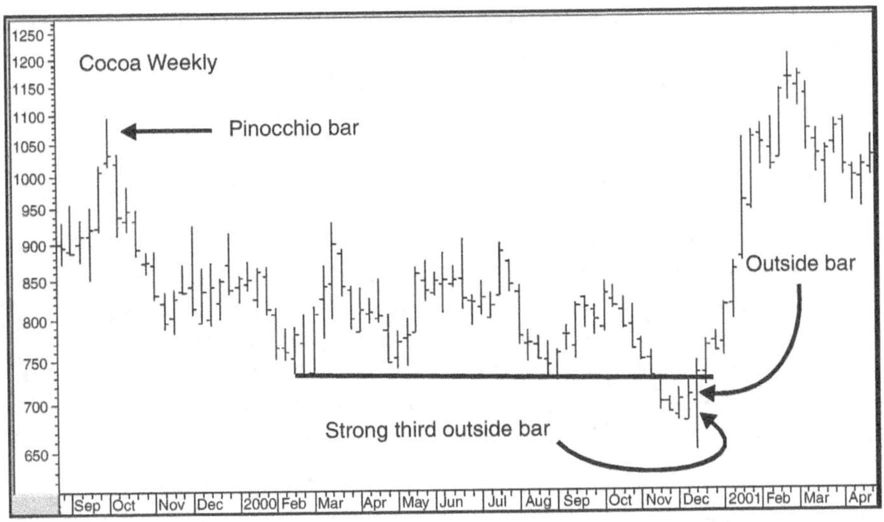

Chart 13-9 S&P Composite, 2002–2003, daily.

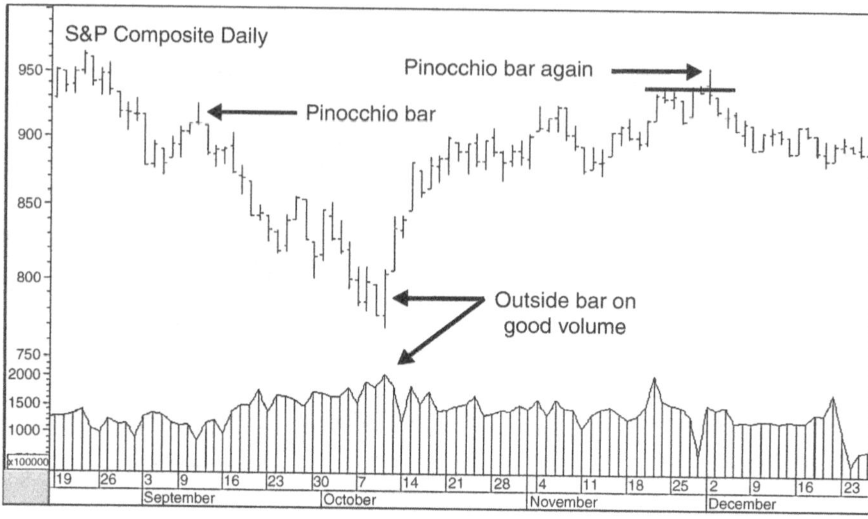

Using Outside Bars as Dominoes or Reverse Dominoes

Earlier in this chapter, it was established that outside bars, like other one- and two-bar patterns, have an influence on prices for only a short period of time. However, when the longer-term technical structure is finely balanced and likely to turn, these patterns can act as a domino at market tops or a reverse domino at bottoms. They can therefore be used to anticipate a reversal in trend, which is of far greater significance than the move implied by the pattern itself.

Chart 13-10, featuring a 60-minute bar for the DJIA, offers an example. Here we can see an outside bar following a small rally. It encompasses three previous bars, so we would expect to see a decline for perhaps 5 to 10 bars. In this case, though, the decline is much greater than that. There are two reasons for this. First, a closer review of the action shows that the upper end of the bar was actually a whipsaw breakout. Whipsaws are typically followed by sharp moves in the opposite direction to that expected from the breakout, as traders scramble to square their positions. Second, the lower part of the bar succeeds in violating a seven-day up trendline, a long time on an hourly chart. The outside bar was therefore in a perfect position to tip the balance of the longer-term technical position.

Our second "domino" example features a daily chart of the DJ Transports in Chart 13-11. The smoothed RSI (a nine-day RSI smoothed with an

Chart 13-10 DJIA 60-minute bar.

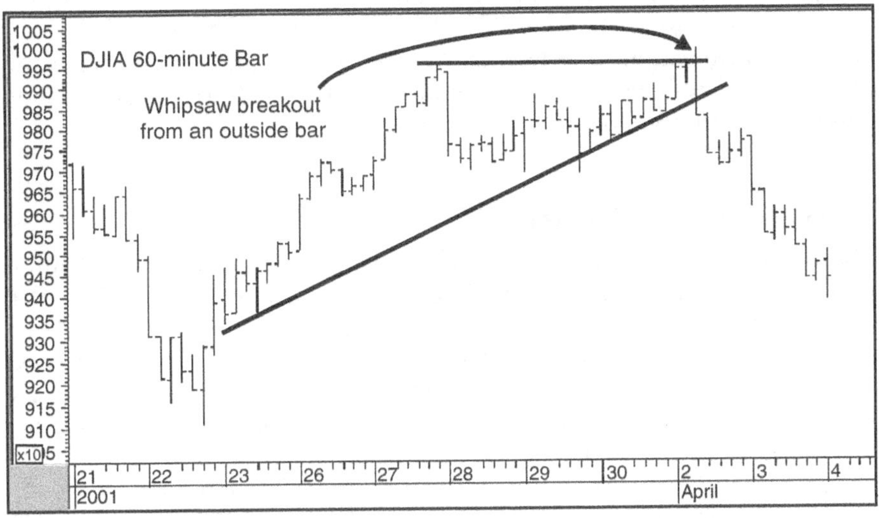

Chart 13-11 DJ Transports, daily.

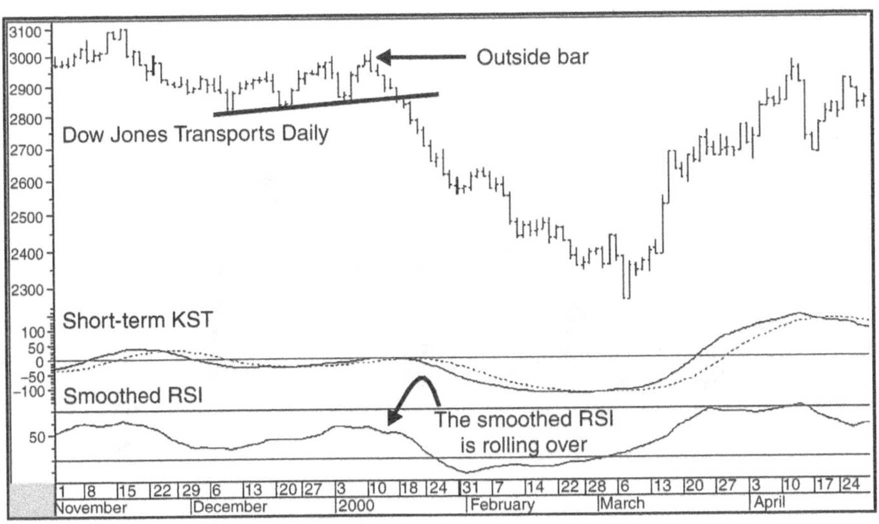

eight-day simple moving average) has started to flatten in early January, so the question becomes whether it will roll over completely, thereby giving a short-term sell signal. A clue is provided by the price, which experiences a bearish outside bar around January 12. This was not an outstanding example, but it was sufficient to push the immediate picture into a negative mode and turn the smoothed RSI into a bearish mode.

Outside Bars and Candles

There is no direct counterpart to outside bars in Japanese candlestick interpretation. A close neighbor is the engulfing pattern, featured in Figs. 13-6 and 13-7. In this situation, it is the open and closing prices that are the determining factors, because such patterns require the real body of the second candle to "engulf" or fully encompass that of its predecessor. The wicks are totally ignored in this concept. If there were such a thing as the outside bar for a candlestick, it would include the wicks as well as the real body. For example, Fig. 13-6 does not reflect a Western outside bar, but Fig. 13-7 does. The underlying psychological principles of the engulfing pattern are basically the same in that they indicate a change in the buyer/seller balance following a worthwhile trend. The two differences are, first, the Japanese use the opening and closing prices for the signal, whereas Western bar charts use the extreme points on a bar. Second, the engulfing candle should be the opposite color from the candle it engulfs. For tops it would be black and for bottoms, white.

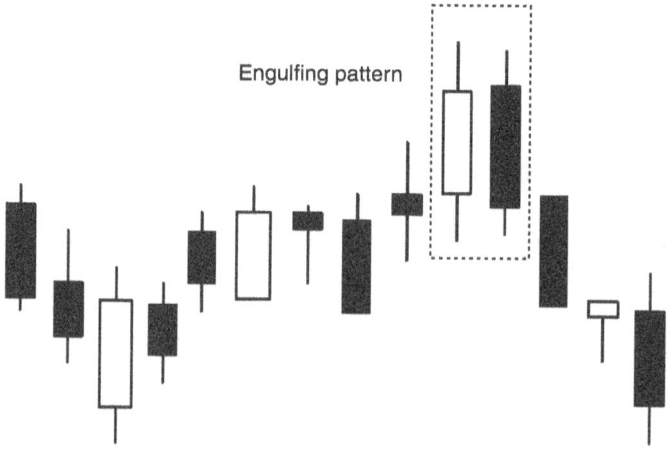

Figure 13-6 Engulfing (top) pattern.

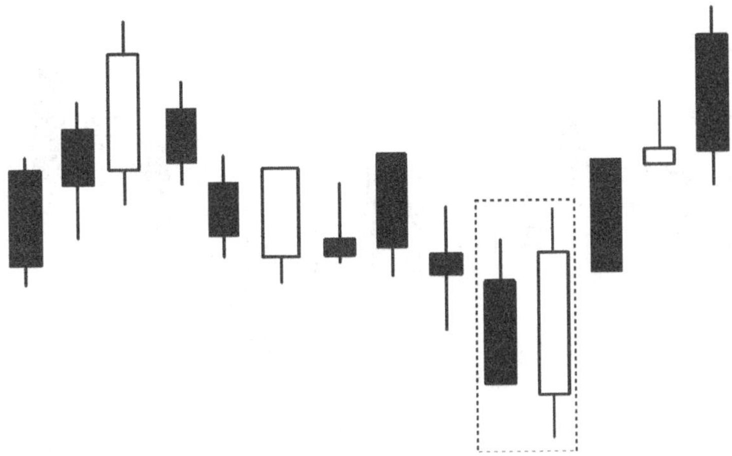

Figure 13-7 Engulfing (bottom) pattern.

A close second to the engulfing pattern is the dark cloud cover (at tops) and the piercing white line (at bottoms). These are shown in Figs. 13-8 and 13-9. At market tops, the first candle should have a reasonably long white real body. The second should have a black real body that has a higher opening, but that closes more than halfway down the first candle. At market bottoms, the exact opposite holds for a piercing white line, as in Fig. 13-9. Once again the wicks (highs and lows) are totally ignored.

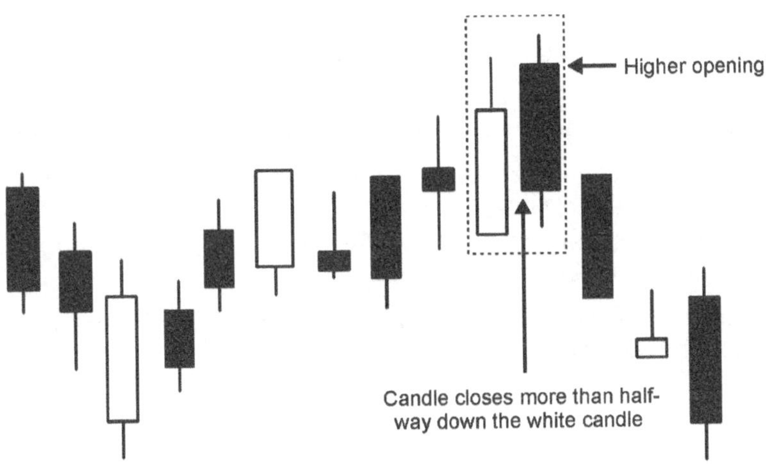

Figure 13-8 Dark cloud cover.

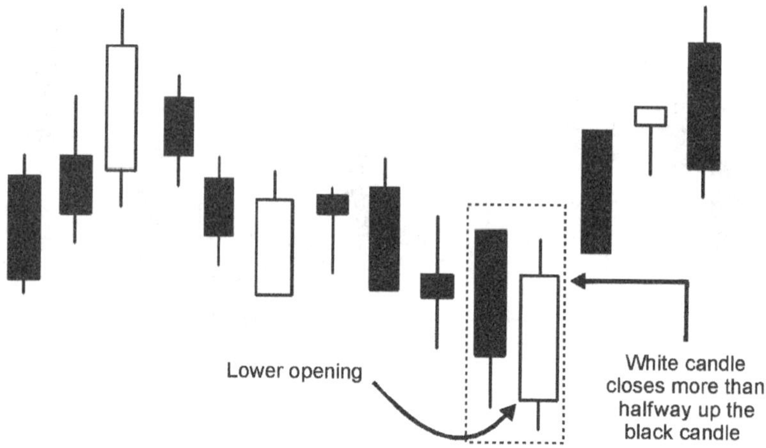

Figure 13-9 Piercing white line.

Thus there are some similarities to outside bars in Japanese candlesticks, but there is no exact match.

Summary

Outside Bars Quick Review

- *Price characteristics:* A single bar whose trading range encompasses its predecessor.
- *Requirement:* Should be preceded by a sharp up- or downtrend.
- *Factors enhancing its significance:* The wider the better; the more bars it encompasses, the higher the volume, the stronger the preceding trend.
- *Factor suggesting failure:* When the close is at the extreme of the bar in the direction of the prevailing trend.
- *Measuring implications:* None, but the pattern should have an influence on prices for 5 to 10 bars.
- *Japanese candlestick match:* None, but engulfing patterns, piercing white lines, and dark cloud cover have close similarities.

14 Inside Bars

Inside bars are the opposite of outside bars, since they form totally within the trading range of the preceding bar. An outside bar indicates a strong reversal in sentiment. An inside bar, on the other hand, reflects a closer balance between buyers and sellers following a sharp up or down move in which one or the other dominated.

In Fig. 14-1, we see a rally in which buyers are very much in control. During the period in which the inside bar is formed, buyers are unable to push prices to a new high. For the first time during the rally phase, the buy side seems to have lost some momentum. By the same token, sellers have not taken over, since they are unable to push the price below the previous bar. In effect, the balance between the two parties is very close, and neither is in control. Such action is a subtle indication that the prevailing trend is about to change. Since inside bars do not reflect as obvious a reversal in sentiment as their outside counterparts, these patterns are often followed by a small trading range, as opposed to a reversal in trend. This trading range is characteristically followed by an actual trend reversal. An example of an inside bar at a market bottom is shown in Fig. 14-2.

Guidelines for Determining the Significance of an Inside Bar

The importance of an inside bar is determined by the following factors:

1. *The sharper the trend preceding the pattern, the better.* In this situation, the strong trend indicates the dominance of one side or the other and is the setup for the reversal. If neither side were in control, sentiment would be indecisive, and there would be nothing to reverse. For example, during a sharp rally, many traders have large paper profits. When they sense

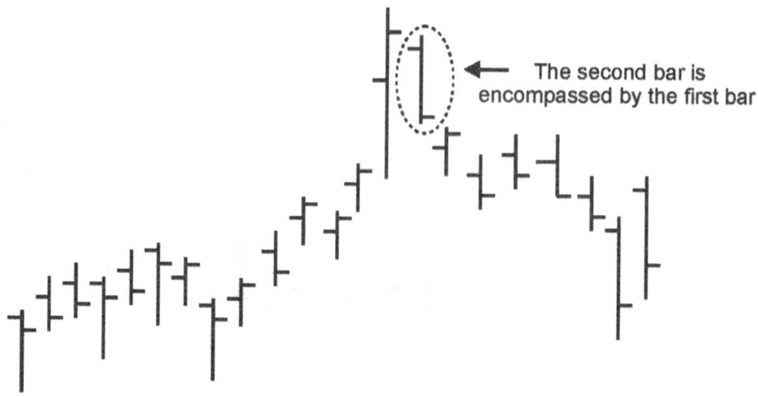

Figure 14-1 Inside bar at a top.

a reversal, it's an easy decision to cash in those profits, rendering the price vulnerable. The opposite would be true for short sellers following a decline. If the inside bar is not preceded by a worthwhile move, this motivation will be absent.

2. *The wider the first bar and its immediate predecessors in relation to previous bars and the inside bar, the better.* This is because the wide bar indicates that the prevailing trend is reaching a climax. An extensive trading range within a bar indicates volatility, and volatility is often a precursor of a trend reversal. Also, at the mature stage of a strong trend, wide bars indicate the probability of exhaustion on the part of those pushing the trend. When

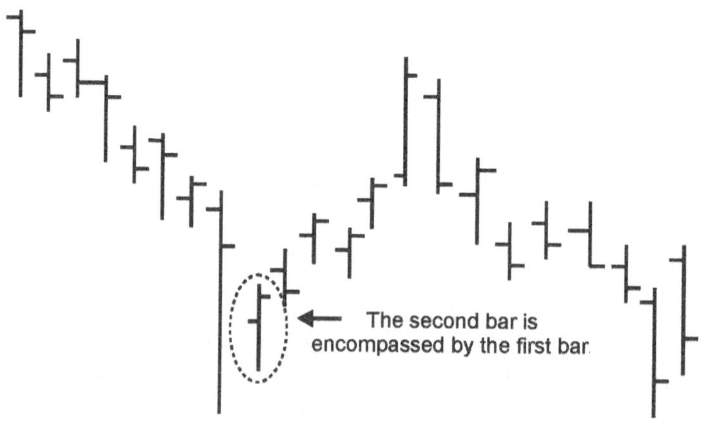

Figure 14-2 Inside bar at a bottom.

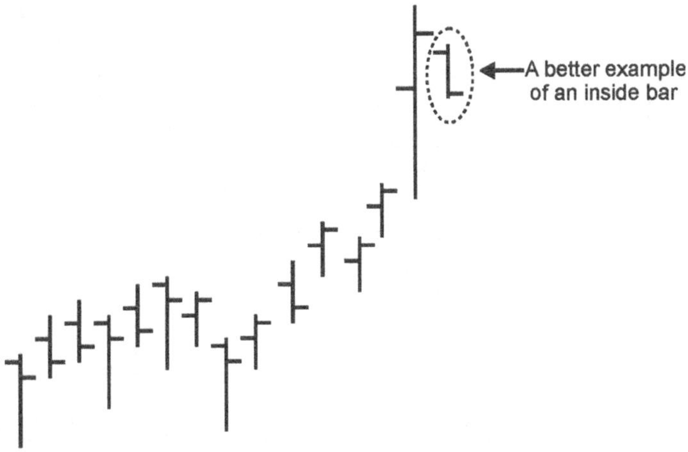

Figure 14-3 Smaller inside bar at a top.

the wide bar is followed by a substantially narrower bar, this suspicion is confirmed.

3. *The smaller the inside bar relative to its predecessor, the more dramatic the change in the buyer/seller balance, and therefore the stronger the signal.* Thus the inside bar in Fig. 14-3 is a much better example than those in Figs. 14-1 and 14-2.
4. *Volume on the inside bar should be noticeably smaller than that for the preceding bar,* since this bar indicates a more balanced situation. If we see heavy volume accompanying the bars preceding the inside bar, this indicates great enthusiasm on the part of those pushing the trend. Then, if volume shrinks noticeably, it means that neither party is in control. Two examples are shown in Fig. 14-4. The example on the left also shows a four-bar consolidation following the inside bar. The price subsequently moves to the upside.

Marketplace Examples

Chart 14-1 shows two examples of inside bars. The first marks the end of the sharp September–November decline. Note the substantial width of the first bar and the paltry range of the actual inside bar. During the formation of the first bar, volume is very heavy and the price declines sharply. There is no doubt here that sentiment is strongly on the bearish side. Then, on

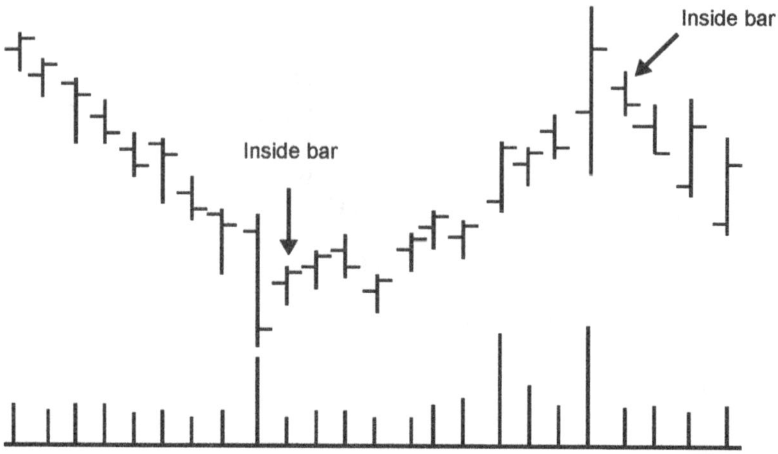

Figure 14-4 Inside bars with volume.

the second day, volume dries up appreciably and the trading range is dramatically reduced, indicating a fine balance between buyers and sellers. While this marked the bottom of the move, the next short-term trend was essentially a sideways one. Quite often we find that with inside bars, there is a change as opposed to a reversal in trend.

Chart 14-1 Oxford Industries, 2000–2001, daily.

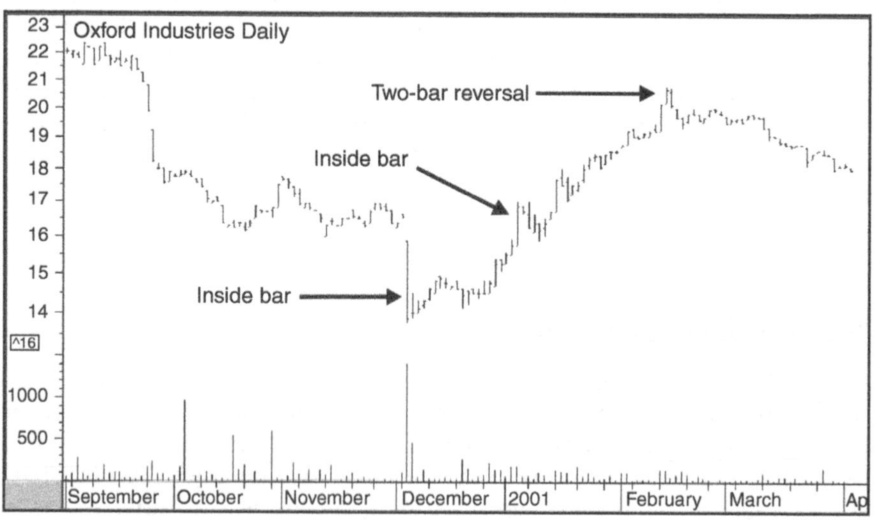

Chart 14-2 S&P Composite 5-minute bars.

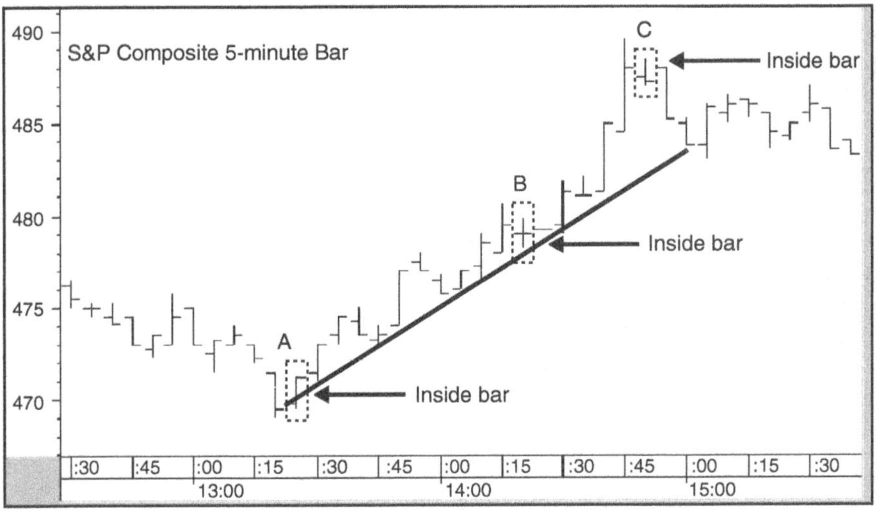

The second inside pattern developed just under halfway up the rally and was followed by a sideways trading range. The move was topped off by a two-bar reversal, which is discussed in Chapter 16.

Chart 14-2 shows some more inside bars, this time on a five-minute bar chart for the S&P Composite. The first example (*A*) was followed by a pretty good rally, although the quality of the signal was not that great, since there was not much of a contrast between the actual inside bar and its predecessor. Example *B* was an outright failure, since the price continued to advance. This goes to show that when a strong trend is underway, price patterns can and do fail. Indeed, their very failure can often be a clue to the strength of the trend. It is often a good idea to see whether one- and two-bar patterns can be confirmed by other evidence, such as a trendline violation. In this case there was no such penetration.

Finally, example *C* was a classic. The two final bars expanded considerably in size. The actual inside bar was relatively small. Note also how the open and close developed at almost identical prices, thereby confirming the idea of a very fine balance between supply and demand.

Chart 14-3 shows an inside bar for weekly cocoa. Note how it was closely followed by an outside bar. In this case, the inside bar indicated that there was a fine balance between buyers and sellers, and the outside bar indicated that buyers were now in control. Later on we see another inside bar, right at the top of the move. This was followed by a small two- to three-week

Chart 14-3 Cocoa, 1991–1992, weekly.

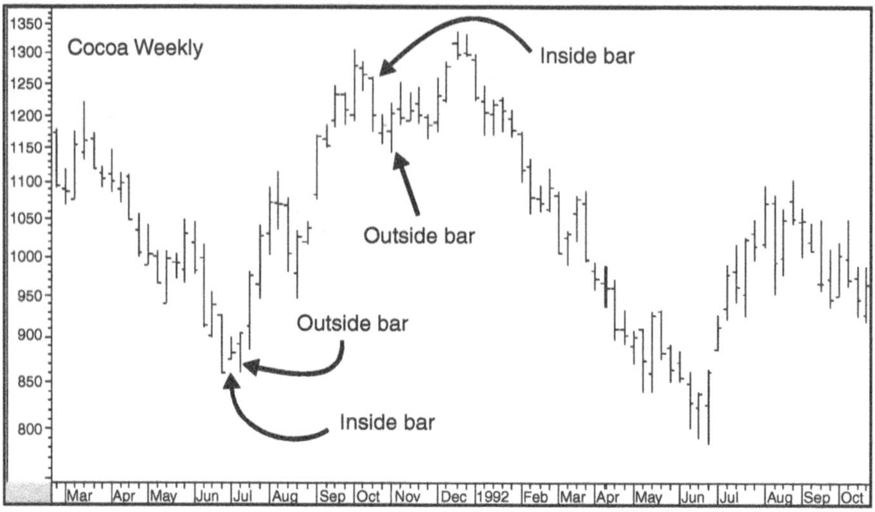

decline, which was part of an overall trading range. Note how the power of the inside bar was later canceled by an outside bar.

Chart 14-4 features the Australian Gold Share Index. An inside bar appears right at the end of a sharp decline. Indeed, the index had been declining for four straight sessions prior to the inside bar. Since these were all relatively wide bars, it indicated that the bears were very much in control. The inside bar was therefore the first sign that this one-way street had ended.

In Chart 14-5, for the Sydney All Ordinaries, an inside bar appears right at the first July low. Strictly speaking, it was not an inside bar, since the low was set at approximately the same place as that for the previous bar. However, it definitely indicated that sellers were not strong enough to send prices any lower. When this happened for a second day and the index closed on its high, more proof was given. The top of this two-day rally was capped by another "almost" inside day, and a four-day correction followed.

Finally, Chart 14-6 shows some more inside days. In the November example, the highs for the wide bar and the inside bar were almost identical. There was no doubt who was in control on the day of the wide bar. However, since the buyers were unable to push prices higher the next day, it was evident that the market had reached a more even state of balance. A bearish inside day in October called the top of a small rally. However, after a quick decline had taken place, what looked like a perfectly legitimate bullish inside

Chart 14-4 Australian Gold Share Index, daily.

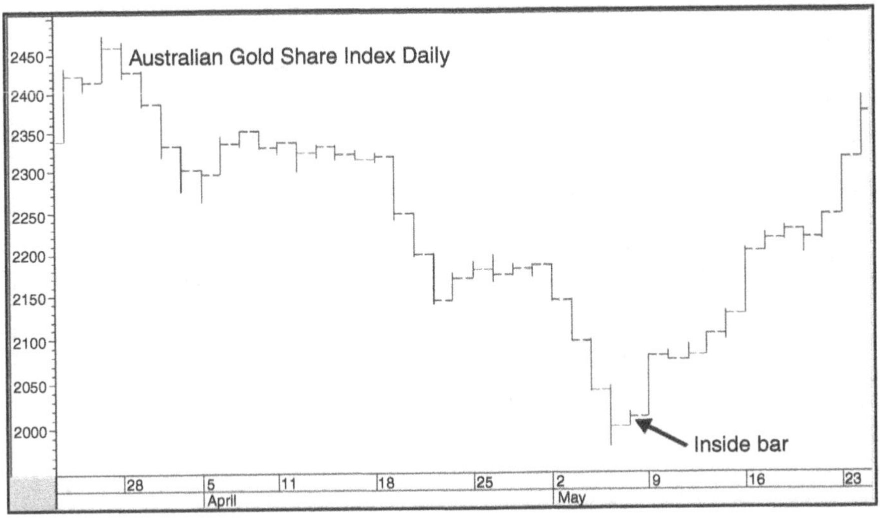

bar did not work. Based on the price action contained in this chart alone, there is no good explanation for this failure. That's why it is always important to look at one or two trends above that which is being traded. Such an investigation might have revealed that the dominant short-term trend (two

Chart 14-5 Sydney All Ordinary Index, daily.

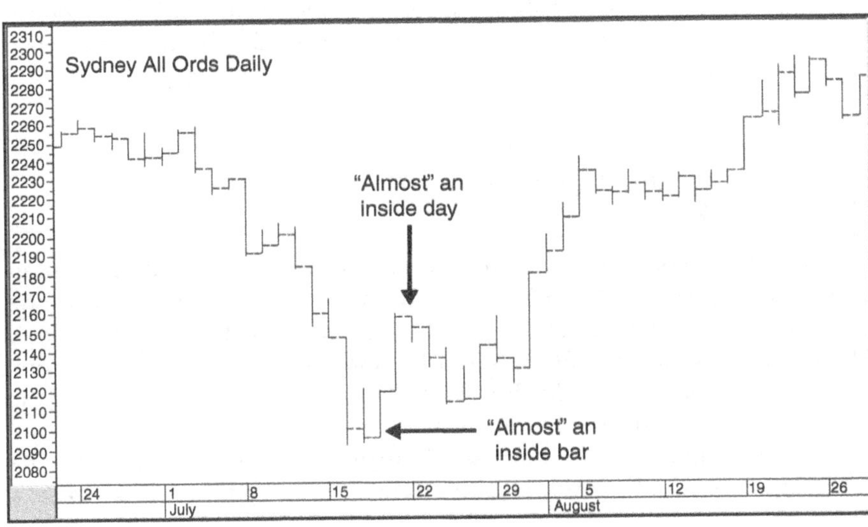

Chart 14-6 Eurodollar, daily.

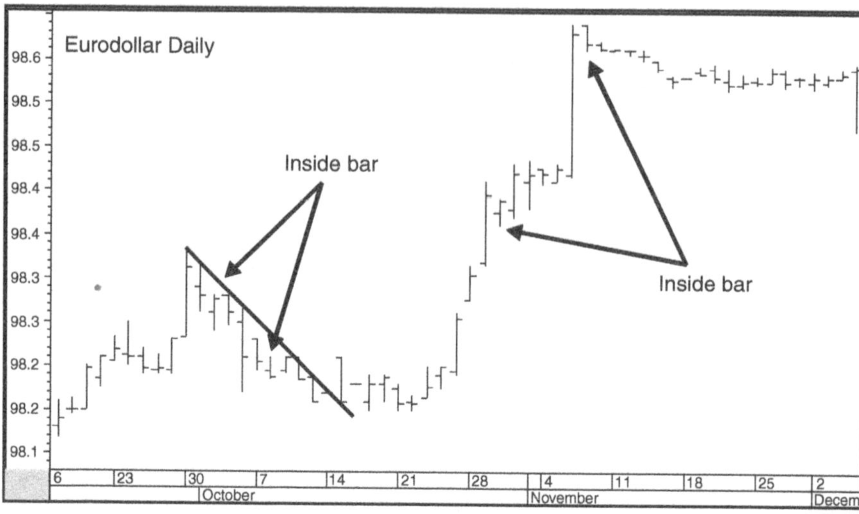

to six weeks) was declining at this point and that the inside bar was a countercyclical signal. Even if that were not so, we need to remember that technical analysis is far from perfect and that perfectly good rules can be and are broken from time to time. I would also add that of all the one- and two-bar price patterns, this one appears to be the least reliable. In this instance, waiting for a trendline violation would have made sense. Finally, another inside bar develops about halfway up the October advance. Once again it failed to trigger a consolidation or a reversal, probably because the short-term trend was strongly positive.

Inside Bars and Japanese Candlesticks

The inside bar corresponds to the harami in Japanese candlestick interpretation (see Figs. 14-5 and 14-6). However, it is different because the Harami ignores the high and low and considers only the open and close. This means that theoretically either or both wicks of a harami could encompass the preceding candle. In situations where both wicks encompassed the entire previous candle, the harami would correspond to a Western-style outside day. It would not be a particularly strong one, however, because the open and close would develop in the middle of the trading range instead

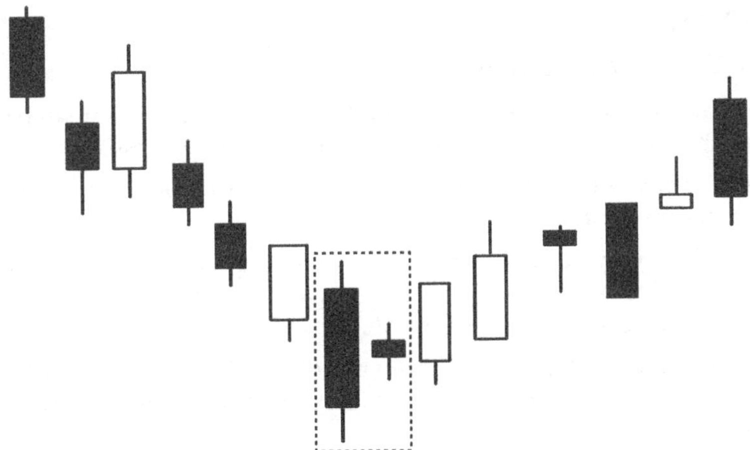

Figure 14-5 Bullish harami.

of at an extreme. Generally speaking, a "good" harami should consist of a relatively wide real body followed by a very narrow real body. Unlike in the engulfing patterns, the color of the second candle is not important, although opposite colors are preferable.

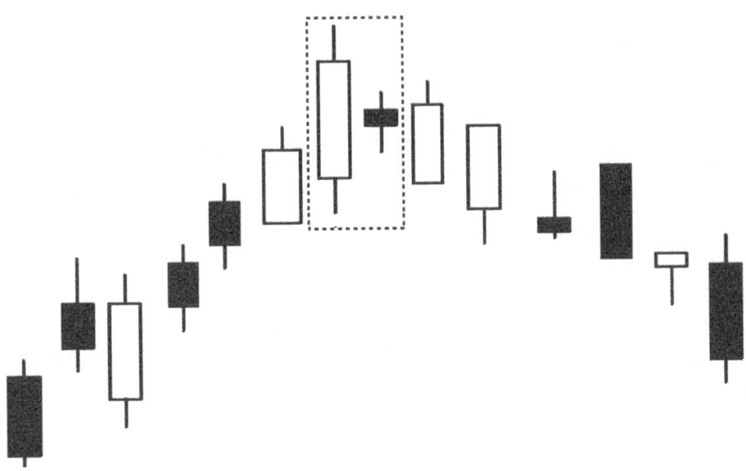

Figure 14-6 Bearish harami.

Summary

Inside Bars Quick Review

- *Price characteristic:* A persistent trend that culminates with a small bar that is totally encompassed by its substantially wider predecessor.
- *Volume characteristics:* Possibly heavy volume on the wide bar; lower activity on the inside bar.
- *Significance increased:* The sharper the incoming trend, the wider the first bar in relation to previous bars, the smaller the inside bar relative to the outside bar, and the greater the volume accompanying the first bar.
- *Implication:* Inside bars are followed by either a 5- to 10-bar consolidation or an actual reversal. It's nice to see confirmation, such as from a trendline break.

15
Key Reversal, Exhaustion, and Pinocchio Bars

Key Reversal Bars

A key reversal bar develops after a prolonged rally or reaction and indicates very strong exhaustion characteristics on the part of the dominating party. By the time the price experiences a really strong key reversal bar, the trend should have accelerated, even taking on parabolic tendencies occasionally.

Basic Characteristics

The classic pattern has the following characteristics:

1. The price opens strongly in the direction of the prevailing trend. Ideally, the open will show up as a gap on the chart.
2. The trading range is very wide relative to the preceding bars.
3. The price closes near or below the previous close (or near or above the previous close in a downtrend reversal).
4. Volume, if available, should be climactic.

Figures 15-1 and 15-2 show two examples of key reversals, one at a top and the other at a bottom.

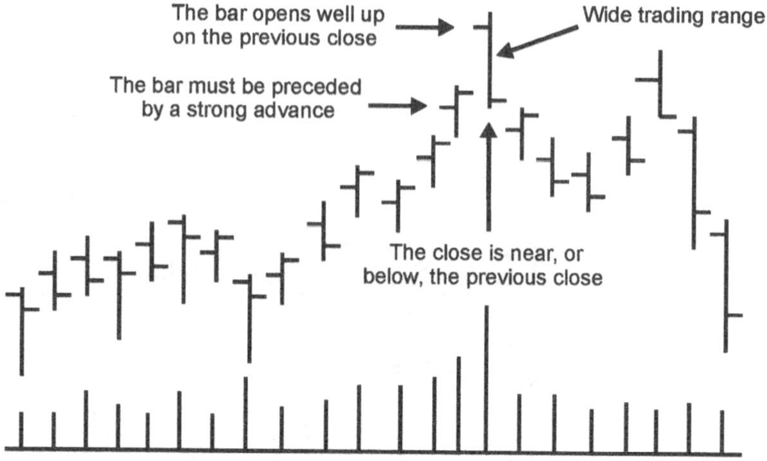

Figure 15-1 Key reversal bar at a top.

Psychological Underpinning

The strong opening emphasizes the urgency with which the dominating party regards the situation. At tops, buyers reach a new high in their level of greed, and at bottoms, sellers are at the height of panic. The gap opening is often associated with unexpectedly good news at a top or bad news at a bottom. The way a market deals with pro-trend developments can be crucial in assessing the short-term technical picture. For example, if a company

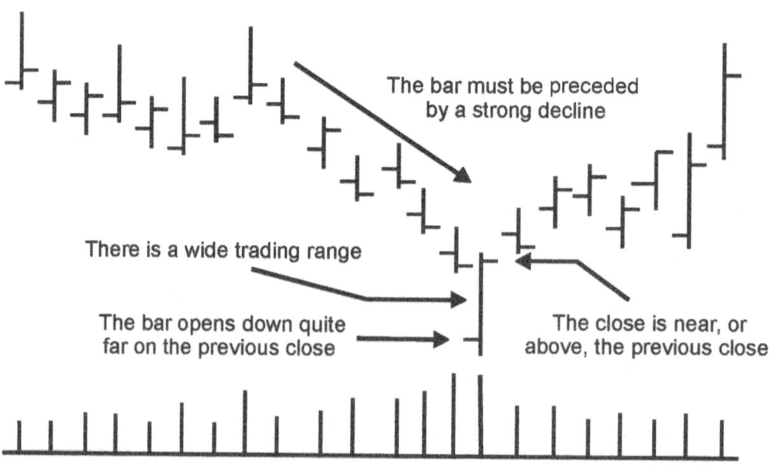

Figure 15-2 Key reversal bar at a bottom.

announces earnings that are above expectations, this could cause the stock price to gap up at the opening. However, if, at the end of the day, the price has returned to a level that is near or just below the previous close, the news has obviously had no new net positive effect on the price. Since the key reversal day is preceded by a strong uptrend, this is really the last gasp of the buyers as weak, uninformed traders, and investors react to the "great" news. It is also the give-up phase for short sellers, many of whom panic out of the security in the frantic activity associated with the early phase of the bar's formation. After all, if good news cannot push prices higher, what will?

At bottoms, the gap lower opening panics the weak longs into liquidation, while short sellers are fully confident as they initiate new positions. Further declines are such a foregone conclusion that the only questions remaining are how low prices will go and when they will get there. When the price returns to a level near the previous close, the careless shorts are locked in at lower prices. Since long liquidation is pretty well complete, prices no longer fall, and the shorts are forced to cover. This is a surprise to them, because the bad news associated with the gap lower opening should have pushed prices lower. However, if bad news cannot invoke further liquidation, what can?

The wide-bar aspect of the key reversal bar is important because it implies volatility, and volatility is often associated with market turning points. When prices open strongly in the direction of the prevailing trend, experience a wide trading range, and close near to where they started, this means that a lot of people are locked into losing positions. The higher the volume, the greater the number of people who are locked in. It also indicates that buyers in an uptrend tried to push the price higher but were able to do so only temporarily. They gave it their very best, but they failed, because at the end of the bar, prices were little changed from the previous close. The opposite would be true for sellers in a downtrend.

Since key reversals develop after a sharp, almost parabolic rally or reaction, they tend to reflect stronger emotions than the average one- or two-bar reversal patterns. For this reason, their effect is usually far more significant, often lasting far longer than the usual 5 to 10 bars.

Key reversal bars are often followed by sharp reversals in trend, but we occasionally find that after several more bars have developed, a retracement move sets it. An example is shown in Fig. 15-3 for a top. This retracement acts as a kind of test. If it fails, it becomes a reinforcement of the change in psychology that has taken place. The retracement also offers sellers at a top another opportunity to get out and buyers at a bottom a second chance to get in.

Normally, the extreme level of the key reversal bar is not exceeded, but if it is, then the pattern is canceled. Since this is an emotional point on the

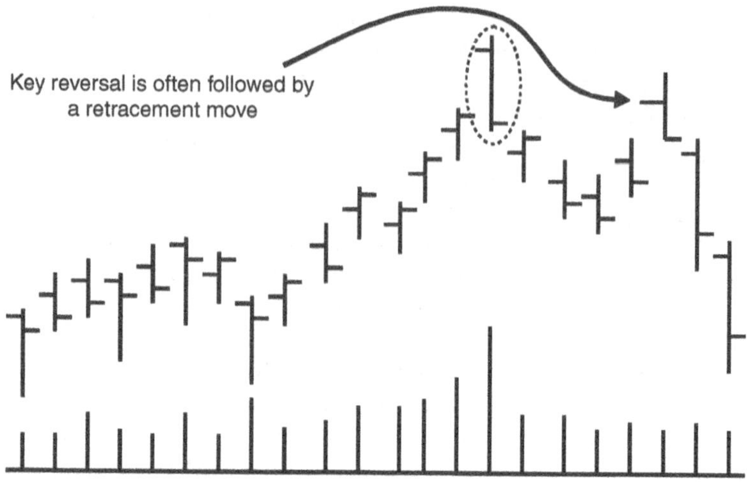

Figure 15-3 Key reversal bar showing a retracement.

chart, it is an important potential support/resistance level, and therefore it represents an intelligent place to set a stop. In the case of a top, this will be slightly above the key reversal bar, and in the case of a bottom, just below it.

Marketplace Examples

The left-hand part of Chart 15-1 shows a classic example of a key reversal for Barrick Gold. Note how the short-term rally is climaxed by an explosion of volume and a wide key reversal bar. The opening price is very near the high. Quite often a key reversal is followed by a sharp change in trend and a subsequent retracement. That is exactly what happened in this case, as the price rallied in the fourth and fifth sessions following the key reversal. The termination of this brief advance was signaled by an outside day. These one-bar patterns have only short-term significance as a general rule, but often they can prove to be the first domino in a major trend reversal. It all depends on the maturity of the trend in question combined with the position of the longer-term indicators. In this instance, the key reversal marked the top for at least six months.

The second example of a key reversal, to the right, is also a good one in that volume expands along with a fairly wide bar. However, it is not preceded by much of a rally. Thus the bullish expectations were nowhere near as strong as on the late September reversal day. This pattern would certainly not warrant as many stars as the first one.

Chart 15-2 features the 1998 bottom for Merrill Lynch. The actual day of the low was a classic case of a key reversal bar. The volume also cooperated

Chart 15-1 Barrick Gold, 1999–2000, daily.

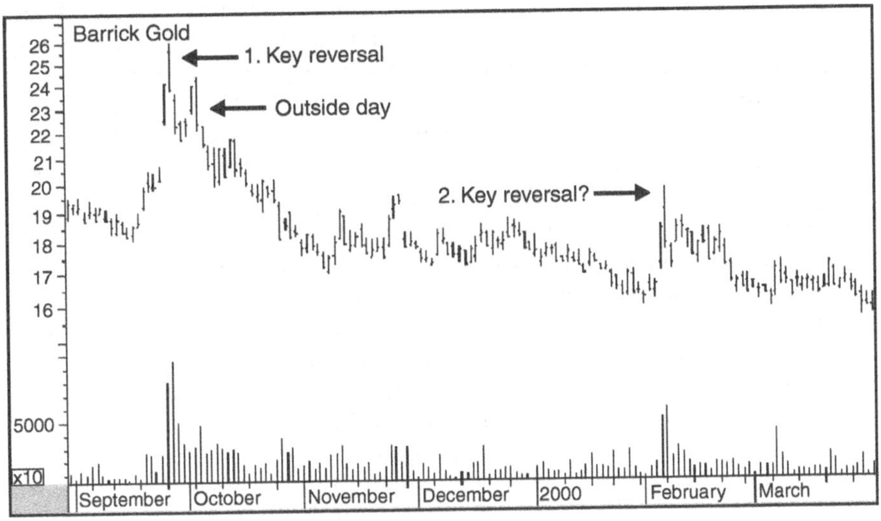

Chart 15-2 Merrill Lynch, 1998, daily.

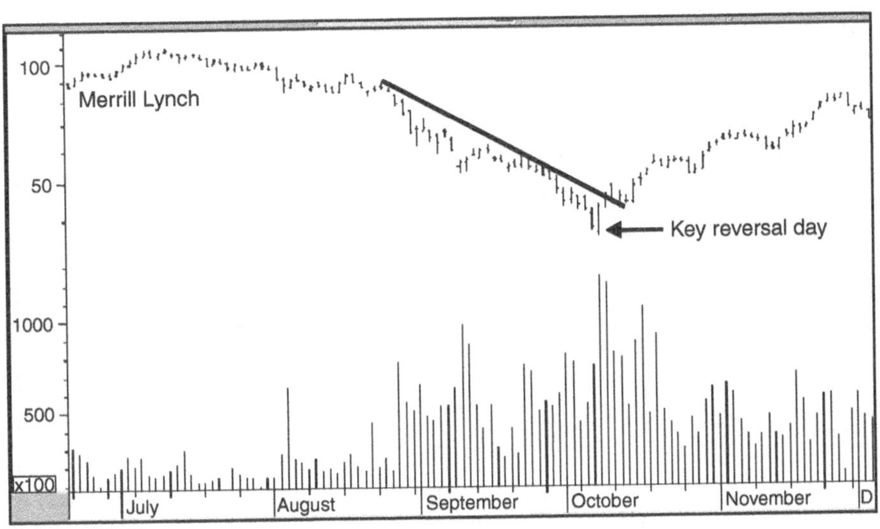

by expanding to a crescendo as the stock bottomed. It was even possible to construct a small down trendline. When this trendline was violated, it confirmed the signal being given by the reversal bar. There was no way of knowing from the bar itself that a bear market low in the stock had just been seen; it merely indicated that a worthwhile rally was likely. The extremely heavy volume would have told us that this particular key reversal would probably reverse the trend for a lot more than the normal 5 to 10 days. On the other hand, had it been possible to establish that the overall market had bottomed on the same day, it could legitimately have been argued that the character of this pattern and its accompanying volume signaled a bear market bottom for the stock. If you look closely you can see that this particular bar was also an outside day. In fact, it could be argued that it bears more resemblance to an outside bar than to a key reversal, since the price closed well above the previous close. This is a semantic point, since we are really concerned with identifying technical phenomena that reflect significant changes in psychology. This bar certainly does, regardless of what it is termed.

Chart 15-3 shows that the July 2002 bottom in the S&P was signaled by a key reversal bar. The opening price appears to be at the same level as the previous day's close, but the chart does not indicate the initial weakness experienced by many issues. This is because the opening price does not reflect stocks that have a mismatch of orders. Since the opening was weak, these stocks experienced a delayed opening, and the "opening" price for the

Chart 15-3 NYSE Composite, 2002, daily.

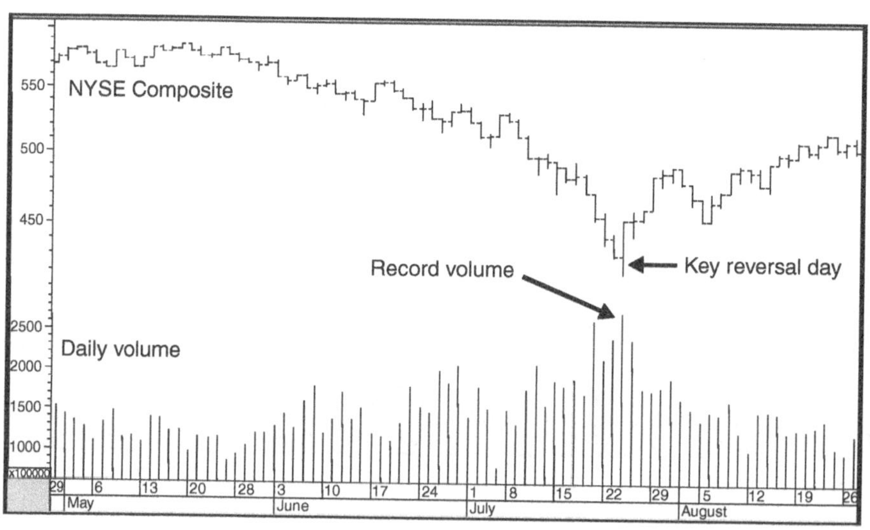

S&P included only those stocks that were trading at the 9:30 a.m. opening. The trading bar was extremely wide compared to anything else on the chart and was preceded by a very sharp and persistent decline. The potential for a reversal in bearish psychology was definitely present. Perhaps the key to this situation was the record volume experienced during this session. Record volume by definition does not happen every day. When it develops after a long bear trend, it is typically a sign of a new bull market. In this case, the index subsequently made a slightly lower low in October, but the July low saw more issues reach 52-week lows and was therefore a more intense bottom.

Exhaustion Bars

Exhaustion bars develop after a really sharp up or down move. They are a form of key reversal and are also a variation on the one-bar island reversal, described in Chapter 12. However, they differ enough to warrant their own category.

Basic Characteristics

The requirements for an exhaustion bar are as follows:

1. The price opens with a large gap in the direction of the then-prevailing trend. That trend is typically quite strong.
2. The bar is extremely wide relative to previous bars. As a general rule, the relative width of these bars is far greater than the average key reversal.
3. The opening price develops in the lower half of the bar in a downtrend and in the upper half in an uptrend. In other words, sentiment is at or very close to its most extreme at the start of the bar.
4. The closing price should be both above the opening and in the top half of the bar in a downtrend and in the lower half and below the opening in an uptrend. This offers a few pointers that sentiment, at least during the bar's formation, has begun to reverse.
5. The bar is completed with a gap to the left still in place. This differs from the key reversal bar, where there is either no gap or an extremely small one.

Examples of exhaustion bars for both a bottom and a top are featured in Figs. 15-4 and 15-5. They differ from the one-bar island reversal (see Chapter 12) in that *there is no gap between the exhaustion bar and its successor.* Also, it is not uncommon for the opening and closing prices in a one-bar island to be near each other and fairly close to the gap.

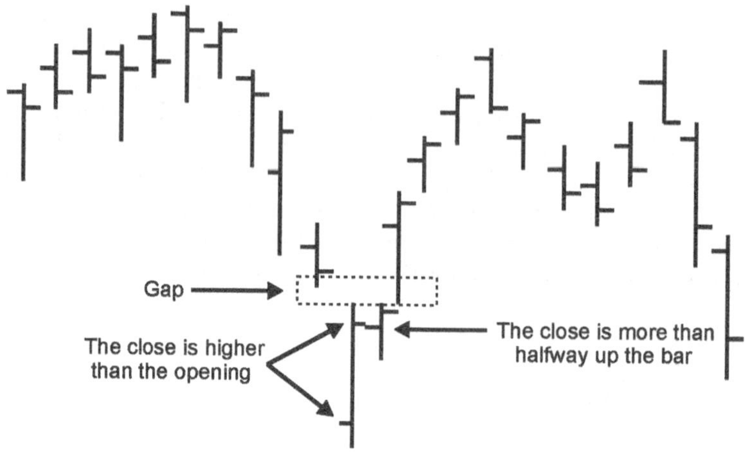

Figure 15-4 Exhaustion bar at a bottom.

Underlying Psychology

When trying to identify an exhaustion bar, look for a very strong trend that is capped with an extension that takes the form of an extreme movement in the price. The idea that the bar opens with a huge gap and closes in the opposite direction reflects the concept of a reversal in psychology. For example, at a market low, we come into the exhaustion bar following a sharp decline. On a daily chart, this could take the form of 5 to 10 days of more

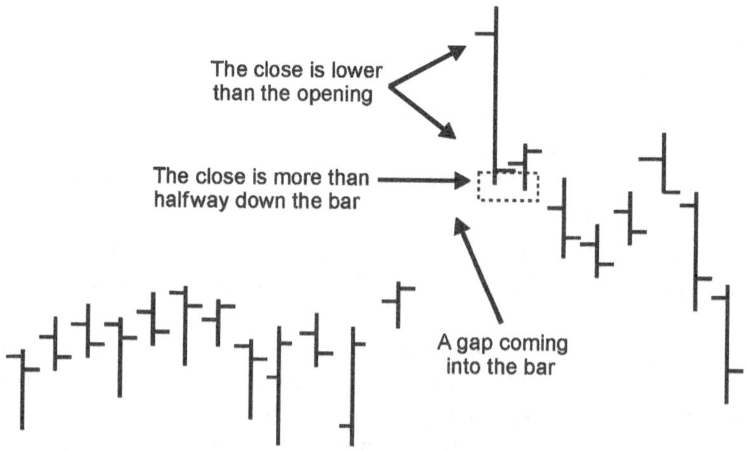

Figure 15-5 Exhaustion bar at a top.

or less persistently lower prices, often reflected by wide bars. The large gap as the price opens in what will turn out to be the lower part of the exhaustion bar reflects the culmination of this bearish psychology and the reality that the sellers are very much in control. However, the fact that prices often drop much further after the opening but then close in the upper half of the bar offers a subtle hint that the selling may be over and that perhaps it is the buyers' turn to take command. The wide high-volume trading range also suggests the kind of frenzied activity associated with a turn.

At market tops, the same kind of psychology is also present, except that greed replaces fear and the opening-closing relationship is reversed.

Marketplace Examples

Chart 15-4 shows an exhaustion bar on a daily chart for Kellwood. It was preceded by a short but sharp decline and became a reversal point for a small rally in an ongoing downtrend. It has the correct price characteristics: gap down, low below the opening of the bar, and close more than halfway up. Generally speaking, it would have been better for the opening to have been in the lower part of the bar, but the extreme width more than made up for this missing ingredient.

Warnaco, in Chart 15-5, had the correct characteristics vis-à-vis the open-close relationship. In this instance, the downside gap would have been a

Chart 15-4 Kellwood, 2000–2001, daily.

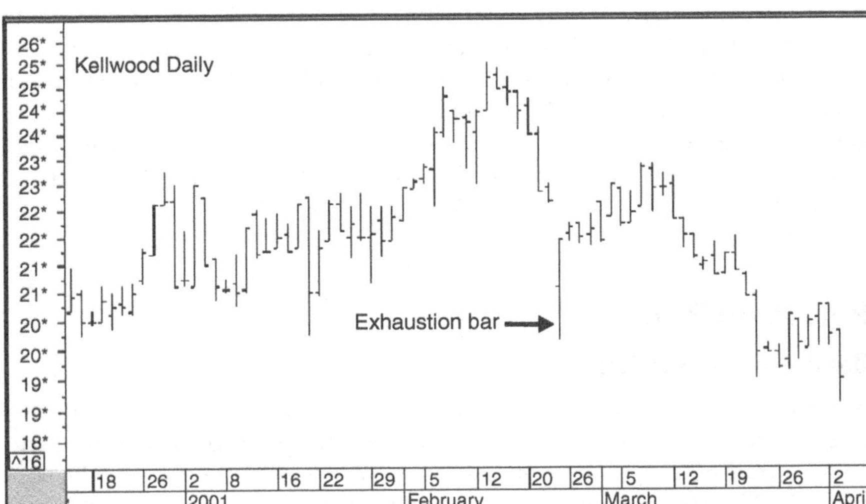

Chart 15-5 Warnaco, daily.

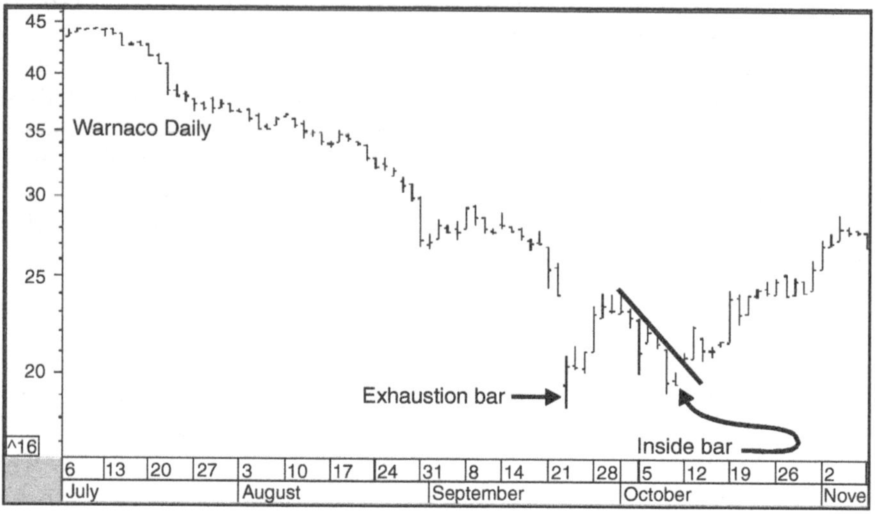

pretty horrific experience for the longs. The price had closed at $24 the night before and opened at $19 on the day of the exhaustion bar, for a $5 gap!

In retrospect, the bar turned out to be the first bottom of a double-bottom formation. Note that the second bottom consisted of an inside bar, which was confirmed when the price broke above the down trendline.

On intraday charts, gaps almost always develop at the open because of some overnight change in psychology. This means that exhaustion bars tend to be more prevalent in these very-short-term charts. Chart 15-6 shows an exhaustion bar for the NYSE Composite. It has all the characteristics: large gap, close higher than the opening, wide range, and so on. It is also followed by an inside bar, which added a further piece of evidence that the trend had changed.

Pinocchio Bars

Basic Characteristics

A pretty common form of exhaustion shows up when a security opens and closes relatively quietly, but during the bar the price breaks temporarily above a trading range, level of resistance, or trendline and then falls back below it. The reverse would be true at a bottom. I call these *Pinocchio bars,*

Chart 15-6 NYSE Composite 5-minute bar.

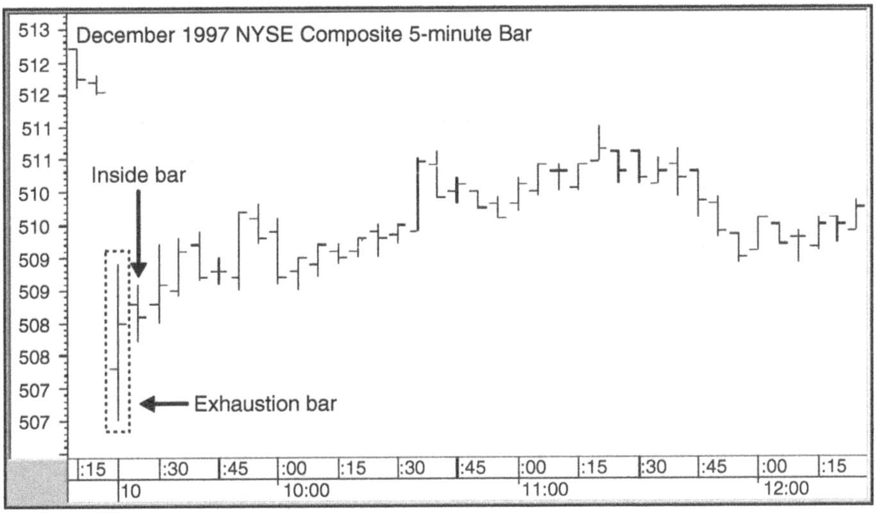

because they give us a false sense of what is really going on. Examples are shown in Figs. 15-6 and 15-7.

Underlying Psychology

Pinocchio bars are bars in which the bulk of the trading takes place outside the previous and subsequent trading range. This means that upside breakouts lock in unwary buyers with a loss at the closing of the bar. Short sellers will be similarly trapped at bottoms. Alternatively, these patterns may develop because the pros on the floor sense that there are a substantial number of stops below the market. The security is then pressured to squeeze out these unwary holders, and the price is subsequently free to move higher.

During the Pinocchio period of trading, when the price is temporarily above resistance in an uptrend or below support in a downtrend, either buyers or sellers have a chance to push prices in their direction, but they fail. For example, if the optimists see an upside breakout, they should be attracted to the security, and the trend ought to continue. However, by the end of the bar, the price returns to below the resistance and they become discouraged.

The character Pinocchio tells us when he is lying because his nose gets longer. In the case of the Pinocchio bar, it is the trading beyond the resistance or support level in question that indicates that the signal is false. We

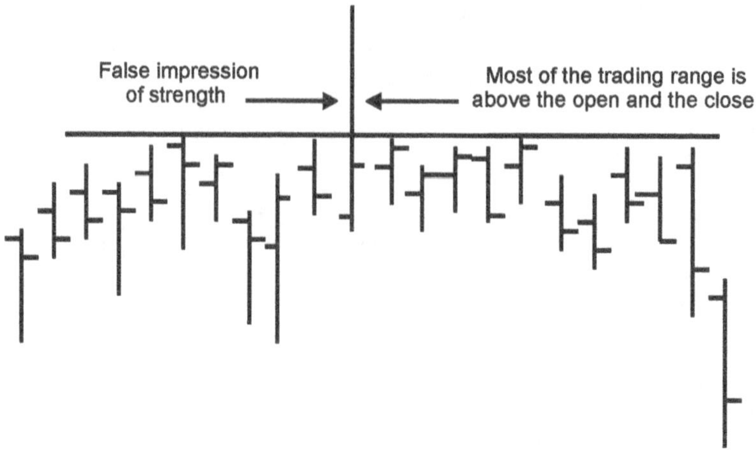

Figure 15-6 Pinocchio bar at a top.

can also take this a step further by saying that the bigger the nose, the bigger the lie. In the case of security prices, the larger the trading range above (below at bottoms) the opening and closing prices, the more false the signal and the greater the move in the opposite direction is likely to be. To put it another way, the wider the bar, the greater the number of traders that have the potential to be locked in at losing prices.

Figure 15-8 reflects the idea that when a false break develops above a down trendline, this is also indicative of exhaustion, since the price cannot hold

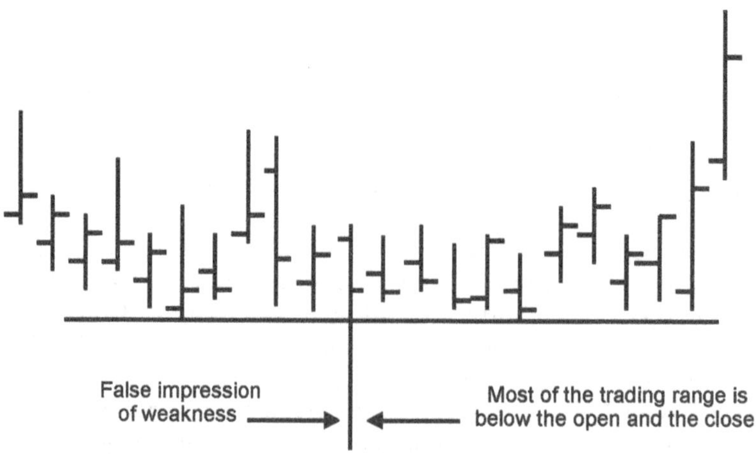

Figure 15-7 Pinocchio bar at a bottom.

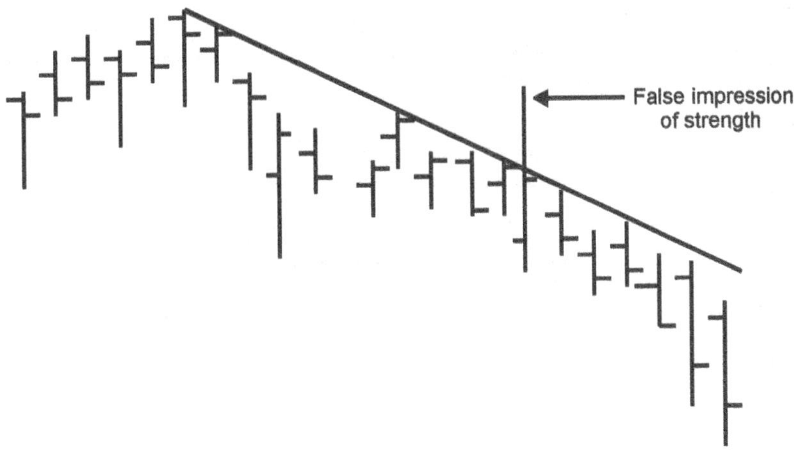

Figure 15-8 Pinocchio bar at a trendline.

above the strong resistance reflected by the line. The same principle would hold true for a false downside break of an up trendline.

Marketplace Examples

Chart 15-7 shows a break above the trading range that was nullified by the time the bar closed. The price moved sideways for a few bars, but, as often happens following false breakouts, it then moved to the downside in a decisive way. Chart 15-8 shows a false break to the downside. Once again this was followed by a strong move in the opposite direction to the Pinocchio "lie."

Chart 15-9 displays a five-minute bar for the S&P December 1998 contract. In this case, the price breaks above the two previous bars' highs, but by the time of the closing it is back below the resistance. This is not as clear-cut a case of temporary resistance violation as Chart 15-7. Even so, it is surprising how many false breaks above resistance (below support) formed by just two or three bars result in a Pinocchio-type whipsaw.

One important fact about an exhaustion move is that the extremity of the bar in question often proves to be an important support or resistance point. Therefore, it is often a good idea to place a stop loss a little bit beyond the extremity of the Pinocchio bar—provided, of course, that the trade still results in a reasonable risk/reward. An example is shown in Charts 15-10 and 15-11, which feature five-minute bars for the S&P futures. Chart 15-10 indicates a Pinocchio break above the dashed trendline. If a trader had had

Chart 15-7 S&P Composite 10-minute bar.

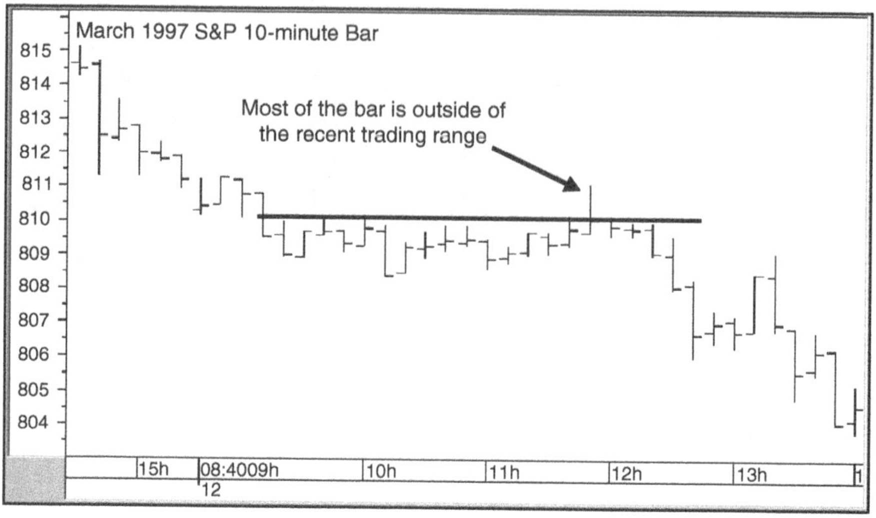

Chart 15-8 S&P Composite 10-minute bar.

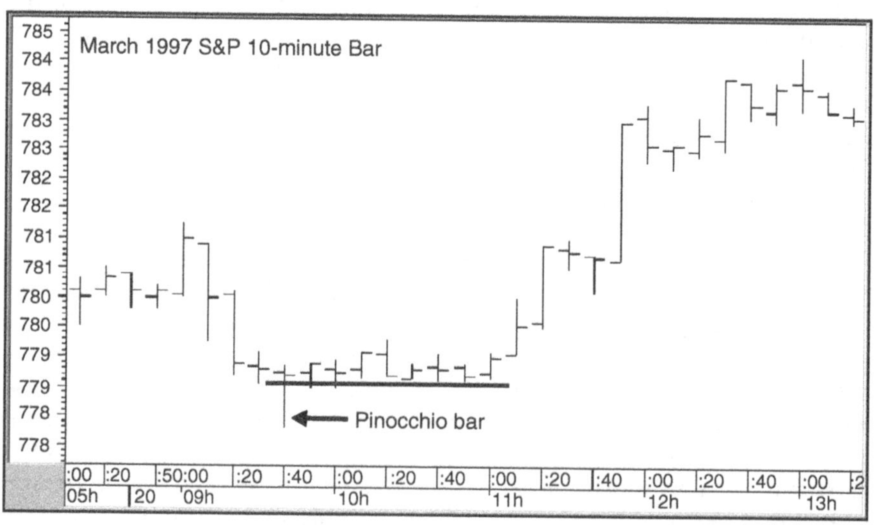

Chart 15-9 S&P Composite 5-minute bar.

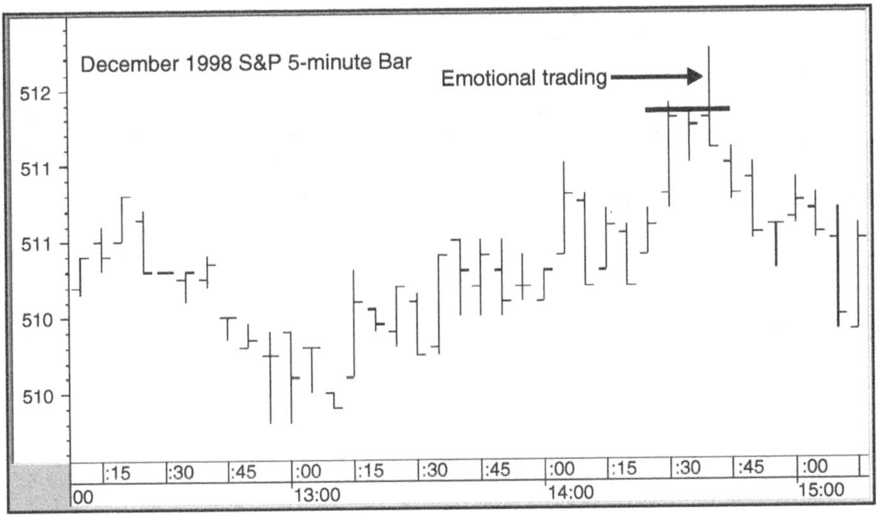

Chart 15-10 S&P Composite 5-minute bar.

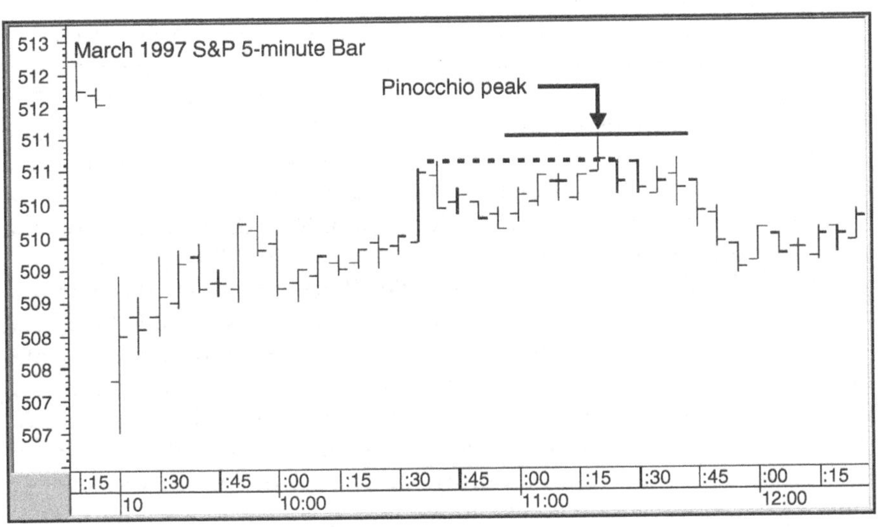

Chart 15-11 S&P Composite 5-minute bar.

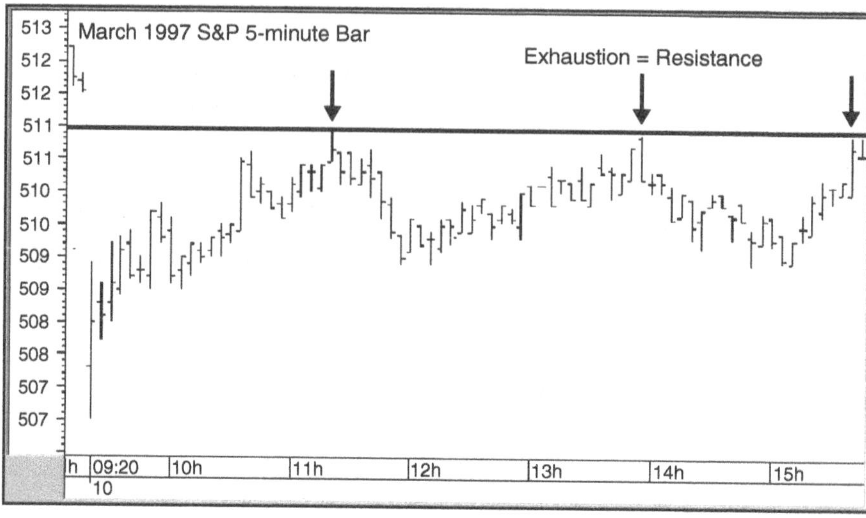

a reason for going short, a stop above the emotional point—i.e., the extremity of the Pinocchio bar—would have made sense. Chart 15-11 shows the same situation, but in this chart the trading period has been extended to show that the Pinocchio high was indeed a great resistance area, since it turned back two subsequent rallies.

Chart 15-12 features a daily graph for the lumber price. A Pinocchio bar develops in early April. It may not have been that obvious at the time, but as the chart progresses, you can see that it was possible to extend the line joining the two pre-Pinocchio highs. This emphasized the fact that a false upside break had taken place. Consequently, it would have been possible to have sold short when a violation of the dashed up trendline confirmed the Pinocchio bar three days after its formation. Note the consolidation outside bar that developed a couple of days after the trendline violation.

In Chart 15-13, featuring the daily crude oil price, an inside day helps the price bounce off its early April low. After a few more days, it would have been obvious that that low was a bottom of some kind. Since previous lows and highs are good candidates for support/resistance zones, it would have been possible to construct a horizontal trendline at the low, indicating potential support. In fact, this trendline was touched or approached twice around June 8, just prior to being temporarily breached as the price experienced a Pinocchio day. After the Pinocchio, the line again acted as support. Then an outside day formed and the price broke above a nice down trendline, thereby confirming the Pinocchio and the outside bar. Finally, note the small

Chart 15-12 Lumber, daily.

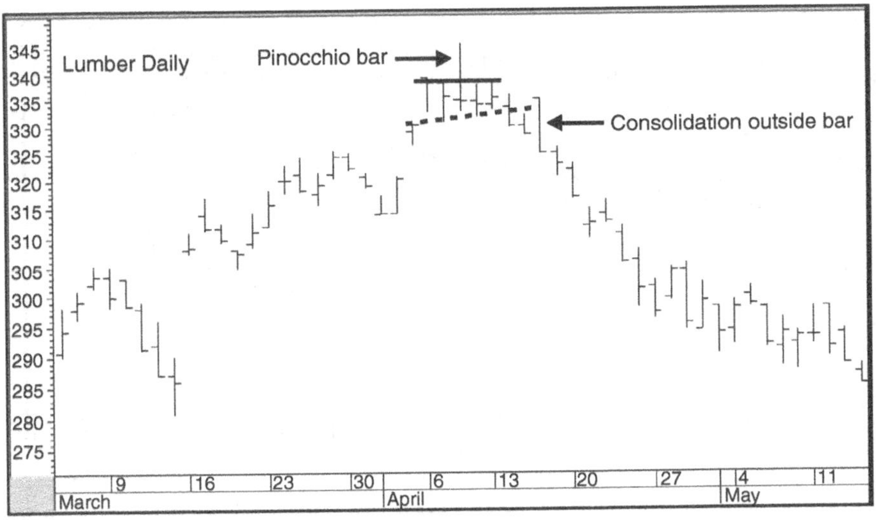

Chart 15-13 Crude oil, daily.

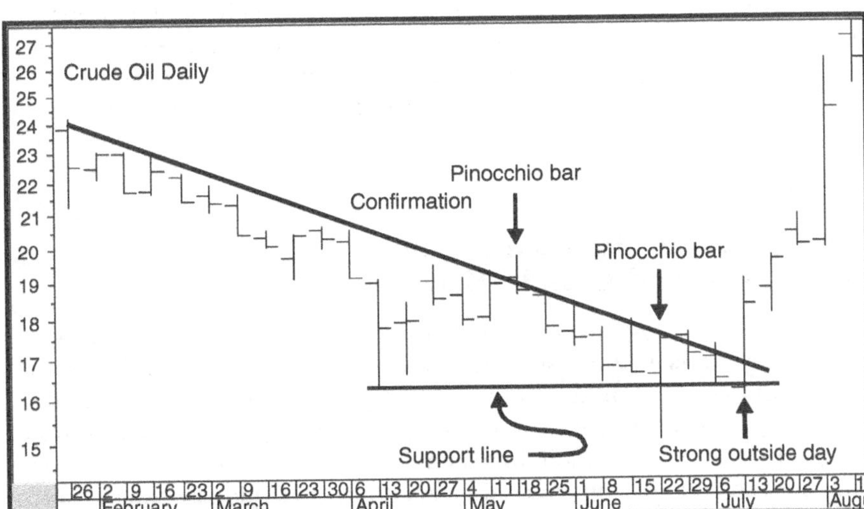

Chart 15-14 Kellogg, 1997–1998, daily.

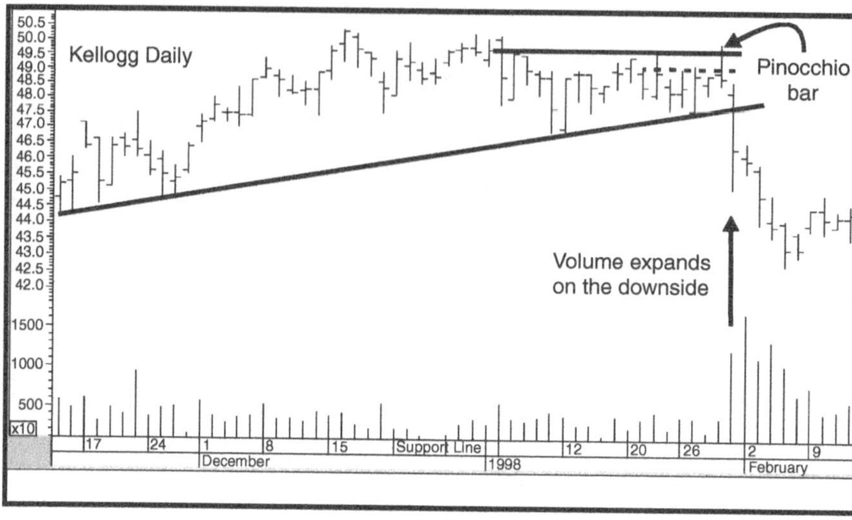

Pinocchio that managed to temporarily break above the down trendline in mid-May. It was initially followed by a decline, as we might have expected. However, the good news is that it enhanced the significance of the down trendline, so when that trendline was finally violated, a terrific rally followed.

Finally, Chart 15-14, for Kellogg, shows a Pinocchio that temporarily pushes above two horizontal trendlines. This bearish action was confirmed the next day as the price violated a good up trendline on extremely heavy volume. The expanded activity emphasized that the sellers certainly had the upper hand at this point.

Key Reversals, Exhaustion Bars, Pinocchios, and Candlesticks

There are no candlesticks that are equivalent to key reversals or exhaustion bars. A key reversal would show up as a very long real body following an advance or decline. Nor are there any direct correlations to Pinocchio bars. The closest is probably a gravestone, dragonfly, or long-legged doji, as shown in Fig. 15-9. A doji is a candle in which the open and close are either identical or extremely close to each other. A Pinocchio could also take the form of a hammer or inverted hammer. In the Pinocchio context, it would be important for the upper wick to temporarily break above resistance in the case of a whipsaw upside breakout, or for the lower one to break below

Figure 15-9 Doji candlesticks.

resistance in the case of a whipsaw bottom. This is because the idea of a false resistance/support violation is crucial to the Pinocchio characteristic, yet none of the candlesticks described here involve such a concept.

Summary

Key Reversals Quick Review

- *Price characteristics:* A wide bar following a strong and persistent trend. In the case of a top, it gaps higher at the opening and may move higher during the remainder of the bar, but it closes near the previous close. At bottoms, it gaps lower at the opening and may move lower during the remainder of the bar, but it closes near the previous close.
- *Volume characteristics:* A heavy-volume day that often climaxes a previous trend of rapidly rising volume.
- *Failure signaled:* When the price moves beyond the extreme point of the bar.
- *Measuring implications:* None. Key reversals often develop at the end of intermediate and primary trends.

Exhaustion Bars Quick Review

- *Price characteristics:* A very wide bar that develops after a strong trend and opens with a large gap At bottoms, the opening is in the lower half of the bar, and the closing is in the top half. At tops, the opening is in the top half of the bar, and the closing is in the lower half. There is no gap on the right-hand side of the pattern unless the exhaustion bar is a one-bar island reversal.

- *Volume characteristics:* Usually volume is heavy and reflects a temporary selling climax.
- *Failure signaled:* When the price moves beyond the extreme of the bar.
- *Measuring implications:* None.

Pinocchio Bars Quick Review

- *Price characteristics:* A bar that temporarily breaks a resistance or support area between the opening and the closing. The longer the "nose," the stronger the signal.
- *Volume characteristics:* Can develop on low volume, but high volume reflects more trapped individuals and tends to be more significant.
- *Significance:* The greater the resistance/support barrier that is penetrated by the "nose" and the stronger the inbound trend, the more the significance is enhanced. Also, the longer the nose, the greater the significance.
- *Failure signaled:* When the price moves beyond the extreme point of the bar. The extreme point often represents strong support or resistance.
- *Measuring implications:* None, but stronger moves tend to develop when a Pinocchio is confirmed within three or four bars by a trendline violation.

16 Two- and Three-Bar Reversals

Two-Bar Reversals

Basic Characteristics

A two-bar reversal is a classic way in which the charts signal exhaustion. Like other one- and two-bar patterns, two-bar reversals develop after a prolonged advance or decline, but the reversal appears to be stronger than the average one- or two-bar formation. Examples are shown in Figs. 16-1 and 16-2. The characteristics of these patterns are as follows:

1. They need to be preceded by a strong and persistent trend. Since two-bar reversals are often followed by dramatic reversals, it is more important for them to be preceded by a strong rally or reaction than for most of the other one- and two-bar formations.
2. Both bars should stand out as having exceptionally wide trading ranges relative to previous bars (see Figs. 16-3 and 16-4). Once again, wide bars reflect volatility and emotional exhaustion. The more we can see of this type of action, the more confidence we can have in the power of the pattern to signal an important reversal.
3. The opening and closing of both bars should be near the extreme points of the bar. This is important, as it reflects the total and unexpected change in sentiment that has taken place. Longs are locked in at two-bar reversal tops and shorts at bottoms.
4. An expansion of volume on both bars enhances the concept of a change in sentiment. High volume after a strong trend is also indicative of buyer

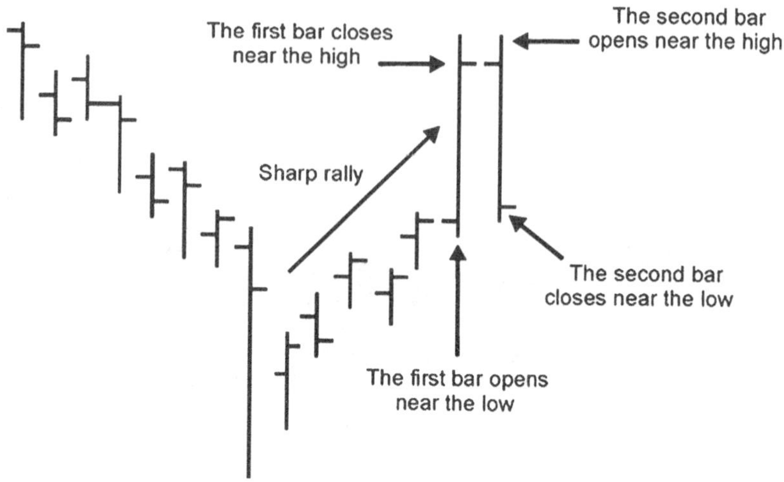

Figure 16-1 Two-bar reversal at a top.

or seller exhaustion, depending on the direction of the preceding trend. It also means that more traders are locked in with a loss at the pattern's completion.

5. A lot of the time, two-bar reversals are followed by an immediate sharp move, with the price reversing on a dime. However, there appear to be equally as many occasions when a small retracement move develops prior to the real trend emerging. Examples are shown in Figs. 16-5 and 16-6. The retracements in these examples have been termed *resistance* zones

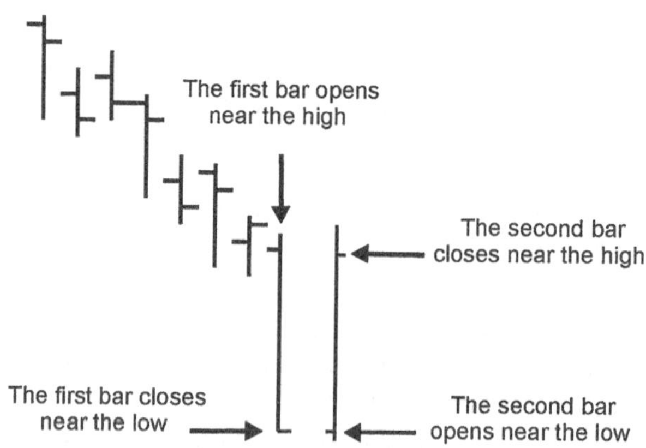

Figure 16-2 Two-bar reversal at a bottom.

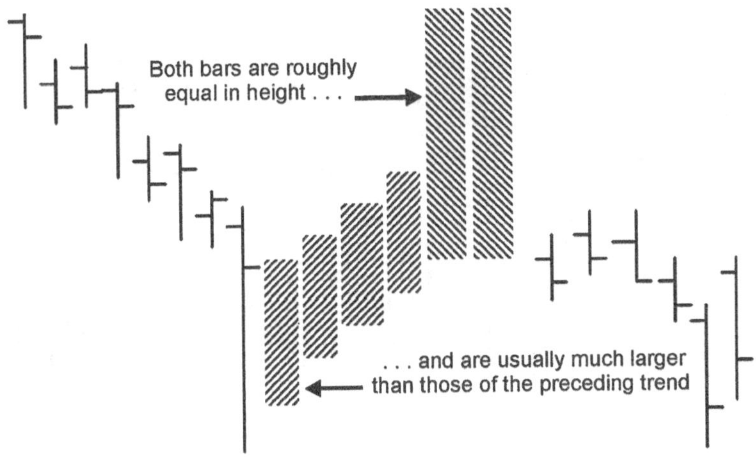

Figure 16-3 Two-bar reversals as rectangles.

for tops and *support* zones for bottoms. The retracements can be as little as one bar or as many as three. However, the longer this process takes, the weaker the pattern is likely to be. I do not have any hard and fast rules as to the degree of retracement that is allowable, but 50 percent appears to be a good starting point. As a rule of thumb, I would say that the smaller the retracement, the greater the ensuing decline (or advance in the case of a two-bar reversal bottom) is likely to be, and the higher the probability that the pattern will work. After all, if there has been a

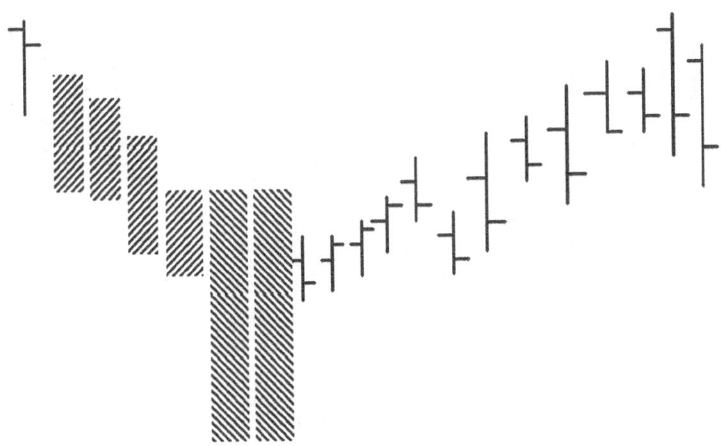

Figure 16-4 Two-bar reversals as rectangles.

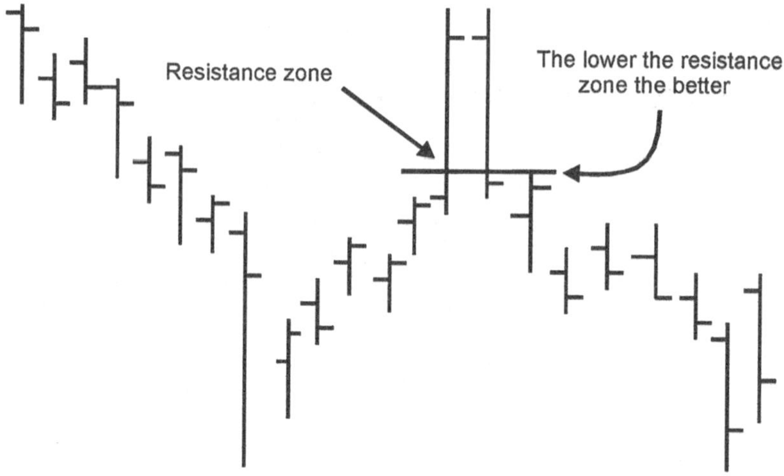

Figure 16-5 Two-bar reversals showing a resistance zone.

dramatic change in sentiment, we do not want the price to act indecisively, since, other things being equal, indecision will indicate a weak signal.

On the other hand, when resistance and support zones develop after the completion of a two-bar reversal, they offer good places above or below which relatively low-risk stops can be placed. The retracements also offer the opportunity to enter a trade at a price closer to the extreme of the two-bar reversal.

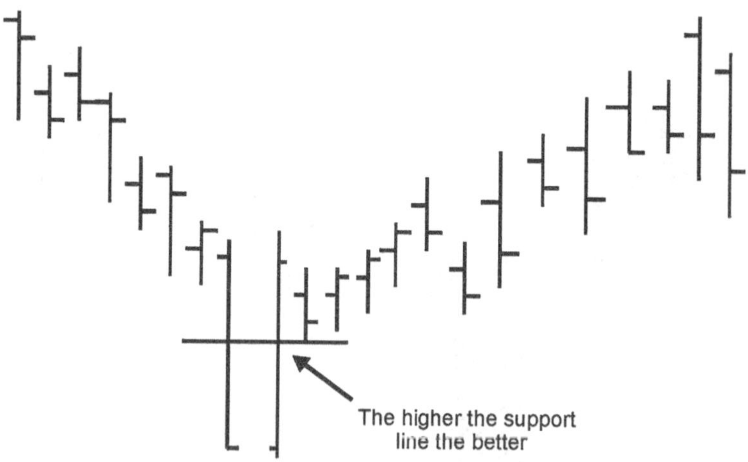

Figure 16-6 Two-bar reversal showing a support zone.

Since the protective stop loss should be placed just beyond the extreme point of the formation, a retracement also reduces the risk associated with the trade.

Underlying Psychology

The first bar of the formation develops strongly in the direction of the then-prevailing trend. For a five-star signal in an uptrend, we need to see the close of the bar at or very near the high. The bar should also be relatively wide. At the opening of the next period, buyers come in expecting more of the same. This means that the price should open very close to the high of the previous bar. However, the underlying concept of the two-bar reversal is that a change in psychology takes place and the second bar closes slightly above or below the low of the first bar. Hence, the high expectations of participants at the opening of the bar are totally dashed by the end of the period, indicating a change in sentiment. People who bought at the upper end of the trading range of the two bars are locked into the position at higher prices and are therefore a potential source of supply on the way down.

The two-bar reversal at market bottoms works exactly the same way, but in reverse. An example is shown in Fig. 16-2. In this case, the pattern should be preceded by a persistent decline, with the sellers remaining very much in control. The first bar opens at or near its high and closes near its low as this pessimistic trend is maintained. However, although the second bar opens close to the low of the first, it ends on a high note, indicating that it is the buyers who now have the upper hand. Once again, it is important for the two bars to be substantially wider than those preceding the pattern. If they are accompanied by very high volume, so much the better. The width adds to the flavor of the formation because wide bars imply volatility, and volatility is associated with reversals. People tend to reach their maximum level of anger right at the end of a row. Markets also tend to reach an extreme in emotion, indicated at the end of a trend with wide bars and lots of volume.

To be really effective, two-bar reversals should reflect a climactic experience. A specific pattern should therefore contain as many of the elements described here as possible.

Marketplace Examples

Charts 16-1 and 16-2 feature a five-minute bar for the S&P Composite. Chart 16-1 shows a classic pattern, with the highs and lows falling at exactly the correct points following a good rally. Chart 16-2 demonstrates a small

Chart 16-1 S&P Composite 5-minute bar.

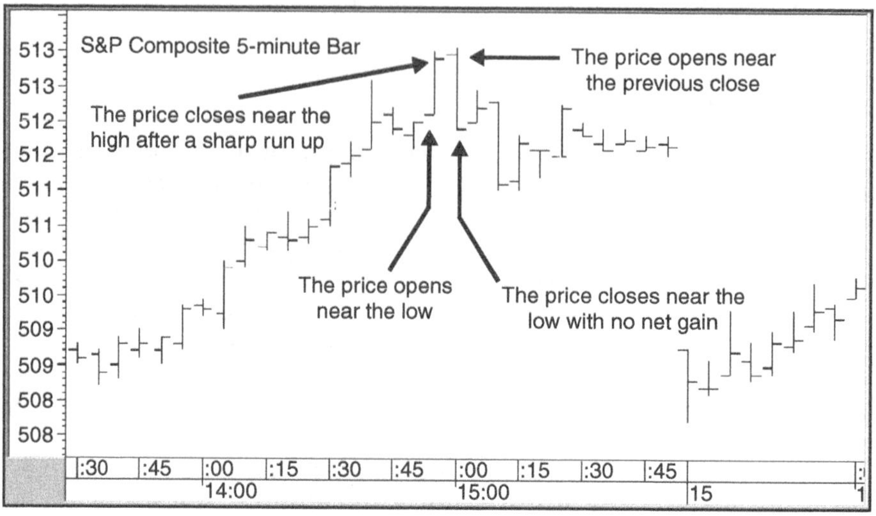

Chart 16-2 S&P Composite 5-minute bar.

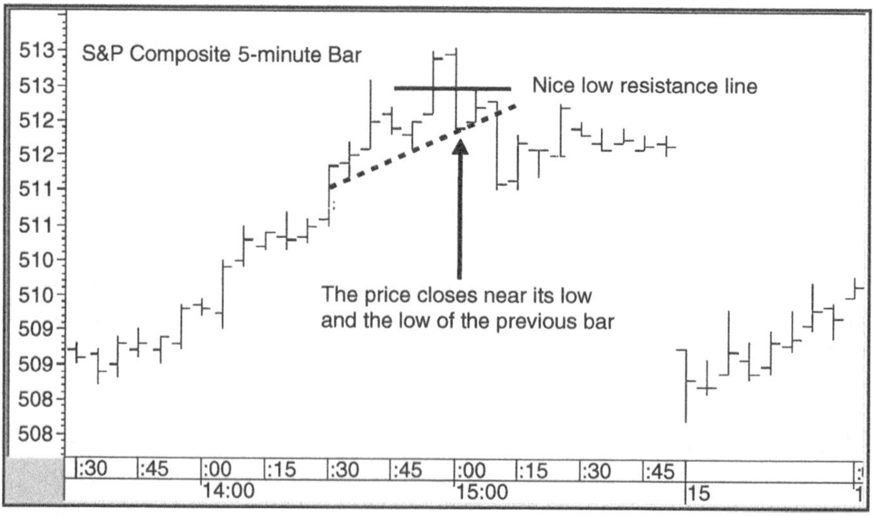

Chart 16-3 June 2001 gold, daily.

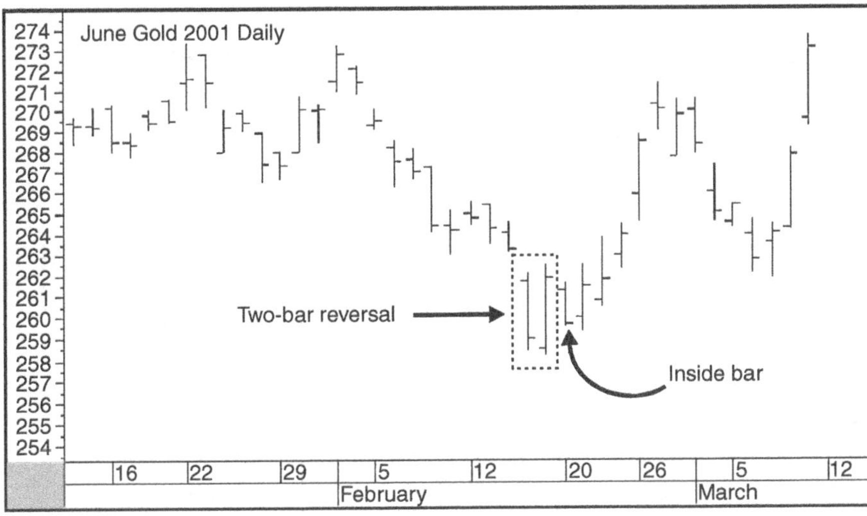

retracement move and violation of the dashed up trendline. Often we do not get confirmation from one- and two-bar patterns, but in this case the downside break indicated that the index had completed a small top, thereby adding further significance to the two-bar reversal top.

Chart 16-3 shows a two-bar reversal for June gold in February of 2001. In many cases, such patterns are followed by an immediate advance. In this case, the advance was delayed a day, as an additional piece of evidence indicated a trend reversal. This came in the form of an inside bar that developed on the day after the two-bar reversal. Such double patterns are often quite effective in signaling changes in trend. In this case, the pattern would probably have been stronger without the inside bar. This is because inside bars indicate a balance between buyers and sellers, and the two-bar reversal ideally indicates a dramatic reversal between them. By the same token, it is possible to argue that the previous weeks had been dominated by sellers and that the inside bar offered another successful test of the idea that the sellers were no longer in control. In this instance, the inside bar was followed by an outside bar (not labeled), so the situation was resolved in favor of the bulls. Note also that the second bar in the two-bar reversal encompasses the first bar. In effect, this is an outside bar. The two-bar reversal pattern rule does not require an outside bar, but the very presence of such a bar reinforces the idea that sentiment has definitely reversed. If we are looking at the quality of a signal, I would certainly add points for this, together with the outside bar that followed the inside bar.

Chart 16-4 US Bancorp, daily.

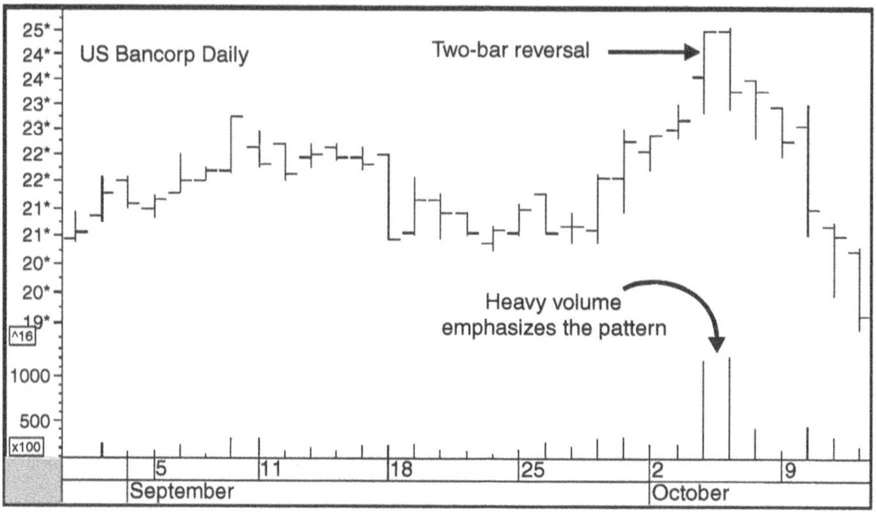

Chart 16-4 shows a two-bar reversal at the climax of a rally in US Bancorp in the fall of 2000. Note the strong expansion of volume, together with the fact that volume on the second day was slightly higher than that on the first. This provided an additional clue that the tide had turned in favor of the sellers.

Sugar offers a very emotional two-bar reversal in Chart 16-5. See how the first day gaps up. It doesn't quite open on the low, but the two bars definitely have the right flavor. The second bar opens right on its high and closes at its low. Three days later, it is apparent that the two-bar reversal is part of an island reversal. (For a full explanation of island reversals, please see Chapter 12.)

A false upside breakout develops in Chart 16-6, for the Dollar/Swiss franc. This adds to the significance of the two-bar reversal, since those who were buying for the bulk of the two days were locked in above the breakout point. This is a slightly different pattern from the classic one that develops after a sharp rally, but the false breakout and fact that the second bar of the two-bar reversal was an outside bar certainly make up for what the rally is lacking. This pattern was also confirmed as the price broke below the dashed support line.

Chart 16-7, for weekly live cattle, shows another false two-bar reversal breakout. In fact, it shows three. The first, on the left (*A*), has the characteristics of a two-bar reversal without much of a rally preceding it. Also, the bars were not particularly wide. It was by no means a classic pattern, but it

Chart 16-5 Sugar, daily.

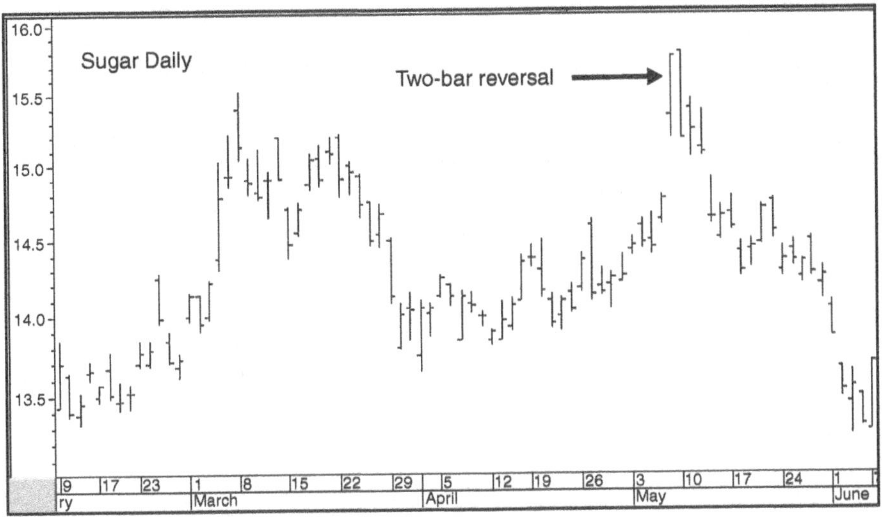

Chart 16-6 Dollar/franc, daily.

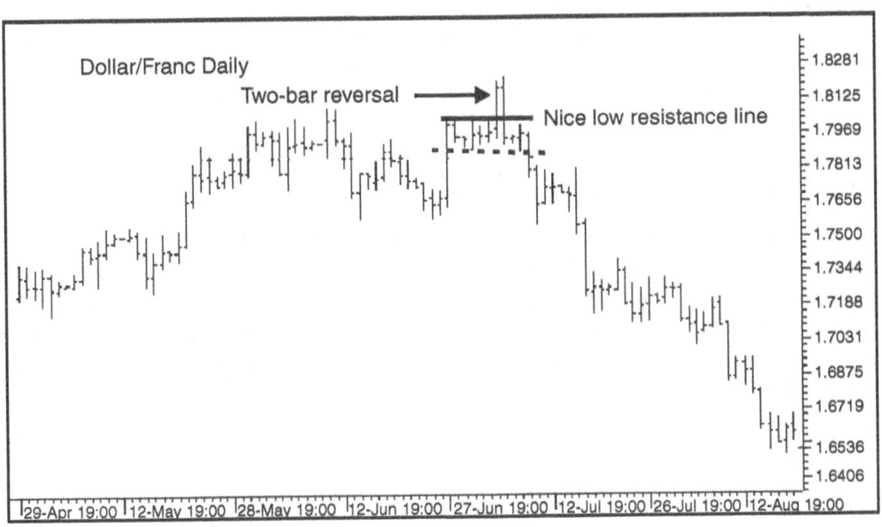

Chart 16-7 Live cattle, 1993–1994, weekly.

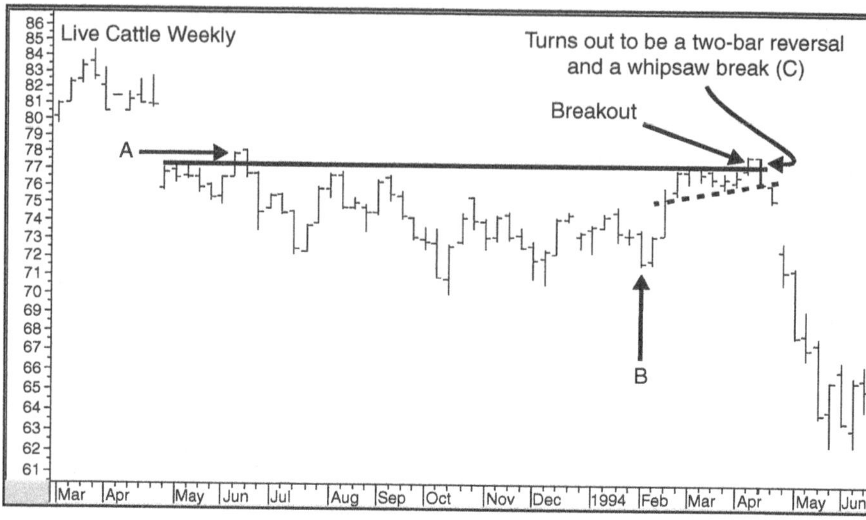

does indicate that when breakouts turn out to be whipsaws and the two-bar reversal forms part of the breakout, then we should expect to see at least a temporary reversal. Later on (*B*), we see a bullish two-bar reversal bottom. Once again it is not preceded by much of a downtrend, so it would not have been given very many stars. However, it did result in a nice rally. Finally, there is another whipsaw (*C*), again characterized by two bars with a two-bar reversal flavor. The whipsaw and two-bar reversal was confirmed in the subsequent week as the price violated a small (dashed) support trendline.

The Importance of Monitoring Several Time Frames

Quite often, patterns will develop in the daily charts that are not apparent in the weeklies or, say, the hourlies, or vice versa. A trader who is simply concentrating on one particular time frame, excluding all others, could easily miss out on some valuable technical information. It therefore makes sense to look at charts constructed above and below the time frame you are actually trading in.

For example, Chart 16-8, for Westvaco, shows a 15-minute time span. Several two-bar reversals are featured in the rectangles. Chart 16-9, on the other hand, shows the same stock, but this time with 5-minute bars. The ellipses indicate the same time periods as the rectangles in Chart 16-8, but they do not contain any technical phenomena that indicate a reversal. Thus,

Chart 16-8 Westvaco 15-minute bar. (*Source: Telescan.*)

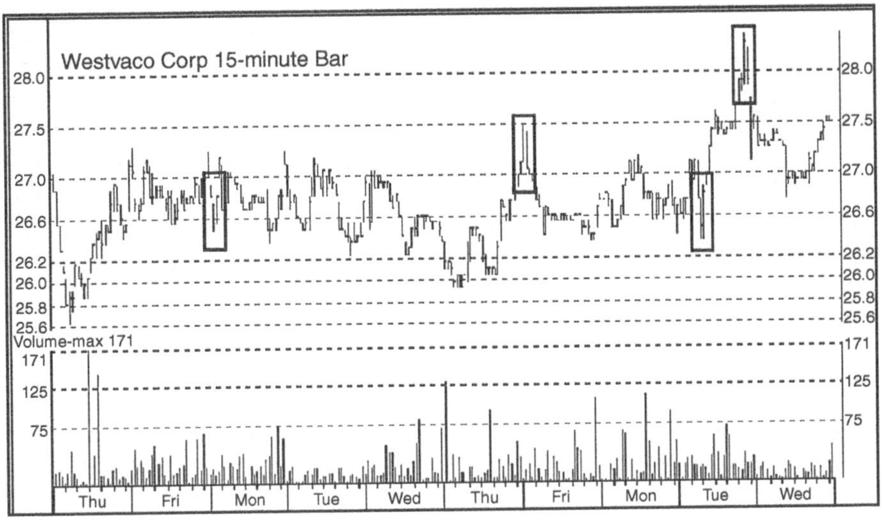

Chart 16-9 Westvaco 5-minute bar. (*Source: Telescan.*)

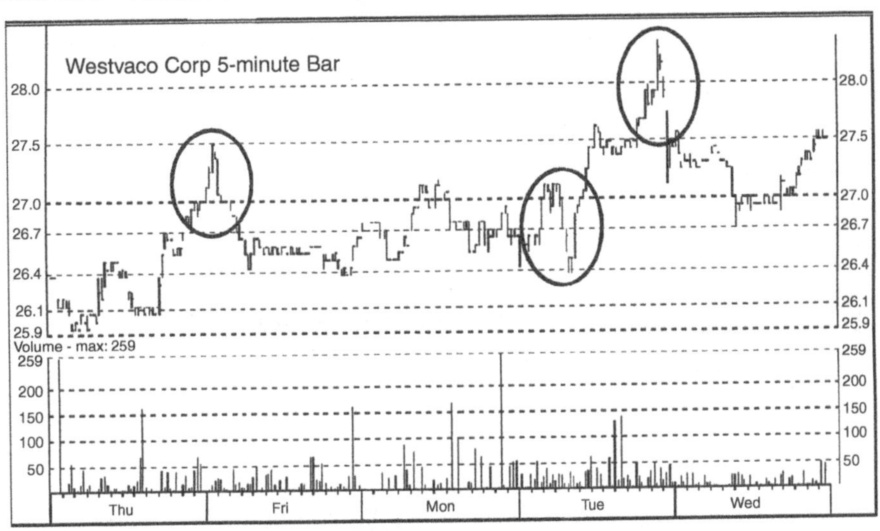

anyone who was just looking at the 5-minute chart would have missed some potential opportunities.

It may be annoying to traders who typically use daily charts to see such small and, they could justifiably say, irrelevant time frames. However, the same principle could be applied by considering hourly or weekly charts. This is because the hourly charts could well reveal important price patterns, such as a head and shoulders, that are not apparent with, say, three or four bars of daily data. Similarly, by looking up one time frame to the weeklies, a daily-based trader could well gain some perspective concerning the more dominant trend. Perhaps the weeklies will reveal an outside bar or a two-bar reversal that is not apparent on the daily charts.

Two-Bar Reversals as a Domino or Reverse Domino

Sometimes these patterns develop at major juncture points on both the intraday and the daily charts. This is because the two-bar reversals (or any other one- or two-bar pattern, for that matter) act as dominoes or reverse dominoes. We examined this concept briefly in Chapter 13 with outside bars. Chart 16-10 features daily price action for the DJ Transports. The bottom panel shows a short-term KST, a smoothed summed rate of change, an indicator that I developed many years ago (for a streaming audiovisual tutorial on the KST, go to www.pring.com, "Charting the KST"). Among other

Chart 16-10 DJ Transports, daily.

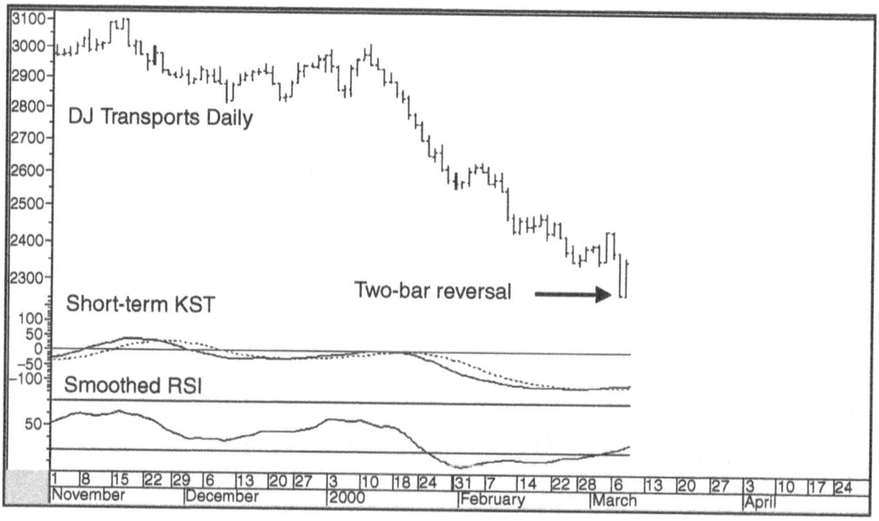

Chart 16-11 DJ Transports, daily.

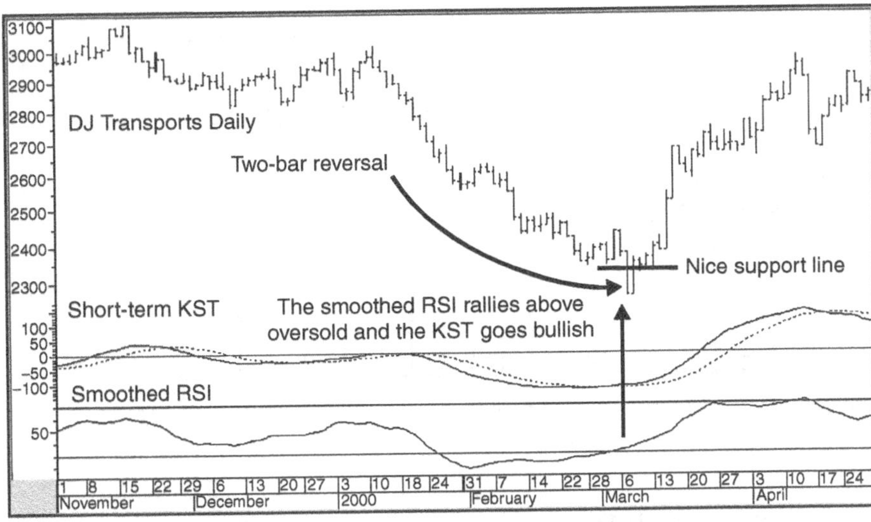

things, this versatile series offers buy and sell signals when it crosses decisively above or below its 10-day moving average. In Chart 16-10, it is trying to give a short-term buy signal, but it is not quite there. Since such signals are typically followed by rallies lasting well over three weeks, they are worth watching for. What clue can we look for that will increase the probability of a reliable signal? The answer lies in the price action, for as the chart ends, the Transports complete a two-bar reversal. Chart 16-11 indicates that this was timely information because the average rallies nicely and the KST eventually gives us a buy signal.

Three-Bar Reversals

Basic Characteristics and Underlying Psychology

A three-bar reversal is essentially a two-bar reversal separated by an exhaustion bar. An example of a top is shown in Fig. 16-7, and an example of a bottom in Fig. 16-8. Coming into a top pattern, the buyers are very much in control. The second bar usually indicates exhaustion in the form of a Pinocchio bar, with most of the trading taking place above the open and close. So it is evident that while buyers are able to push prices significantly higher during the bar's formation, they are unable to keep it there. In order to reflect the abrupt change in psychology that takes place, it is important

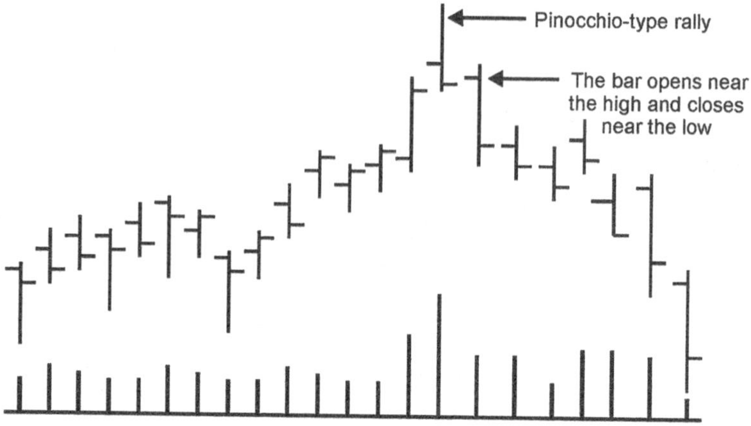

Figure 16-7 Three-bar reversal at a top.

for the first and last bars to be as wide as possible relative to those preceding them during the trend leading up to the pattern. If the bar in the middle is a Pinocchio type, then the wider the trading above the open and closing price, the better, because that implies exhaustion. The opposite would be true for a bottom. In addition, a three-bar pattern will gain a few stars if the center bar is accompanied by a noticeable expansion in volume.

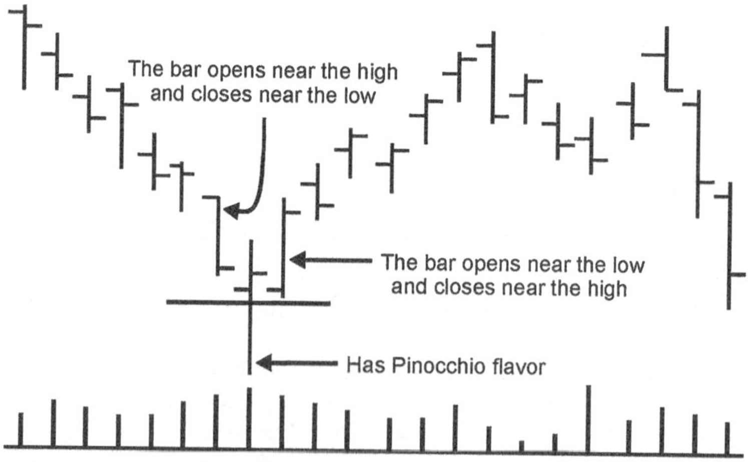

Figure 16-8 Three-bar reversal at a bottom.

This also underlines the idea of buyer or seller exhaustion, depending on the direction of the trend.

Marketplace Examples

Chart 16-12, featuring Cisco, shows a three-bar bottom reversal. It's not really a classic formation because it is missing one element, and that is substantial width in the third bar. However, the center bar is accompanied by lots of volume and is unusually wide, which more than compensates for the lack of width in the third bar.

Chart 16-13, for sugar, shows another three-bar reversal. This time the center bar turns out to be a one-day island. Note that the open and close are right at the low, so all the trading that occurred that day was done at higher levels. At the end of the day, virtually everyone who had bought was locked in with a loss. This was hardly what they expected given the sharp run-up preceding this pattern.

Cintas, in Chart 16-14, provides us with a nice three-bar reversal top. The arrow shows the relatively high level of volume on the Pinocchio day. Note that all the trading took place above the other two bars, as indicated by the dashed horizontal trendline. The violation of the up trendline the day after this pattern was completed provided strong confirmation that the formation was valid.

Chart 16-12 Cisco, daily.

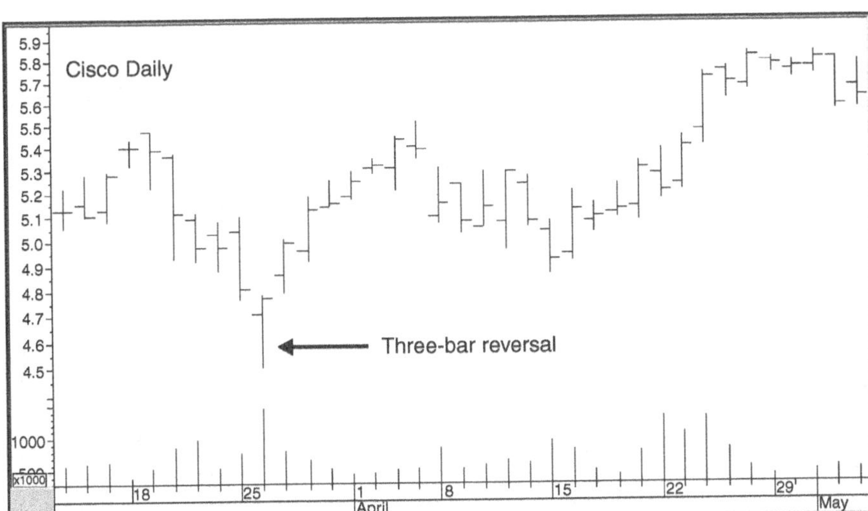

Chart 16-13 Sugar, daily.

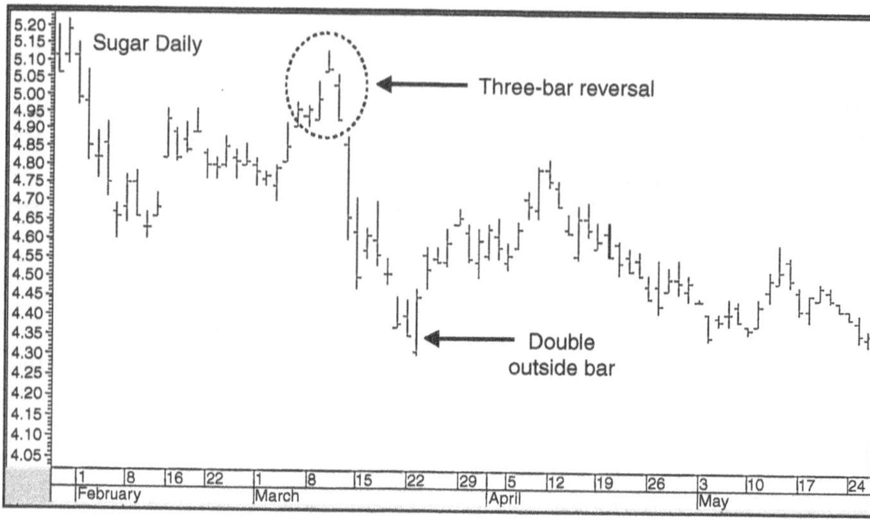

Chart 16-14 Cintas, daily.

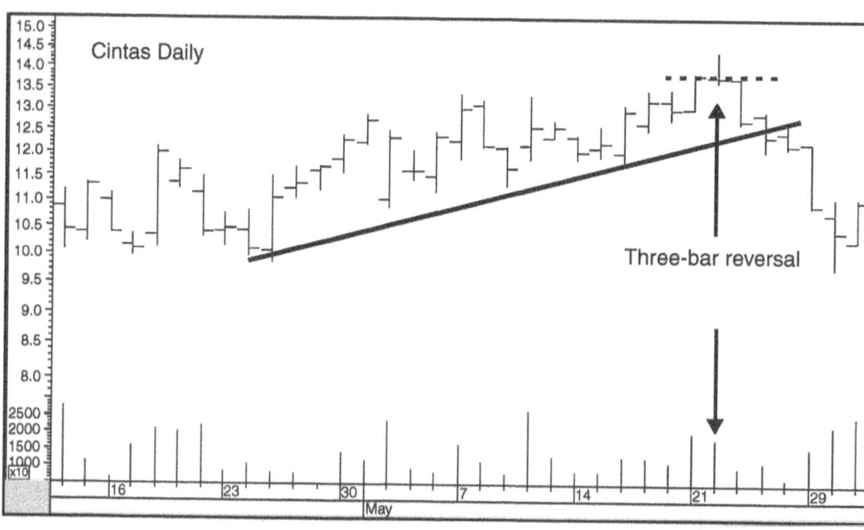

Chart 16-15 Cnet, daily.

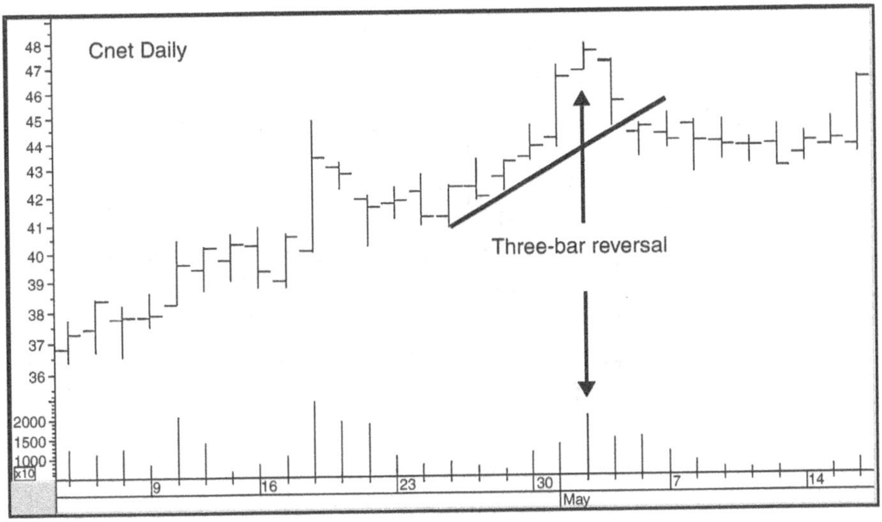

Chart 16-15, featuring Cnet, is missing some of the ingredients. First, the center bar is not a true Pinocchio, since the open and close are not close to each other relative to the bar's width. Also, the close is higher than the open. The volume on this center bar is pretty heavy, and the width of the flanking bars is acceptable. Normally we would expect to see more of a decline following a three-bar reversal than the eight or so days indicated on the chart. The real point of showing this example, though, is that even a high-volume center bar does not necessarily have to take on Pinocchio characteristics in order to work, though it is preferable for it to do so.

Quiet Three-Bar Reversal

A variation on the three-bar reversal is what I call a quiet three-bar reversal (see Fig. 16-9). The "quiet" part refers to the center bar, which is not a Pinocchio, but is very narrow relative to the two-bar reversal flanking it. Volume, unlike that in the standard three-bar reversal, is often quite low. This, of course, indicates a distinct lack of interest on the part of both parties. It also acts as a contrast to the wide bar that precedes it, where the dominant party is urgently buying or selling, depending on the direction of the trend. Typically the open and close of the center bar will be very near each other. The implication of this proximity is that both parties are pretty evenly matched following the strong up- or downtrend that precedes it. The narrow

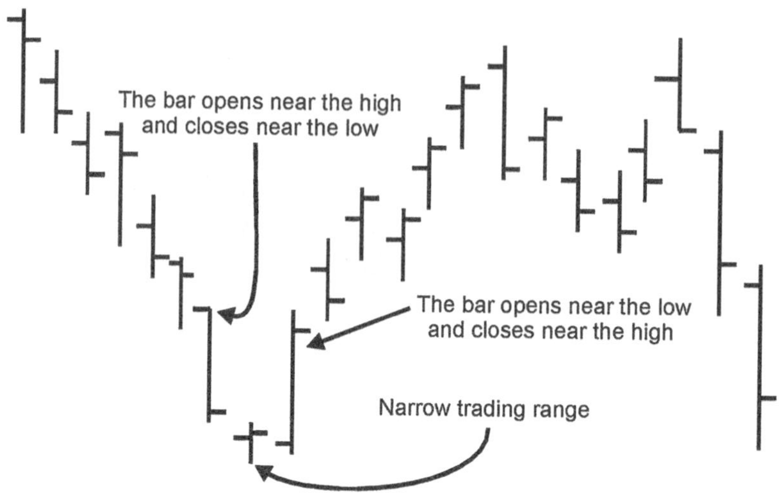

Figure 16-9 Quiet three-bar reversal at a bottom.

bar therefore warns that whoever was previously in charge may no longer be in control. It is a less strong signal than the Pinocchio bar, but a subtle one nonetheless. The clincher comes on the third bar, which opens close to the first bar's closing price and closes near that bar's opening. Thus, by the time the third bar closes, there has been little or no net gain, despite all the volatility involved in the pattern's formation.

Figure 16-10 shows a comparison of a regular three-bar reversal with a quiet three-bar reversal, with the trading ranges being represented by rectangles.

Chart 16-16, for Cisco, shows a quiet three-bar reversal following a short-term rally. The arrow indicates that the center bar was accompanied by very low volume, reflecting a fine balance between buyers and sellers following the previous dominance of the buyers. This pattern was immediately confirmed by a trendline break, which left little doubt that a short-term downtrend was underway.

Three-Bar-Plus Reversal

This is a variation on the quiet three-bar reversal that includes more than one quiet bar, hence the inclusion of the word *plus*. Examples are shown in Figs. 16-11 and 16-12.

The concept remains the same, whether we have one, two, or three narrow trading bars. They all indicate a fine balance between buyers and sellers flanked by two very decisive wide bars.

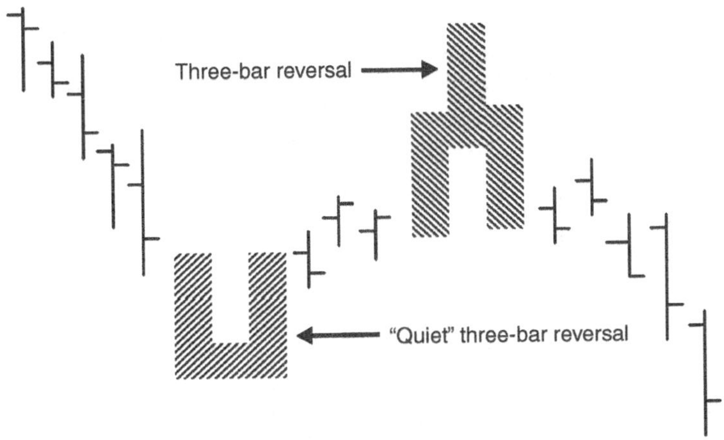

Figure 16-10 A three-bar and a quiet three-bar reversal as rectangles.

In order to work well, these three-bar-plus patterns really need to be preceded by a sharp price movement because they should reflect a quick transition in sentiment between one trend and another.

Apple Computer produces a three-bar-plus reversal in Chart 16-17. I would have liked to have seen a wider trading range for the bar preceding the two center bars, but there was no question that the sessions preceding

Chart 16-16 Cisco, daily.

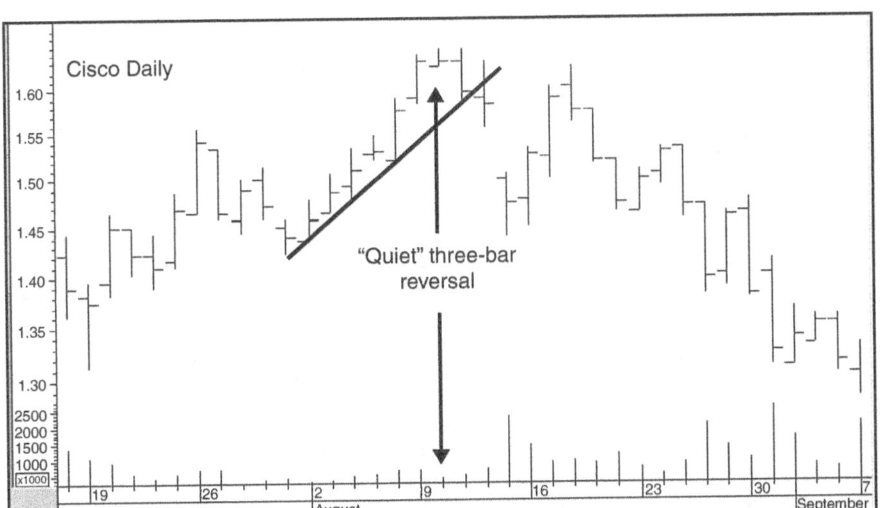

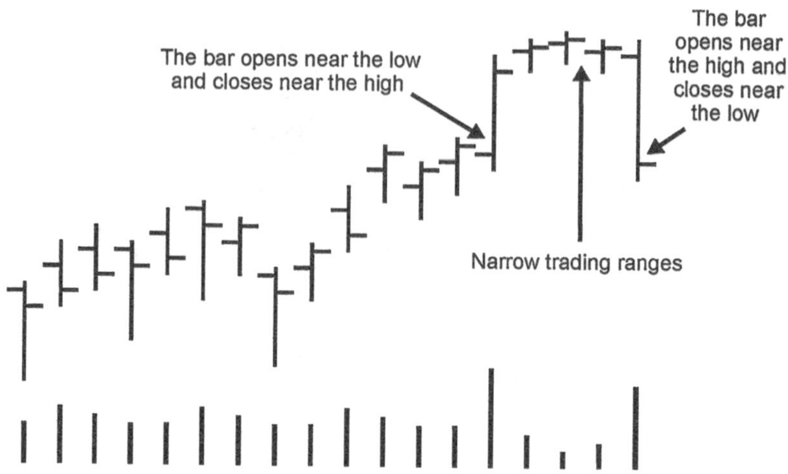

Figure 16-11 Three-bar-plus reversal at a top.

it were dominated by sellers. However, the final bar in the formation more than made up for this. The volume configuration for this pattern shows a rounding formation, which is just what we like to see. If the volume had expanded a bit more on the final day, this would have been great, but you can't have everything!

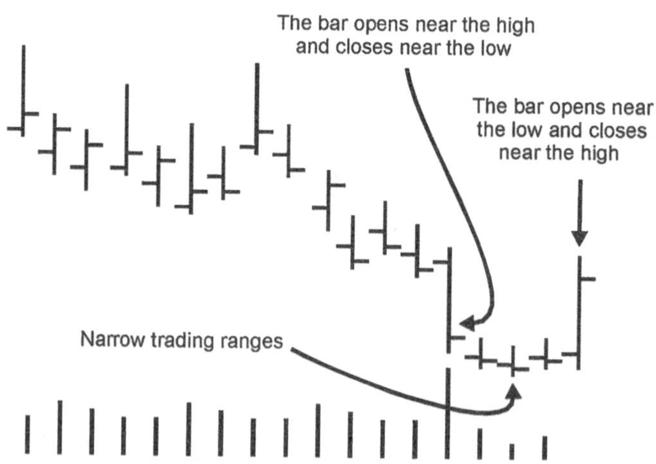

Figure 16-12 Three-bar-plus reversal at a bottom.

Chart 16-17 Apple, daily.

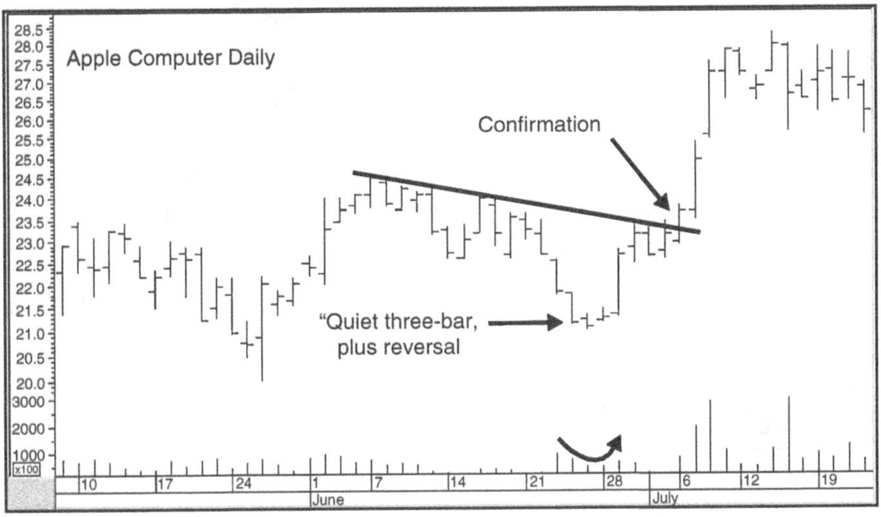

Two-Bar Reversals and Candlesticks

There are no well-known Japanese candlestick patterns that correspond to a two-bar reversal. The closest is an engulfing pattern, described in Chapter 13. Two-bar reversals would show up in the candles as two very wide real bodies with little or no upper and lower wicks (see Figs. 16-13 and 16-14). The first real body would be colored in the direction of the prevailing trend, and the second would have the opposite color. A top would therefore consist of a black candle followed by a white one, and vice versa.

Three-Bar Reversals and Candlesticks

Three-bar reversals are close to a doji star, although the Pinocchio aspect of the three-bar reversal means that the center bar is usually wider than in the doji star. Examples of morning and evening dojis are shown in Fig.16-15. Quiet three-bar reversals are more like the morning and evening star. A morning star is featured in Fig. 16-16. The underlying psychology of all these patterns is very similar: A strong trend gives way to a balance between

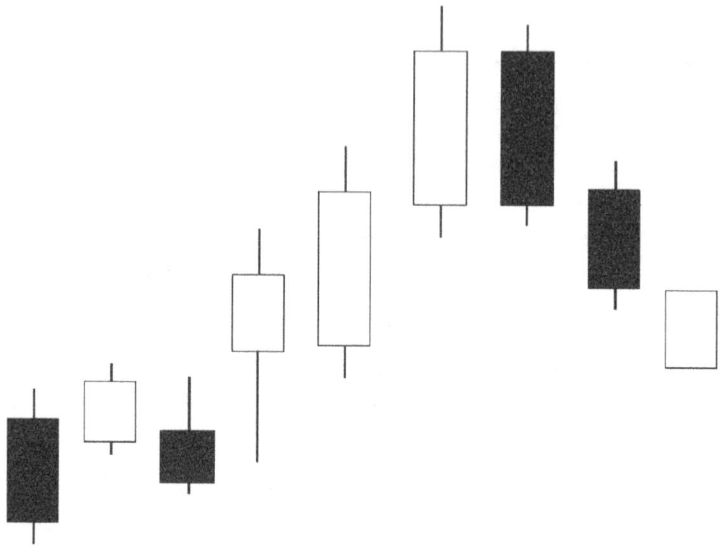

Figure 16-13 Candlestick rendition of a two-bar reversal top.

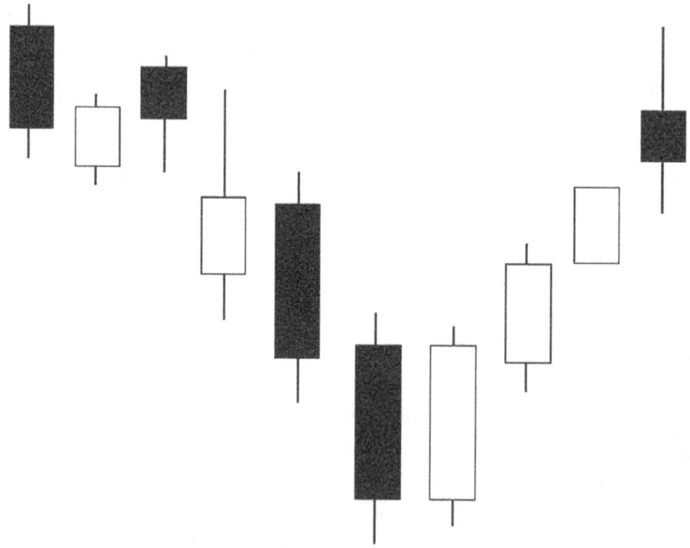

Figure 16-14 Candlestick rendition of a two-bar reversal bottom.

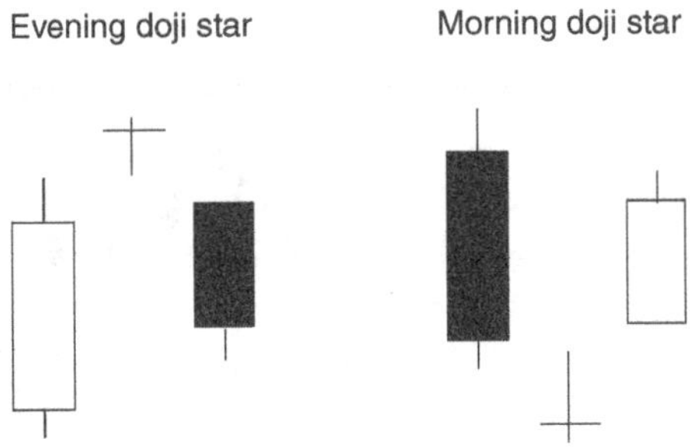

Figure 16-15 Doji stars.

buyers and sellers, which then leads to a new trend favoring the party that was dominated in the previous trend.

The three-bar-plus reversals are in many instances like tower tops and bottoms (see Chart 16-18). These patterns involve a very narrow, saucer-like trading range flanked by two very wide real bodies of differing colors. The idea of the two wide candles sandwiching several smaller ones is again indicative of two strong trends being separated by a fine balance between buyers and sellers. The principal difference, as you can see from Chart 16-18, is that the top of a tower takes a lot longer to form than a quiet three-bar-plus reversal.

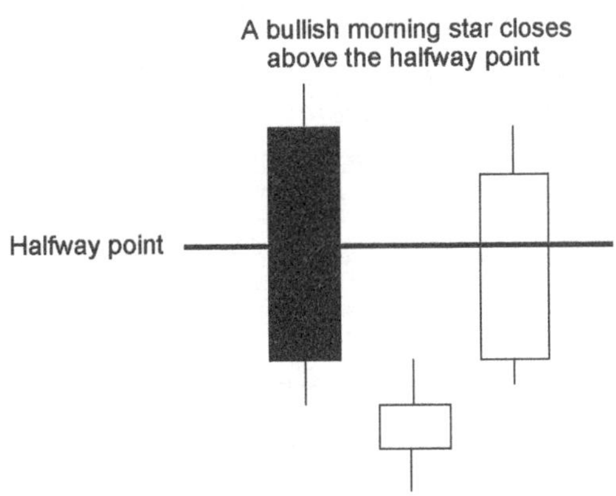

Figure 16-16 Morning star.

Chart 16-18 General Motors, 1994–1995, and a tower top. (*Source: pring.com.*)

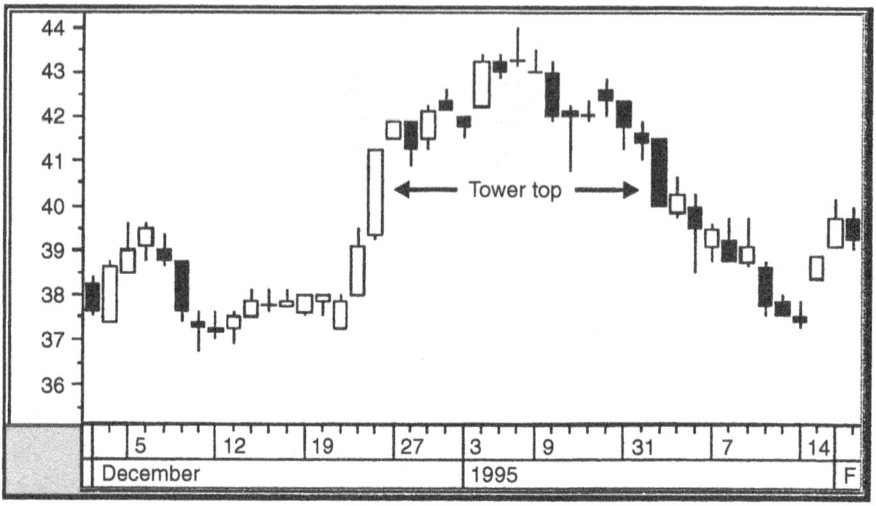

Summary

Two-Bar Reversals Quick Review

- *Price characteristics:* Two wide bars of roughly the same height following a strong trend. At a top, the first bar opens near its low and closes near its high. The second opens near its high and closes near its low. For a bottom, the first bar opens near its high and closes near its low, and the second opens near its low and closes near its high.
- *Volume characteristic:* Both bars at tops and bottoms should be accompanied by higher-than-average volume.
- *Measuring implications:* None, but usually followed by a strong short-term reversal.
- *Reliability:* Usually good when preceded by a strong inbound trend.

Three-Bar Reversals Quick Review

- *Price characteristics:* Two wide bars of roughly the same height following a strong trend. They are separated by either a Pinocchio-type bar or a narrow bar (quiet three-bar reversal) that forms toward the high of the two wide bars at a top or toward the low of the two wide bars at a bottom. The first wide bar at a top opens near its low and closes near its high. The second wide bar opens near its high and closes near its low. For a bottom, the first wide bar opens near its high and closes near its low, and the second wide bar opens near its low and closes near its high.

- *Volume characteristic:* Above-average volume on the two wide bars and the Pinocchio bar. Small volume on the narrow bar in the quiet three-bar reversal.
- *Measuring implications:* None, but usually followed by a sharp short-term reversal.
- *Reliability:* Usually good when preceded by a strong inbound trend.

Quiet Three-Bar-Plus Reversal Quick Review

The same as quiet three-bar reversals except that a single narrow bar is replaced with two to four narrow bars.

PART IV
Miscellaneous Issues

17
How to Assess Whether a Breakout Will Be Valid or False

When most traders or investors commit money to the marketplace based on a price pattern breakout, they always assume that the trade will be profitable. However, it is widely understood that most professional traders—or should I say successful professional traders—expect to lose as many times as they win. What makes them successful is the fact that the losing trades are small relative to the winners. "Cut your losses and let your profits run" is a hackneyed expression, but the principle definitely works. Throughout this book, I have tried to emphasize that technical analysis does not deal in certainties, but only in probabilities. It is therefore important that whenever we take action, we look over our shoulders and ask ourselves the question, What if? What if the pattern fails? Where should we get out, or what technical action would we have to see in order for the situation to revert from bullish to neutral, or even bearish?

There are two reasons why we need to go through this process. First, price trends are nothing more than people in action. People can and do change their minds, and thus so do markets. Consequently, it's important to be prepared *ahead* of time to deal with such situations. Second, if we mentally rehearse what our reaction might be if the technical evidence were to change, we will be in a more objective psychological state if this actually happens. Failure to prepare in this way will result in small losses turning into large ones. For example, if we buy a stock on a breakout, and the next day it sells off into the body of the pattern on bad news, what do we do? Most people will hold on; after all, they have just experienced a loss when they were expecting a profit. In most instances, they will convince themselves that the trend is still up, even though the breakout has been invalidated. The tendency of most people is to stubbornly hold on in the *hope* that the price will come back. The right thing to do is to recognize that false breakouts are a fact of life and a cost of doing business. Therefore, it is important to *anticipate* potential adversity by planning ahead and placing stops in the market in the event that the worst does happen. This chapter is concerned with learning to anticipate when a failure might develop and pointing out some intelligent places to put stops. In the meantime, let's take a few moments to demonstrate why cutting losses is so important.

Why Cutting Losses Is Important

Table 17-1 shows a hypothetical example of a trading experience that begins with a large loss—50 percent, in fact. The next four trades gain a total of 80 percent. You would think that this would be more than sufficient to offset the initial loss and earn a nice profit. However, the table clearly shows that the trader is barely back to breakeven. His record is 4-1 on the winning side, and yet he has failed to make any money. Add to this the fact that we have not included commissions and slippage from poor executions, and you can appreciate why it is important to cut those losses to a minimum.

You may be saying to yourself that if our hypothetical trader had lost the 50 percent at the end instead of the beginning, he would have been OK. However, Table 17-2 shows that the end result is virtually identical. A large loss is a large loss however you cut it. The point of the exercise is to show that it is mathematically much harder to come back from a large loss than from a small one. Therefore, while we cannot avoid losses, we should at least take the time when trading price patterns to plan ahead and provide for false breakouts in our trading plan.

Table 17-1

	Capital	Profit/Loss %	Profit/Loss Amount	Ending
Trade 1	100	(50)	(50)	50
Trade 2	50	50	25	75
Trade 3	75	10	75	82.5
Trade 4	82.5	10	83	90.8
Trade 5	90.8	10	9.1	99.9

Table 17-2

	Capital	Profit/Loss %	Profit/Loss Amount	Ending
Trade 1	100	50	50	150
Trade 2	150	10	15	165
Trade 3	165	10	16.5	181.5
Trade 4	181.5	10	18.15	199.65
Trade 5	199.65	50	99.825	(99.8)

When Do False Breakouts Most Commonly Occur?

The most common reason why price pattern breakouts fail is that they develop in a contra-trend way. That means bullish breakouts in bear trends and bearish breakouts in bull trends. If the security you are following is experiencing a primary bear trend, that trend is the dominant one, so far as the short- and intermediate-term trends are concerned. That means that most of the magnitude of these shorter trends is on the downside. Reactions are large and rallies short. As a result, in most cases, bullish price patterns have used up most, if not all, of their positive potential by the time the breakout develops. After the breakout, the dominant primary trend once again takes over, and prices slip. After they fall below the lower part of the pattern, a new down leg in the bear market gets underway. The reverse would be true for downside breakouts in a bull market. We cannot say that every contra-trend breakout results in a whipsaw, but it is certainly surprising how many do,

This can be appreciated from Chart 17-1, featuring Echostar. The chart has been divided into two parts, a primary bull market and a primary bear market. The idea is to demonstrate how buyers dominate during a bull market and sellers during a bear market. Underneath is a nine-day RSI smoothed with an eight-day moving average. [For a full explanation of the RSI, please see *Martin Pring on Market Momentum*, Volume 1 (McGraw-Hill, 2002.)] We would expect bullish psychology to dominate during a primary uptrend and bearish sentiment to have the upper hand during a negative trend. Since oscillators, such as the smoothed RSI, closely reflect psychology, we would also expect to see the character of this indicator change as the primary trend changes direction. The two thick sets of parallel lines attempt to illustrate this by showing that the oscillator appears to have a bullish upside bias in an uptrend and a downside bias during a bear market. The point here is that if an upside breakout takes place in a contra-trend manner, it is not likely to hold because the oscillator does not have much potential to remain overbought.

Chart 17-1 Echostar, 1997–2002, daily.

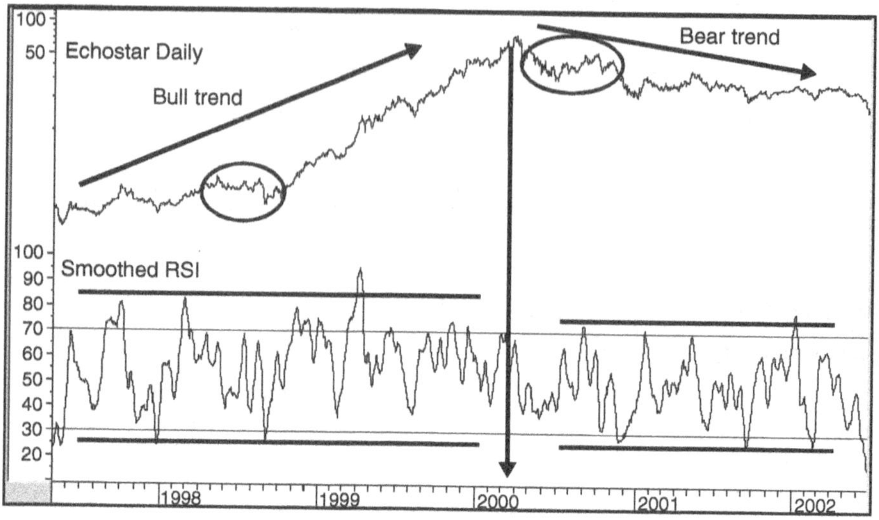

Charts 17-2 and 17-3 focus on the two ellipses highlighted in Chart 17-1, since each of these contains a contra-trend breakout. The first reproduces the action in the ellipse on the right and shows an upside breakout during the bear market. Note that the RSI was at an overbought reading at the time of the completion of the pattern. If you refer back to Chart 17-1, you can see that during the primary bear trend, the price was extremely sensitive to overbought conditions. The actual high for the move, which was marginally above the breakout high, was associated with a negative divergence in the smoothed RSI.

If a purchase had been made on the basis of the breakout, where should the protective stop have been placed? The answer would be below the breakout level, since that marked the low point between the late August and late September highs. It was also the point at which the dashed up trendline was intersecting. A violation of that line would have confirmed the negative divergence as well.

The other ellipse, featured in Chart 17-3, shows a downside breakout. Referring back to Chart 17-1 again, you can see that this developed in a bull market, when the oscillator was very sensitive to oversold conditions but not to overbought ones. It is questionable whether this was a whipsaw, since the price did achieve the pattern's minimum ultimate downside objective. However, since it reversed on a dime, the trader would have had to be extremely nimble to make much of a profit. If a short trade had been initiated on the breakout, a protective stop should have been placed above the

Chart 17-2 Echostar, 1999–2000, daily.

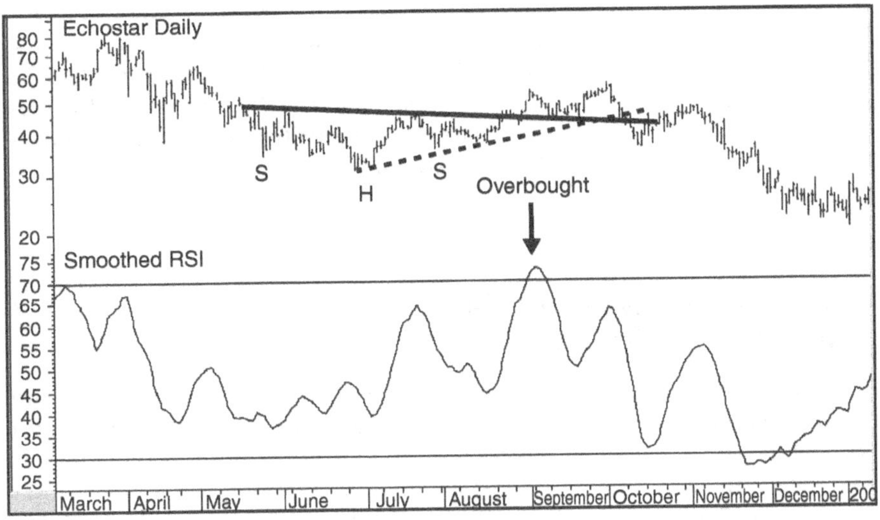

Chart 17-3 Echostar, 1997–1998, daily.

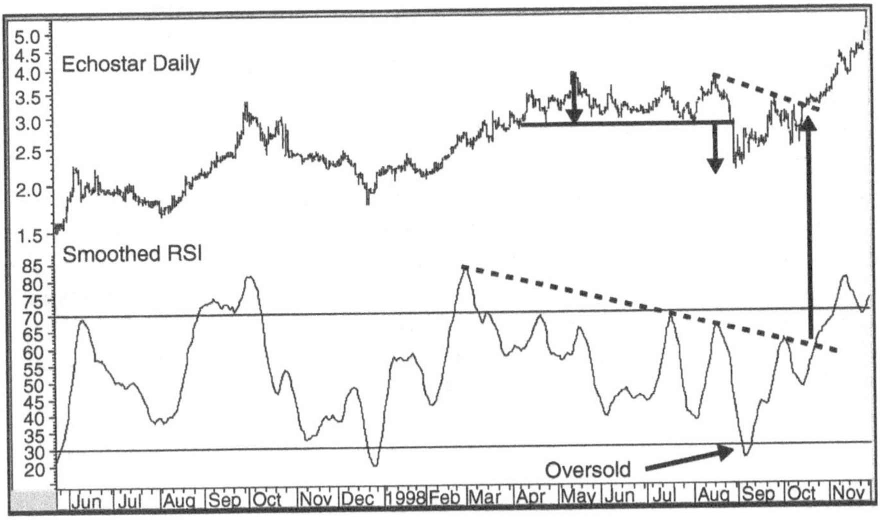

point where the probabilities favored the pattern's no longer having any downside influence on the price. In this instance, that would have occurred when the two dashed down trendlines were violated.

We must continue to emphasize the point that *contra-trend breakouts do not always result in whipsaws, and pro-trend breakouts are not always valid.* However, as is fairly evident, oscillators tend to be very sensitive to contra-trend overbought/oversold extremes. This means that the ability of most contra-trend breakouts to hold is relatively limited.

Further Pointers to Invalid and Valid Breakouts

For a breakout to stand a better chance of being valid, it needs to be decisive. What is decisive is very much in the eye of the beholder, a call made on the basis of judgment and experience. Unfortunately, it is not possible to give a percentage beyond which a breakout can be said to be decisive because different securities have different volatility. A breakout for a low-volatility utility would not have to be as decisive as, say, one for a highly volatile mining or technology stock.

A second consideration is time frame. A breakout of 3 percent on a 10-minute bar may well constitute the whole move. On the other hand, such a breakout on a monthly chart would be reasonable, since the implied new trend would be expected to last for nine months or much longer and have far greater magnitude than a trend on a daily or intraday graph.

One benchmark used by many technicians is to allow the breakout to maintain itself for at least two bars. If it holds for only one bar, it is argued, then this is a sign of exhaustion. Holding for two bars represents a sign of strength and confirmation. This rule will certainly filter out a lot of whipsaws, but definitely not all of them. The disadvantage is that by the time the second bar has been completed, prices may well have moved a long way from the breakout point. Unless you are long the security in question and have to liquidate, or are short and forced to cover, this is not that important, because the only thing you have lost is an opportunity. Markets being what they are, there will always be another opportunity around the corner. The key is to have the patience and the discipline to wait for it.

Divergences and Breakouts

Sometimes prices work their way higher, but an oscillator does not. This provides us with a clue that the upside breakout might fail. Chart 17-4 features

Chart 17-4 Comcast, 1995–1996, daily.

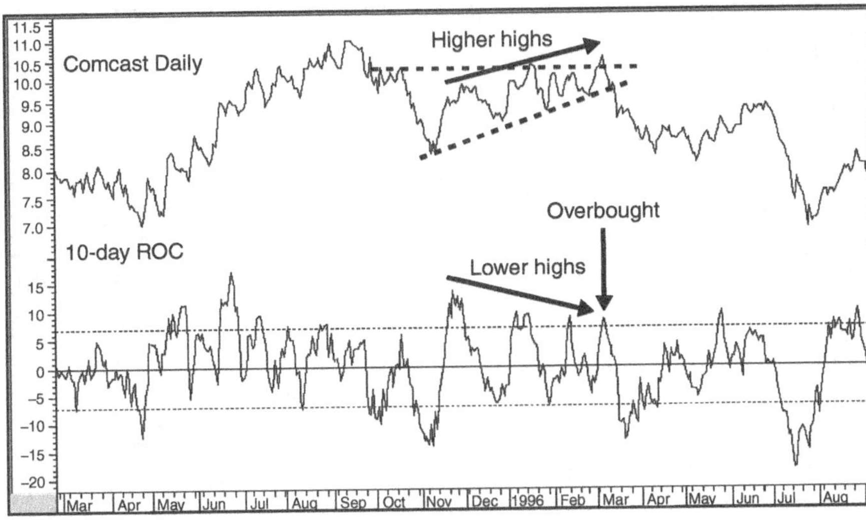

a breakout by Comcast. The price had been rising in a series of higher peaks between November 1995 and March 1996, but the 10-day rate of change had experienced a series of lower peaks. This is known as a negative divergence and is a bearish sign, since it indicates that the breakout was not accompanied by much in the way of upside momentum. When the price returned to the body of the pattern and the rate of change peaked, that should have been enough to indicate a failed breakout. However, the issue was placed beyond reasonable doubt a couple of sessions later when the price violated the dashed up trendline.

The same principles are true for downside breakouts, but here the conditions would be reversed: Falling prices and a false downside would be associated with a positive divergence between the price and the oscillator.

Volume and Breakouts

Having established what we might call macro guides to potential whipsaws, it is now time to turn our attention to smaller and more subtle guides to whether a breakout will lead to success or failure.

One of the most obvious of these guides is volume. It has already been established that it is better for upside breakouts to be accompanied by a noticeable expansion of activity, since this is an indication of enthusiasm on

Chart 17-5 Merrill Lynch, daily.

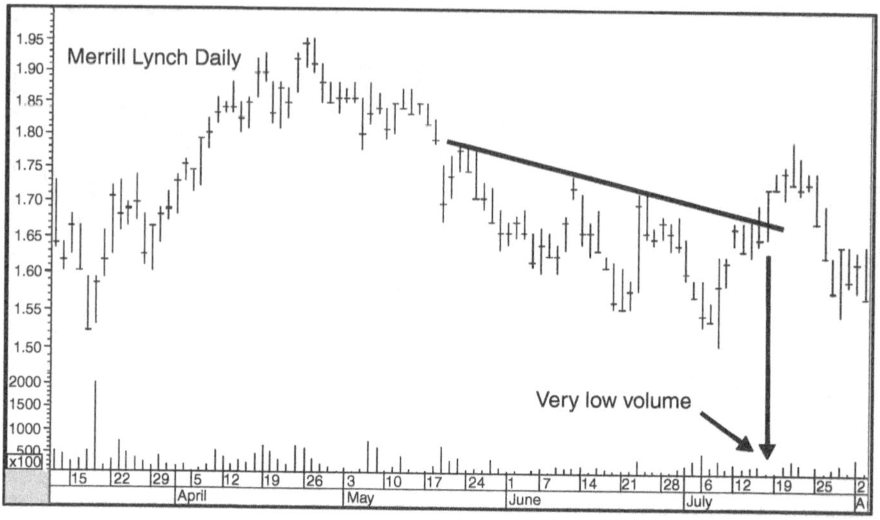

the part of buyers. However, many upside breakouts that are not accompanied by high volume are successful, so normal volume is not necessarily a "pattern killer." It's just that heavy volume increases the odds that this is a valid breakout. The thing to look out for in this regard is a definite decline in volume as the price breaks to the upside. This is a bear market characteristic and is a definite red flag suggesting that the breakout is developing more because of a lack of selling pressure than because of buying enthusiasm. Chart 17-5, featuring Merrill Lynch, shows a breakout above a down trendline, but on the day of the breakout there is virtually no volume. The price bounced around for a few days before heading south in a big way.

It is normal for volume to contract during declines, so a decline on downside breakouts does not provide any clues to whether the breakout will be invalid or not. On the other hand, if volume picks up on the downside penetration, then this is abnormal and indicates selling pressure. The expanding volume is therefore a plus in terms of increasing the probabilities of a valid signal.

One- and Two-Bar Price Patterns

A false breakout is, by definition, the end of a trend, and for this reason many whipsaws show up as exhaustion moves. These are reflected on the charts in the form of two-bar reversals, Pinocchio bars, and so forth. Such

Chart 17-6 Merrill Lynch, 1981–1982, daily.

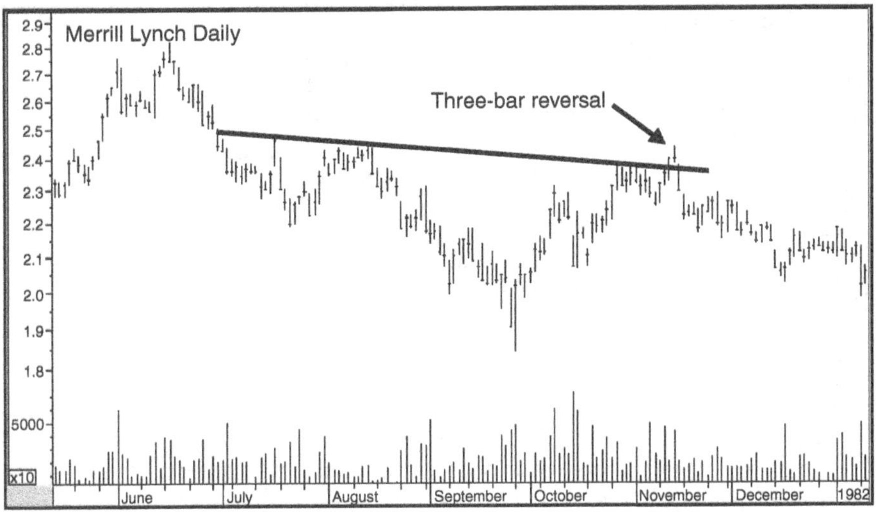

formations have only short-term implications, but their very presence at breakout time warns us of more significant trouble than the pattern considered in isolation. This is because we do not expect to see an exhaustion pattern as the price is breaking out, for exhaustion comes at the end of a move, not the middle. When the price breaks from a pattern, it is reasonable to anticipate an extension of that trend. The appearance of a one- or two-bar reversal should alert us to the fact that the probabilities of failure have definitely increased. It is not possible to say that *every* time one of these formations develops right after a breakout, the signal will turn out to be a whipsaw, but it is definitely a red flag.

Chart 17-6, for Merrill Lynch, offers an example. The price breaks out from a base, but the very next day it experiences a Pinocchio. This becomes evident the day after, when it gaps down and closes well within the base. The flavor is that of a three-bar reversal, but the gap, though bearish, does not exactly meet our definition of this formation. In a sense this chart is misleading. If you look carefully, you will see that the way the data are being reported, the opening and closing for each day are identical. Consequently, the opening data are incorrect, so we really do not know where any of the openings took place. In reality this may not have been a Pinocchio at all, but prices certainly broke in the expected way.

Chart 17-7, for Knight Ridder, features another whipsaw. This time the opening and closing prices are recorded, and they definitely reveal a

Chart 17-7 Knight Ridder, 1992–1993, daily.

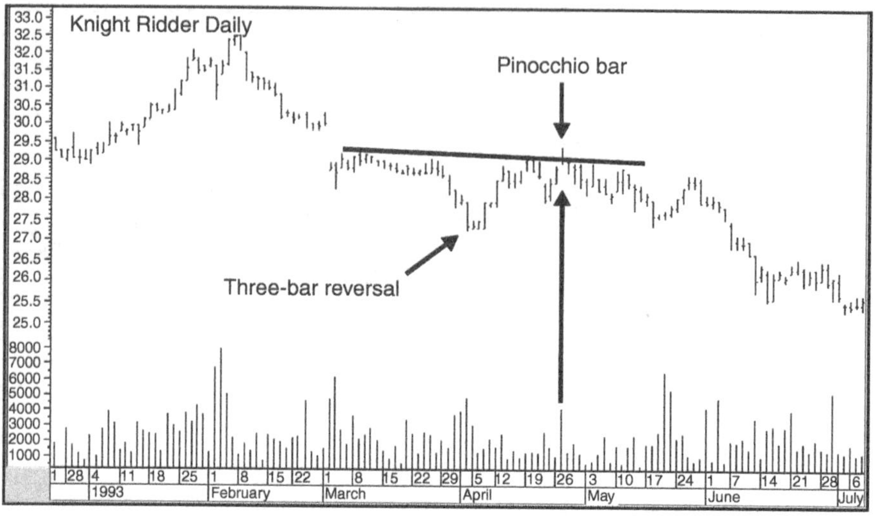

Chart 17-8 Knight Ridder, daily.

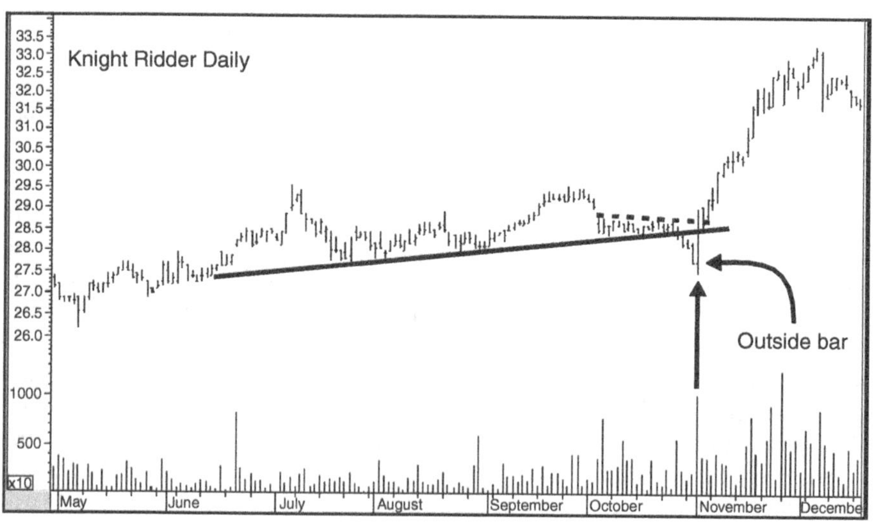

Pinocchio bar ending in a failed breakout. Note that the volume on the day of the whipsaw was pretty heavy. The technical position certainly looked good as the breakout was taking place, but since the price ended up where it started, below the breakout trendline, the volume became a negative factor because it showed that there was overwhelming selling pressure at higher prices. Note also the three-bar-plus reversal at the end of March that signaled the start of the April rally.

Chart 17-8 shows another false breakout for Knight Ridder, this time on the downside. The whipsaw was signaled by a very wide outside bar accompanied by a huge level of volume. If there had been any doubt that this formation was going to fail, it would have been cleared up at the close of the outside bar, because the price was well above the dashed down trendline at that time.

Anticipating Breakouts That Are More Likely to Be Valid

Just as it is possible to look for signs that indicate a possible whipsaw, we can also look for signs that increase the odds that a breakout will be valid. One approach is to look for a potentially strong one- or two-bar price pattern that develops just prior to a potential breakout point and use that as an indication that the next trend is likely to have the power to result in a move that is strong enough to result in a valid breakout. In reality, we are looking for one of those reverse domino-type effects discussed earlier.

Chart 17-9, for NCR, offers a good example. The price traces out an upward-sloping head-and-shoulders pattern. At the time it would have been reasonable to anticipate a valid breakout because of the strong Pinocchio bar that marked the top of the head. It was a classic pattern, first, because it was preceded by a very strong and persistent advance, and second, because of its wide trading range. Finally, the huge volume that accompanied it was icing on the bearish cake. In actual fact, the Pinocchio bar and the two bars surrounding it were really an island reversal. The right shoulder of the head-and-shoulders top was a good-faith effort to close the gap, after which the price was free to make a new low. The chart also supports the idea that exhaustion extremes are important potential resistance areas. The horizontal trendline shows that the level experienced by the Pinocchio extreme turned back the next advance several months later.

The pattern in Chart 17-10, for Newmont Mining, is really a failed bullish right-angled triangle. Its demise could have been anticipated by the two-bar reversal that developed on the rally preceding the downside breakout. This two-bar formation was not a particularly strong pattern because it was not accompanied by a lot of volume or preceded by much of a rally. However,

Chart 17-9 NCR, 1998–1999, daily.

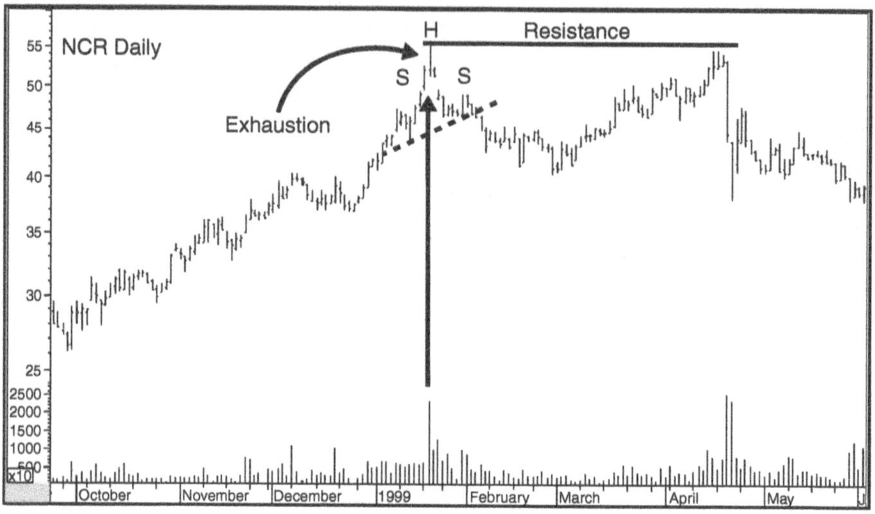

Chart 17-10 Newmont Mining, 1995–1996, daily.

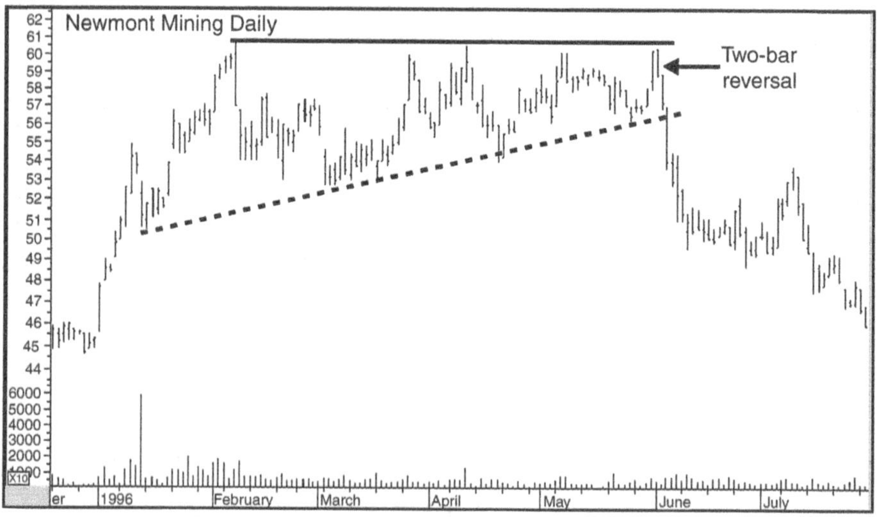

the bars were reasonably wide, and it developed at an important resistance level. The two-bar reversal told us two things. First, the late May attempt at an upside breakout would probably fail and require further regrouping. Second, the abrupt turn of fortune, reflected by the characteristics of a good two-bar reversal, ought to result in a test of the up trendline. When this came and failed two days later, the decisive downside breakout indicated that many traders had anticipated a break above the solid trendline and were forced to liquidate their positions. Incidentally, if this information had shown up on the candle charts, it would have revealed a dark cloud cover, since the opening of the second day was above the close of the first, and the second day closed more than halfway down the real body (i.e., the difference between the opening and closing prices) of the first.

We have to use a little common sense when using these patterns to predict a legitimate breakout. If they form a long way from the breakout point, they are far less likely to work, since they will not provide sufficient momentum to act as a springboard for a successful breakout. Chart 17-11, for Nabors, shows an example. We see a strong outside day on huge volume in early May. This could certainly have been used to anticipate a good rally, but the outside bar developed so far from the breakout trendline that it would not have been reasonable to use it as evidence to project a successful breakout. On the other hand, a two-bar reversal developed just after a whipsaw breakout. When the price broke above the horizontal trendline for

Chart 17-11 Nabors, daily.

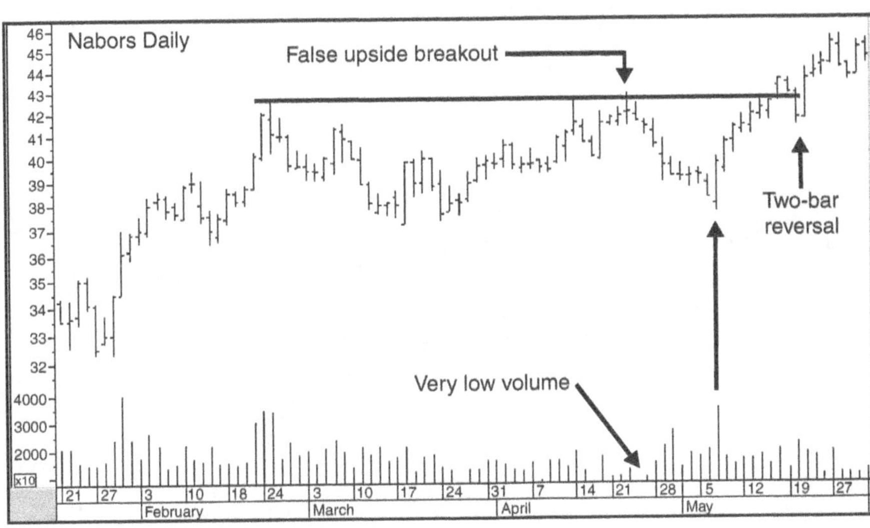

a second time, this provided ample proof that this second breakout would not turn out to be a whipsaw. Thus we have a breakout, a cancelled breakout (whipsaw) on the first day of the two-bar reversal, and a cancelled whipsaw on the second. Although the two-bar reversal was not preceded by much of a decline, the fact that the price was able to make a new high after such an indecisive period was a strong signal indicating that the buyers were now in control.

The Importance of Using Perspective

It doesn't matter what time frame you are trading or investing in; it is always a good idea to monitor the time frame above and the one below your chosen time frame. Considering the time frame above your chosen time frame gives you the perspective of a more dominant trend and will help to either validate any signals you obtain or give you a stronger and more reliable indication of a whipsaw.

For example, Chart 17-12 shows a false breakout for the Nasdaq on a 10-minute bar. The false breakout became apparent when the price broke below the previous minor low. On the other hand, if we look up to a higher level, as in Chart 17-13, which features a 30-minute bar, we can see that the

Chart 17-12 Nasdaq 100 10-minute bar.

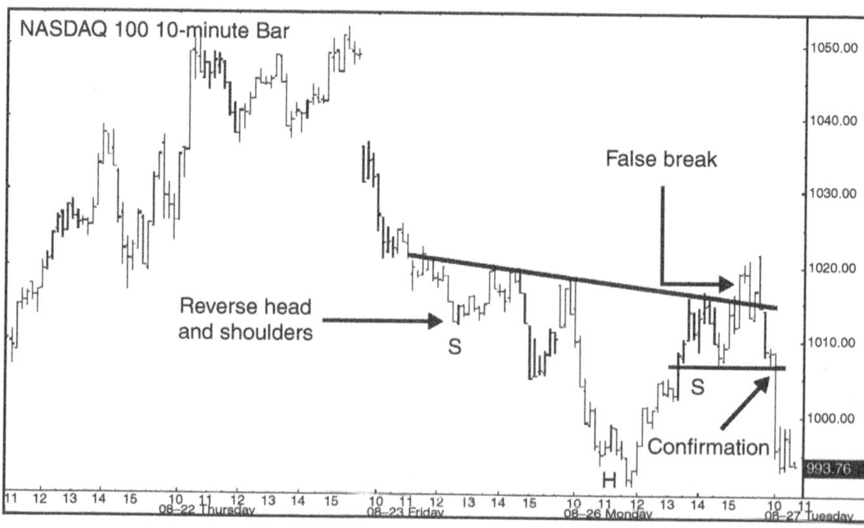

Chart 17-13 Nasdaq 100 30-minute bar.

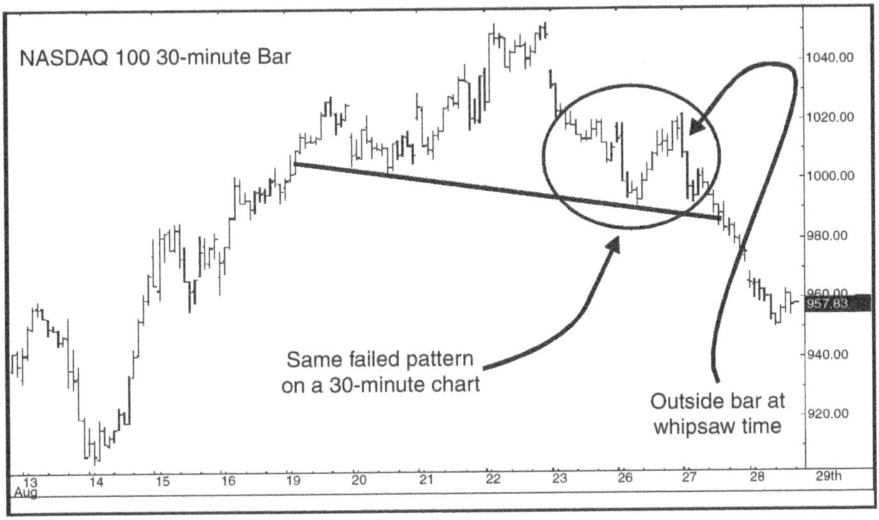

whipsaw was an outside bar. The two indications of whipsaws developed at roughly the same time, but the outside bar being formed at a higher and more dominating time frame represented a much stronger signal.

Chart 17-14 features the U.S. Government 10-year yield. The head-and-shoulders reversal indicates that the yield is headed higher, but this gives us only part of the picture. That's because Chart 17-15 showed that on a weekly basis, a large double bottom had yet to realize its full indicated upside potential. In other words, Chart 17-14 tells us that the situation is positive, but Chart 17-15 indicates that it is actually substantially better than what is shown by the shorter-term chart. Note that on the gap up day of the breakout the price action has many of the ingredients of an exhaustion bar. A cautious trader would have been justified in staying away from the trade. However, when the price broke above the high for the exhaustion day it was definitely canceled. Unfortunately, there was not a low risk point underneath which a stop could have been placed.

In this example we looked up to see what a longer-term trend was signaling. In Charts 17-16 and 17-17, we look the other way.

The large ellipse in Chart 17-16 shows a three-bar-plus reversal. However, for the purpose of this exercise, we are concerned with the trading activity contained within the smaller ellipse. Looking at this daily chart, there is no indication that a reversal is in progress; that does not come until the closing of the three-bar-plus reversal. However, had we taken the trouble to look at

Chart 17-14 10-year government bond yields, daily.

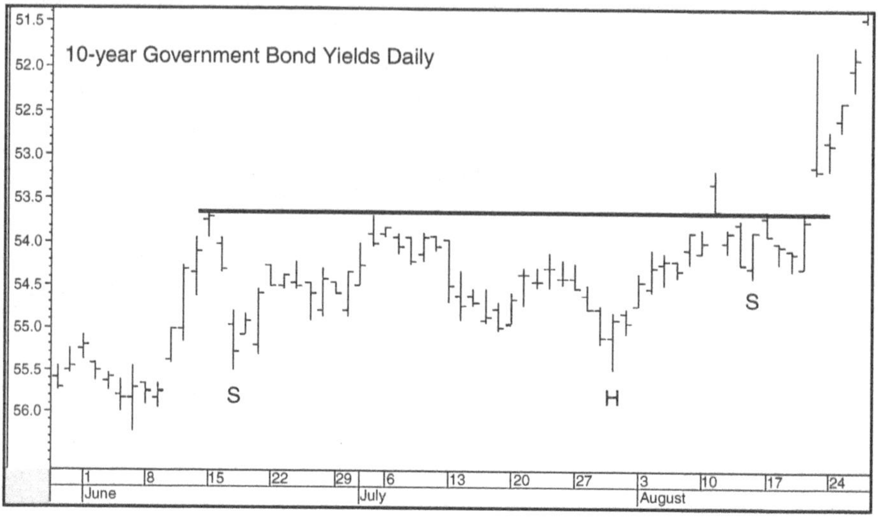

Chart 17-15 10-year government bond yields, weekly.

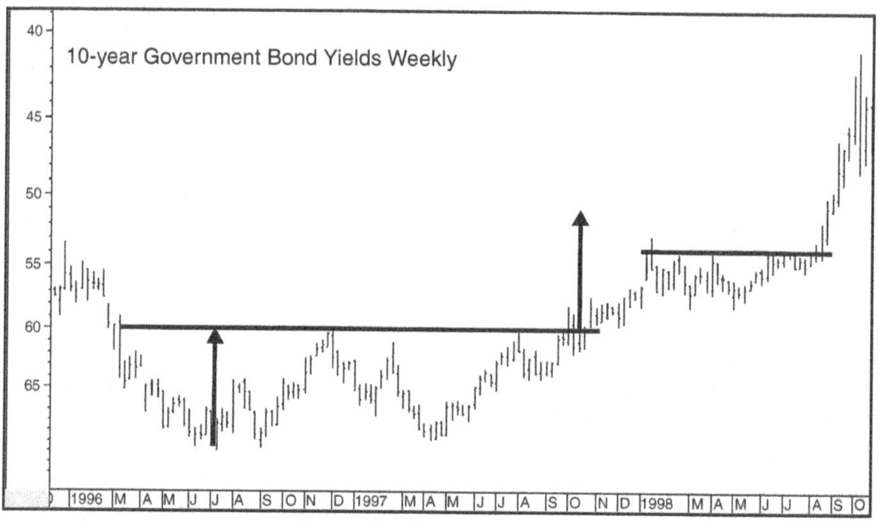

Chart 17-16 September 2003 Euro FX, daily.

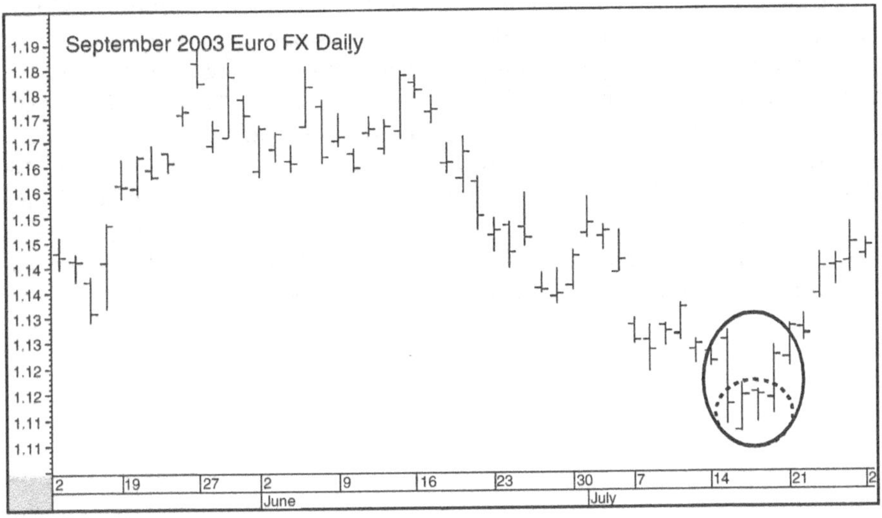

Chart 17-17 September 2003 Euro FX 10-minute bar.

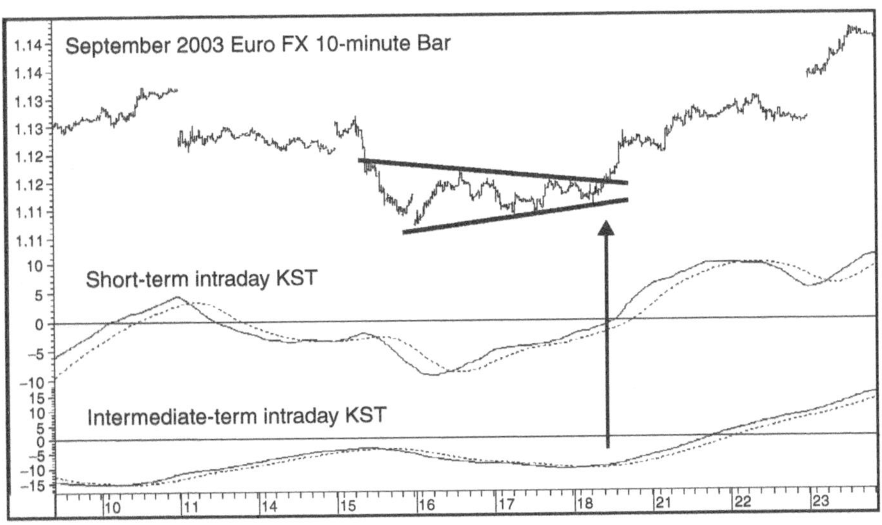

the intraday activity, as shown in Chart 17-17, we would have seen that the price was forming a triangle bottom. Note that the breakout confirmed the rising trend of the two momentum indicators, which were both in the type of subdued position that could support a good short-term rally. (For a description of the KST momentum indicator, please go to the "Trader's Den" section at www.pring.com.) The example used here compared a daily to an intraday situation, but it could easily have been a monthly-weekly or a weekly-daily comparison. The important point is that longer-term charts do not always reveal potential reversal patterns, but a study of short-term time frames often does. Therefore it's a good idea to look not only at time frames above the one that you are trading or investing in, but also at those below.

18
How Do Price Patterns Test?

This chapter sets out the results of computer-recognized price patterns in several U.S. industry groups. The research was based on criteria that I defined and was conducted by Rick Escher and his team at Recognia Inc. (http://www.recognia.com), to whom I owe a big debt of gratitude. Historical data used for the testing were kindly provided by Bob Peltier, president of Commodity Systems Inc. (http://www.csidata.com), the world's most comprehensive provider of commodity futures data. Recognia is an investment research company devoted to stock screening using sophisticated analytics, principally technical event analysis and chart pattern recognition. The technology was originally developed for British military use, and Recognia has enhanced it for the financial markets. Recognia's research and its online tools are available through several brokerage houses and through a special subscription service whose principal objective is price pattern screening at www.pring.com.

Basic Problems in Price Pattern Evaluation

At first glance, one might think that the recognition process is fairly simple. This is certainly true for evaluation of, say, moving-average crossovers or other statistically derived indications of trend changes. Evaluating price patterns, on the other hand, is not an easy process, because the interpretation of these patterns is a very subjective. Patterns first have to be recognized, and what is one man's head-and-shoulders top may not be another's. As an example, I defined a head-and-shoulders top earlier as a final rally

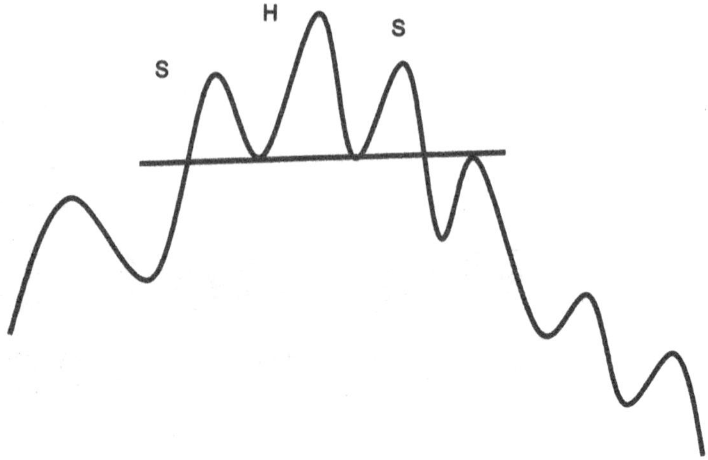

Figure 18-1a Symmetrical head and shoulders.

separated by two smaller rallies. Figure 18-1*a* offers a classic symmetrical example that virtually everyone could agree on. Figure 18-1*b*, on the other hand, meets the criteria of a final rally separated by two smaller ones, but it would be far more controversial because of the steepness of the neckline and the extremely small left shoulder. A judge in a vice case some years back said when defining pornography, "I know it when I see it." The same is really true of most price patterns, since very few are formed with the classic appearance defined in the textbooks.

Designing software to interpret price patterns is therefore an extremely difficult and complex task. Recognia has a parameter that allows its patterns

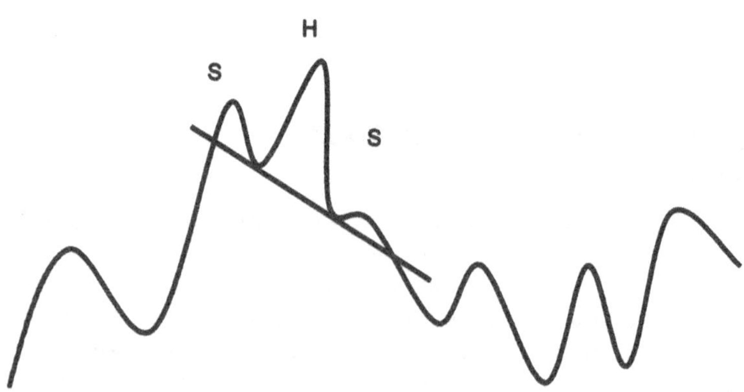

Figure 18-1b Downward-sloping head and shoulders.

to be classified according to a consensus rating—a fuzzy logic measure of a pattern's closeness to the pattern ideal and of the strength of the prior trend (Recognia calls this the "inbound trend"). In our research, we originally ignored the consensus rating, which meant that all patterns, regardless of the prior trend and the pattern's closeness to the ideal, were included. It is reasonable to ask the question, "Why not search for patterns with a consensus rating of 50 percent or 100 percent?" The answer is that this resulted in so few patterns that it rendered the research statistically invalid. In the end, we chose to use patterns that had a consensus rating of zero or higher. This meant that the prior trend was taken into consideration when selecting bottom and top patterns, but that all patterns meeting the recognition threshold were considered in the statistical analysis. From a practical point of view, though, the patterns returned by the Recognia search engine at pring.com have been filtered with a 50 percent consensus rating.

Once a pattern has been correctly identified, there is also the question of measuring whether the formation has been successful. If a bullish pattern immediately rallies to its price objective, there will be little dispute (Fig. 18-2*a*). On the other hand, if the price breaks up, declines well into the body of the pattern, and subsequently advances to the objective (Fig. 18-2*b*), is this a profitable situation? After all it is quite probable that in the interest of good risk management, any responsible trader would have liquidated the position during the postbreakout decline, when it appeared that the pattern might have failed.

Recognia devised a way to get around this problem by treating all patterns equally, basing the results on price as a percentage of the pattern's confirmation price and projected time periods of pattern length. In this way, it was possible to statistically compare patterns of differing duration and price

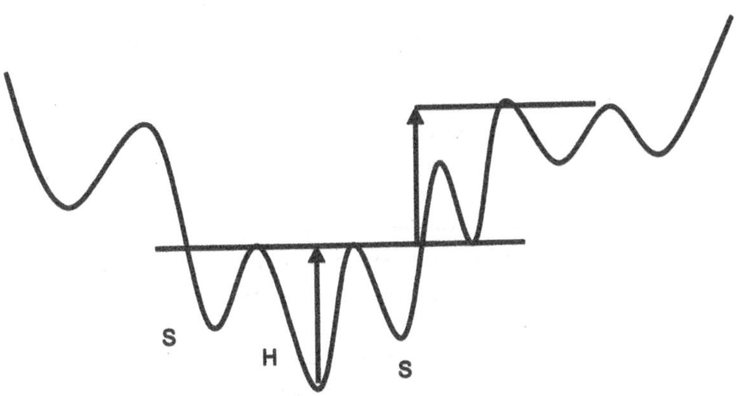

Figure 18-2a Head-and-shoulders bottom.

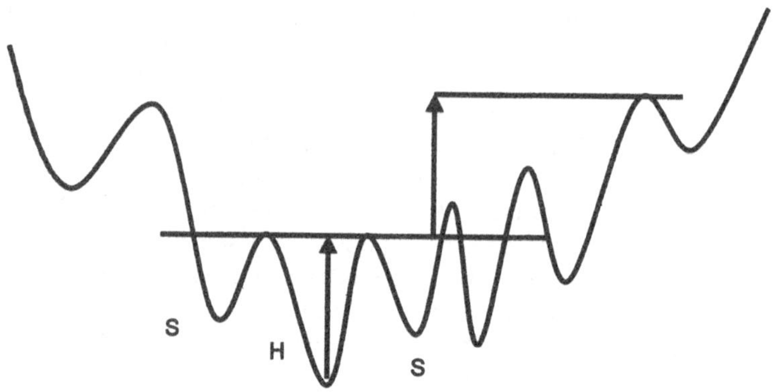

Figure 18-2b Head-and-shoulders bottom with hesitant breakout.

and to offer a statistical projection of reliability for all breakouts. Had we used some form of loss limitation, it is very probable that the results from these patterns would have been far better. I will explain the pattern length concept later.

What Was Tested?

For the purpose of this test, we decided to use two patterns, head-and-shoulders and double bottoms and tops. Recognizing the influence of industry trends on individual stocks and the importance of the direction of the primary trend, we chose four major sectors: financial, energy, transportation, and retail. With the benefit of hindsight, we were able to categorize primary-trend bull and bear markets for each sector during the 1982–2003 period. Stocks from individual sectors were identified from a database of close to 14,000 U.S. equities.

In order for a pattern to qualify as a legitimate reversal pattern, there had to be something to reverse. For purposes of identification, therefore, the Recognia consensus rating allows for the existence of what Recognia called an inbound trend.

In one way, the results are biased in that we already knew the direction of the primary trend, which is obviously not possible in real time. On the other hand, since the testing permitted a theoretically unlimited loss from short sales or a 100 percent loss from long positions, the research results are adversely affected, since they did not take into consideration the possibility of limiting the losses from failed patterns through prudent money management.

The Concept of L

The price behavior following a pattern's confirmation was evaluated in segments that reflected the time taken for the pattern to form. This permitted patterns of differing duration to be compared on an equal basis. For example, if it took 50 days to complete a formation, this time duration was defined as one L, or length. The period following the breakout was then measured in units of L, up to a maximum of 5 L. In the example of a 50-day pattern, 5 L would be 250 days. This approach made it possible to appraise performance over several time segments for individual patterns of varying length.

The price behavior following a pattern's breakout was evaluated in segments of time that represent 10 percent of the pattern's length (0.1 L). Thus, if a 52-day head-and-shoulders bottom pattern was identified, then its postbreakout prices were evaluated in segments of 5 days (52 divided by 10 rounded down to a whole number).

The closing prices for these 5 days were averaged, then the result was divided by the closing price on the day of pattern confirmation (breakout). Multiplying by 100 yielded the average price over the interval expressed as a percentage of the pattern's closing price on the day of confirmation (breakout). This process was continued for each 5-day interval through to 5 L, or 50 intervals (10 intervals per L times 5 Ls equals 50).

One factor that could potentially affect the analysis was when some part of the 5 L projection developed after a primary-trend reversal had taken place. Thus the results of, say, a bullish pattern could well be partially evaluated after a bear market was underway. This was addressed by terminating the analysis at the bull/bear boundary. This ensured that the post-turning point results were excluded from the calculation for subsequent periods of 0.1 L.

Aggregate Results

In total, 5,235 patterns were identified. Chart 18-1 shows the average and median length for tops and bottoms in both bull and bear primary-trend environments. The average length did not vary very much, though the time taken to form patterns was slightly less in primary bear markets than in primary uptrends. For all 5,000 formations, the average was around 49 trading days or 10 calendar weeks. This is interesting, since 10 weeks or 50 days is a moving average that is widely used by many technicians.

Since we were able to split the data into primary bull and bear markets, it was possible to categorize the results as pro- and contra-trend signals. Note that the standard of success in this research is based on the percentage of

Chart 18-1 Tested pattern durations in different environments.

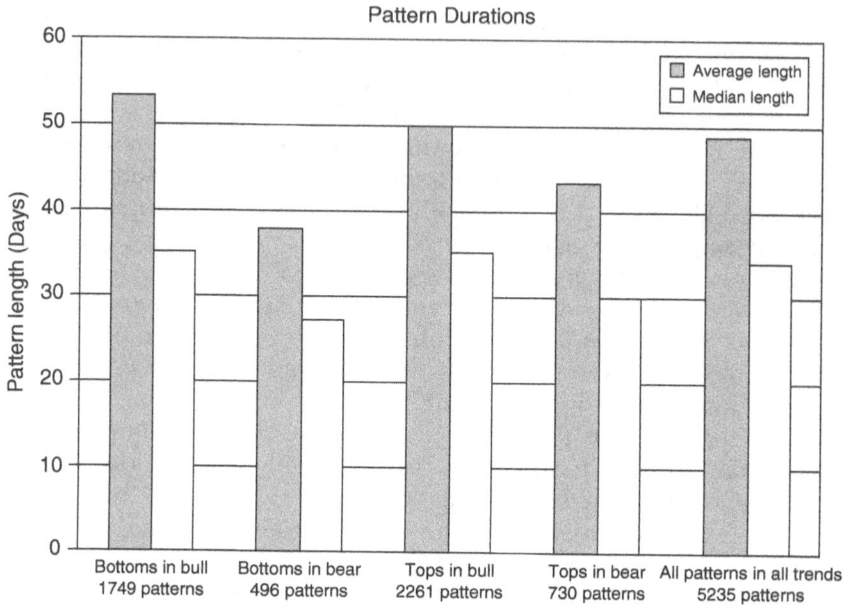

the objective being attained, not on profitability. This is a stricter assessment, since a profitable pattern could fall well short of the objective.

Pro-Trend Signals

Aggregate results for all four patterns (head-and-shoulders tops and bottoms and double tops and double bottoms) are shown in Charts 18-2 and 18-5 to 18-7. Chart 18-2 reflects the bottoming patterns during primary bull markets. The *Y* axis represents multiples of the price objective. Thus, the 100 percent line is the price objective, the 200 percent line is twice the objective, and so on. Objectives were calculated by projecting the point depth of the pattern upward from the point of breakout. The *X* axis shows the percentage of patterns reaching a particular level. Finally, the six curves represent the results for a specific multiple of the pattern length (L). Thus, at point *A* we can see that approximately 15 percent of all patterns had reached their price objective within half the time that the pattern itself took to form, i.e., 0.5 L. At point *B*, about half the sample (50 percent) had reached their objective within twice the time that it took for the pattern to

Chart 18-2 Bullish breakouts in bull markets.

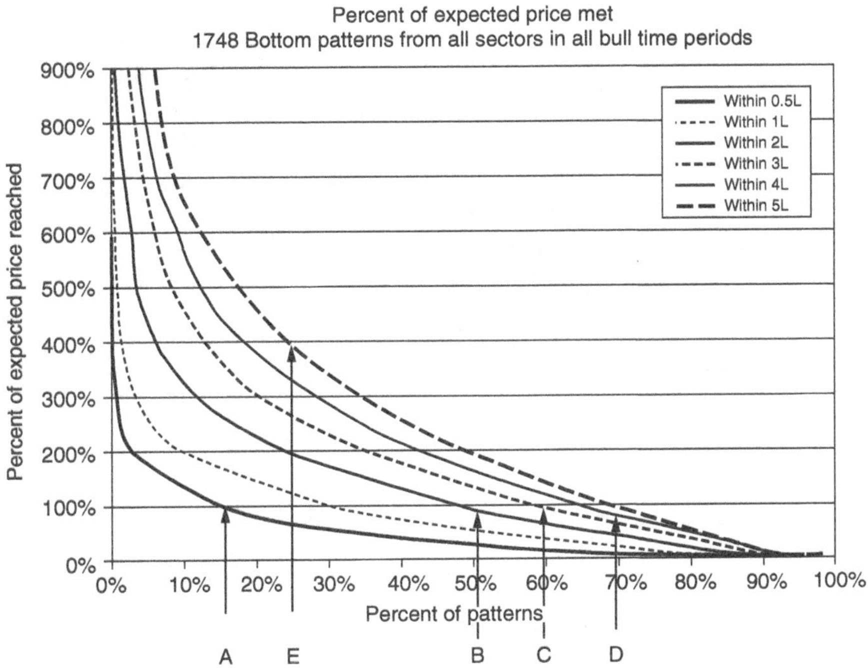

develop (i.e., 2 L). By point *C*, for 3 L, approximately 60 percent of all patterns had achieved their objective. Finally, nearly 70 percent of all patterns in bull markets had achieved their objective by 5 L (point *D*).

To put it another way, there was a 70 percent chance that the price objective would be achieved within five times the time needed to form the pattern. For example, if a pattern took 30 days to complete, there was a 70 percent chance that the objective would be achieved within 150 days. Some objectives would be achieved earlier, say in 30 days, but in this example, 70 percent of all patterns would have attained their objectives by day 150. Arguably more impressive is the fact that approximately 25 percent of all patterns (point *E*) achieved 400 percent of their objective (four times the objective) within five pattern lengths (5 L).

It's important to understand that from a practical point of view, some of these results are not as good as they look. This is because the path to the objective is rarely a straight line and can often be quite fickle. In other words, a pattern may reach its objective or a multiple thereof, but its volatility before it gets there could easily frustrate the trader, resulting in liquidation

Chart 18-3 Bullish breakout—good example.

Chart 18-4 Bullish breakout—bad example.

before the objective is reached. That is one reason why it does not make sense to trade on price patterns alone. It is important to also check that momentum is not *unduly* overextended at the time of the breakout and so forth. The word *unduly* has been emphasized because it is very likely that momentum will be partially overextended to some degree at the time of most breakouts. It is often a good idea to check the momentum calculated from a time frame higher than the one that is being traded. For example, anyone who is trading off the daily charts with a two- to three-week horizon should check momentum indicators based on intermediate time frames, and so on.

Charts 18-3 and 18-4 illustrate the point made earlier concerning volatility. Chart 18-3, for example, offers a classic result with a more or less immediate move toward a multiple of the objective. On the other hand, Chart 18-4 shows a far more difficult situation. The objective was easily obtained, but not before a nerve-shattering decline well into the body of the formation.

Chart 18-5 shows that the results from tops in primary bear markets were not as reliable as those from bottoms in bull markets, since it took 3 L before half the sample reached its objective. This compares to only 2 L for the bottoms in bull markets. By the same token, point *B* shows that it took 4 L

Chart 18-5 Bearish breakouts in bear markets.

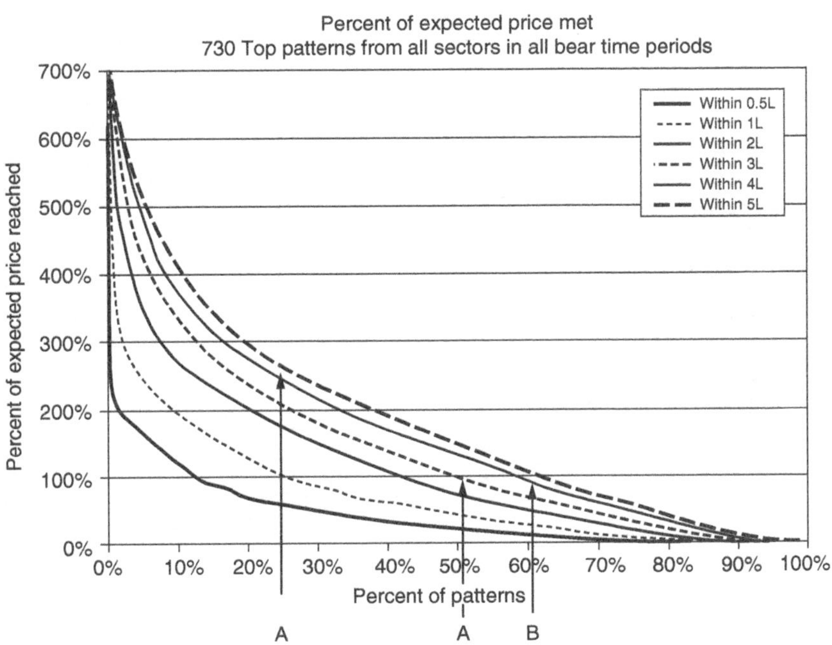

before 60 percent of tops reached their target, whereas bottoms took only 3 L. Finally, 25 percent of all patterns reached approximately 270 percent of their objective by 5 L. This compared to a 400 percent achievement for 25 percent of bullish patterns in bull markets.

Contra-Trend Signals

Not surprisingly, contra-trend signals (e.g., bullish patterns in bear markets) did not perform as well as breakouts that developed in the direction of the primary trend. In Chart 18-6, we see that only about 55 percent of all bullish breakouts in bear markets achieved their objective by 5L (point *A*). This compares to 70 percent for positive breakouts in bull markets. Moreover, the magnitude of most breakouts was far less. In the case of the pro-trend moves, 25 percent of patterns achieved 400 percent of their target, but for positive breakouts in bear markets, the corresponding percentage sank to just over half that level (point *B*).

In Chart 18-7, only about 43 percent of tops in bull markets reached their objective within 5L, compared to around 62 percent in bear markets (point *A*).

Chart 18-6 Bullish breakouts in bear markets.

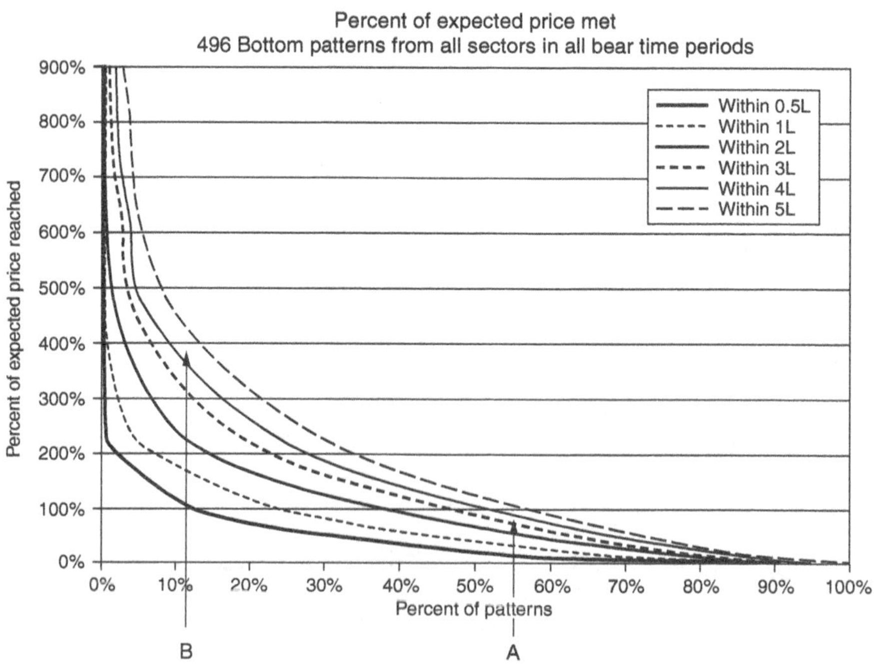

Chart 18-7 Bearish breakouts in bull markets.

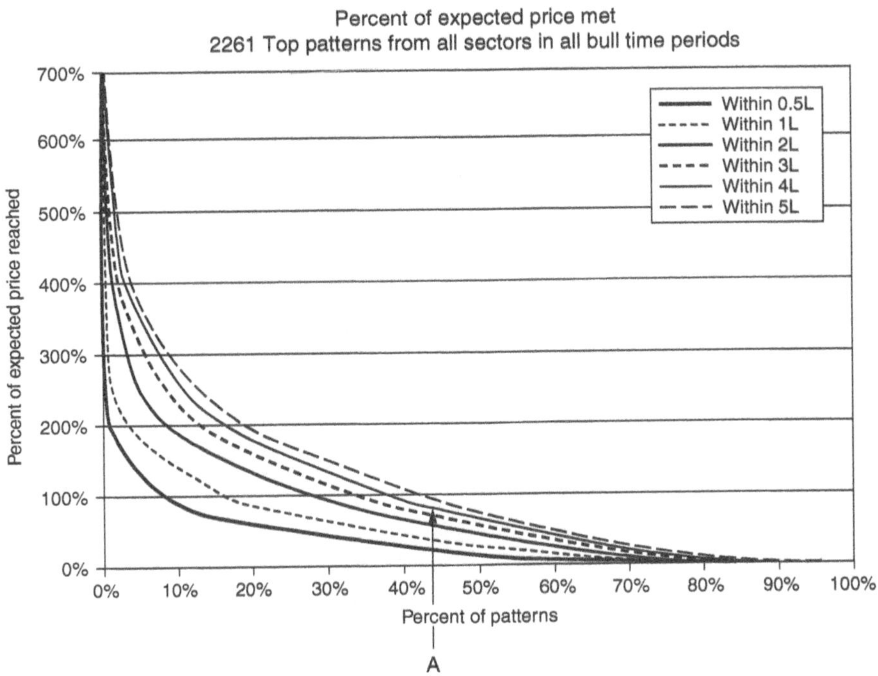

While we obviously cannot say that all contra-trend breakouts will fail, the research definitely confirms that the odds of success are greatly increased with signals that develop in the direction of the prevailing primary trend.

Conclusion

This research strongly suggests that price patterns, at least the head-and-shoulders and double varieties, work. Pro-trend signals are much more likely to result in positive returns than contra-trend signals. Unfortunately, a tight publishing schedule did not permit a more thorough examination of the results or the possibilities of testing for other ideas—for instance, objectives based on percentage measurements as opposed to point or dollar moves, or the ability to limit losses once a price had seriously broken back into the body of the formation. It would also have been interesting to assess the results by limiting the identified patterns to slightly more stringent consensus ratings to see if the results would have changed any.

Appendix
Individual Patterns Summarized

Chart A-1

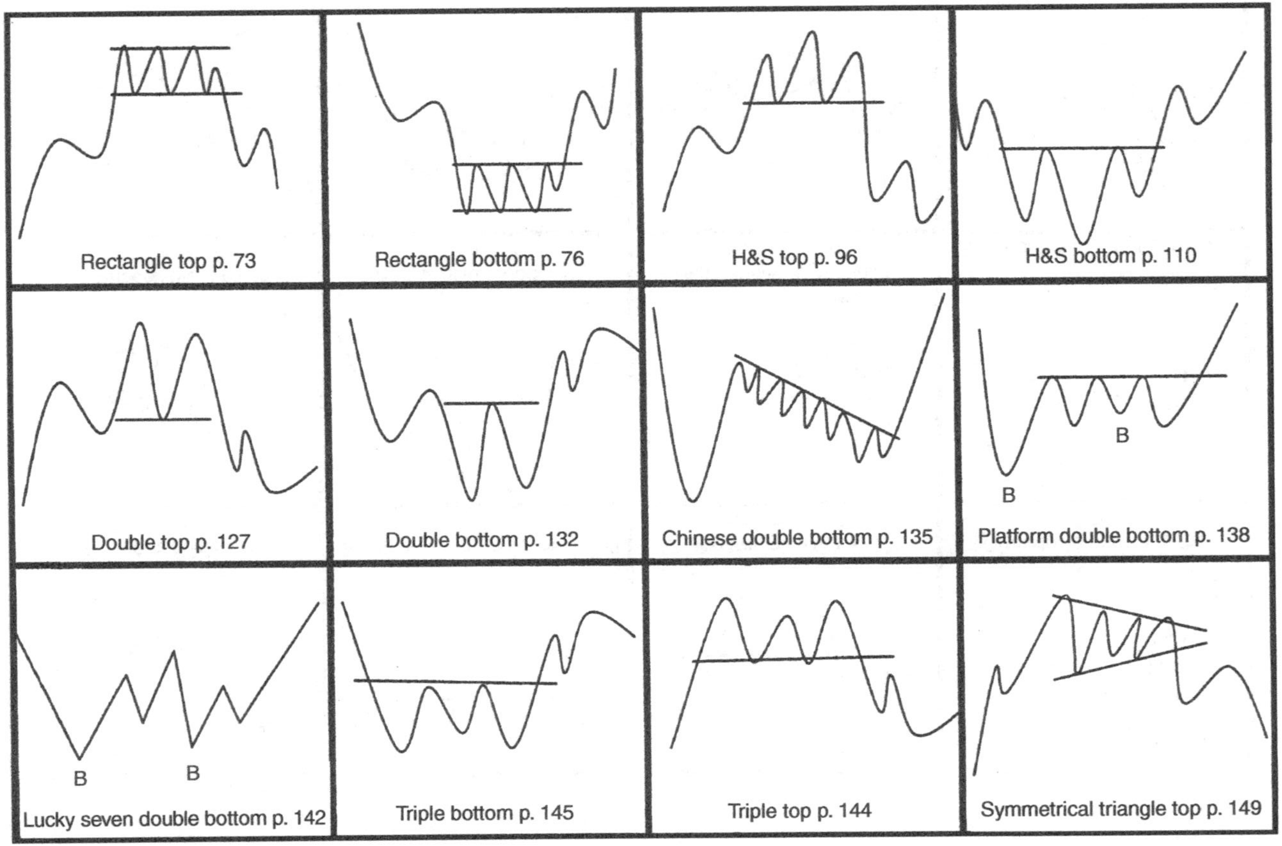
Rectangle top p. 73
Rectangle bottom p. 76
H&S top p. 96
H&S bottom p. 110
Double top p. 127
Double bottom p. 132
Chinese double bottom p. 135
B
B
Platform double bottom p. 138
B
B
Lucky seven double bottom p. 142
Triple bottom p. 145
Triple top p. 144
Symmetrical triangle top p. 149

Chart A-2

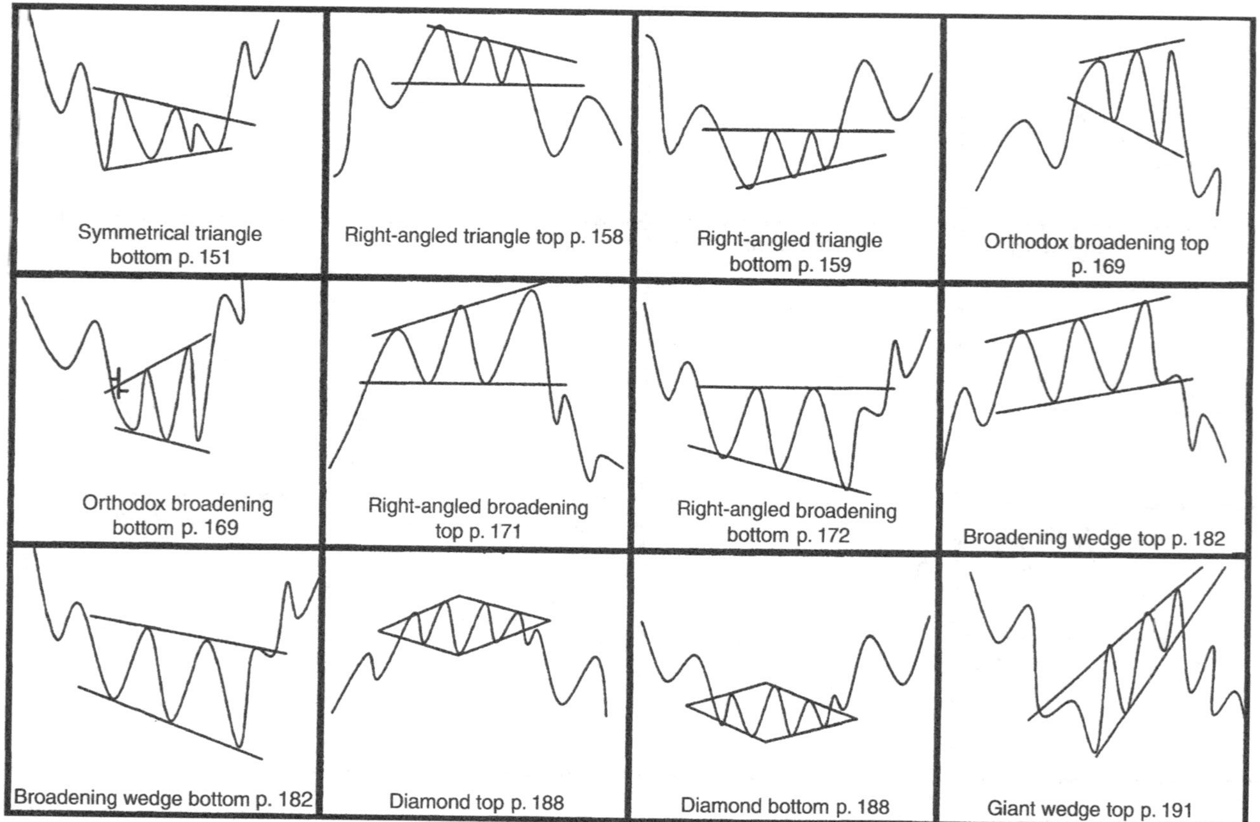
Symmetrical triangle bottom p. 151
Right-angled triangle top p. 158
Right-angled triangle bottom p. 159
Orthodox broadening top p. 169
Orthodox broadening bottom p. 169
Right-angled broadening top p. 171
Right-angled broadening bottom p. 172
Broadening wedge top p. 182
Broadening wedge bottom p. 182
Diamond top p. 188
Diamond bottom p. 188
Giant wedge top p. 191

Chart A-3

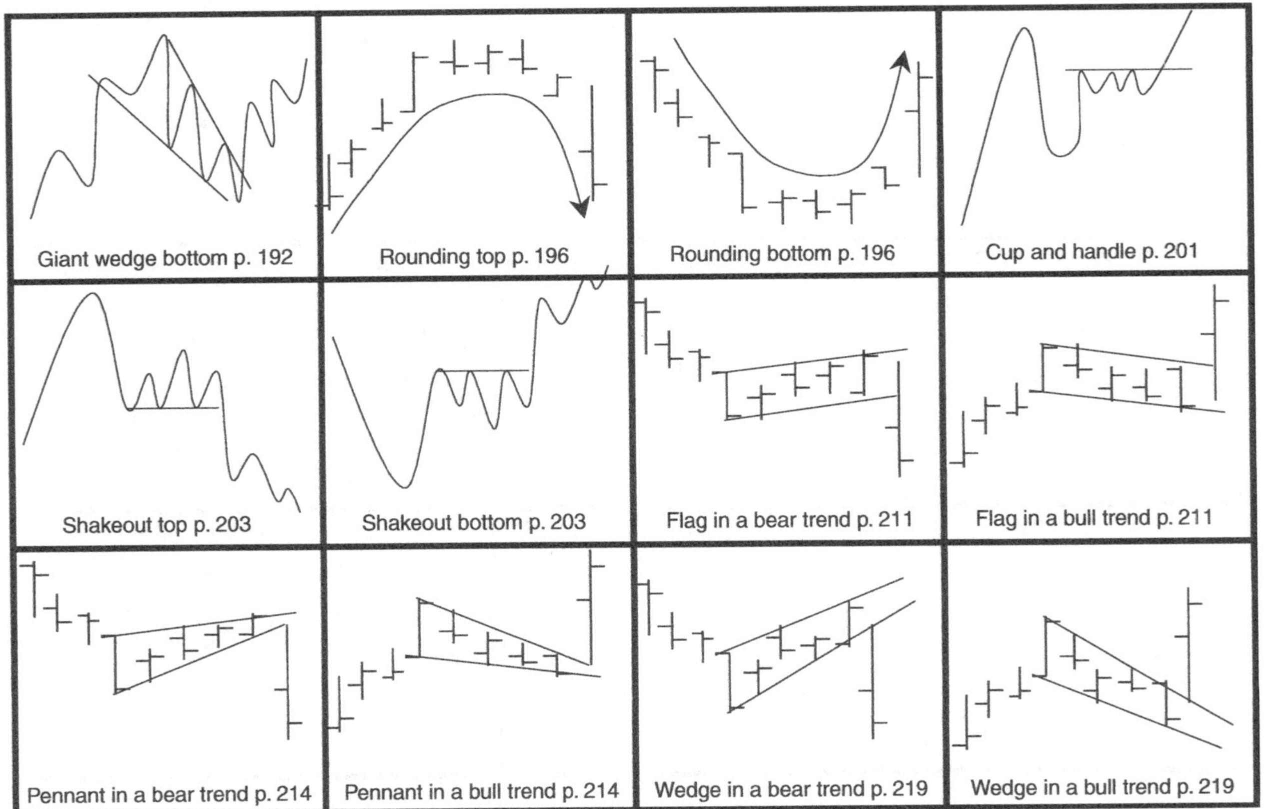
Giant wedge bottom p. 192
Rounding top p. 196
Rounding bottom p. 196
Cup and handle p. 201
Shakeout top p. 203
Shakeout bottom p. 203
Flag in a bear trend p. 211
Flag in a bull trend p. 211
Pennant in a bear trend p. 214
Pennant in a bull trend p. 214
Wedge in a bear trend p. 219
Wedge in a bull trend p. 219

Chart A-4

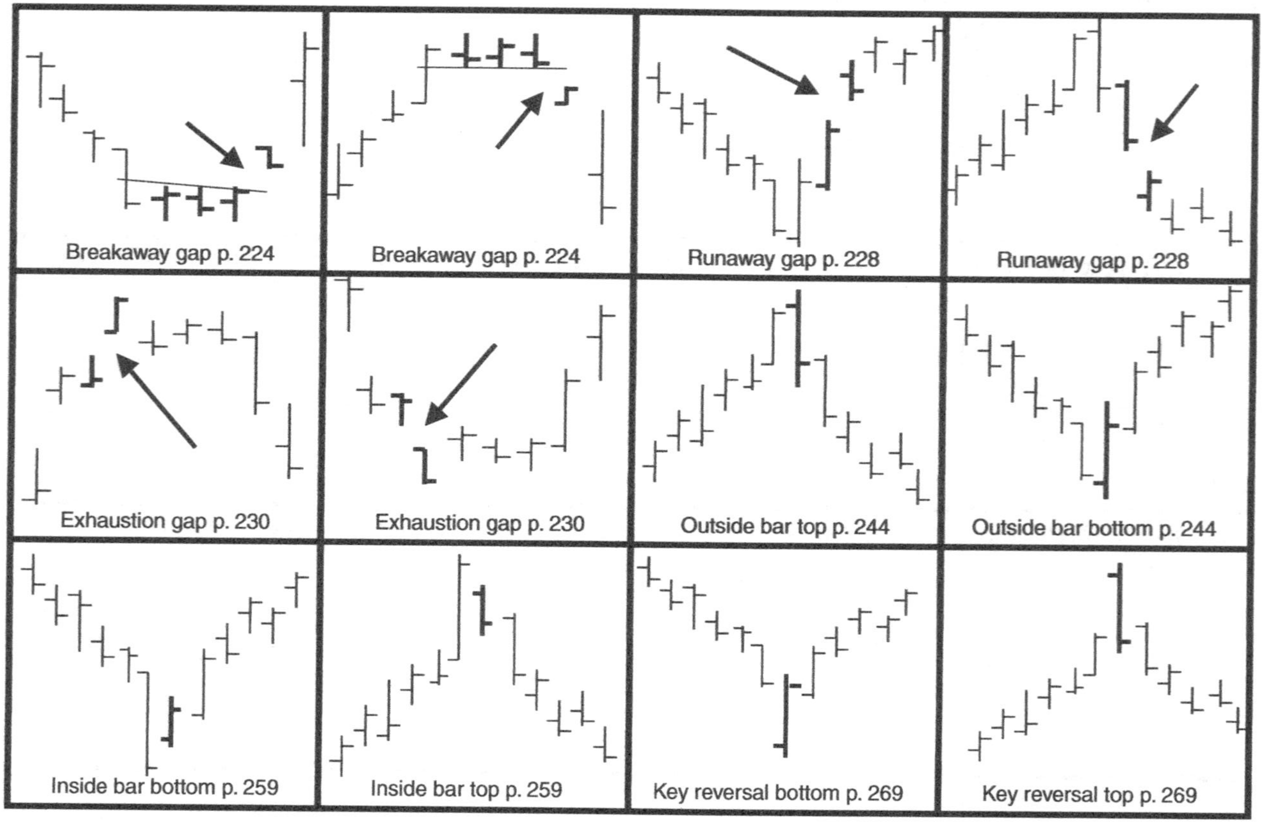
Breakaway gap p. 224
Breakaway gap p. 224
Runaway gap p. 228
Runaway gap p. 228
Exhaustion gap p. 230
Exhaustion gap p. 230
Outside bar top p. 244
Outside bar bottom p. 244
Inside bar bottom p. 259
Inside bar top p. 259
Key reversal bottom p. 269
Key reversal top p. 269

Chart A-5

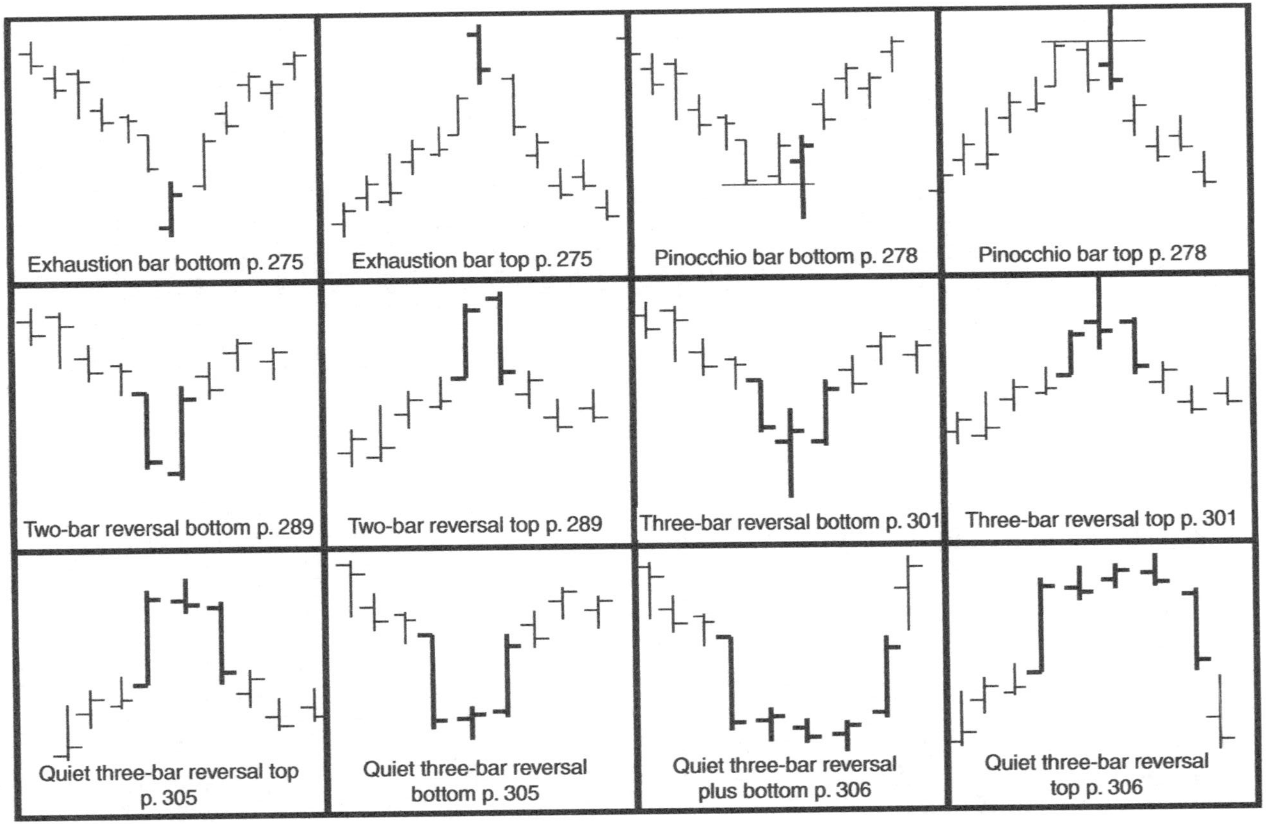
Exhaustion bar bottom p. 275
Exhaustion bar top p. 275
Pinocchio bar bottom p. 278
Pinocchio bar top p. 278
Two-bar reversal bottom p. 289
Two-bar reversal top p. 289
Three-bar reversal bottom p. 301
Three-bar reversal top p. 301
Quiet three-bar reversal top p. 305
Quiet three-bar reversal bottom p. 305
Quiet three-bar reversal plus bottom p. 306
Quiet three-bar reversal top p. 306

Index

About the Author

Martin J. Pring entered the financial markets in 1969 and has grown to become a leader in the global investment community. In 1981, he founded the International Institute for Economic Research and began providing research for financial institutions and individual investors around the world. Since 1984, he has published a monthly market review offering a long-term synopsis of the world's major financial markets, and since 1988 has been actively involved in Pring Turner Capital Group, a money management firm.

Demanded as a speaker worldwide, he is the author of several outstanding books, including the classic *Technical Analysis Explained*, now in its fourth edition. Since this unique book first appeared in 1979, *Technical Analysis Explained* has established itself as the number one guide of its kind, and it is used as a training tool by international technical societies and many universities. It is one of the three main books for Level 1 CMT certification for the Market Technicians Association. Translated into more than eight languages, the book is, as quoted in *Forbes*, "widely regarded as the standard work for this generation of chartists." According to *Futures Magazine* "it is one of the best books on technical analysis to come out since Edwards & Magee's classic text in 1948 ... belongs on the shelf of every serious trader and technical analyst." It has since become the text on which other works in the field have been based.

Martin pioneered the introduction of videos as an educational tool for technical analysis in 1987, and was the first to introduce educational, interactive CDs in this field. His latest releases include *Introduction to Technical Analysis*, an eight-hour workbook CD-ROM course, *Technician's Guide to Day Trading*, the *Introduction to Technical Analysis, Breaking the Black Box, Introduction to Candlesticks, How to Select Stocks Using Technical Analysis*, and a two-volume course on market momentum.

Recognized by his peers as a technical leader and innovator, he was awarded the A. J. Frost Memorial Award by the Canadian Technical Analysts Society in 2000, and in 2004 was honored with the Market Technician's Association (MTA) Annual Award.

Described by *Barron's* as a "technician's technician," Martin's articles have been featured in *Barron's*, and he has been quoted in the *Wall Street Journal*, the *Financial Times*, the *International Herald Tribune*, the *New York Post*, and the *Los Angeles Times* newspapers as well as the *National Review*.

Over the past 31 years, his research has led to the development of reliable financial and economic indicators for timely and effective forecasting. Martin's personal Barometers for the Bond, Stock, and Commodity markets have identified major turning points since the 1950s on a timely basis and have outperformed the buy/hold approach by a wide margin.

For many years, Martin's primary interest has been educating students of technical analysis in the basic and finer points of this art. He enjoys mentoring students of technical analysis from the college level to professionals already in the field, sharing the wealth of knowledge he has gained through his own experience and research. In this regard, he has spoken on technical analysis to the Darden Business School, Golden Gate University, and University of Richmond, Virginia.

DVD WARRANTY

This software is protected by both United States copyright law and international copyright treaty provision. You must treat this software just like a book. By saying "just like a book," McGraw-Hill means, for example, that this software may be used by any number of people and may be freely moved from one computer location to another, so long as there is no possibility of its being used at one location or on one computer while it also is being used at another. Just as a book cannot be read by two different people in two different places at the same time, neither can the software be used by two different people in two different places at the same time (unless, of course, McGraw-Hill's copyright is being violated).

LIMITED WARRANTY

Customers who have problems installing or running a McGraw-Hill DVD should consult our online technical support site at http://books.mcgraw-hill.com/techsupport. McGraw-Hill takes great care to provide you with top-quality software, thoroughly checked to prevent virus infections. McGraw-Hill warrants the physical DVD contained herein to be free of defects in materials and workmanship for a period of sixty days from the purchase date. If McGraw-Hill receives written notification within the warranty period of defects in materials or workmanship, and such notification is determined by McGraw-Hill to be correct, McGraw-Hill will replace the defective DVD. Send requests to:

McGraw-Hill
Customer Services
P.O. Box 545
Blacklick, OH 43004-0545

The entire and exclusive liability and remedy for breach of this Limited Warranty shall be limited to replacement of a defective DVD and shall not include or extend to any claim for or right to cover any other damages, including, but not limited to, loss of profit, data, or use of the software, or special, incidental, or consequential damages or other similar claims, even if McGraw-Hill has been specifically advised of the possibility of such damages. In no event will McGraw-Hill's liability for any damages to you or any other person ever exceed the lower of suggested list price or actual price paid for the license to use the software, regardless of any form of the claim.

McGRAW-HILL SPECIFICALLY DISCLAIMS ALL OTHER WARRANTIES, EXPRESS OR IMPLIED, INCLUDING, BUT NOT LIMITED TO, ANY IMPLIED WARRANTY OF MERCHANTABILITY OR FITNESS FOR A PARTICULAR PURPOSE.

Specifically, McGraw-Hill makes no representation or warranty that the software is fit for any particular purpose and any implied warranty of merchantability is limited to the sixty-day duration of the Limited Warranty covering the physical DVD only (and not the software) and is otherwise expressly and specifically disclaimed.

This limited warranty gives you specific legal rights; you may have others which may vary from state to state. Some states do not allow the exclusion of incidental or consequential damages, or the limitation on how long an implied warranty lasts, so some of the above may not apply to you.